Jewish Cooking in America

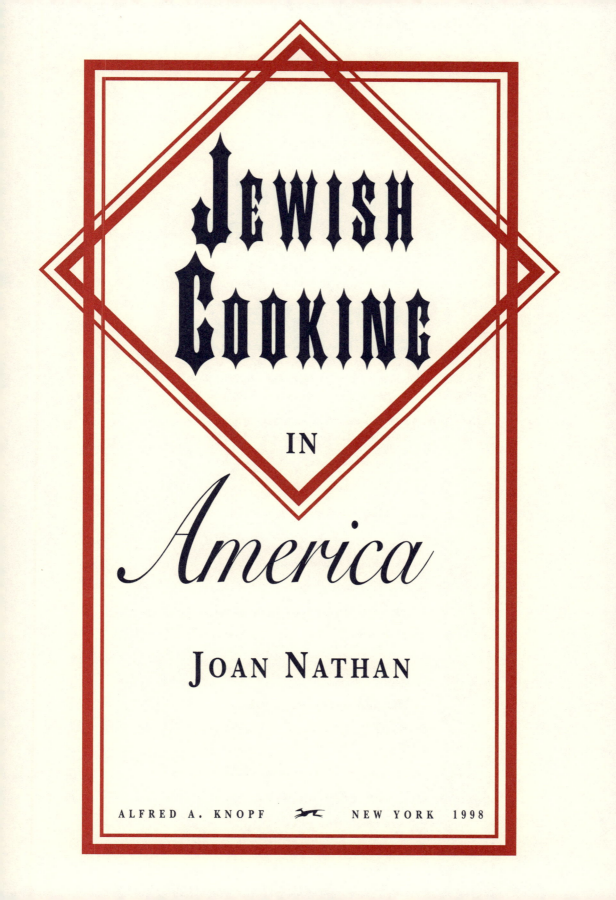

Jewish Cooking

IN

America

Joan Nathan

ALFRED A. KNOPF   NEW YORK   1998

THIS IS A BORZOI BOOK
PUBLISHED BY ALFRED A. KNOPF, INC.

Copyright © 1994, 1998 by Joan Nathan

All rights reserved under International and Pan-American Copyright
Conventions. Published in the United States by Alfred A. Knopf, Inc.,
New York, and simultaneously in Canada by Random House of Canada
Limited, Toronto. Distributed by Random House, Inc., New York.

Owing to limitations of space, all acknowledgments for permission to
reprint previously published material may be found on page 517.

Library of Congress Cataloging-in-Publication Data

Nathan, Joan.

Jewish cooking in America / by Joan Nathan.

p. cm.

Includes bibliographical references and index.

ISBN 0-375-40276-4

1. Cookery, Jewish. 2. Jews—United States—Social life and customs.
I. Title

TX724.N368 1994

641.5'676'0973—dc20   93-38581 CIP

Manufactured in the United States of America

(The Knopf Cooks American series; 13)

PUBLISHED MARCH 17, 1994
EXPANDED EDITION PUBLISHED
SEPTEMBER 1998

To the memory of my father, Ernest Nathan,
who taught me that eating is a shared experience

Born in Augsburg, Germany, June 21, 1905
Died in Providence, Rhode Island, November 2, 1991

In America you can have challah every day.

—a Yiddish lullaby

Contents

Preface to the Expanded Edition of *Jewish Cooking in America*

Rarely does a writer have the opportunity of repeating all the wonderful experiences that contributed to creating a book—visiting again with the people who shared their stories and their favorite recipes. And it is even rarer that a writer can add something new and different to the original book while retaining its initial integrity. Maryland Public Television has given me this unique opportunity by creating a twenty-six-part series based on my book. In scouting locations and sources for the television production and in speaking to groups around the country, I have been able to further illustrate the story I told in *Jewish Cooking in America,* which came out in 1994. Usually, the television series creates the book. In this case, the book created the series, *Jewish Cooking in America with Joan Nathan.*

Out of the TV series, new stories evolved that I want to share:

Recreating the preparations for the Sabbath with Cyrel Deotsch in the Lubavitcher community of Crown Heights, Brooklyn, was an eye-opener for our mostly Christian crew. Cyrel, a sylph-like forty-eight-year-old mother of twelve, feeds fifty people the way I do ten, never skipping a beat and never becoming unnerved. In her community, I also participated in *kapparot,* the custom, which dates back to the ninth century, of swinging a chicken symbolically over your head to transfer your sins in preparation for Yom Kippur, the Day of Atonement.

In Coral Gables, Florida, the entire crew broke down when Hungarian-born Aggie Stern, while making a multilayered *palachinta* torte for her grandchildren, told us about her loss of faith in God when she was in Auschwitz as a sixteen-year-old girl. Having relocated to Mexico after the war, and now living in Miami, Mrs. Stern has regained her faith through the lives of her children and her eleven grandchildren.

I had the rush of excitement that a journalist experiences when I finally tracked down—through a limo driver—Uzbekistan Tandoori Bread, a kosher bakery in Kew Gardens, Queens. The search for this fabulous flat Bukharan bread, baked in a traditional Tandoori oven, began in Tel Aviv's Carmel Market more than two years ago.

Having discovered an old-time baker Benny Moskovitz of Star Market in Oak Park, Michigan, I was thrilled when, on camera, the natural actor in him came to life. He told me a story that he had not revealed during previous interviews. It was the tale of his mother in Apsha, Czechoslovakia, making bread all night long and letting it rise in the warmest place of the house: under the feather comforter where Benny, her young son, was sleeping.

Then there are the thirty-plus new recipes, many of which were demonstrated on-camera. Edda Servi Machlin's Italian *Carciofi alla Giudia,* artichokes Jewish style, is the kind of dish that is better learned by watching an expert demonstrate it on-screen than on paper. Now everyone will be able to try this delicacy, as well as many others: a stunning kasha, vegetable loaf, six-braided challah, marvelous pickled lox, and a guava *mandelbrot,* to name a few. On television, fifty-two recipes, two per show, are woven in with Sabbath dinners, visits to cheesecake factories, pickle stores, appetizing stories, and myriad delicatessens and Jewish kitchens throughout the country. Some of these recipes are scattered through the book as they appeared in the original edition; others will be found in the New Recipes section of this expanded edition.

When John Potthast, senior vice president of Maryland Public Television, asked me to do a series using food as a way to tell the story of the Jewish experience in the United States, I thought it was a great idea. Fortunately, potential funders thought so as well. Our major sponsors include a charitable trust established by Joseph S. Steinberg and Diane H. Steinberg, Hebrew National, Lender's Bagels, and over a dozen individuals, including Beverly B. Bernstein, Melvin and Ryna Cohen, Libby Fain, Elaine Frank, Estelle Gelman, Henry and Carol Goldberg, Janice Goldsten, the Jesselson family, Robert and Arlene Kogod, Jerome and Nancy Kohlberg, and Ann P. Rosenberg, as well as the Nash, Ben and Esther Rosenbloom, Smelkinson, and Wasserman Foundations. Through their generosity, we were able to travel the country, visiting real American Jewish cooks in their homes.

It takes a truly professional and dedicated team to produce a series of this magnitude. Fortunately, I had the best, thanks to the Maryland Public Television staff members Margaret Sullivan, Tina Waganer, and Mary Helford. What a crew! Thanks also goes to Susan Barocas, Fern Berman, Marilyn Nissenson, the series writer, and to Andy Statman for his musical talent, which helped make each episode come alive. Families coast-to-coast welcomed us into their homes and, of course, experts throughout the country shared their cooking expertise and stories on television.

None of this could have happened without the cooperation and creativity of many people. First and foremost, Charlie Pinsky, the director and my co-producer, conceived and crafted the series. He brought with him a great team, assembled by Jeff Cirbes and Lewis Rothenberg, consisting of Robert Benedetti, Benjamin Gerstein, Craig Haft, Mark Mandler, Peter McEntyre, and Chris Truno. Bill Dukes, Bob Mixter, Gary Ledet, and Virginie Danglades deserve special praise for editing and reediting those hundreds of hours of tapes. Not only were they professionals in every sense, they provided personal support for me every single step of the way.

Judith Jones at Knopf once again understood the story I am telling and has made me feel, as she does all her lucky authors, that my project is special. Thanks also to her assistant, Ken Schneider, and to my assistant, Eve Lindenblatt, who shepherded this project to fruition with me.

Most of all, I want to thank my family—Allan, Daniela, David, and Merissa—who have understood and have been indulgent of the time I have been away during the past year. I hope that the final product has made it worthwhile for them.

Acknowledgments

When I first started working on this book five years ago I received a fellowship from the American Jewish Archives in Cincinnati. This enabled me to spend invaluable concentrated time at the Archives and the Hebrew Union College Library. While there I met the late Dr. Jacob Rader Marcus, the walking encyclopedia of American-Jewish history who gave me hours and hours of his time. Kevin Profitt, the Archives' librarian, and Karla Goldman, now teaching at Hebrew Union College, were both helpful to me there as well. The Quincentennial Foundation of Istanbul also awarded me a fellowship to study the food of the Jews of Turkey. I thank them, too, for the time spent in Istanbul and Izmir.

So many people have gone out of their way for me. Many I have mentioned in the text. Others I want to thank here. Peggy Pearlstein, librarian at the Hebraic Section of the Library of Congress, steered me in the right direction and saved me many hours of digging out documents. Everett Larson of the Library's Hispanic division helped me with old Ladino and Spanish texts. Food historian Karen Hess unearthed for me many old American culinary documents that mentioned Jewish food; and Dalia Carmel fed me wonderful new information and encouraged me throughout this long period.

The late Rabbi Eugene J. Lipman, Pamela Nadell, Susan Goldman, and Jennifer Breger read the manuscript. And my dear friend Henry Goldberg at Artery Organization in Bethesda, Maryland, gave me a quiet space in his office to complete the manuscript.

I want to thank Nancy Becker of the Cleveland Jewish Archives at the Western Reserve Historic Society; John Coski, staff historian of the Museum of the Confederacy; Ed Rider, archivist at Procter & Gamble; Lilly G. Schwartz, archivist, Philadelphia Jewish Archives Center at the Balch Institute for Ethnic Studies; the National Museum of American Jewish Military History; Western Jewish History Center at the Judah Magnes Museum; Susan Stein, curator, and Suzanne M. Olson, assistant curator, at Monticello; Ruth Semler at the

Portland (Oregon) Jewish Historic Society; Elinor Hurwitz at the Rhode Island Jewish Historical Society; the late Nathan Kaganoff of the American Jewish Historical Society; The New-York Historical Society; the New York Public Library; the Schlesinger Library at Harvard University; David Young at the St. Louis Jewish Archives; The Yivo Institute; Barbara Kuck, Culinary Library, Johnson and Wales; and Cynthia N. Krumbein of the Congregation Beth Ahabah Museum and Archives Trust in Richmond, Virginia.

Other people who have helped me with research, recipes, and rituals are the following: Marian Arkin, Jacky Samuels Baboussa, Sandy Berler, Mitch Berliner, Ann Brody, Michael and Ruth Cernea, Roberta Colton, Giselle Dahan, Cara De Silva, Hasia Diner, Sue Dolan, Lynn Downey, Jay Feron, Carol Field, Susan Gelman, Sally Godfrey, Ellen Gold, Carol Goldberg, the late Jean Hewitt, Stanley Hordas, Allie Ince, Estelle Jacobs, David Joseph, Lori Kimble, Grace Kirshenbaum, Barbara Kirshenblatt-Gimblett, Freya Koss, Susan Koss, Alan Kraut, Donna Lee, the late Leo Lerman, Edward and Dalya Luttwak, John Mariani, Sidney Mintz, Miriam Morgenstern, Edmond Morris, Ronni Neckes, Marilyn Nissenson, Dov Noy, Trina Rubenstein, Elinor Sachse, Jonathan Sarna, Molly Schuchat, Arthur Schwartz, Carol Sinton, Dorothy Golub Spira, Herbert Spira, the late Malcolm Stern, Cathy Sulzberger, Fernanda Torres, Nach Wachsman, Jan Weimer, and Rabbi Jeff Wohlberg.

Some articles that appeared in *The New York Times, Moment Magazine,* and the *B'nai B'rith International Jewish Monthly* are in part reproduced in the book. I want to thank my editors Eric Asimov, Penelope Green, Jeff Rubin, Herschel Shanks, and Margot Slade who encouraged me.

Six years ago when I talked with my agent, Susan Lescher, she told me that I should only write a book on a subject about which I feel passionate. My editor, Judith Jones, found that subject for me. For years I had wanted to work with her on a book—and now I know why. She is a real pro. I have learned from her and I hope that she has learned something about Jewish food from me. Others at Knopf who have been there for me are Kathy Zuckerman and Iris Weinstein.

As in my other books my mother, Pearl Nathan, a retired English teacher, has read through the manuscript carefully, occasionally recalling memories of her own American Jewish experience. My mother-in-law, Paula Gerson, with her M. F. K. Fisher–like memory, has taught me about small-town life in pre-war Poland. She sat with her late husband, Morton, who patiently translated articles on food in early Yiddish newspapers.

My children, Daniela, Merissa, and David, will be the happiest that this book is finally finished! Again, I want to thank my husband, Allan, who, as ever, has been such a good sport in tasting so many different incarnations of bagels, briskets, and bialys.

Jewish Cooking in America

Introduction

When I worked for Mayor Teddy Kollek of Jerusalem in the early 1970s, I learned how varied Jewish cooking could be. With Jews from seventy different countries living in Israel, Jerusalem seemed to me the epicenter of Jewish cuisine. Until then, I thought all chicken soups were like my mother's. I had never imagined one with fresh coriander and fenugreek as eaten by the Jews of Yemen. The fluffy dumplings floating in the chicken soup had always been matzah balls, not the Persian *gundi* made from onions, ground chicken, and chick-peas, flavored with cardamom and turmeric, or the Kurdish variety made from bulgur and meat. I quickly learned the differences between Ashkenazic (Western and Central European, Yiddish-speaking Jews), Sephardic (Ladino-speaking Jews of the Iberian peninsula and the Levant), and Oriental Jews from the Middle East.

Today one doesn't have to travel as far as Israel to see how varied Jewish food can be. While the United States, with almost six million Jews living here, is the major cultural center of the Diaspora, it has also, in many ways, become its culinary center. Not only has America welcomed Jewish immigrants from all over the world, but it has also incorporated their foods into the diet. Because this country's culinary traditions are always evolving, Americans are equally at home with Italian pizza, Portuguese sausage, and Jewish bagels.

Throughout their wandering history, Jews have adapted their life-styles to the local culture. Food is no exception. Following the same dietary laws, Jews, relying on local ingredients, developed regional flavors. Because they have lived in so many places, there is no "Jewish" food other than matzah; *haroset* (the Passover spread); or *cholent* or *chamim* (the Sabbath stews that surface in different forms in every land where Jews have lived).

Since more than two thirds of the millions of Jews in America today can trace their roots to greater Poland, including parts of Austria and Hungary (Galicia), the Ukraine, Lithuania, and Russia, "Jewish food" came into its own with the arrival of these immigrants. Because Jews lived in Poland and Russia for so many centuries, many Russian and Polish dishes, not considered Jewish in Europe, like herring in sour cream, rye bread, and borscht, became identified here as Jewish. Others, like gefilte fish and bagels, though not necessarily created by Jews, are all considered Jewish.

In America, all immigrant foods became enriched: sweet challah, overstuffed deli sandwiches of pastrami and corned beef, large bagels filled with cream cheese and lox, New York cheesecakes made from commercial cream cheese are today as American as apple pie.

Like many other immigrants, Jews went through several stages in the preservation and adaptation of their culinary culture. The first generation brought the traditions of the past with them. Depending upon how they felt about their Jewishness and the degree to which they wanted to assimilate, they either cherished or rejected the cuisine from home, including the dietary laws.

In this country, as in many parts of the world, the majority of the Jewish population does not wholly adhere to dietary laws. But most Jews retain some awareness of them and may even be aware that they are breaking a taboo by eating a cheeseburger or a ham sandwich, or by cooking on the Sabbath. Others, in some way, see these laws as an integral link to their identity as Jews.

For second- and third-generation American Jews, what was once daily subsistence became a special occasion food. In Europe, knishes, like *kugels* and latkes, were a way of varying the daily monotony of potatoes for the poor. Here during the sweatshop era, knishes, a portable food like pasties—lunchtime meat-filled small pies for Welsh ironworkers—were eaten for lunch every day. Thereafter these foods disappeared as daily fare. Now they are in vogue again, having reappeared in miniature form as hors d'oeuvres at weddings and other ceremonial events, and as fast-food snacks.

As "scientific" vegetable shortenings and shortcut foods like *phyllo* dough became available for the Jewish housewife, and as "healthy" has replaced "heftiness," some traditions like rendering schmaltz (chicken fat) or stretching strudel dough have become obsolete outside the Orthodox community.

It is often the members of later generations who want to return to their roots and who question elderly relatives or track down cookbooks in seeking out the original recipes. This explains the transformation of Jewish food in the 1990s with *baalei tshuvah,* returnees to the faith. These Jews, often from nonobservant homes, are studying Orthodoxy and are creating a new kosher cuisine mindful of new health guidelines. It also explains why I myself, passionately interested in studying the roots of Jewish cuisine, am trying, through cooking, to provide a link to the past.

THE JEWISH DIETARY LAWS

What makes the Jewish diet unique is the Covenant given by God to Moses on Mount Sinai and spelled out in the Hebrew Bible. Modern Jewish culinary traditions date back three thousand years to the sacrifices at the Temple in Jerusalem. It was in that context that the dietary laws were promulgated.

Kashrut, the Jewish dietary laws, govern the selection, preparation, and consumption of all food of observant Jews. A number of these principles are mentioned in the Bible. They have been codified and elaborated upon throughout the centuries. The rules and the rabbis' commentaries are listed in the Shulhan Arukh, the standard code of Jewish law. The following are some of the major regulations governing food.

According to the Bible, Jews are permitted to eat meat only from an animal that has completely cloven hooves and chews its cud. "Whatsoever parteth the hoof and is wholly cloven-footed and cheweth the cud, that may you eat" (Leviticus 11:3). The biblical permission includes beef, venison, mutton, lamb, and goat and excludes, among others, rabbit or hare, horse, dog, cat, whale, and, of course, pig.

Edible fowl include turkeys, quail, squab, Cornish hens, chicken, and doves. These fowl have in common a projecting claw, a crop, and a gizzard or stomach whose inner lining can be readily peeled. Birds of prey are excluded.

To understand the kosher slaughtering of meat today I visited the David Elliott Poultry Farm, a small, highly respected company in Lake Ariel, Pennsylvania. David Fink, the owner, told me that he is as fussy about the way his chickens are raised as he is about the way they are slaughtered. "We insist that the chickens have good feed," he said.

He explained that there are distinct and explicit rules governing the way in which animals are slaughtered. These rules spring from ethical principles and are also designed to reject the sacrificial practices of paganism. "Thou shalt kill thy herd and thy flock, which the Lord hath given thee, as I have commanded thee, and thou shalt eat within thy gates, after all the desire of the soul" (Deuteronomy 12:21).

The knife used by the *schochet* (ritual slaughterer) must be twice as long as the width of the animal's throat, extremely sharp and smooth, without the slightest perceptible notch so that it will slide cleanly. Even a fraction of a second's delay makes the killing invalid.

After the slaughter, chickens are put in a cone to drain the blood. Then the feathers are removed by machine in cold water, the chickens rinsed and put in a chill. According to Mr. Fink, employing a professional kosher slaughterer rather than using an automatic electric machine adds to the final cost of the bird, as do the quality of the chickens and their feed.

Both a government inspector and a *mashgiach* (Jewish inspector) check the chickens. Although I did not observe the inspection at the David Elliott Poultry Farm, I did see it at the Empire Chicken Factory in Mifflintown, Pennsylvania. There the *mashgiach* removed at least twice as many unacceptable chickens as the USDA representatives.

After the slaughter of beef, lamb, or veal, the lungs are checked for abnormalities. The *schochet* rejects cattle with certain types of adhesions, cuts, and bruises. The term "glatt kosher" refers to the smoothness of the lungs. Today the very Orthodox use the term to define extremely kosher. Only the grainier forequarters of the approved cattle are used, since the sciatic nerve must be removed in order to eat the meat of the hindquarters. Because it takes many hours to remove this nerve, the process is prohibitively expensive.

This means that filet mignon, rump and sirloin steaks, leg of lamb, and London broil are all considered non-kosher cuts, because they come from the hindquarters of beef, lamb, or veal.

Once the animal is slaughtered, all blood must be extracted from the meat through salting or, with liver, broiling. To the Jew, blood is sacred, a gift of God. "I have given it (the blood) to you upon the altar to make an atonement for your souls" (Leviticus 17:11). "Therefore, I said unto the children of Israel: No soul of you shall eat blood. . . . Ye shall eat the blood of no manner of flesh . . . whosoever eateth it shall be cut off" (Leviticus 17:12, 14). The reason for the salting is to rid the body of blood, following the Biblical prohibition against the pagan tradition of drinking blood.

To rid the animal of blood after the kill, the meat is put through a process called *melihah,* which consists of first soaking it in water for one-half hour and then covering it with coarse kosher salt for one hour, before it may be prepared for food. (Fine-grained salt, which is also kosher, would dissolve instead of drawing out the blood.) After that, the salt is shaken off and the meat is washed three times in cold water so that no blood remains. Some people dislike the salty taste of kosher chickens because they fail to soak them before cooking. In the old days a wooden board used while the meat was salted was a familiar sight in Jewish homes. Today, most kosher meat and poultry are presalted.

"These may ye eat of all that are in the waters: whatsoever hath fins and scales in the waters, in the seas, and in the rivers, them may you yet eat" (Leviticus 11:9). Kashrut-observing Jews may eat only fish that have both fins and scales—scales, that is, which are detachable from the skin. Thus all shellfish, such as shrimp, scallops, crabmeat, clams, and oysters are forbidden. Sturgeon, although famous for caviar, is not considered kosher because its scales are not removable unless the skin is also removed; nor is swordfish for some, since it has one set of scales.

Milk (*milchig*, dairy) dishes must be cooked and eaten separately from meat (*fleishig*) dishes. (No French cream sauces over meat for kashrut-observing Jews.) Three times, in Exodus and Deuteronomy, the Hebrew Bible states that a kid cannot be cooked in its mother's milk. "Thou shalt not seethe a kid in its mother's milk" (Deuteronomy 14:21). Although the reason for the prohibition is unknown, the law may have kept the ancient Hebrews from participating in pagan customs of animal sacrifice.

Neutral or pareve food, such as fish, eggs, and vegetables, may be eaten with either milk or meat. As we shall see in the story of Jewish food in America, the role of a pareve or neutral cooking fat, such as olive oil and later vegetable shortenings, became increasingly important. Religious Jews in the eighteenth and nineteenth centuries were uneasy about eating with non-Jews because they feared that lard might have been used instead of kosher oil. Today, labeling and identification of products in supermarkets makes it easy to check ingredients before purchasing.

Two sets of utensils and dishes, one for milk meals and one for meat, are used, stored, and cleaned separately, and table linens are separate, too. Between a milk meal and a meat meal, one must rinse out the mouth or eat a morsel of bread. For this there is no waiting requirement. But if the meat meal precedes a milk meal, the normal wait is about three hours. However, some Jews wait as long as six hours after eating a meat meal before having milk products.

THE JEWISH HOLIDAYS

When my children asked why we don't celebrate Christmas, I told them how lucky we are. We have Shabbat, a holiday every single week. Not only that, but this Sabbath springs directly from one of the Ten Commandments, where God told the Israelites to rest on the seventh day, linking the present with the remote past. So it is with all the Jewish festivals. Each one is layered historically with the original holiday linked to the Bible and the natural cycle of the year. The holidays and the weekly Sabbath have meant a great deal to Jewish people throughout history. They are a means of binding families and community. And food plays a major part in each one, given the importance of the dietary laws and the table-centered rituals involved in Judaism. The symbolism and inherent qualities of food are kept in the consciousness of observant Jews every day. One can see that even where some of the more stringent commandments have been forgotten, the festive holiday get-togethers are scrupulously and lovingly perpetuated.

The Sabbath is usually marked by two symbolic loaves of bread, wine, fish and/or meat, and other special foods. Since no cooking is permitted, for religious Jews, on the Sabbath, the day of rest, dishes have been created like the traditional *cholent* (a robust stew), or *kugels* (vegetable or noodle puddings), which can be prepared in advance and can stay warm overnight over a low flame. In Europe, white flour for challah, fish, and even chicken were reserved to make the one day a week important. The Sabbath celebration varies widely in America today. At the least, candles are lit, blessings said over the wine, and a festive meal is prepared on Friday night. At the most, an entire twenty-four-hour period is spent in rest and ritual, with three meals on the Sabbath, before the *Havdalah* ceremony—including wine, spices, and a candle—starts the new week on Saturday evening just after sunset.

In addition to the weekly Sabbath, the three major seasonal harvest festivals include Passover, beginning the barley harvest in ancient times. Because Passover is the one holiday the overwhelming majority of American Jews celebrate, I have devoted an entire chapter to it in this book and will describe it in depth there.

At Shavuot, a second harvest festival in the late spring, when there is an abundance of cheese and milk products, dairy dishes like cheesecakes and blintzes are served. And at Sukkot, celebrating the grain harvest at the commencement of autumn, all kinds of stuffed vegetables and stews are eaten. As signs of the plentiful harvest, meals are served in huts open to the sky, reminding us of the temporary shelters in the desert thousands of years ago.

Sukkot encompasses Rosh Hashanah and Yom Kippur. At Rosh Hashanah dishes like apples and honey and other sweet vegetable dishes are traditionally eaten with the hope for a good New Year. Yom Kippur, the Day of Atonement, is the major fast of the Jewish year. In many American Jewish homes, kreplach (pasta-wrapped meat morsels known as Jewish *tortellini*) are traditionally eaten at the meal before the fast and herring and honey cake to break the fast. Historically, all three festivals are associated with the Exodus from Egypt— Passover representing the release from bondage; Shavuot, the giving of the Torah at Mount Sinai and the completion of the Covenant between God and the people; and Sukkot, the sojourn of the Israelites in the wilderness on their way to the promised land. In ancient times these three festivals, commemorating the covenant between God and the Jews, were marked by pilgrimages to the Temple in Jerusalem and special offerings of food to God in thanksgiving.

During the winter solstice period, Hanukkah, the festival of lights commemorating the victory of the Maccabees over Antiochus of Syria less than 2200 years ago, is celebrated. It also commemorates the miracle when the oil in the synagogue lasted not one but eight days. Foods fried in oil are served, including latkes and other pancakes as well as deep-fried pastries dipped in honey.

Another beloved festival is Purim, a month before Passover, when the yearly store of flour must be used up. This festival—when Jews can let go—is a reminder of the Jewish people's deliverance from the wicked Haman, who wanted to annihilate the Jews, and was the favored minister of the Persian King Ahasuerus. It was Queen Esther, a Jewess, who cleverly saved her people day after day with a series of pretexts. Her story is recounted every year in the synagogue, when the biblical book of Esther is read. Charity to the poor, gifts of food, and a festive meal afterwards mark the holiday. In this country, starting in the early nineteenth century, Purim fund-raising balls for charitable institutions became very popular, a custom that is being revitalized today.

NEW FOODS FOR OLD TASTE BUDS: FIRST JEWISH IMMIGRANTS ARRIVE IN AMERICA

Not too long ago, while on a family vacation, I visited Mill House, the earliest known standing Jewish residence in the United States. This flintstone block house, built around 1720, is adjacent to Route 9W, about twelve miles north of Newburgh, New York, in the Hudson Highlands. The house, part of a trading station, was built by Luis Moses Gomez, the first of a distinguished Sephardic family to emigrate from Spain to America. Outside, near what became known as Jew's Creek, Mr. Gomez, known in Ulster County as "Gomez the Jew," traded furs with the Indians.

Inside are two open-hearth fireplaces, which kept Gomez, his assistants, and visiting Indians warm in winter and, more important for my quest, were used for cooking. One of the fireplaces includes a Dutch oven for baking, possibly used to warm the Sabbath stew or *chamim*—in those days a simple mixture of beans, onions, and beef. After simmering for several hours in an iron pot, which hung over the open fire on an iron chain with a hook or sometimes rested on three long legs within the fire itself, the stew would be kept warm in the dying embers of the closed oven until the Sabbath lunch. This oven may also have been used to bake bread. The flour was ground in the mill just down the hill along Jew's Creek, where Mr. Gomez fished for his trout. Ceramic crocks in the kitchen were probably used for the pickling of tongues and beef that were eaten by the early Jewish settlers.

No doubt Mr. Gomez, like many of his Sephardic brethren, slaughtered his own beef, lamb, and chickens, since it was impossible to hire a *schochet* in this remote area.

I had already seen the Gomez Bible, a leather-bound tome with the dates of births and deaths of Gomez ancestors recorded in Portuguese, Spanish, and English. This Bible dates from Spain in the sixteenth century when the family became Marranos (secret Jews). It mentions Gomez as well as his granddaughter's husband, Uriah Hendricks, who came to the Colonies in 1755. A Dutch-born Jew, who emigrated from England, he bartered goods against American raw products, primarily West India sugar. Very observant and devout, he looked contemptuously on anyone who desecrated the Sabbath and ate forbidden food. He became president in 1791 of Shearith Israel, the Spanish and Portuguese Synagogue in New York, which had supervised kosher slaughtering in the city of New York since 1752.

Ruth Hendricks-Schulson, an active member of Shearith Israel today, and a great-great-great-granddaughter of Uriah Hendricks, is the custodian of this Bible as well as the family recipes, which she shared with me. For me Jewish and American history blended at that moment. I knew that this kitchen, along with Mrs. Schulson's recipes, would provide clues to the early Jewish culinary past in the United States.

The story of Jewish food in America begins, however, sixty years earlier, when twenty-three Sephardic Jews arrived in New Amsterdam in 1654. As a result of the expulsion from the Iberian peninsula in 1492, Sephardic Jews had fled to Greece, the Middle East, England, the Netherlands, and the Americas. This particular New Amsterdam band first sought haven from the Spanish Inquisition in Recife, Brazil.

Under the Dutch, about one thousand Jews prospered in Recife, calling it the "New Jerusalem." Although the majority were petit shopkeepers, some were involved in sugar mills and sugar plantations. But when the Portuguese took over again, bringing with them the Inquisition, the Jews faced the choice of either going back to Amsterdam or to parts of the Dutch West Indies, such as Suriname and Jamaica, where some of their kinsmen had fled. Instead, this time they sought refuge in Dutch New Amsterdam. Their relocation took place during the time when the discoveries of exotic and unfamiliar foods in the Americas and the production of sugar changed forever the cuisines of the Old and New Worlds. The triangular trade route, established to satisfy the world's craving for sugar, involved ships that picked up slaves in Africa and brought them to the West Indies and the Americas to work the sugar plantations. From there sugar, molasses, rum, vanilla, and foods, such as white and sweet potatoes, turkeys, chocolate, peppers, corn, tomatoes, and kidney and string beans, which had all been discovered in the Americas with the voyages of Christopher Columbus and Hernando Cortés, made their way to Europe. Later, these foods returned to the Americas with immigrants bringing new ways of using them.

For centuries Jews and Muslim Arabs had been sending almonds, olive oil, dates, chickpeas, fava beans, grapes, pomegranates, lentils, and other Mediterranean goods from the Middle East to the Iberian Peninsula. It was the Jews who introduced their ways of preparing these foods to the New World. As a result, some dishes like *escabeche* (pickled fish) and almond desserts, prepared by Jews and Arabs alike, became known in England and the New World as Jewish foods.

The business of food continued when Jews came to the Americas. On the boat in 1654 there were several butchers, including one Asser Levy.

For the most part, Jews during the Colonial period cooked and ate like everyone else. They learned to use corn, beans, and the abundant halibut, cod, shad, herring, and salmon. Their diet was seasonal: fresh food in the summer, dried and preserved fruits and vegetables in the winter, pickled vegetables in the late summer and fall, and dandelion greens and even meats and fish dressed with a vinegar sauce in the spring—a popular pickling practice frequently used in the days before refrigeration.

But unlike other colonists, most Jews observed the laws of kashrut in their homes. Some of their dishes, like cod or haddock fried "Jewish style" (in olive oil, not lard), soon became popular among non-Jews.

Before Jewish communities were well organized, most Jewish men learned how to slaughter meat according to the dietary laws. If they did not, they went without meat. Mordecai Sheftall of Georgia, for example, one of the most famous American Jews during the Revolution, received a letter from a Christian friend, John Wereat, on December 2, 1788: "Don't forget to bring your sharp knife with you," he wrote. "And then you shall not fast here unless 'tis your own fault, as I am putting up some sheep to fatten."

As opportunities arose, some of these kosher butchers, who lived on the Atlantic seacoast, expanded their businesses and became merchants. They included kosher meat as a commodity to sell on their voyages. Before the days of refrigeration, the kosher way of preserving beef by carefully selecting the animal, slaughtering it, washing the meat in cold water, then salting it, ensured safer meat for transport.

Probably the most famous of these merchants during the Revolutionary period was Aaron Lopez, Newport's largest taxpayer. Mr. Lopez came in 1752 from Portugal, where his family had been New Christians and secret Jews for two generations before returning to Judaism. Having made his initial fortune in whale oil and the spermaceti candle industries, he was one of the few American Jews active in the slave trade. A distiller of rum and manufacturer of clothing, barrels, ships, and foods, he built an extensive transatlantic mercantile empire. From the West Indies he brought commodities like sugar, molasses, cocoa, coffee, pimento, ginger, nutmeg, allspice, pepper, and cloves to satisfy the tastes of the colonists.

When the British took Newport, Mr. Lopez, a rebel sympathizer, fled the city, but on his return, in 1782 after the Revolution, drowned in quicksand. His now-tattered leather-bound ledger books contain accounts showing items sold in his shop and other goods included in cargoes sent to Suriname and Jamaica. Kosher articles in the ledgers were marked with a "cashier" (kosher) stamp for "Jew beef" (salted beef), meat tongues, rendered fat, smoked beef, "chorissa" (smoked beef sausages), as well as cheese, all packed in barrels. Chorissa is defined in *The Jewish Manual,* the first Jewish cookbook in English, published in London in 1846, as "that most refined and savoury of all sausages." It may have been the chorissa sausages that the Portuguese still talk about as the smoked beef, not pork sausage, of northern Portugal drying in the chimneys of New Christian homes. To this day, in Portugal, a pork-loving land, there are small towns that specialize in beef, rather than pork, sausage.

Aaron Lopez had a ready market in the Jewish community of Newport, the Colonial Jewish settlement second only to New York. Clearly his relationship to the Jewish community was more than mere business. In a letter dated 1779, he wrote, "The Jews in particular were suffering due to a scarcity of kosher food. They had not tasted any meat, but once in two months. Fish was not to be had, and they were forced to subsist on chocolate and coffee." Of the two thousand or so Jews living in the Colonies during the Revolutionary period, there were many Ashkenazim, perhaps more even than Sephardim. Even so, it was the Sephardic Jews in Newport, New York, Philadelphia, Charleston, and Savannah who set the tone of Judaism in this country, both in the synagogues and in the kitchens.

Because many of their dishes were holiday foods, bound for centuries to tradition, they were the last to go during cultural and culinary assimilation in this country. Allspice or hot pepper might have been added to a fish or meat stew during their sojourn in Brazil or a stopover in the West Indies, but the basic recipes of stewed and fish fried in olive oil, beef and bean stews, almond puddings, and egg custards come directly from the Iberian peninsula and represent the most authentic Sephardic foods we know in this country. *Jewish Cookery* by Esther Levy, the first kosher cookbook in America, which appeared in Philadelphia in 1871, included many of these old recipes.

At the same time that Sephardic Jews were setting the tone on the East Coast, there were in the Southwest the descendants of crypto or hidden Jews who had fled the Inquisition. They had come from Mexico even before the New Amsterdam group, in the sixteenth century. Anthropologists are now discovering that crypto Jews retained many of their three-centuries-old cultural and culinary traditions, which they continued to practice in secret. Many of them have no idea of the origin of their customs.

Some still light candles on Friday night while attending Catholic churches on Sunday. Some salt meats, others eschew pork, using beef for tamales and *albondigas* (meatballs). Even their *empanaditas* (an empanada is often stuffed with pork in Spain today) are filled with chopped beef and with ground tongue. At Passover some secret family customs include eating crackers that they call "pan de semite." While it is important to keep this group in mind when studying the foods of the early Sephardic Jews, I have used instead the recipes that I have found on the East Coast, since many of the foods were the same and the evidence about the crypto Jews of New Mexico is still very tentative.

THE SECOND WAVE — JEWS FROM GERMANIC LANDS, 1830 TO 1880

> The peddler took from his pack a kosher sausage and the remains of a loaf of bread. These he inspected carefully to see that the snow had not soaked through his pack and spoiled them. He next took from his bag a cheap, silver-plated candle holder with eight arms which he set in one of the high windows of the barn. Into the first arm on the right side he placed a candle which he lit . . .
>
> "Petravsky on the Road," *Hearst Magazine,* March 1913

While early American Jewry settled along the Atlantic Coast, after 1830 the second wave forged westward, crossing the mountains to the Ohio and Mississippi rivers. Many, like Levi Strauss, strapped packs on their backs and headed all the way across the continent to San Francisco, peddling textiles, kitchen wares, and other non-perishables as they went along. Jews have always been in the backpack business, selling spices, fabric, precious stones, anything that could be packed up easily when they were expelled from a country. It was a natural occupation for them, as they were rarely allowed to own land. In America, they became a familiar sight in the countryside before mail-order catalogues, like the Jewish Sears Roebuck, put them out of business.

Food, especially kosher food, posed a problem for them when they were traveling. Peddlers would often roast herrings, wrapped in newspaper, over an open fire, or subsist on preserved or hard-boiled eggs and kosher sausage, as long as those supplies lasted. On Saturdays the men created Sabbath communities in little towns where they met to pray. Often, as they made a little money peddling, they would buy a wagon and eventually settle in these communities, bringing their families from abroad.

"The Jewish heart with its most beautiful blossom, parental love, thought in its happiness of parents living in need in the old country and would bring them over from Germany," wrote I. J. Benjamin, an observer of American Jewish life in the mid-1850s. "But the old father and the pious little mother, would not, in the late evening of their lives, have any part in eating forbidden food. The sons had no choice, then, but devoutly to accommodate themselves to true Jewish piety, according to the wishes of their parents, and also to appoint a schochet. The institutions that a Jewish community usually organizes were, accordingly, soon in existence. So arose one Jewish institution after another."

While Jews were trying to balance Judaism and assimilation, great inventions were changing the United States. Coal and wood-burning stoves rapidly outdated open-hearth cookery, the steam engine took the place of the horse and buggy, ready-made clothing eliminated handmade dresses, and refrigeration replaced endless salting, smoking, and preserving.

Of the ten million immigrants to this country between the years 1830 and 1880, three million were Germans and 200,000 were Jews from German-speaking lands. The most important German Jewish center of commerce, culture, and cuisine was Cincinnati,

The peddler's wagon

Ohio. By 1872 Cincinnati had nine *schochetim,* five Jewish restaurants, sixteen abattoirs for kosher meat, and three matzah bakeries.

Until World War I, German immigrants—Jews and non-Jews alike—thought of their native culture as superior to that of America. German was the first language in many homes, a required subject in elementary school and the language of sermons in synagogues and churches. Students even had a choice of a German or English curriculum. By the end of the nineteenth century these Jews became American-German-Jewish. This tri-ethnicity played itself out in both culture and cuisine. In Jewish homes, foods like chicken-noodle or vegetable soup, roast chicken, and goose graced the tables for Friday-night dinner or Sunday lunch when the entire family gathered together.

Because baking had reached a more sophisticated level in Germany than it had in the United States at that time, these immigrants brought with them marvelous kuchen, breads, and tortes. In addition, as whole Jewish communities from Bavaria emigrated, they carried their own German regional recipes such as *Lebkuchen* or *Dampfnudeln,* a wonderful brioche-like cake soaked in caramel and served with a vanilla sauce. It was no coincidence that Cincinnati became the home of Fleischmann's yeast and Crisco, a vegetable-based shortening for which Procter & Gamble advertised the Jews had waited four thousand years.

In nineteenth-century America, traditional Jews and those wanting a more "enlightened American Judaism" were having a hard time. Since laws prohibited shops from being open on Sunday, Jews usually had to keep their shops open on Saturday, often either postponing the Sabbath meal to Sunday dinner or having a Friday evening get-together.

Time was ripe for a rabbi to try to unify the "secularists and the conservateurs" who had broken away from Orthodoxy. It was Isaac Mayer Wise, the leader of the reform movement, who tried to present a practical American Judaism. He called for many changes in the old order: for women to come down from the balcony, for hats to come off in the synagogue, and for many people to realize that the dietary laws were an archaic relic of the past.

Born in Bohemia in 1819, Wise immigrated as a young man to the United States, where he became a rabbi in Albany, New York, and in 1854 moved to Cincinnati. Founder of the Hebrew Union College, the Union of American Hebrew Congregations, and the Central Conference of American Rabbis, Wise also edited *Die Deborah,* a German language paper, and the *American Israelite,* which he claimed to have "the largest circulation of all Jewish papers published between the Atlantic Coast and the Rocky Mountains" by 1886. His daughter, Effie, later married Adolph Ochs of Chattanooga who, in 1896, bought *The New York Times.*

Isaac Mayer Wise

Believing that Orthodoxy would disappear within one or two generations, he resented "the zealous orthodoxy, (who) make of these (dietary) laws a matter of religion, a test of orthodoxy, a touchstone of Judaism . . . A man can be a conscientious believer in Judaism and a religious Israelite without obeying any laws which are not contained, expressed or implied in the Sinai Revelation."

One of the many subjects upon which he wrote frequently was the dietary laws. Although Wise himself refrained from pork on sanitary grounds and excluded in his home almost all shellfish, he had a passion for oysters. In an editorial in the *American Israelite* on April 4, 1895, he wrote, "There can be no doubt that the oyster shell is the same to all intents and purposes as the scales are to the clean fish, protecting against certain gases in the water. In fact, the oyster shell is a close connection of scales. It is the scales only which the Talmud acknowledges as the sign of cleanliness. . . . Oysters grown in ponds outside of the sea are certainly kosher, also according to Maimonides." It is not surprising, then, that by the end of the century a reform temple in Alabama held an oyster dinner fundraiser and *Aunt Babette's Cookbook* of Chicago in 1889 included an entire oyster chapter, as did many of the Council of Jewish Women's fund-raising cookbooks from Boston to Portland, Oregon.

Wise's ambivalence toward the laws of kashrut and the growing gap within the Jewish community with regard to dietary laws contributed to an event that has become known as the "Treif Banquet." It led to the final schism between traditional and Reform American Jews. On July 12, 1883, the graduation of the first class of American rabbis was celebrated with an eight-course dinner for two hundred people at the Highland House in Cincinnati. "Knowing that there would be delegates from the various parts of the country present who laid stress upon the observance of the dietary laws, the Cincinnati committee engaged a Jewish caterer," wrote Dr. David Philipson, one of the rabbinical graduates. "The great banqueting hall was brilliantly lighted, the hundreds of guests were seated at the beautifully-arranged tables, the invocation had been spoken by one of the visiting rabbis, when the waiters served the first course. Terrific excitement ensued when two rabbis rose from their seats and rushed from the room. Shrimp had been placed before them as the opening course of the elaborate menu."

Actually it was littleneck clams, but it could have been the soft-shelled crabs, shrimp salad, or frogs' legs with cream, all non-kosher foods, which were also served at the banquet. Although the departure of the two rabbis did not cause much of a stir at that dinner, it did in the Orthodox press throughout the country. This event became a factor in the creation of Conservative Judaism. Five years later, the conservative Jewish Theological Seminary opened.

It has never been clear who was responsible for the banquet. The dinner was supposedly supervised by Gus Lindeman, caterer for Cincinnati's wealthy German Jewish Allemania Club, and some of the members had arranged and paid for the ceremonial repast. After the event *Die Deborah*'s correspondent in Denver wrote, "kitchen Judaism should be relegated to the antique cabinet where it belongs . . . the humbug of the dietary laws must go." And a Chicago paper took blame for this second mortal sin against the Jewish stomach: "Why feign compliance with dietary laws in public when privately no one observes them?"

After the event Rabbi Wise wrote, "The fact is that the said chief cook, himself a Jew, wool-dyed, was placed there to bring before the guests a kosher meal. So it was understood in Cincinnati all along, and we do not know why he diversified his menu with multipeds and bivalves. . . . There is a law which stands higher than all dietary laws, and that is 'be no fanatic,' which translated in our vulgar language would sound somewhat like this: 'Be intelligent, and allow your reason to govern your passions, propensities and superstitions.' "

While Reform Jews were tasting American produce, their family recipes were becoming regionalized. In Mississippi and Alabama pecans replaced almonds in tortes and cookies; in Ohio molasses or brown sugar replaced honey in *Schnecken;* in the state of Washington salmon appeared instead of carp on Northwest Sabbath tables; and in Louisiana hot pepper and scallions were used instead of mild ginger in matzah balls.

Crossover foods were already beginning to affect the non-Jewish public as well, often being mentioned in mainstream American nineteenth-century cookbooks. The introduction to *Smiley's Cook Book and Universal Household Guide,* published in 1901, notes: "Jewish cookery is becoming much like that of their Christian neighbors, as, except among the more denominationally strict, the old restrictions are melting away, and they often employ Christian servants. From having been forbidden to use butter with meat, oil enters more largely into their cookery of both meat and vegetables. Their fish fried in oil, and so cooked that it can be eaten cold or hot, enjoys a deservedly high reputation. As the Mosaic law forbids the use of any flesh as food which is not free from 'spot or blemish' the meat supplied by the Jewish butchers is of the best quality."

BAGELS TRIUMPHANT: THE RISE OF
EASTERN EUROPEAN JEWRY

For my first meal in the New World I bought a three-cent wedge of coarse rye bread off a huge round loaf, on a stand on Essex Street. I was too strict in my religious observances to eat it without first performing ablutions and offering a brief prayer. So I approached a bewigged old woman who stood in the doorway of a small grocery-store to let me wash my hands and eat my meal in her place. She looked old-fashioned enough, yet when she heard my request she said, with a laugh:

"You're a green one, I see."

"Supposed I am," I resented. "Do the yellow ones or black ones all eat without washing? Can't a fellow be a good Jew in America?"

"Yes, of course he can, but—well, wait till you see for yourself."

Abraham Cahan, *The Rise of David Levinsky,* 1960

Abraham Cahan's autobiographical David Levinsky was not the only Eastern European Jew who was thrown off base on his first day in the New World. Between 1881 and 1921, the year of the first restrictive law cutting off Jewish immigration, there were perhaps 2,500,000 like him, all looking for a new life, many hoping to hold onto their Orthodoxy (which, of course, included their dietary laws).

With European pogroms, forced military conscription, lack of civil rights, periodic expulsion from towns and villages, and displacements from the industrialization of the 1870s, millions of Jews sought a freer life in America. They came here carrying with them their brass candlesticks, mortar and pestles, pots and pans, as well as century-old recipes.

Not surprisingly, even on the journey over, food became a major issue for the Orthodox immigrants. According to the *Jewish Messenger* of November 25, 1881, "Some of the emigrants who arrived on the Helvetia, of the National Line, last week, complained of the food given them on the voyage, asserting that it was not prepared according to the Mosaic dietary laws, as promised by the agents of the line in Europe. This is the second time this complaint has been made."

Not all passengers, of course, observed the dietary laws. Many were radicals who rebelled against this Orthodoxy. But no matter what their attitude was towards kashrut, they all complained about the food on the journey over. "We had the desire to fill our stomachs but nothing to fill them with," said one immigrant, Harris Rubin. "It was not because there was any lack of quantity. The tables were loaded with bread, butter, herring, cake and potatoes in their skins and we were free to take as much as we wished. But the trouble was that we could not put the stuff in our mouths. The butter smelled like old wax, the herring like raw fresh fish. The cake was mouldy. The bread and potatoes without good reason had a nauseating taste."

Overcoming the ocean voyage, the passengers arrived at Ellis Island. Whole Jewish communities were transplanted, including the rabbi and the *schochet*. They crowded into New York's Lower East Side, Chicago's West Side, Boston's North End and south Philadelphia. At one time there were almost four thousand kosher butcher shops in New York City alone. The immigrants were successful at finding work and housing and became a part of a network of familiar social and cultural institutions, such as landsmanshaftn, the Jewish mutual aid societies that were formed by immigrants originating from the same villages, towns, and cities in Eastern Europe.

A square block in an immigrant area in any American city would include overcrowded

Turn-of-the-century Jews on the Brooklyn Bridge throwing bread into the water for tashlich, an ancient cleansing ritual at Rosh Hashanah

tenements, sweatshops, basement synagogues, saloons, and cafés. In the typical tenement, tiny apartments burst with large families, boarders, and little air.

As the immigrants adjusted to new food habits, they quickly forgot some of the foods of their poverty like *krupnick,* a cereal soup made from oatmeal, sometimes barley, potatoes, and fat. If a family could afford it, milk would be added to the *krupnick.* If not, it was called "*soupr mit nisht*" or supper with nothing. Today, *krupnick* is considered a health food. Bagels, knishes, or herring in a newspaper would be taken back to the sweatshop, providing a poor substitute for the midday lunch they were used to in Eastern Europe. "The dietary routine of life changed when I came to America," wrote Benjamin Lee Gordon in his autobiography, *Between Two Worlds.* "The dinner which at home had been served at noon and was the main meal of the day, changed into lunch and consisted, like as not, of two slices of bread simply concealing a scanty piece of cheese, meat, or canned fish—the kind of food we boys used to take along in our pockets to hold us over from breakfast to dinner."

To combat all these changes and the rise of Reform Judaism in America, many Orthodox Jews clung to their old traditions, including kashrut. It was not always easy. In 1 8 8 1 in Denver, for example, Jews were unable to acquire kosher meat so they either had to practice ritual slaughtering for themselves or eat no meat. Many quickly abandoned their Orthodoxy and joined the "reformed temple." Later, many of them would become Conservative Jews.

One Orthodox Jew, Rabbi Hyman Sharfman, went from Kennebunkport, Maine, to Corpus Christi, Texas, in a gearless cycle car, sometimes on horseback, kashering meat and teaching people in the community how to do it themselves. Another, Dov Behr Manischewitz, hearing of the huge center of Reform Judaism in Cincinnati, decided to settle there as a *schochet.* He later made his fortune in the matzah industry.

For all the diverse Orthodox immigrant groups, there was no unified Jewish leadership. In a small town in Russia, for example, the rabbi was the leader. Meat was kosher because everyone went to the same *schochet*, but in New York, with millions of people and thousands of kosher butchers, not to underestimate the importance of the separation between church and state, there was no central authority to whom to turn for validation of the religious laws.

Finally, eighteen Orthodox synagogues in New York, Philadelphia, and Baltimore organized themselves and brought over Jacob Joseph, the chief rabbi of Vilna, in 1 8 8 8 as their head. Among his other duties he was supposed to organize the kosher-meat business. By 1 9 1 7, at the height of Orthodoxy in America, there were a million Jews eating 1 5 6 million pounds of kosher meat annually. With no central authority, individual rabbis were putting their "*hechsher*" or kosher stamp on the meat. Some was kosher, some was not. Because of dietary abuses and escalating prices, kosher meat and bread riots broke out at the turn of the century. One boycott was dubbed the "war of the women against the butchers." The battle cry became "1 2 cents instead of 1 8 cents a pound."

Against such odds, Joseph's efforts at organizing a central kosher authority failed miserably. It was not until 1 9 4 4 that a food-inspection bureau to authenticate kosher meats was

Maxwell Street, Chicago

formed in New York State. Still in operation to this day, inspectors regularly spot-check all kosher meat markets across the country . . . yet there are still occasional problems.

Despite the riots and lack of unification, the United States gave these Eastern European immigrants, deeply interested in the way food was prepared, great opportunities in the food business. The butchers, bakers, and pushcart peddlers of herring and pickles soon became small-scale independent grocers, wine merchants, and wholesale meat, produce, and fruit providers.

Not only did these immigrants go into the business of food, but they also adapted their Eastern European food ways to the new environment. Sunday, for example, a second day of rest, provided them with new gastronomic opportunities like a dairy brunch, an embellishment of their simple dairy dinners in Europe.

THE MAKING OF AMERICAN JEWISH FOOD—
FROM LOX AND BAGELS TO LINDY'S CHEESECAKE

Who, today, would put up tomato catsup when there are Heinz's "57 varieties" to choose from? And who would corn or spice beef when a tempting delicatessen shop is at the corner? In those days (the 1880s) housekeepers went to market. No one gave orders over the telephone. . . . There were no women's club activities in the 'eighties. We had no civic duties, no public meetings to distract us from our homes and social duties. . . . As I look back to those days, the distinguishing feature of our receptions—which contrast so strongly with the receptions of today—is the fact that we entertained our friends in our own home. Today, clubs and hotels take the place of home entertainments. This is largely due to the present custom of living in apartments, the increasing problem of efficient domestic service, and the modern habit of thought—to accomplish results with a minimum of responsibility. I wonder whether the modern hostess derives the same thrill and joy from her vicarious methods of hospitality as did the hostess of forty years ago, who planned with care and foresight every detail of the entertainment. It may not have been "grand" or so "smart" as a modern function given at Sherry's, but at least in its fruition it was the expression of the hostess' own individuality. Herein lay its charm.

Maud Nathan, *Once Upon a Time and Today,* 1933

For Maud Nathan, a direct descendant of one of the first Jews to set foot on American soil and the sister of Annie Nathan Meyer, the founder of Barnard College, cooking changed dramatically from the 1880s, when she married, to the 1930s, when she wrote her autobiography. Not only did women have the right to vote, but the first national Jewish women's organization, the National Council of Jewish Women, was founded in the fall of 1893 as an outgrowth of a national Jewish women's congress. By 1900 the 7,080 members in fifty-five cities helped support the rights of women, mission and industrial schools

Suffragist Group: Maud Nathan is standing second from the right.

for poor Jewish children, free baths in Kansas City and Denver, and, of course, cooking classes in the settlement houses, such as Mrs. Kander's in Milwaukee. Council cookbooks were put out nationwide with proceeds to help support their projects. Like the *Settlement Cook Book,* these books often had a German slant and included many goose recipes as well as other American dishes such as chicken chow mein, often made from leftover chicken soup, and Saratoga chips, a turn-of-the-century potato chip.

Other organizations followed suit. In September 1905, for example, the Montefiore Lodge Ladies Hebrew Benevolent Association of Providence, Rhode Island, published the following in its newsletter: "It was voted that 'this lodge publish and sell a cookbook of favorite recipes.' Two separate committees were appointed, one for the cooking recipes and the other to solicit advertising."

While the women's organizations were working to help the less fortunate, another revolution was taking place—that of food technology and scientific discovery. Slowly the kitchen was transformed, liberating women from time-consuming chores. Not only was Heinz producing its bottled ketchups and fledgling companies making kosher canned foods, but companies were manufacturing a white vegetable substance resembling lard—the shortening that would change forever the way Jewish women cooked. The inventions of cream cheese, rennet, gelatin, junket, Jell-O, pasteurized milk, Coca-Cola, nondairy creamer, *phyllo* dough, and frozen foods would all affect Jewish cooking in America.

With the growth of food companies, delicatessens, school-lunch programs, and restaurants, American food and American Jewish food became more processed and more innovative. In 1925 the average American housewife made all her food at home. By 1965, 75 to 90 percent of the food she used had undergone some sort of factory processing.

As the latest wave of Eastern European Jews became more Americanized, they began trying new dishes like macaroni and cheese and canned tuna-fish casseroles. Jewish cookbooks included recipes for creole dishes, for chicken fricassee using canned tomatoes, and shortcut kuchen using baking powder. Many of these Jews cared little about the import of scientific discoveries on kashrut. Others cared deeply. At the turn of the century, the Union of Orthodox Jewish Congregations, the umbrella organization for Orthodox Jews, was established as a means of bringing cohesion to the fragmented immigrant Jewish populations. In 1923, the year it created its women's branch, and four years after women won the right to vote, the Union's official kashrut supervision and certification program was introduced.

At about that time, a New York advertising genius named Joseph Jacobs encouraged big companies to advertise their mainstream packaged products in the Yiddish press. Jacobs' mission was to change the way Americans thought about Jewish dietary practices. The chains and the big food companies did not know how to promote to a Yiddish-speaking population since they employed no Jews.

One day he approached Joel Cheek, the founder of Maxwell House Coffee. Mr. Cheek, who had started selling his coffee from saddlebags off a horse in Tennessee, was searching for ways to widen his Eastern market. Mr. Jacobs suggested to him the Jewish Passover

clientele. For some reason, Eastern European Jews thought that coffee beans, like other beans, were forbidden during Passover. Mr. Jacobs consulted a rabbi who told him that coffee beans were technically berries and were kosher for Passover. After the rabbi approved Maxwell House, Jacobs hired men to go into independent stores with the coffee. The merchants were delighted to sell the coffee, which became such a success that in 1934 the company started producing Maxwell House haggadahs for Passover, another Jacobs idea.

When canned products like H. J. Heinz Company's baked beans and pork came on the market, an inventive advertising man named Joshua C. Epstein, an Orthodox Jew, had a thought: What if Heinz made kosher vegetarian baked beans? Company officials liked Epstein's suggestions, but they balked at the idea of writing kosher in Hebrew or English on the package. "Heinz wanted something identifiable, but not too Jewish: they didn't want to antagonize the non-Jewish population," recalls Abraham Butler, the son of the late Frank Butler, Heinz's first *mashgiach*. With Jacobs and Rabbi Herbert Goldstein, one of the founders of the Union of Orthodox Hebrew Congregations of America, the three devised the Orthodox Union Ⓤ symbol, today the best-recognized trademark of the some 120 symbols for kosher certification.

Jews went into the packaged-food business, too. In this land of opportunity, some food merchants struck it rich. One Chicago baker named Charley Lubin made a luscious cheesecake; it was the beginning of the age of frozen food so he tried freezing his cake. It worked and he named it "Sara Lee" after his daughter. Another Jew in the advertising business tried to think of what to do with a bumper crop of oranges so he invented frozen orange juice.

The fast-growing influence of radio and television affected how Americans saw each other and how products were sold. "The Goldbergs," a program about a fictional Bronx family, reached a radio audience of ten million in the thirties and at least forty million two decades later on television. Just as *I Remember Mama* taught us about Scandinavians, "The Goldbergs" familiarized non-Jews with a simple, everyday Jewish family. Sometimes Molly Goldberg just cooked throughout the whole program, cutting up a chicken, chopping fish or herring, as the problems of her family paraded through her kitchen.

After World War II another "cooking lady" stepped onto television. Her name was Edith Green, whose popular "Your Home Kitchen" ruled the airwaves in the San Francisco Bay area from 1949 to 1954. Although this "queen of the range" was Jewish, her cooking was American . . . and it was "gourmet." A week's recipes might include veal scallopini, coffee chocolate icebox cake, coconut pudding, or frozen tuna mold. She showed her viewers how to use new gadgets, such as electric mixers and electric can openers, all products of the post-war period of affluence.

As Jews became more Americanized, notions of "Jewish food" changed with the availability of regional ingredients. Taste buds adjusted to local spices and new dietary guidelines. While Jews in Burlington, Vermont, ate potato latkes with maple syrup, Californians preferred theirs with local goat cheese. Gefilte fish was made with whitefish in the midwest, salmon in the far west, and haddock in Maine. The matzah balls, gefilte fish, even the Passover desserts American Jews eat today are certainly very different from those eaten in Europe or in this country a century ago.

Molly Goldberg

TWENTIETH-CENTURY IMMIGRATION — FROM THE CASBAH, THE CAMPS, THE KIBBUTZ, AND THE CAUCASUS

. . . there has sprung up during the past few years another group of kosher eating houses which cater to the needs of the Oriental (Jew) who hails from Saloniki, (sic) parts of Turkey and the Levant . . . Occasionally you will see in these restaurants a newly arrived Oriental still wearing a fez and his wife still adorned with some of the jewelry and embroidered fabrics of the Near East.

Montague Glass, "Kosher Restaurants,"
Saturday Evening Post, August 5, 1929

When Sephardic Jews from Syria and Turkey came here at the beginning of the twentieth century, most American Jews already knew about knishes and pirogi. But now they would learn about other "Jewish" finger-food pastries. Syrian Jews brought cheese *sambousek* and date *adjwah* and Turkish Jews eggplant *burek.*

Later, with the rise of Hitler, refugees from Germany and Eastern Europe fled to America, and they brought with them updated versions of recipes that had come to this country one or two generations before. We sometimes forget that food in the "old country" was

*Child refugees of the Holocaust
arrive in New York Harbor.*

*An immigrant family's Lower
East Side kitchen*

evolving just as it was in the United States. Many old immigrant recipes have what I call a "culinary lag" in this country. Because they were handed down, brought out for special occasions, they were not changed. In the old country these dishes were constantly evolving.

Most of the Chasidim arrived after the war, following their leaders. In 1940, the story goes, the State Department intervened with the Nazis to allow the Lubavitcher Rabbi Joseph Schneerson and his followers to leave in a train from Germany to Switzerland. The other Chasidim came by harder routes carrying their belongings in kerchiefs and cardboard boxes. In Crown Heights, in Borough Park, in Williamsburg, they resettled in their own shtetls, U.S. style. Now, a generation later, their numbers are expanding, reaching out to assimilated second- and third-generation American Jewish youth, with religious centers in cities coast to coast. Their influence has increased in many areas, including that of the demand for a strict adherence to kosher foods.

Political and economic upheavals brought more Jews who were beleaguered and badgered in other countries by regimes unfriendly to them in the decades after World War II. In a sense, the creation of Israel spurred a worldwide awareness of Jewish food. Before 1948, many of the dishes now appearing on Israeli tables had been eaten for hundreds, even thousands, of years, only by Jews in isolated little villages of the Atlas Mountains, the kitchens of Izmir, or the shtetls of Poland. Now some of the children of these immigrants to Israel are setting foot in the United States. These Mediterranean Jews have enriched the tapestry of Jewish cuisine here. They have contributed new "Jewish" dishes with such treats as Syrian tamarind-flavored meat pies, fresh cumin-accented carrot salads from Morocco, and Israeli falafel. Americans are attracted to their cuisines because of the many vegetable-based dishes—the kind of cooking that is in keeping with our new dietary guidelines.

While masses of Jews came to the shores of the United States during pogroms and the Holocaust, others went to Mexico, to Cuba, to China, to Australia, and to Argentina. As political problems swept through these lands many Jews moved to America, or as they visited relatives here they stayed on. And they brought still more new dishes with them.

With the upheavals in the former Soviet Union, a new kind of Russian Jew arrived, one who knew very little about the Jewish religion and customs, which had been outlawed in 1917. Settling in large cities, converting places like Brighton Beach, Brooklyn, into a new kind of ghetto, they are learning quickly about Jewish foods.

NEWISH JEWISH FOOD—
TRANSFORMATION—1980S AND 1990S

Since the 1980s, kosher food has had an astonishing revival from coast to coast. People respond to an advertisement for a kosher hot dog "answering to a higher authority" or identify with "You don't have to be Jewish to like Levy's." To many Americans the word *kosher* is synonymous with better and safer. But 90 percent of Americans do not even know—nor do they care—that they are buying "kosher" when they pick up a box of Pepperidge Farm cookies or a bottle of Heinz ketchup, only two of the thousands of kosher products that are on the market today.

Of the 6,500,000 people who purposely buy kosher foods, only 1,500,000 are kashrut-observing Jews. The great majority are Black Muslims, vegetarians, and Seventh-Day Adventists, as well as regular supermarket shoppers, because the kosher sign proves to them that the food is not pork or a pork by-product.

A shot in the arm to kosher food has been the Baalei Tshuvah, returnees to the faith. Baal Tshuvah restaurateur Sol Kirschenbaum of New York's Levana restaurant has introduced his kosher clientele to rare beef and kosher quail. These formerly non-observant Jews, who are returning to their Jewish roots, observe the laws of kashrut, but are anxious to try the new, lighter tastes and dishes that they knew before they became kosher. They have welcomed new look-alike products such as mock shrimp and lobster made of pollock and prefer *radicchio* with *shiitake* mushrooms without the prosciutto.

Gone are the days of stuffed *derma* (stomach casings) and stuffed *helzel* (chicken neck), cooked with schmaltz—all representing heavy, time-consuming traditional Jewish foods. First-class kosher wines are being produced in California, kosher meals are prepared for all airlines, and the kosher product market is expanding rapidly.

Although Jews have long been in the food business, only recently did they become chefs. Today, many second- and third-generation Americans are cooking professionally instead of becoming doctors and lawyers. Some of them are reaching back to their own traditions for Jewish tastes in their cooking. Chef Janos Wilder of Janos Restaurant in Tucson, Arizona, has adapted his mother's traditional apple and nut *haroset,* adding mangos and chopped toasted pecans. Some cooks, like David Leiderman in New York and Jim Cohen in Vail, Colorado, although not observant Jews themselves, swear by kosher chickens. And many non-Jewish chefs have become intrigued with Jewish customs, preparing Roman Jewish menus and even seders in their restaurants.

Jewish chefs often express their Jewishness in preferences for kasha, potato pancakes, kosher chickens, chicken soup, or a good New York cheesecake. There are also new kosher restaurants, where the word is taken seriously—not just metaphorically as in kosher-style delis, a term coined in the fifties. You can eat kosher Hunan, Indian, Italian, Moroccan, French—whatever you want—in New York, in Los Angeles, as well as in some cities in between.

Not only are there many Jewish chefs today, whole chapters in professional cookbooks are devoted to cooking for the kosher market, and there have never been so many Jewish cookbooks, including low-cholesterol kosher.

Since, unfortunately, many second-generation Americans have lost the recipes and the traditions of the past in their race for assimilation, it is my hope that this book will take them back to their roots and that all readers will try the new as they understand the old tastes.

As I have done in my other cookbooks, I do not treat recipes as isolated phenomena. Each one has a story that connects it historically and culturally to its Jewish past. I have structured within each chapter an interweaving of cultures, starting with older recipes and ending with more contemporary interpretations of these dishes. Although the sequence of the over three hundred kosher recipes is chronological, I have divided the book into a "cookable order"—appetizers, soup, fish, meat, vegetables and salads, dairy dishes, breads, desserts, and beverages as well as a chapter devoted to Passover. Each chapter, just as American Jewry is today, is an interweaving of different cultures.

Without destroying the traditional flavors of these recipes, which were lovingly handed down from generation to generation, I have tried to reduce fat and sugar wherever possible. Often, I have included tips for variations of a recipe, shortening the cooking time or reflecting my own feelings about the dish. Each recipe is designated with a P for pareve, D for dairy, and M for meat. If I enjoy serving dishes together, I have indicated my favorite combinations and have also provided menus at the end of the book.

Recipes have come from a variety of sources. Many were in response to a "letter to the editor" I ran in Jewish newspapers and historical society newsletters across the country. Others came from people who knew my quest, and wanted to share their own family recipes. Still others are treasures from eighteenth-, nineteenth-, and twentieth-century private papers and cookbooks, which I have adapted for present-day use.

Whenever I could, I conducted direct interviews, traveling from coast to coast, sometimes staying with my hosts, as I did with the Lubavitcher Deitsch family of Crown Heights, Brooklyn. I visited Ernie Weir's Hagafen vineyards in Napa Valley and Ruth Hendricks-Schulson's living room on New York's West Side, where portraits of her ancestors looked down at us as she showed me a folder with heirloom recipes of the first Sephardic families.

While watching eighty-five-year-old David Sofaer of San Rafael, California, carefully stirring dates into a jam used as *haroset* for Passover, I listened to the life story of the Baghdadi Jew who was born in Burma and lived in Bombay; I visualized his mother reducing this delicious compound in huge copper pots, a recipe that most likely originated in biblical times. From Emme Sue Frank of Dallas, I discovered how American Jews were influenced by regional foods, how pecans, for example, worked their way into matzah balls. From Kora Bloom Potatnik of Dawson City, Alaska, I learned how Jews in that remote area made their own matzah and gefilte fish from greyling and Mackinaw trout. And from Harvey Potkin, Executive Officer of Hebrew National, I listened to the tale of a Lower East Side family of butchers that became the largest producer of kosher meat in America today. This book is about all these people, their food and their stories. These past five years have been a great adventure for me, and I hope the reader enjoys the fruits of this odyssey as much as I have enjoyed the trip.

Appetizers—From Herring to Hummus

The Jewish appetizing store (in Brownsville, Brooklyn) was a fixture of all these Jewish neighborhoods. They were quite marvelous, barrels of pickles, smoked fishes, slightly seedy. They also carried barrels of sunflower seeds, halvah and dried fruit. They were pareve and strictly Jewish institutions. Appetizing stores never had tables, they specialized in these fishes, ancillary products, whitefish. Where I grew up we were too poor for sturgeon.

Norman Podhoretz, editor of *Commentary,* 1993

In several of the cafes of the quarter these old fellows gather. With their long beards, long black coats, and serious demeanor, they sit about little tables and drink honey cider, eat lima beans, and jealously exclude from their society the socialists and free thinkers of the colony who, not unwillingly, have cafes of their own.

Hutchins Hapgood, *The Spirit of the Ghetto,* 1892

Boulettes de Poissons (Sephardic Fish Balls with Saffron and Fresh Coriander)

Because of the prohibition against cooking on the Sabbath, Jews devised fish dishes that could be made several days ahead. A recipe that goes back to at least medieval times was fish balls, fried or simmered in water, and served cold. It came to this country with the early immigrants from Spain and Portugal. Because the recipe was adapted to British ways en route to America, the fish balls were often coated with an egg-lemon sauce rather like hollandaise. But descendants of the Jews from Spain, who went to Morocco and other countries, are now bringing recipes for fish balls spiked instead with hot pepper, coriander, and garlic. I have tasted variations in Moroccan and Egyptian Jewish homes in the United States. Although gefilte fish may have evolved from this dish, I don't recommend serving these spicy balls with horseradish. You won't need it. It is great as a fish appetizer at parties.

2 pounds sole or white fish
*   fillets*
10 cloves of garlic
1 fresh hot pepper or to taste,
*   seeded*
2 cups fresh coriander
1 teaspoon salt or to taste
2 teaspoons cumin or to taste
¼ teaspoon turmeric
1 ¼-inch slice challah or other
*   white bread*
1 cup and 1 tablespoon water
2 large eggs, beaten
Pinch of saffron
3 tablespoons vegetable oil
Juice of 1 lemon

1. Place the fish, garlic, pepper, coriander, salt, cumin, and turmeric in a food processor fitted with a steel blade and process until smooth.

2. Put the challah in a bowl with the cup of water and soak. Drain thoroughly, add along with the eggs to the fish, and process until smooth.

3. Soften the saffron in the remaining tablespoon water, then add that with 1 tablespoon of the vegetable oil and the lemon juice to the fish, and process until smooth.

4. Cover the pureed fish mixture and put in the refrigerator for an hour or so.

5. Shape the fish into balls the size of a walnut. Heat the remaining oil in a frying pan over medium heat and brown the fish balls on all sides. When brown, cover with aluminum foil and bake in a preheated 350-degree oven for about 25 minutes. Eat either immediately or at room temperature, serving with toothpicks.

Yield: about 40 fish balls (P)
Note: You can also deep-fry these fish balls.

Salmon Ceviche — *Mexican Food Goes Kosher*

Keeping a kosher kitchen in the Kittrie family does not mean traditional Jewish cooking. "We find great pleasure in discovering multi-cultural recipes that can be easily made at home," said Sara Kittrie. Mexican-born from a Polish Jewish family, Ms. Kittrie has also introduced her family to the food of her native land.

At the Kittries', ceviche is made from red salmon laced with green avocado—pretty and delicious.

1 pound skinless, boneless
  fillets of red salmon,
  bluefish, red snapper, or
  mackerel
Juice of 3 limes
1 cup peeled, seeded ripe
  tomatoes, cut into ¼-inch
  cubes and drained
1 to 2 fresh serrano chilies,
  chopped
½ cup finely chopped scallion
1 tablespoon olive oil
2 teaspoons finely chopped
  fresh coriander
1 teaspoon fresh oregano
Salt and freshly ground pepper
  to taste
½ cup avocado, cut into small
  cubes
Grated rind of 1 lime

1. Cut the fish into ½-inch cubes. Place in a bowl and add the lime juice, making sure it penetrates throughout. Cover and refrigerate 12 hours or longer, stirring occasionally.
2. Add the remaining ingredients, toss, and chill until ready to serve.

Yield: 6 to 8 servings (P)

"If I lived in America for a hundred years I couldn't get used to the American eating. What can make the mouth so water like the taste and smell from herring and onions?"

One by one, as their cups of tea were filled, the hungry workers dispersed into groups. Seated on window-sills, table-tops, machines, and bales of shirts, they munched black bread and herring and sipped tea from saucers. And over all rioted the acrid odor of garlic and onions. . . . "If I lived in America for a hundred years I couldn't get used to the American eating. What can make the mouth so water like the taste and the smell from herring and onions?"
                                                    Anzia Yezierska, "Hunger," 1920

Although herring is in no way exclusively Jewish, it earned its reputation in this country as a Jewish fish served by Jews on New York's Lower East Side. Herring was the everyday staple food of the new immigrants as described by Yezierska, the "Sweatshop Cinderella" who wrote poignantly about the Eastern European immigrant experience. Wrapped in newspaper with a pickle and a piece of black bread, herring was a healthy lunch at the sweatshop. Some immigrants loved this preserved fish staple or hated it, depending on whether they wanted to break with their past or not. "How grand it felt to lean back in my chair, a person among people, and order anything I wanted from the menu," wrote Ms. Yezierska in the *Bread*

Market on Rivington Street, Lower East Side

Givers. "No more herring and pickle over dry bread, I ordered chops and spinach and salad. As I spread out my white, ironed napkin on my lap, I thought of the time only four years before, when I picked herring pieces out of the loaf, and wiped my mouth with a corner of a newspaper and threw it under the seat."

Visiting the herring dealers in the heavily Chasidic neighborhood of Williamsburg, Brooklyn, is like a voyage back to the turn of the century. Flaum Appetizing store, for example, has been pickling herring in its back room on Lee Avenue in Williamsburg since 1935. "Herring is a big item here," said Sonny Flaum, son of the family which founded the

Russ & Daughters

business in the 1930s. In the store—a thriving relic of a bygone era when appetizing stores with smoked fish, pickles, dried fruits, and halvah were a living part of each neighborhood—the sharp aroma of pickling brine rises to the white-tin ceiling and hovers around the old-fashioned scales.

Flaum carries a traditional line of items, like *matjes* and schmaltz herring fillets in oil and onions. In Dutch, *matjes* (pronounced *mat-jiz*) means maiden or young tender herring; in this country it has come to mean a Dutch, Swedish, or Icelandic herring cured in sugar and salt and often pickled in a red sauce with sandalwood. The male has milt that looks creamy when soaked with vinegar and water. Schmaltz is a fat herring from Iceland or Norway that is packed in barrels and cured with salt and sugar. For the most part, herring for pickling, which has a lower oil content than schmaltz, comes from Canada and is cured in salt.

Like Flaum, a half dozen or so other "appetizing" stores in New York, including Zabar's, Russ & Daughters, and the Murray Sturgeon Shop on the Upper West Side of Manhattan, buy barrels of herring from distributors in the Greenpoint section of Brooklyn. "When I stick my hand in the barrels to feel the plumpness of the herring, I feel like I am going back to the time of my grandfather," said David Zabar, the grandson of the founder of Zabar's, who often journeys to Greenpoint to handpick herrings for pickling.

"At one point there were maybe fifty jobbers in Brooklyn," said Emanuel Sklar, whose family founded Novie Herring. "Now there are a handful." At the turn of the century, the Sklar family sold whole herrings from a horse and wagon by the barrel, pail, or individually, wrapped in newspaper. Customers would then pickle the fish themselves at home.

For some, like food impresario Joseph Baum, herring is as sophisticated as any smoked salmon. "I know how elegant herring can be. I love to go to Russ & Daughters or Murray Sturgeon Shop. I buy a herring with skin and bones and fillet it at home. It is a great feeling when I cut off the belly part and lift up the skin. I don't put the marinated onions in too soon; I add a little red pepper, a pickled carrot, a little allspice, a bay leaf. It's not so bad."

Pickling Your Own Herring

The trick to pickling today is to find fresh herring or fresh salted herring. Once you've pickled it, use the herring in any favorite recipe, or just mix it as I do, with sour cream, red onion, and dill, to break the fast of Yom Kippur. It will keep for weeks.

6 Canadian herrings

1 tablespoon to ½ cup sugar

1 cup white vinegar or to cover

1 large onion, sliced

1 thinly sliced lemon (optional)

2 cloves

6 peppercorns

4 bay leaves

1. Remove the heads from the herring and scale the fish. Wash well, open them, and remove the milt (roe of male fish). Clean the fish well, drain. Lay the herring and milt in water to cover in the refrigerator overnight.

2. The next day rub the milt glands through a sieve or mash them well, and mix with 1 tablespoon of the sugar and a few tablespoons of the vinegar.

3. Place in a 1½-quart jar in layers the herring, onion, lemon slices, cloves, peppercorns, and bay leaves.

4. Add the milt gland mixture, the remaining vinegar, and as much of the remaining sugar as your taste dictates.

5. Cover the jar and keep in the refrigerator for at least 4 days.

Yield: about 6 cups (P)

Herring Salad with Beets, Potatoes, and Apples

We were very poor and my first interest in food was merely to get enough of it. I can remember living on boiled potatoes and as an extra treat dipping them into the brine in which cucumbers were pickled. We finally reached the stage of having herring with our potatoes. And, by the way, wouldn't I love a plate of good herring right now. We sliced some raw onion over the herring and then poured a little oil and vinegar over it. The potatoes were boiled in their jackets and peeled by my mother at the table. I especially loved new potatoes with the tender skin. They were easier to peel.

Eliot Elisofon, *Food Is a Four Letter Word,* 1948

This would have been a favorite of the late Mr. Elisofon, a *Life* photographer.

1 cup pickled herring

2 beets, boiled, cooled, and peeled

4 medium new potatoes, boiled, cooled, and peeled

1 large Granny Smith apple, cored but not peeled

¼ cup diced red onion

2 tablespoons red-wine vinegar

1 teaspoon Dijon-style mustard

3 tablespoons olive oil

2 tablespoons chopped walnuts

1 . Remove and discard any onion that might come with the herring and drain. Cut the herring, beets, potatoes, and apple into ½-inch cubes and place in a bowl with the red onion.

2 . Put the vinegar and the mustard in a small bowl. Slowly whisk in the olive oil.

3 . Place the herring salad on a plate, pour the vinaigrette over, and sprinkle with the walnuts.

Yield: 4 to 6 servings (P)

Pickled Herring with Mustard Sauce

This more sophisticated herring salad can be found in many "appetizing" or "delicatessen" stores. I like it as well as traditional recipes.

4 salted herring fillets

5 tablespoons white vinegar

½ cup water

2 tablespoons sugar

1 tablespoon salt

1 tablespoon Dijon-style
    mustard

1 tablespoon honey mustard

5 tablespoons vegetable oil

2 tablespoons heavy or sour
    cream

2½ tablespoons chopped
    fresh dill

1. Remove any bones from the herring and soak overnight in water to cover in the refrigerator. Drain.

2. The next day, combine 2½ tablespoons of the vinegar, water, 1 tablespoon of the sugar, and salt and pour the marinade over the herring. Let sit overnight in the refrigerator.

3. Mix the remaining vinegar, both mustards, and the remaining sugar. Whisk in the oil until a thick consistency is reached. Add the cream and dill.

4. Drain the herring and cut into 1-inch slices. Cover with the mustard sauce and serve in a bowl.

Yield: 8 servings as an appetizer (D)

Sour Cream Sierras, Derma Road, and the Borscht Belt

The Borscht Belt was so christened because one of the most popular dishes served thereabouts was a red beet soup called borscht. Proper borscht, incidentally, comes with sour cream and boiled potatoes, and some people claim that the white line on Route 17, the four lane path that leads from Seventh Avenue to the Catskills, is made of pure sour cream.

Joey Adams

The names "Bagel Aristocracy," "Sour Cream Sierras," "Derma Road," and "Borscht Belt" did not just happen by chance. Jewish entertainers and comedians like Al Jolson, Fannie Brice, Paul Whiteman, George Jessel, and Sophie Tucker parodied every aspect of Jewish life in the mountains, especially the food. Tummlers or entertainers at the hotels continued the jokes, and newspaper columnists sharpened their pencils with new ways to characterize the Catskill resorts.

"Most people don't eat borscht here," said Milton Kutsher, owner of Kutsher's, one of the last of the family-run resorts. "It is a very derogative term. A journalist thought of the acronym. What with the farm belt, the corn belt and the Bible belt, why not have the borscht belt?"

Copious amounts of food, not necessarily borscht, have always been central to life at the Catskill resorts. The open sew-

ers and overcrowded tenements of the Lower East Side, exacerbated by the stifling workshop conditions, bred disease. To escape the heat and the "workers' disease," tuberculosis, Jews came to the Catskills for fresh air and fresh food at kosher boardinghouses and sometimes at *kochalein,* which meant places where you had to cook for yourself. For about sixty dollars a season a whole family could rent a bed-room in a large house with cooking and food-storage privileges in a communal kitchen with half a dozen wood stoves and daily delivery of groceries from the vil-lage. "We ate at two long tables. There was ample and delicious food. We had meat twice a day," wrote the Yiddish poet Joseph Rolnik. "Big pitchers of milk stood on the table at all three meals. The guests ate and drank more than they needed, because we all believed that the more we ate, the sooner we would get well. In ten weeks I gained thirty-eight pounds."

Later, as the Jews moved out of the Lower East Side, the Catskill resorts became playgrounds for the privileged with Grossinger's, coined "Lindy's with Trees" by Damon Runyon, the most famous. Galician-born Selig and Malke Grossinger, restaurateurs from Manhattan, began their empire with nine boarders in a seven-room boardinghouse on one hundred acres of rock-strewn land. Even-tually, their daughter Jennie and her husband, cousin Harry, attracted thousands of Jews and non-Jews to their kosher kitchen with all-you-can-eat matzah balls, gefilte fish, and lox.

Russ & Daughters Pickled Lox

Whenever I went to Grossinger's, I always chose pickled lox as an appetizer. "The belly is the filet mignon of salmon," said Mark Federman, owner of Russ & Daughters on New York's Lower East Side. "When pickling, feel the fish to see when it is ready. We pickle our fish and onions separately and thin the sour cream with a little buttermilk." Although it will not taste as good as wild salmon that has been salt-cured for months, you can cure lox on your own with farm-raised salmon. Rub 4 tablespoons of kosher salt into the surface, cover, weigh it down, and keep it in the refrigerator, turning occasionally for 2 days. Those who are truly adventurous can make a pastrami-lox cure as they do at Ossie's Table in Boro Park, Brooklyn, with white and black peppercorns, ground black pepper, whole and ground coriander, sugar, vegetable oil, and fresh chopped garlic. For this you need a smoker. But, for those who love a good pickled salmon, there is no recipe better than that at Russ & Daughters, who will also ship overnight the real thing if you place an order at 1-800-RUSS229.

2 pounds salt-cured wild Pacific salmon, aka belly lox, with enough cold water to cover

2 large Spanish onions, peeled and sliced in rounds

5 cups cold water

1 cup white vinegar

1 cup sugar

1/2 cup mixed pickling spices, including coriander seed, mustard seed, dill seed, allspice, bay leaf, and dried chili pepper

1. Soak the lox overnight in cold water in the refrigerator, changing the water once.
2. Cut the lox pieces into half-pound chunks. Place in a glass bowl, layering them with the onion slices.
3. In a mixing bowl, place the water, vinegar, sugar, and mixed pickling spices. Stir by hand until the sugar dissolves. Pour the mixture over the salmon and let stay out on the countertop overnight so that the pickling process starts to work. In the morning, place it in the refrigerator and let it marinate for 2 days or until ready to use. Serve as is or with the cream sauce below.

Yield: 8 servings (P or D)

Sour Cream Sauce

2 cups good quality sour cream

1/2 cup buttermilk (approximately)

2 tablespoons marinade from above

1. In a glass bowl place the sour cream, buttermilk, and marinade. Mix well. If it is too thick, add a little extra buttermilk.

Yield: about 2 1/2 cups (D)

What Is Lox? A Delicate Jewish Fish, You'll Like It

When I went to the Carnegie Delicatessen in New York one day, two men sat down at a Formica table nearby. "I'm going to order lox," said one of the gentlemen, a non-Jewish businessman from the midwest. "What is lox?" asked his companion. "It's a delicate Jewish fish, you'll like it, it's not dry," said the first with conviction. "Try it with bagels and cream cheese."

Had the surly delicatessen waiter overheard this conversation, he may have told the gentleman that "lox" comes from the German "*lachs*" for salmon, and it is not particularly Jewish. He may also have said that most people are eating the more expensive Nova, short for Nova Scotia salmon, and imported smoked salmon, often cured with salt and brown sugar, then smoked.

Before refrigeration was efficient and widespread, the salmon that went into the Jewish delicatessens of the eastern United States came from Alaska packed in salt-brine barrels. It was then soaked in water to remove a good bit of the salt before it was sliced and sold as lox. "In the beginning there was lox," said Mark Federman, owner of Russ & Daughters.

Since World War II the salmon that provides lox for the East Coast market usually arrives frozen and is treated with salt for three days to months, then desalted, lightly smoked, sliced, and sold. Today when people say lox, chances are they mean Nova.

Cream Cheese, The Perfect Spread for Bagels and Matzah

Cream cheese, the perfect spread for bagels and matzah . . . the ideal complement to lox, whitefish and all other smoked fish.
        Breakstone's cream cheese advertisement, *Hadassah Magazine,* 1954

In 1882 Isaac and Joseph Breakstone, Jewish immigrants from Lithuania, opened their first dairy store on New York's Lower East Side to sell butter, soft cheeses, and sour cream. In those days dairy products were sold in bulk; consumers would often bring their own containers or use the wooden boxes, metal cans, and glass bottles supplied by Breakstone's. By World War I, Breakstone's was one of the

Breakstone's truck delivering milk and cheese

largest producers of condensed milk for the armed forces. But it was the firm's cream cheese, developed in the 1920s under Isaac's supervision, that made Breakstone's a big success. Isaac Breakstone did not invent cream cheese. It was an upstate New York dairyman in 1872 who created the white cheese made from cream and milk, similar to creamy cheeses eaten in Eastern Europe. Eventually James Lewis Kraft bought Breakstone's as well as Philadelphia Cream Cheese, which had been introduced in 1880 and was named after America's cradle of liberty and first capital.

As early as 1911 Kraft was advertising in Chicago's elevated trains, using outdoor billboards and mailing circulars to retail grocers. In 1933, the company ventured into radio advertising on an extensive scale when it sponsored a two-hour musical and variety show entitled "Kraft Musical Review," later changed to the "Kraft Music Hall," which headlined notable persons in show business. In addition to such newly processed products as Miracle Whip salad dressing, Kraft Macaroni and Cheese dinner, and Parkay margarine, cream cheese was promoted in a series of weekly Thursday night broadcasts, highlighted by such stars as Paul Whiteman and Al Jolson. Mr. Kraft's instructions were to include the word cream cheese as often as the comedians could in as many jokes about the product and the sponsor as possible. Unfortunately, the early shows predated devices for recording them. "It would have just been like Jolson to use the words cream cheese as a springboard into some quick joke about lox and bagels," said Herbert Goldman, Mr. Jolson's biographer. "That may have been the start of the new Jewish trilogy of bagels, lox, and cream cheese, sort of a Jewish answer to the old Sunday triumvirate of bacon, eggs, and pancakes."

Both the jokes and the product worked. Jews and non-Jews alike loved cream cheese. By 1938 several brands, including Breakstone's and Kraft, were included in the Kosher Food Guide.

"Jewish" Savory Salmon and Dill Cheesecake

Savory cheesecakes, often with artichokes and Roquefort cheese or with goat cheese, have been very popular as hors d'oeuvres in the past few years. Although smoked salmon and dill sounds Scandinavian, when you add cream cheese the combination seems Jewish. Thus, when I first tasted this knockout smoked salmon and dill cheesecake, I thought Jewish. So will you.

4½ tablespoons unsalted butter

½ cup fine dry bread crumbs

¾ cup grated Gruyère cheese

1 cup snipped fresh dill

1 cup chopped onion

28 ounces cream cheese at
room temperature

4 large eggs

1 cup heavy whipping cream

½ pound smoked salmon
trimmings, chopped

Freshly ground pepper to taste

Garnish: pitted black olives,
fresh dill, slices of roasted
red pepper

1. Using 1½ tablespoons of the butter grease a 9-inch-diameter springform pan with a 2½-inch-high side. Mix the bread crumbs, ¼ cup of the Gruyère, and 1 tablespoon of the dill. Coat the bottom and side of the pan well with this mixture. Wrap foil around the bottom and the outside of the pan.

2. Melt the remaining 3 tablespoons of the butter in a skillet over medium heat. Add the onion and sauté until tender, about 5 minutes. Cool slightly.

3. Using an electric mixer or food processor, beat the cream cheese, eggs, and cream until well blended. Fold in the onion mixture, salmon, remaining Gruyère, and remaining dill. Season with lots of pepper.

4. Pour the batter into the springform pan and place in another baking pan large enough to hold it. Add enough boiling water to the larger pan to come halfway up the side of the cheesecake.

5. Bake in a preheated 325-degree oven for about 40 minutes or until it seems solid. Leave the cheesecake in the water bath and turn the oven off. Let stand for 1 hour with the door ajar.

6. Transfer the cheesecake, still in the mold, to a rack and cool for at least 2 hours. Refrigerate overnight. Before serving, unmold and decorate with cut black olives, fresh dill, and slices of roasted red pepper. Serve at room temperature with crackers.

Yield: 20 servings (D)

Avas or Arbes, Boiled Chick-peas
By Any Other Name

In the famous Orchard Street Pushcart Market, which stretches for several blocks above and below Delancey Street, fruits, vegetables, bread, hot knishes (boiled buckwheat groats or mashed potatoes, wrapped in a skin of dough and baked), bagels (doughnut-shaped rolls), and hot arbes (boiled chickpeas) are offered for sale. WPA, 1939

Avas or *arbes,* boiled yellow chick-peas, are probably the earliest snack food of the Jews. Once served from paper spills kept warm in little tin stoves on pushcarts in this country, they have been eaten throughout the Middle East for centuries. Munched the way we would salted peanuts, they are traditionally served by Jews at Purim. In Europe, they were also eaten with roast garlic to ensure potency.

1 cup raw chick-peas

Salt and freshly ground pepper to taste

1. Soak the chick-peas in water to cover overnight. Drain and boil in water to just cover until *al dente,* about 20 minutes.

2. When cooked *al dente,* spread on a clean towel to dry, removing excess moisture.

3. Sprinkle with salt and pepper. Put into small serving bowls and place them around the room with bowls of olives, nuts, etc., for finger foods.

Yield: about 3 cups (P)

In the Beginning the Bat Mitzvah Ceremony Was a Learning, Not an Eating, Experience

We knew about the bar mitzvah confirmation ceremony for boys, but we had not realized that our rabbi was departing from the orthodox ritual to add a bat mitzvah for girls. I had always felt that the female was given rather cavalier treatment in Jewish religious ceremonies: in really orthodox Temples—of which ours was not one—she was exiled to the balcony; she was not allowed to share the sacramental wine on Saturday evenings; there were a great many prayers that could be said only by men. I had once complained to my sister that we might as well be Chinese for all the consideration girls got in the Jewish religion, but I would never have started the reforms by introducing the bat mitzvah.

Felicia Lamport, *Mink on Weekdays, Ermine on Sundays,* 1950

Felicia Lamport proceeded to describe her own double bat mitzvah with her rabbi's third daughter at the Society for the Advancement of Judaism in New York in the late 1920s. In 1922 Judith Kaplan Eisenstein, the eldest daughter of the rabbi, Mordecai Kaplan, was the first American girl to become a bat mitzvah. Blessed with four daughters and a staunch advocate of women's rights, Rabbi Kaplan sought a new kind of Judaism that would include the participation of women in the service. "Part of the Revolution in those days," said Mrs. Eisenstein at her home in Woodstock, New York, "was to get women out of the kitchen, to try very hard for them to do something other than to cook." Needless to say, the Jewish press of the time thought this idea of bat mitzvah blasphemous.

In those days the food after a bat mitzvah service was basic. "My father was always against these splashy things anyway. He tried to simplify the whole thing and made it a learning, not an eating, experience," recalled Mrs. Eisenstein. The unadorned food included gefilte fish made by her mother and aunts and *kichels* (crackers) that her aunt made by the hundreds. "Afterward we had a party at home with rugelach, tea, and hot dogs for the children. The greatest treat in the world for me at that time was a kosher hot dog."

Poppy-seed Kichels

There are all kinds of *kichel* and all kinds of Jewish poppy-seed recipes, but I especially like these savory crackers studded with poppy seeds, adapted from Bobbi Meisel.

4 cups all-purpose flour

½ cup dry poppy seeds

2 onions, chopped

1½ teaspoons baking powder

1 teaspoon salt

Freshly ground pepper to taste

2 large eggs

¾ cup vegetable oil

*¼ cup water plus enough
    additional water to make a
    pliable dough*

1 egg yolk

1. Put the flour, poppy seeds, onions, baking powder, salt, and pepper in the bowl of an electric mixer or a food processor.
2. Add the eggs and mix well, using the kneading attachment or the steel blade.
3. Add the oil slowly and mix until absorbed into the dough.
4. Slowly add the water, starting with a quarter of a cup and adding a few teaspoons at a time, mixing until the dough is pliable. The dough should be easily workable, neither dry nor sticky. If dry, add water; if sticky, add flour, a little at a time.
5. Roll the dough out ⅛ inch thick on a wooden board or smooth surface that has been dusted with flour.
6. Cut into 2-inch diamond shapes, then brush the *kichels* with an egg wash of egg yolk and a little water.
7. Bake in a preheated 350-degree oven for 25 minutes or until a light tan color.

Yield: 90 kichels (P)

Isaac Bashevis Singer's Vegetarian Pâté

A short time ago a schochet . . . told the readers of the *Warheit,* how in the course of his professional practices he had been converted to the vegetarian idea and has ceased to kill, as well as to eat of, any living thing. Now, a group of Jewish vegetarians have addressed a call to some paper urging the abstinence from flesh foods and appealing to all other persons similarly inclined to help them in organizing a society of Jewish vegetarians.

American Hebrew, July 16, 1909

In the nineteenth century many Jewish peddlers were obligatory vegetarians unless they found Jewish families with whom they could eat. A renewed interest in vegetarianism arose in the early twentieth century when many Jews espoused radical ideas on politics, literature, and religion. "Dairy" restaurants catered to this population as did early Yiddish vegetarian cookbooks. In 1926 Abraham B. and Shifrah I. Mishulow called his *Vegetarische Kochbuch:* "Rational Eating, a book of knowledge for the right preparation and combination of natural vegetarian health foods, according to the latest scientific methods."

Mock Chopped Liver or String Bean Vegetarian Pâté

In the *Daily Forward* there were occasionally "health" recipes in Yiddish for new immigrants. One of the most popular vegetarian dishes was and still is a chopped "liver" made from eggplant, lentils, or string beans. The recipe was one of the favorites of the late Isaac Bashevis Singer. He ate it at least once a week after he walked down Broadway to the Famous Dairy Restaurant on Seventy-second Street.

We taped the actor and singer Mandy Patinkin at his apartment a few blocks from that of the late Mr. Singer's. Mandy's mother and cookbook writer, Doralee Patinkin Rubin, made for us this same vegetarian chopped liver with string beans, peas, and walnuts. The secret to this version—and to all good chopped liver—is the flavor that comes from slowly cooked caramelized onions. This is the only time that Mrs. Rubin, who lives in San Diego, uses canned vegetables other than tomatoes. She also uses only the whites of the eggs.

¼ cup peanut oil

4 large onions, sliced

2 cups canned string beans, drained

½ cup canned peas, drained

4 hard-boiled eggs

½ cup walnuts

Salt and freshly ground pepper to taste

1. In a deep-frying pan, heat the oil. Add the sliced onions and sauté slowly for at least 1 hour or until the onions are caramelized.

2. Place the caramelized onions, string beans, peas, eggs, and walnuts in a food processor and process until slightly chunky. You want some texture in this dish. Place in a bowl in the refrigerator for several hours. Serve with cocktail rye or crackers.

Yield: 6 to 8 servings (P)

Chopped Liver Sculpture on Ice — The Jewish Wedding in America

Weddings (in Chicago) were mostly "at home," but the feast was cooked by "mother," the mother of the bride. A home was a busy place the week before the wedding with the neighbors coming in to help clean the poultry and bake the cakes. Friends came to set the bridal table, to decorate it, to dress the bride, and the better educated men came prepared with speeches, mostly very long and very dull. A fashionable wedding had ice-cream, and there was a naive informality in the way the good mothers took pieces of cake, or any goodies, in their handkerchiefs to take home to their children.

Jennie Gerstley, "Reminiscences, Chicago, Illinois, 1859–1934,"
American Jewish Archives

A few years ago, I had just finished performing at a Bar Mitzvah out on Long Island, and headed over to the buffet. On the table was a life-size sculpture of the bar mitzvah boy rendered in ice. As I ladled fruit salad onto my plate, I heard the women behind me commenting on the sculpture:

"It's beautiful," said the first woman.

"It's a perfect likeness," agreed the second woman. "Who did it? Epstein?"

"Don't be silly. Epstein only works in chopped liver."

Henny Youngman

The Jewish wedding in America changed tremendously with the Eastern European migration. In the old country a wedding was a time of celebration with symbolic foods including a *goldene yoikh*, a chicken soup with golden ringlets of *schmaltz* (chicken fat), symbolizing luck and wealth. Everyone wished the new couple a "*schmaltz-grub*," a Yiddish expression meaning falling into a pit of fat.

Never did a group of Jews fall so fast into this *schmaltz-grub* as they did in America. The wedding scene in Philip Roth's *Goodbye, Columbus,* a post–World War II description of prosperous Jewish life in suburban New Jersey and New York, showed how the wedding more than any other event was transformed. "These people were grappling with kosher laws and assimilation," said Judith Siegel, who was married in a synagogue in Brooklyn in 1967. "A grandparent and sometimes a parent might say to the couple, 'I don't care where the wedding is as long as it's kosher.' Life cycle events meant 'going out' to lots of people. They never went to a restaurant, they never went to Europe, so they bought expensive clothes for weddings and bar mitzvahs."

Bar mitzvah for the son of the owners of Dubrow's Restaurant in Brooklyn

To this day a typical "gourmet" wedding might start with a smorgasbord of heavy, meat appetizers before the ceremony, including chopped liver sculptures on ice. Waiters serve trays of sweet and sour meatballs, mock spareribs, knishes, stuffed kishka, potato pancakes, mock shrimp made from fish cut like a curve, spinach puffs, Jewish rumaki from chicken liver and water chestnuts, as well as kosher egg rolls. Today, nouvelle kosher caterers are offering more exotic and lighter appetizers like sushi or satays.

While the guests eat, the bride and groom often sit in separate rooms, sometimes on thrones, having fasted all day. Weddings sometimes feature the traditional *tenaim,* or betrothal ceremony, in which the bride and groom formally accept the conditions of engagement. Following the reading of the *tenaim* agreement, the mothers of the bride and groom crack a plate together to symbolize the severity of breaking the conditions of marriage.

In traditional Orthodox weddings the bride and groom, separated for several days, meet at the ceremony. After Judith Siegel and her husband, Mark, were married, the newlyweds went together to a separate room to symbolically eat their first meal together. When all the guests had sat down, the bride and groom made their entrance. "The sit-down dinner was fairly heavy," recalled Judith Siegel. "There was a pretentiousness of trying to be both American and continental. French service meant white gloves, which cost an extra dollar or so per person. There was soup, salad, overcooked prime rib au jus which was, of course, not prime rib at all but a kosher cut, roasted potatoes, carrots, and a big ornate challah." The Siegel wedding ended, as did many, with sherbets and cakes and the continental Viennese table with ornate "butter" pastries made out of pareve margarine, vegetable shortening, and nondairy creamer.

Bookie's Chopped Chicken Liver

This recipe comes from Hyman Bookbinder, the retired lobbyist for the American Jewish Committee and the man many politicians considered, until his retirement, the most listened-to professional Jewish spokesperson in the United States. Since his daily tasks seldom afforded him the satisfaction of immediate tangible results, Bookie, as everyone calls him, turned to cooking. One of his favorite recipes is this *"meichel,"* or delicacy: chopped chicken liver with a totally unorthodox ingredient—green pepper.

When we taped Bookie, one of his fans, ABC's Cookie Roberts, dropped in with a bottle of Tabasco—she likes to add a few drops to her version.

4 large eggs

3 to 4 tablespoons vegetable oil

3 medium onions, diced

¼ green pepper, diced
  (optional)

1 pound fresh chicken livers

Salt and freshly ground pepper
  to taste

1 tablespoon chicken fat
  (optional)

1. Put the eggs in cold water in a saucepan. Bring to a boil and simmer for about 10 minutes. Cool rapidly in iced water and peel.

2. Heat the oil in a 10-inch skillet. Sauté the onions and green pepper over a high heat for about 5 minutes, until the onions start turning brown.

3. Add the chicken livers to the sautéed onions and green pepper and cook, tossing the livers occasionally, until they are firm, about 5 minutes. (Don't let them become tough by overcooking.)

4. Chop together the livers, hard-boiled eggs, sliced or quartered, and the sautéed onions and green pepper, using an old-fashioned manual chopper or food processor until of even consistency, but not pureed. Season with salt and pepper.

5. If you want, add a tablespoon of chicken fat to the mix.

Yield: 10 to 12 servings as a pre-dinner nosh or as an appetizer on a leaf of lettuce (M)

Mock Stuffed Derma or Falshe Kishka

Two delicacies cooked in the *cholent* and served as accompaniments or appetizers at the Sabbath lunch meal in Europe were *helsel* (a stuffed goose-neck pâté) and stuffed *kishka* or *derma* (intestine casings filled with bread crumbs or flour, goose or chicken fat, and minced onion). The Sephardic equivalent of this dish is *nakahoris*, with a filling of ground meat, pine nuts, cinnamon, and sharp pepper, which was also served at weddings. Because it is practically impossible to obtain intestine casings anymore and the dish is very fatty, it is fast disappearing in this country.

George Lang, a Hungarian Jew who lives in New York, where he owns Café des Artistes, serves stuffed *helsel* in his newly renovated Gundel's Restaurant in Budapest. The food at Gundel's, once a palace of gastronomy, is updated Hungarian with some flavors that Mr. Lang has resurrected from his Jewish past. "Stuffed goose neck is a dish that my grandmother made," he said. She may very well have served this goose pâté with her goose-based *cholent,* which appears in Mr. Lang's authoritative *Cuisine of Hungary.*

In America few people make authentic *helsel* or *kishka* because of the fat, the time it takes, and the difficulty in obtaining intestine casings. Instead, false *kishka*—using pureed crackers, chopped celery, carrots, margarine, and onions—is the leading American replacement. People love this appetizer popularized by a recipe on the box of Manischewitz' Tam Tams in the 1960s. Just don't tell your guests how simple it is!

2 carrots

1 stalk celery

1 onion

½ stick (4 tablespoons)
   margarine, melted

½ pound crackers, such as Tam
   Tams or Ritz
   (about 90)

Salt and freshly ground pepper
   to taste

1. Peel the carrots.
2. Cut the vegetables into 4 pieces. Place all the ingredients in a food processor with a steel blade and process the mixture until it reaches the consistency of dough. Taste and adjust seasonings.
3. Shape the dough into 2 logs about 1 inch in diameter and 12 inches long. Wrap with aluminum foil and place on a greased baking sheet. Bake in a preheated 425-degree oven for 30 minutes. Let cool on a rack. Slice into half-inch rounds and serve with toothpicks.

Yield: about 16 slices, serving about 8 people (P)

Leo Lerman's Mother's Pierogen

A generation or so ago every country had its *pierogen* or *piroshki,* empanada, *bureka,* pastie, or other meat turnover. And every cook had his or her own savory pastry, be it *phyllo* or a short lard, chicken fat, or sweet butter dough for enclosing leftover meat or potatoes and sweet jams. The different shapes of circles, crescents, triangles, and squares varied the monotony of the same dish at different times of the year.

The late Leo Lerman, editorial advisor and social chronicler, kept a smudged handwritten recipe for his mother's *pierogen* in his Condé Nast office. "It was my mother's agility with her fingers that made this so good," he said. "She could work the dough quickly to make something scrumptious and flaky out of simple ingredients. On Friday nights in Jackson Heights she made a feast—chicken soup with these *pierogen,* roast chicken, pot roast, hand-cut noodles, *tzimmes,* and all kinds of cakes. She controlled her family through their stomachs."

Pierogen, cont.

2 cups all-purpose flour

7 tablespoons chicken fat or
    vegetable shortening, such
    as Crisco

1 large egg

Salt and freshly ground pepper
    to taste

About ¼ cup ice water

1½ cups leftover pot roast,
    coarsely shredded

½ cup cooked chicken, coarsely
    shredded

1 onion, sliced in rounds

1 egg yolk, beaten

1. Mix the flour and 5 tablespoons of the chicken fat or vegetable shortening with a fork until crumbly. Make a well in the center and drop the egg in. Add a pinch of salt and mash everything together with a fork. Stir in enough water to make the dough stick together in a ball. Refrigerate overnight. This dough can be frozen.

2. To make the filling, season the pot roast and the chicken with salt and pepper.

3. In a sauté pan melt the remaining 2 tablespoons of chicken fat or shortening and sauté the onion until golden. Add to the meat mixture.

4. Divide the dough into 12 balls. Roll each ball out to 3-inch-diameter circles and fill with a tablespoon of meat and onions. Brush the edges with water, fold over like a half moon, and crimp edges. Brush with the egg yolk and bake on a greased cookie sheet in a preheated 375-degree oven for 20 minutes. Serve immediately. You can also freeze the *pierogen* after forming. Defrost and then bake.

Yield: about 12 (M)

Note: Besides being a good appetizer, this is a fine accompaniment to cabbage soup for a during-the-week evening meal.

A Yiddishe Mama's Knishes in Daytona Beach, Florida

I'm not supposed to eat any of it but I do. I am a man of no dietary will power. I like liver knishes, meat knishes, potato knishes. I am a great traditionalist when it comes to Jewish food.   Justice Arthur Goldberg

Farther on I came upon another, laboriously pushing a metal box on wheels and offering baked potatoes and hot knishes to the hungry, cold-bitten passers-by.

M. E. Ravage, *An American in the Making: The Life Story of an Immigrant,* 1917

Potato, kasha, liver, or cheese knishes may once have been a celebratory food in the Ukraine, where the potatoes were encrusted in a flaky pastry. But on New York's Lower East Side, most specifically lower Second Avenue, nicknamed "knish alley," the knish became a convenient hot finger food that sweatshop workers could buy and take to work for a filling snack or lunch. Knishes were often sold outside so they became a visible Jewish food. Because of the guttural "k" in knish, they were also an obvious target for vaudeville comedians.

Mama Batalin is not the only queen of knishes. Meet Fryma Gorenstein of Los Angeles.

Today knishes have gone mainstream. Yonah Shimmel, who has been selling his since 1913, sells flavored broccoli and spinach knishes. Whoever heard of vegetable knishes in Europe! Before knishes became chic, Schleider's Caterers sold them at Baltimore Oriole games. Blazer's market, catering to every ethnic group in Atlanta, sells freshly baked potato, spinach, and vegetable knishes along with empanadas and Vietnamese spring rolls.

In Daytona Beach, Florida, eighty-nine-year-old Betty Batalin is the queen of knishes. Born in Odessa, Russia, Mrs. Batalin came to New York at the age of nineteen and made a vow that "no one would ever go hungry in her house." No one has. Before a recent stroke slowed her down, she cooked up a storm in the kitchen of the local synagogue and at her daughter's home where she now lives. She crafted her finger pastries from a paper-thin strudel dough, cutting them with her little finger. Fortunately, unlike many mavens, she shared her recipe.

Mama Batalin's Potato Knishes

Don't be intimidated by this strudel dough. It is easy and fun to make. Try doing it with a friend.

FILLING

4 large onions, sliced

2 tablespoons vegetable oil

2½ pounds russet (baking)
  potatoes

Salt to taste

1 large egg

½ cup chopped parsley

1 teaspoon salt or to taste

Freshly ground pepper to taste

DOUGH

2 large eggs

½ cup vegetable oil plus
  additional for rolling the
  dough

1 cup water

1 tablespoon white vinegar

½ teaspoon salt

4 cups all-purpose flour
  (about)

1. Slowly cook the onions in the oil in a skillet, covered, over a low heat. Let the onions "sweat" for about 20 minutes, or until they are soft. Then remove the cover and let fry over a medium heat until golden brown. Don't drain.

2. Meanwhile peel the potatoes and cut them in half. Put them in a large pot filled with cold water and salt to taste. Bring to a boil, then turn the heat down, and cook until soft, about 15 minutes. Drain and cool for 5 minutes.

3. Mash the potatoes and add the egg, the parsley, salt, and pepper. Add the onions with the oil and mix well with your hands. Set aside while preparing the dough.

4. Beat the eggs and reserve about 1 tablespoon of egg for the glaze. Mix the rest with the oil, water, vinegar, and salt. Add the flour gradually, beating first with a spoon and eventually your hands as you knead the dough. Continue to add enough flour to make a smooth dough. Shape into 4 balls and let rest, covered with a cloth, about a half hour to relax the gluten.

5. Roll each ball of dough out as thin as possible into a flat rectangle. Flour well and place between 2 sheets of waxed paper. Let sit for about 15 minutes.

6. Using your hands carefully stretch each rectangle as thin as possible, about 12 to 14 inches long by 4 to 5 inches wide. Spread one quarter of the filling (about 1½ cups) onto approximately one third of the dough, leaving a 1-inch border.

7. Holding onto the waxed paper, roll up the dough like a jelly roll, brushing oil across the top a couple of times as you roll. Using the side of your hand like a knife, divide the roll into 2-inch knishes. Then pinch the open ends shut. Repeat with the remaining balls and dough. Place the knishes, flat side down, on a greased cookie sheet, leaving a 2-inch space between each. You will have to bake in batches.

8. Mix the reserved tablespoon of egg with a little water. Brush the tops with the egg wash and bake in a preheated 375-degree oven for 25 to 30 minutes or until golden brown.

Yield: approximately 60 knishes (P)

The Cheese of Salonika Does Not Exist Anymore

Huseein Agha of Seslovo . . . had given Nono a gift of several pounds of sheep's milk cheese packed in five-gallon tins. Such a superlative cheese was not to be found at the marketplace! Yussefico would be summoned to bring in a large piece then and there, and everyone must sample it and exclaim at its unusual creaminess. . . . Rachel, standing by the kitchen door, would announce that with such a creamy cheese she would bake pastels and borrekitas for Saturday. "Why, with cheese like this, they will melt in your mouth!" Nono's face would beam with pride. One would think he had made the cheese himself!

Leon Sciaky, *Farewell to Salonika,* 1946

"Cheese like this does not exist anymore," said Lilly Modiano, eighty-seven. "We called it 'white cheese' in Salonika. Here we buy feta cheese." World War II changed the cheese and the life that Leon Sciaky wrote about in his *Farewell to Salonika.* It also changed Lilly Modiano's life. Of the approximately fifty thousand plus Jews who were in Salonika at the beginning of the war, about two hundred or so survived. Luckily both Mr. Sciaky and Mrs. Modiano were able to come to the United States.

Almost fifty years later, Mrs. Modiano reflected on her life in Salonika. "We ate *burekas* for Friday at lunch and Saturday morning when my father came home from synagogue with raki (a licorice-flavored drink) and huevos haminados, the roasted eggs which my mother took from the top of the fijones." (Fijones—meaning beans—was the Ladino name for *chamim*, the Sabbath stew with beans and meat.) "We made fijones with very fatty meat, the breast of the cow and homemade sausages because it gives a very beautiful taste, but they don't do that anymore because it is too fat. They would first cook it on top of the stove and then put it in the wood-burning oven after they made the bread when the fire was already spent and left it warm until Saturday at lunch."

Burekas de Berencena *(Turkish Eggplant Burekas)*

When Mrs. Modiano makes the *burekas,* she boils oil and water and then beats in flour to make a very flaky dough. Her friend, Ida Dana, formerly of Istanbul, whose ancestors came from Salonika, adds to the dough a little *kasseri* cheese, which she uses instead of feta in her pastry. Both fill their *burekas* with eggplant, spinach, and béchamel or a combination of ricotta, feta, and *kasseri, kafalograviera,* and Parmesan. *Phyllo*-dough, which was hand-made in Salonika and Turkey, is a shortcut to making your own dough. *Phyllo* is Turkish or Greek, not Jewish.

FILLING

3 medium eggplants (about 2½ pounds)

1 tablespoon salt

½ cup Greek kasseri cheese

½ cup grated mozzarella cheese

DOUGH

½ cup vegetable oil

1 cup water

½ cup Greek kasseri cheese

2½ cups all-purpose flour plus extra for kneading the dough

Dash of salt

¼ cup grated Parmesan cheese

1. To make the filling, pierce the eggplants with a fork. Place them on a baking sheet in a preheated 450-degree oven and roast for about 20 minutes or until the skin is charred.

2. When cool enough to handle, peel off the skin and put the eggplant and a tablespoon of salt in water to cover. Let soak for 30 minutes, then rinse, place in a colander, and press with paper towels to drain out the water. Chop the eggplant pulp with a fork or pastry blender, but do not use a food processor; it will make the pulp too mushy.

3. Mix the eggplant with the *kasseri* cheese and the mozzarella and set the filling aside.

4. To make the dough, mix together the vegetable oil, water, and the *kasseri* cheese. Gradually add the flour and a dash of salt, mixing until a very wet dough is formed. Place on a floured board and knead.

5. Putting flour on your hands, take a piece of dough the size of a walnut and flatten it to a 4-inch-diameter circle. Place a teaspoon of eggplant filling in the center. Fold the dough over and press into a plump crescent shape, sealing the edges from the sides. Do not touch the top. Sprinkle with Parmesan cheese and place on a foil-lined baking sheet about 2 inches apart.

6. Bake them about 25 minutes in a preheated 375-degree oven or until light golden brown.

Yield: about 32 (D)

Note: You can freeze the burekas before baking. Defrost slightly and bake as above or a few minutes longer.

Moroccan Bastilla San Francisco Style

This glorious finger pastry filled with chicken, cinnamon, nuts, and ginger is used as an hors d'oeuvre for bar mitzvahs and other life-cycle events at the Magen David Sephardic Synagogue of San Francisco. *Bastilla,* one of the great dishes of Moroccan cookery, is traditionally served in a big pie shape made of thin *warka* dough, and eaten with the right hand. The Jewish version of this dish came to this country with the two waves of Moroccan immigrants: the first in the early 1900s and the second, via France and Israel, where they immigrated in the fifties and sixties after Israeli and then Moroccan independence. In California cooks have reduced the eggs from about twenty to two and replaced the traditional *warka* with commercial egg-roll wrappers. It is a great way to use up leftovers.

1 3-pound boiled chicken
   (about 3 cups)
2 medium onions, chopped
¼ cup vegetable oil plus oil for
   deep frying
1 cup blanched almonds,
   coarsely chopped
Pinch of saffron
½ cup warm water
1 cup parsley, finely chopped
½ cup fresh coriander, chopped
½ cup currants
1 tablespoon sugar
¼ teaspoon turmeric or to taste
1¼ teaspoons cinnamon
1 teaspoon ground ginger
Salt and freshly ground pepper
   to taste
1 to 1½ cups chicken broth
2 large eggs
100 3-inch-square egg-roll
   wrappers
1 egg white (optional)

1. Remove the skin and bones from the chicken. Cut the meat into bite-size pieces. You will need about 3 cups of the cut-up chicken and 1½ cups of the broth.

2. Brown the onions in the oil until golden. Remove and add the almonds, browning well.

3. Soak the saffron in the water in a small bowl, letting sit for a few minutes, and add to the onions.

4. To the onions, almonds, and the saffron add the chicken, parsley, coriander, currants, sugar, spices, and 1 cup of the broth. Simmer on a very low heat for 5 minutes, stirring occasionally, adding more broth if too dry.

5. Beat the eggs and slowly add to the mixture. Stir for a minute or two until the eggs become custard-like. (They should not be runny.) Taste and adjust seasonings.

6. Place approximately 1 heaping teaspoon of the filling in the center of an egg-roll wrapper and fold the top and bottom over like an envelope. Seal from right to left using a dab of egg white or water on your finger. You can refrigerate or freeze them at this point. It will be easier to fry them if they are cold.

7. When ready to cook, defrost the frozen *bastillas* for about an hour. Heat about 3 inches of vegetable oil in a deep saucepan or deep fryer until it reaches 375 degrees. Add a few *bastillas* at a time, turning after a minute or two when they are brown. Drain on paper towels and serve immediately.

Yield: about 100 (M)

A Tortilla Press, Ravioli, and Spaghetti?— Syrian Food in America

In 1919 Egyptian Rose, a Jewish Aleppan restaurant, opened in New York on the Lower East Side. "It was one of those restaurants with no printed menu," said Joseph A. B. Sutton, author of *Aleppo Chronicles*. "You'd go in the back, past the backgammon players, to see what was cooking and order that way."

"It was more than a restaurant," said Sarina Missry Roffe, the great-niece of Rose Missry. "It was a social plaza for the Syrian Jews to play backgammon, have Turkish coffee, and talk to each other. Limited by the lack of Yiddish, these Sephardic Jews spoke only Arabic and some French."

Rose Missry outside the kosher restaurant she ran at the Chicago World's Fair in 1933

Two generations later Mrs. Roffe still makes her great-Aunt Rose's dishes, learned from her own grandmother, Esther Salem, a Syrian kosher caterer in Brooklyn. "For us," said Mrs. Roffe, "food is carried through the generations because our dishes are the traditions of the Syrian Jews. Foods reflect our culture."

Mrs. Roffe, in her late thirties, stocks her freezer with the dishes of her past. She tunnels out zucchinis to stuff with rice and meat. She makes her own tamarind paste for *la ham agene,* a Syrian meat pie, sometimes substituting commercial ravioli or mini pizza doughs for the crust as a time saver.

Except for a few shortcuts, Mrs. Roffe sticks to tradition, serving Syrian food at least twice a week in her own home in Brooklyn. On Jewish holidays her table is laden with a variety of different symbolic dishes. "For me, part of each holiday is making these foods like for Passover it is cleaning the house. It is important for my children to know that these Syrian foods are our culture."

Sarina Roffe's Syrian Cheese Sambusak

This is one of those recipes that started out in Syria with *kashkeval* (sheep's cheese). When the immigrants came to this country they used the most interesting cheese they could find—kosher Muenster. Today the varieties of kosher cheeses have greatly expanded so that the recipe can again become more authentic. Mrs. Roffe often flattens the semolina dough with a tortilla press rather than a rolling pin. The semolina adds a pleasant crunch to the crust. Her cheese *sambusak* has become my daughter Daniela's favorite.

DOUGH

1½ cups smead (semolina, not semolina flour)

3 cups all-purpose unbleached flour

Dash of salt

3 tablespoons vegetable oil

1½ sticks (¾ cup) unsalted butter, softened

¾ cup cold water

FILLING

2 large eggs

1 pound Muenster cheese, grated, or a combination of feta, kashkeval, and Muenster

Dash of salt

2 tablespoons farmer cheese

½ cup black or plain sesame seeds

1. Mix the semolina with the flour. Add the salt, oil, and butter. With a fork or your fingers, mix in the butter until the dough is lumpy. Do not overmix. Add the water, a little at a time, bringing the dough together until it is smooth and pliable. You can also pulse on and off with a food processor until a ball is formed.

2. Beat the eggs and combine with the grated cheese, salt, and farmer cheese. The mixture should be slightly dry.

3. Place the sesame seeds in a flat plate. Roll the dough into 1-inch balls. Flatten slightly and dip one side into sesame seeds. Flatten to ⅛-inch thickness with a rolling pin or tortilla press. If using the tortilla press, cover with plastic wrap so dough does not stick to the press.

4. Place 1 tablespoon of the filling in the middle of the circle. Pull one side over the other to form a half moon. Press the edges to close. Flute edge, if desired, for a better presentation.

5. Bake for 20 to 25 minutes in a preheated 350-degree oven until slightly golden on bottom. Do not overcook.

Yield: about 3 dozen (D)

Syrian La Ham Agene *(Syrian Meat Pie with Tamarind)*

I was delighted when Sarina Roffe showed me how she makes *la ham agene,* a Jewish equivalent of the Armenian flat meat pizza pie I loved so much in Jerusalem, and one of the traditional dishes for her Sabbath and holiday *mazza,* an array of appetizers served in the Middle East. Before tomatoes were common, tamarind was often used as a sauce. Serve the pies as a snack or with kibbe, avocado, bean and potato salads, or pickled vegetables.

FILLING

2 medium onions, finely
   chopped

1½ teaspoons salt

1½ pounds ground beef
   (regular is fine for this)

1 3-ounce can tomato paste

Juice of ½ lemon

½ teaspoon white pepper

¼ teaspoon cinnamon

¾ teaspoon Syrian allspice*

½ to ¾ cup tamarind paste*
   (according to taste)

¼ cup chopped walnuts

DOUGH

1 package active dry yeast

2 cups warm water

1 teaspoon sugar

6 cups all-purpose flour

2 teaspoons salt

6 tablespoons vegetable oil

*Available in Middle Eastern
grocery stores

1. Sprinkle the chopped onions with the salt. Let them rest.

2. Mix together the meat, tomato paste, lemon juice, spices, the tamarind paste, and the walnuts.

3. Squeeze the water from the onions and add the onions to the meat. Set aside.

4. To make the dough, dissolve the yeast in the water and sugar in a large bowl. Let sit a few minutes until the yeast starts to bubble. Gradually add the flour, salt, and vegetable oil. Turn the dough out onto a floured board and knead until a soft dough is formed. Place in a greased bowl, cover, and let rise for about 1½ hours or until doubled. Punch down.

5. Tear off walnut-size pieces of dough. Roll each into a ball and place in a tortilla press. Flatten to a circle 3 inches in diameter; or roll out the dough ⅛-inch thick and cut into 3-inch circles with a cookie cutter.

6. Put 2 tablespoons of filling in the center of each circle and pat down to the edge of the dough, leaving a ⅛-inch border like a pizza. At this point you can freeze the *la ham agene* if you like or bake on a greased cookie sheet for 30 minutes in a preheated 350-degree oven.

Yield: about 3 dozen (M)

Tip: To freeze, place the patties on waxed paper and on a cookie sheet. When frozen, take them off and put in plastic bags. You can also substitute the crust with packaged ravioli or mini pizza dough obtainable at most grocery stores today.

Polish Mushroom and Sour Cream Dip

"At last the Bronx Park! . . . I am smelling out the mushrooms," she (my mother) explained. "I know how to do that. I learned it in Hungary. Each mushroom has its own smell. The best ones grow under oak trees."

"I want to pick some," said Esther.

"No!" said my mother, sharply, "you must never do that. You are an American child, and don't know about these things. Some mushrooms are poison! They will kill you! Never pick them!"

"Do they come on strings?" I asked.

"Those are the grocery store mushrooms," explained my mother. "Ach, America, the thief, where children only see dry, dead mushrooms in grocery stores! Wait, I will show you!"

Michael Gold, *Jews Without Money*, 1930

The following Polish mushroom and sour cream dip came to this country a half century after the recipes of Michael Gold's immigrant mother. It is a specialty of Holocaust survivor Helen Ciesla Covensky. Her many other recipes are a celebration of life and are served frequently by her daughter Aviva Kempner, director of the film *The Partisans of Vilna*.

2 onions, diced

½ stick (4 tablespoons) salted butter

1 pound wild or cultivated mushrooms, coarsely chopped

Salt and freshly ground pepper to taste

1 cup sour cream

2 tablespoons fresh dill, snipped

Paprika to taste

1. In a frying pan sauté the onions in 2 tablespoons of the butter until they are golden. Remove from the pan and set aside.

2. Place the remaining butter in the pan and add the mushrooms. Sauté for about 10 minutes, stirring occasionally until the water evaporates.

3. Mix the onions and the mushrooms together in a serving bowl, seasoning with salt and pepper to taste. Fold in the sour cream and sprinkle with fresh dill and paprika. Serve as a dip with dark rye bread, pita, or fresh vegetables.

Yield: about 3 cups (D)

Mushrooms Stuffed with Mushrooms

If you have any dried mushrooms, use them for extra flavor. Soak them for a few hours in cold water before cooking.

1 teaspoon dried mushrooms (optional)

1 pound large cultivated mushrooms (fresh and firm)

2 tablespoons minced onion

3 tablespoons butter or margarine

1 tablespoon finely chopped parsley

Salt and freshly ground white pepper to taste

3 tablespoons dry white bread crumbs

2 tablespoons flour

2 egg yolks

1 cup vegetable broth

¼ cup dry red wine

1. Place the dried mushrooms in cold water to cover a few hours or overnight. When soft, dice.

2. Remove all the stems from the fresh mushrooms and chop the stems finely. Gently squeeze the chopped stems in a clean dish cloth to remove any excess moisture.

3. In a small saucepan sauté the onion, dried mushrooms, and mushroom stems in 1½ tablespoons of the butter over medium heat until golden brown, about 10 to 15 minutes. Stir in the parsley, salt, and pepper. Reduce the heat to low; add the bread crumbs and flour; cook and stir the mixture for 5 more minutes.

4. Remove the saucepan from the heat and let it cool for 3 minutes. Stir in the egg yolks.

5. To prepare the mushrooms for stuffing, slice off a thin piece of the bottom of each one which will be the cap. Fill each mushroom cavity with the filling and cover with the sliced mushroom bottom.

6. Heat the remaining butter in a heavy skillet over medium heat. Place each mushroom, stuffing-side up, in the skillet and cook until the bottoms are lightly browned, about 3 minutes. Remove the browned mushrooms, stuffing-side up, to an ovenproof casserole just large enough to hold all of them without crowding.

7. Add the stock and the wine to the skillet—along with any remaining filling—and cook over high heat until the liquid is thickened and reduced by about half; taste for seasoning and adjust if necessary. Pour the sauce over the mushrooms in a casserole. (Note: The mushrooms can be prepared ahead of time to this point and finished just before serving.) Bake in a preheated 350-degree oven for about 10 minutes or until lightly browned on top; serve immediately.

Yield: 4 appetizer servings (M)

Jewish Culture at the Hungarian Embassy in Washington

In 1991 the Hungarian embassy in Washington held a landmark event: a celebration of Hungarian Jewish culture. "We wanted to show what the Hungarian Jews have contributed to the world in science, the arts, and the kitchen," said Ann Marshall Zwack, whose husband was the Hungarian ambassador to the United States, Peter Zwack. In addition to having Jewish songs, a lecture on Hungarian Jewish culture, and even the blowing of a shofar at the reception, the embassy's chef, Kalman Kalla, prepared a sumptuous buffet of Hungarian Jewish dishes for two hundred guests, most of whom were familiar with the slightly sweeter American versions of every dish.

"Hungarian Jewish food is similar to Eastern European Jewish food," said Mr. Kalla. "The only difference is that Hungarians make a peppery gefilte fish and a savory stuffed cabbage and they don't make sweet and sour dishes." On the other hand, Hungarians might make a cabbage strudel with caraway and a slight amount of sugar to bring out the cabbage taste as an accompaniment to meat. All Hungarians like Chef Kalla's stuffed mushrooms, which we tasted again in Budapest.

Hagafen's Dolmeh
(Stuffed Grape Leaves)
Adapted from Batia Davidyan

Hagafen, meaning "vine" in Hebrew, was a natural name for Ernie Weir and his wife, Irit, to choose for their kosher wines from their Napa vineyard. Although Mr. Weir grew up in Los Angeles, he met his Iranian-born wife in Israel, where he was living on a kibbutz. Partners in the family-run business, they often play host to Irit's parents. "When my mother comes," said Irit, an acupuncturist, "she picks the grape leaves and stuffs them or else she makes a grape sauce with rice." Of course with the meals that this good-hearted grandmother prepares, the Weirs serve one of their prize-winning Chardonnays, Pinot Noir Blancs or Cabernets Sauvignons.

Dolmeh, cont.

2 large or 4 small white
    onions, chopped

1/2 cup olive oil

1 1/2 cups basmati rice

3/4 cup chopped parsley

3/4 cup chopped mint

1/2 cup raisins

Juice of 2 lemons

2 1/2 tablespoons apricot jam

Salt and freshly ground pepper
    to taste

1/2 teaspoon cumin or to taste

About 40 grape leaves

1 1/2 cups water or enough to
    almost cover stuffed grape
    leaves

1. Sauté the onions in the oil until light brown. Remove from the heat and add the uncooked rice and the other ingredients except the grape leaves.

2. Scatter the bottom of a heavy casserole with a few grape leaves.

3. Place a leaf, dull side up and stem removed, on a flat surface, with the stem end away from you. Place a tablespoon of filling on the leaf near the stem end; flatten out to the width of the leaf. Fold the stem end over the filling. Press the filling firmly underneath the leaf. Fold the sides in and roll from the top toward you. Place the stuffed grape leaves in alternate layers in the casserole. Add the water.

4. Cover with a plate to keep the grape leaves down, and then place a lid on the casserole. Steam the grape leaves over very low heat for about 40 minutes or until cooked.

Yield: about 3 dozen (P)

V A R I A T I O N : *Egyptian-born Elise Akouka, living in Miami, Florida, includes a filling of 2 cloves fresh garlic, 1 pound ground lamb or beef, 1 cup rice, 1/2 cup tomato sauce, 1 tablespoon vegetable or canola oil, and salt and freshly ground pepper to taste. The stuffed grape leaves are simmered in a sauce made of 2 whole cloves of peeled garlic, 1 cup tomato sauce, 1 cup water, the juice of 1 lemon, salt and freshly ground pepper to taste. Then cook them like the Iranian version.*

*Hagafen Vineyard's Ernie
Weir picks grape leaves for his
Persian mother-in-law to stuff.*

Israeli Eggplant Salad

Every Israeli has a recipe for eggplant salad. This one comes from Dassi Stern, the former Attaché for Women's Affairs at the Israeli Embassy in Washington.

3 large eggplants (about 5 pounds)
Juice of 2 lemons
1 bunch scallions, including the green tops, diced
Salt and freshly ground pepper to taste
¼ cup vegetable oil (about)

1. Pierce the eggplants with a fork and place in a pan with a rim. Turn on the broiler and place the pan on a rack about 3 inches from the broiler. Grill for about 10 minutes on each side or until charred on the outside.

2. Remove from the broiler and place the eggplants in a wooden bowl. Slit open with a knife and pour off some of the water. Immediately squeeze the lemon over the eggplants and remove the rest of the water. Chop the eggplants with a knife and place in a wooden or ceramic bowl with the scallions, salt, and freshly ground pepper to taste; dribble with the vegetable oil. Serve with rye or pita bread as a dip.

Yield: 3 cups dip (P)
Tip: This is also good with slivers of roasted red pepper in it.

Moshe's Falafel— The Best Stretch Pushcart in New York City

"Moshe's, the Best in Town" says the sign above the stretch pushcart stand at the corner of Forty-sixth Street and Sixth Avenue in New York City. Business is brisk and at least twice as busy as at the kosher hot-dog stand on the opposite corner. Chasidic Jews, Arabs, Indians, Americans, Israelis—they all line up to buy a pita sandwich with falafel, pickles, tahina, shredded lettuce, and hot tomato sauce. From eleven to five, Monday through Friday, the Bangladeshi, Egyptian, Mexican, and Afghan helpers dip ice-cream scoops into the chick-pea batter and fry the fritters in hot white oil.

"My family has been making falafel for the past sixty years in Israel and Syria," said Moshe Mizrachi, thirty-five, the owner of Moshe's. "When I came to this country in 1980, falafel was a natural, especially when my English was so poor. I chose this area because it is known as the Jewish diamond center." Moshe, who usually sits in a van nearby, pays a few hundred dollars each year to the city for a permit and more money to Kosher K, the kashrut certifying agency that he chose to approve his vegetarian stand.

As the fourth generation in the falafel-making business, Mr. Mizrachi is certainly an expert. "For falafel to be fresh," he advised, "the color should be gold. If it is black it is no good. Either the oil, the chick-peas, or the spices are not fresh." He also recommends using soybean oil, which he changes each day. The only difference between his falafel stand and that of his father's in the Bezalel marketplace in Tel Aviv is the number of spicy sauces. In Israel, reflecting the taste buds of Jews from seventy different countries, his father showcases many. In New York Moshe uses one all-purpose hot sauce.

Moshe's stand may be one of the most successful, but it is not the only one. With hundreds of thousands of Israelis in this country, there is an increasing demand for Israeli food. In Crown Heights, Cleveland, and Los Angeles, I have stumbled on many kosher vegetarian restaurants. They have almost all been run by ex-Israelis, especially if they are selling hummus, *zhug* (a Yemenite hot sauce), or *burekas*.

Moshe's Falafel

Serve this falafel alone or with the following Israeli salads. Don't forget the heated pita—and the hot sauce.

1 cup dried chick-peas

½ cup fine bulgur

1 large onion, chopped

2 tablespoons finely chopped parsley

1 large egg

1 teaspoon salt

2 teaspoons dried hot red peppers or to taste

2 cloves garlic

1 teaspoon cumin

Dash of coriander seed

Soybean or vegetable oil for frying

1. Cover the chick-peas with water and let soak overnight. Drain.

2. Cover the bulgur with water in a mixing bowl and let sit a half hour or until moist.

3. Meanwhile, mix the drained chick-peas and the onion. Add the parsley, egg, and spices. Whirl in a blender or food processor until blended but not smooth.

4. Add enough of the bulgur to the chick-pea mixture until the dough forms a small ball and no longer sticks to your hands. Refrigerate at least one hour.

5. Form the chick-pea mixture into balls about the size of a walnut or use a falafel measuring gadget available in Middle Eastern markets.

6. Flatten the patties slightly. Heat 3 inches of soybean oil in a deep pot to 375 degrees and fry about a half dozen at once until golden brown on each side. Drain the falafel on paper towels. Stuff the pocket of a half pita with falafel and chopped salad (see page 274). Dribble with tahina sauce. Accompany it with hummus (see next page), eggplant salad, tabbouleh (see page 292), and lots of *zhug* (see page 127).

Yield: about 30 (P)

Jerusalem Hummus

Hummus and falafel are not only popular as street food, they are also served at "falafel or hummus stations" at bar mitzvahs and are becoming an everyday staple with the ever-increasing number of vegetarians. There is an art to making good hummus. Start with dried, not canned, chick-peas. Once you have prepared the hummus, you spread it on the plate and dribble with the olive oil so some of it flows on the depression in the center. Then you scatter the pine nuts on top. The pita must be warm; cold pita is for tourists and amateurs. Tear off a piece of the warm pita, dip it in the olive oil, and then scoop up the hummus.

¾ cup dried chick-peas

1 cup tahina (sesame paste)

½ cup lemon juice or to taste

2 cloves garlic

1 teaspoon salt

Freshly ground pepper to taste

¼ teaspoon cumin

Olive oil

Toasted pine nuts

Paprika

Fresh parsley

Olives for garnish

1. Soak the chick-peas in water overnight. Drain the water, add fresh water to cover by ⅓, and simmer, covered, for about 1 hour or until the skin separates. Drain. There should be 1½ cups cooked chick-peas.

2. Reserving ¼ cup of the chick-peas for garnish, place the rest in a food processor or blender with the tahina, lemon juice, garlic, salt, pepper, and cumin. Process or whirl until smooth. If too thick, add a bit of water. To serve, place the hummus on a large, flat plate. Smooth it down with the back of a spoon, making a slight depression all around the center. Dribble with olive oil and sprinkle with the reserved chick-peas, pine nuts, and paprika. Garnish with parsley and olives.

3. Serve with a large basket filled with hot pita cut in wedges.

Yield: 6 to 8 servings (P)

TWO

לחם

Breads, Bagels, and Biscochos

Good flour should be white with a faint yellow tinge;
if wet and kneaded, it should work dry and elastic; if a
lump of dry flour is thrown against the wall it should
adhere altogether and not fall apart; good flour when
squeezed in the hand should retain the shape thus given.

American Jewess, 1895

Ai vos? Men nemt a teigel un men macht a bagel.
So what! You take a lump of dough and you make a bagel.

GOOD BREAD

For Friday Dinner
There Was the Fresh-Baked Berches

The Sabbath began at sundown Friday, just as soon as it was dark, but the preparations began on Thursday morning. The good housewives did the marketing, and worked ahead feverishly and hard. The house had to be immaculate, the "kuchen" baked, the children in their good clothes, to welcome the Sabbath—the day of rest and peace and gladness. How hard our mothers worked on Friday! There was evening service and then we had supper—we didn't call it "dinner" in those far-off days. Never was the linen more snowy, never the meal more perfect. We had either chicken, or fish, and there were no better cooks anywhere than our mothers. There was the fresh-baked "berches," the loaf of bread—twisted and huge, and the yeast kuchen.

Jennie Gerstley, "Reminiscences, Chicago, Illinois, 1859–1934,"
American Jewish Archives

Aunt Babette's Berches

Mrs. Gerstley, a communal worker in Chicago at the end of the nineteenth and beginning of the twentieth century, may have used the recipe for *berches,* the German Jewish name for challah, from *Aunt Babette's Cook Book of Foreign and Domestic Receipts for the Household, A Valuable Collection of Receipts and Hints for the Housewife, Many of Which are not to be Found Elsewhere,* first published in Chicago in 1889. Aunt Babette was the nickname for Mrs. Bertha F. Kramer, a Reform Jew, mother, and grandmother, who "hoarded [the recipes] up as treasures for my own daughters and grandchildren."

Aunt Babette gave a dairy version of *berches* in her book as well as one for a meat meal with "a little shortening of nice drippings or rendered suet." Of course she meant beef suet in this era before vegetable shortening.

Berches was usually shaped in one long braid with a smaller braid on top. Some of the old recipes called for an initial rising of a sponge of flour and yeast, a step unnecessary with the kind of yeast we use today. Usually a potato-based savory bread, it is possible that the sweeter, more stollen-like variety, called fruit bread in nineteenth-century Charleston, South Carolina, was reserved for the New Year and Hanukkah, close to Christmas. This recipe, studded with grated lemon rind, almonds, and raisins, makes a loaf large enough to feed fifteen people. Any cookbook today would divide the dough into two loaves.

2 tablespoons dry yeast

2 cups warm water

½ cup sugar

8 to 9 cups all-purpose flour

1 teaspoon salt or to taste

2 whole eggs, lightly beaten

½ cup vegetable shortening

¼ cup raisins

Grated peel of one lemon

¼ cup almond slivers

1 egg yolk

1 tablespoon poppy seeds

1. Dissolve the yeast in 1 cup of the water with a teaspoon of the sugar. Let sit for 10 minutes or until bubbles form.

2. Place 8 cups of the flour in a bowl. Add the salt, the remaining sugar, and the dissolved yeast. Then add the 2 eggs, the shortening, the remaining water, the raisins, the lemon peel, and the almonds, working the dough well with the heel of your hand. Turn out and knead, adding more water and, if necessary, flour until the dough is smooth.

3. Place the dough in a greased bowl, cover, and let rise for an hour or until doubled in bulk.

4. After the dough has risen, punch down and knead again briefly. If you want to make 1 large loaf, take the dough and divide into 2 parts, one slightly larger than the other. Divide each part of the dough into 3 equal pieces. Roll each piece out into a rope-shape strand and braid the 3 rolls together. Place the larger braid on a greased cookie sheet and cover with the second braid. For 2 loaves, divide the dough into 4 parts, 2 larger than the others, and proceed as above.

5. Let the loaf rise once again, about a half hour, then brush with the egg yolk and sprinkle with poppy seeds.

6. Bake in a preheated 350-degree oven for about 1 hour for 1 loaf and about 35 minutes for 2.

Yield: 1 large or 2 smaller loaves (P)

Fleischmann's Yeast—A Rising Success

It was a Hungarian Jewish immigrant, arriving in this country while the Civil War was still raging, who changed the way Americans made bread. Charles Louis Fleischmann's family had been in the distilling and yeast business in Hungary. Astounded by what he considered to be the poor taste of American bread, he returned to Europe and brought back his brother and a variety of yeast strains derived from a Hungarian method, long used in his family. At first the compressed yeast, made from the froth formed during the manufacture of malt, was slow in finding a market.

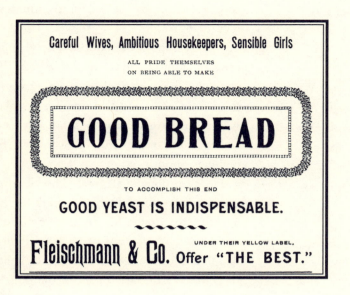

Careful Wives, Ambitious Housekeepers, Sensible Girls

ALL PRIDE THEMSELVES
ON BEING ABLE TO MAKE

GOOD BREAD

TO ACCOMPLISH THIS END

GOOD YEAST IS INDISPENSABLE.

Fleischmann & Co. Offer "THE BEST." UNDER THEIR YELLOW LABEL,

Then the Fleischmann brothers had an idea: They would show off their yeast at a special "Vienna Bakery" booth at the Philadelphia Centennial Exposition in 1876. In those days German culture and cuisine were very popular. While sipping hot coffee, visitors to the booth watched the yeast being made, the dough kneaded and set to rise, and the bread baked. The exhibit was successful; the bakery yielded a cash profit and the advertising value of the enterprise was enormous. So many people were impressed by the samples of Fleischmann's Old World baked foods that the demand for the brothers' yeast soared.

Soon the Fleischmann yeast cart with its neatly groomed horse was as common a sight on American streets as it had been in Hungary. In the late nineteenth century people were so accustomed to buying their yeast that the amount listed in cookbooks was one or two cents' worth, probably equivalent to one or two packages today.

Until the 1930s all yeast was sold in fresh cakes. Then Fleischmann's perfected a dry yeast that did not require refrigeration and had an extended shelf life.

Only a few years after he developed his yeast, Fleischmann prepared Old World recipes for consumers that he advertised in such newspapers as Isaac Mayer Wise's *American Israelite* and the *American Hebrew Almanac*. Included in a 1920 Fleischmann recipe pamphlet was a recipe for potato biscuits. A more Jewish form of these biscuits was a potato-based *berches,* a bread Mr. Fleischmann no doubt remembered from his mother's Budapest kitchen.

Yeast from Grape Leaves
The New York Times, 1870

Until the end of the nineteenth century, housewives were still making their own bread and even their own yeast. In the mid 1870s *The New York Times* included several "receipts" to make yeast from grape leaves, from peas, from potato, and from hops. The recipe for grape yeast assured the reader that "grape leaves make a yeast in some respects superior to hops, as the bread rises sooner, and has not the peculiar taste which many object to in that made from hops."

Cincinnati Potato Berches

This was a savory loaf with a hard crust covered with poppy seeds, probably eaten for normal Sabbaths throughout the year. It is very similar to the recipe handed down in my own family from Bavaria. This one is adapted from the Pritz family papers.

1 tablespoon active dry yeast

2 cups warm water (about)

1 tablespoon sugar

*8 cups all-purpose flour
(about)*

1 tablespoon salt

*3 medium boiled potatoes,
mashed (about 1½ cups)*

1 egg yolk

1 tablespoon poppy seeds

1. Dissolve the yeast in ½ cup of the water with the sugar. Let sit for at least 10 minutes until the mixture starts to bubble slightly.

2. Combine the dissolved yeast with 2 cups of the flour and the salt. Then add the mashed potatoes. Continue to add flour and water until the dough is stiff. Turn out on a board and knead until the dough is smooth. Place in a greased bowl and cover with a cloth. Put in a warm place and let the dough rise for about 1½ hours or until doubled in bulk.

3. After the dough has risen, punch down and knead again briefly. To make one large loaf, take two thirds of the dough and divide it into 3 equal pieces. Roll each piece out into a rope-shape strand as thick as a thumb and then braid the 3 strands together. Then take the remaining third of the dough, divide and shape it into 3 strands and braid. Place the small braid on top of the large one.

4. To make 2 smaller loaves divide the initial dough in 2 and then proceed for each loaf as you did in step 3.

5. Let the loaf rise once again on a greased cookie sheet, for about a half hour, then brush with the egg yolk and sprinkle with poppy seeds.

6. Bake in a preheated 350-degree oven for about one hour for a large loaf and about 30 minutes for 2 smaller loaves.

Yield: 1 very large loaf or 2 small loaves (P)

How Can One Recognize a Reform Jew in a Bakery on Friday? He Orders a Challah and Says, "Slice It."

Leo Rosten, *The Joys of Yiddish*

There are two words for bread in Hebrew: *lechem* and challah. *Lechem* is the everyday bread—the rye pumpernickel of Eastern European Jews, the pita for Middle Eastern ones, bagels, the bought bread, and now the crunchy, chewy bakery breads that are being made all around the country. Challah is the special, usually white egg bread reserved for the Sabbath. Challah is also the word that refers to the portion of dough set apart for the high priests in the Temple of Jerusalem. One of the three commandments incumbent upon women, "taking challah," evolved sometime following the destruction of the Temple by the Romans in 70 C.E. Following the rising of the dough, women would separate a piece and burn it to remind them of the offerings to the Temple. For nearly two millennia it has symbolically replaced the sacrificial offerings. All challah that is baked today is kosher only if "challah has been taken." You'll often see that sign in a kosher bakery. Jews seem to be masters at imbuing ordinary acts with symbolism—or creating symbols out of almost anything.

It was the Eastern European immigrants who put challah on the gastronomical map in this country. In biblical times, however, the Sabbath bread was probably more like our present-day pita. Through the ages and as Jews moved to different lands the loaves varied. But only in America could Jews eat challah or, as some call it, *cholly,* every day of the week.

All breads were sweetened in the late nineteenth century and early twentieth century in the United States. Sugar was a sign of affluence so why not add more to challah?

Elsewhere a round challah at Rosh Hashanah became a symbol of life. Usually the Rosh Hashanah bread is formed in a circle, to signify the desire for a long life. At this point local traditions diverge. Some people add saffron and raisins to make the bread just a little bit more special than a typical Friday-night loaf. In certain towns of Russia, the round challah was imprinted with the shape of a ladder on top, to symbolize the ascent to God on high. A Midrash states that on Rosh Hashanah, the "Holy One, blessed be He, sits and erects ladders; on them He lowers one person and elevates another."

In the Ukraine bread for the holidays was baked in the form of a bird. This symbolized God's protection of the people, as stated in Isaiah 31:5: "As birds hovering (over their fledglings), so will the Lord of hosts protect Jerusalem." Jews from Lithuania baked challahs topped with a crown, in accordance with the words of the great liturgical poet Eleazar Kalir: "Let all crown God."

Many challot traditions were lost as a result of the Holocaust or because of Soviet religious suppression. Some, thankfully, have survived. When Manfred Loeb, a German Jew from Cologne, came to this country to escape Hitler, he apprenticed at Zouderer's Bakery in Bridgeport, where he learned how to make a sweet six-braided Russian challah. Mr. Loeb eventually opened his own very successful bakery in Silver Spring, Maryland. His entire clientele—whether of German, Moroccan, or Russian background—bought the Russian-style six-braided challah. Today Mr. Loeb is retired and for fun makes challah for his friends in a bakery set up in his own basement.

Manfred Loeb's Six-Braided Challah

2 packages active dry yeast

¼–½ cup sugar

1¼ cups warm water

5 to 6 cups bread flour

2 teaspoons salt

3 large eggs

¼ cup vegetable shortening

Handful of sesame or poppy
    seeds

Cornmeal for dusting

1. In a large container dissolve the yeast and a pinch of sugar in 1 cup of the warm water (105 to 115 degrees) and let stand for 10 minutes.

2. Place the flour in a large bowl. Add the dissolved yeast and stir with a spoon. Add the remaining sugar, salt, 2 eggs,* and the vegetable shortening. Beat about one minute and then mix by hand. When the dough begins to leave the side of the bowl, turn it onto a lightly floured surface to knead. You can also use a dough hook in a mixer to blend and knead.

3. Knead for about 15 minutes or until soft, adding more water or flour as necessary.

4. Place the dough in a lightly greased bowl, turning the dough over so that the entire surface is lightly greased; cover the bowl with a cloth. Let rise in a warm place (75 to 80 degrees) for about an hour or until the dough doubles in size. Punch down and divide into 2 balls.

5. Divide each ball into 6 snake-like pieces and roll out, about 12 inches long.

6. Place all 6 strands on a board side by side, pressing the 6 ends together. Divide into 2 groups of 3 strands.

7. Now braid the 6 strands. Take the strand from the extreme left and place it over the other 2 and into the center. Take the second from the right and place it over the top to the far left. Take the one from the far right to what is now the center of your 6 strips. Then take the second one from the left and put it to the far right and take the far outside on the left to what is now the center. Go back to the right side and take the second from the right and put it over to the far left. Always work with the 2 outside strands. Continue braiding until the dough is used up. When you have finished squeeze the ends together. Repeat with the second loaf.

8. For those who want less of a challenge, divide each ball into 3 strands and braid. Place the outside strip over the middle one, then under the third. Pull the strips

*To reduce the cholesterol you can use 1 egg white and 1 whole egg instead of 2 eggs.

*Manfred Loeb shows the
author's children and others
how to braid challah.*

tight. Continue braiding. (Mr. Loeb braids half way
through and then flips the challah, continuing to braid to
the end. This way he gets a more even braid.) When finished braiding, tuck in the ends. Repeat with the
remaining 3 strips.

9. Using a pastry brush, brush the challah with the
remaining egg mixed with water and sprinkle with
sesame or poppy seeds. After you have brushed the
bread, dip your second finger in the egg wash and indent
the top of the braids. Then dip your finger in the seeds
and touch the indented area again to make a more strik-
ing design.

10. Sprinkle a cookie sheet with cornmeal and place the
loaves on top. Cover with a plastic sheet and let rise for
30 minutes in a warm place.

11. Bake in a preheated 375-degree oven for about 30
minutes or until golden.

Yield: 2 loaves (P)

A Chez Panisse Busgirl Turned Lubavitcher's Healthy Whole-Wheat Challah

Shulamis Nadler, a Chasidic caterer in Brooklyn, started her cooking career as a busgirl at Chez Panisse in Berkeley, California. Like other *baalei tshuvah* who were followers of Meir Abehesera, a macrobiotic cookbook writer turned Lubavitch, she has introduced her Lubavitcher friends and clientele to untraditional spices and grains as well as tofu.

Many new Lubavitchers, members of a Chasidic sect, grew up eating international and non-kosher foods. "Today the Lubavitcher movement is very international, with Sephardim and Jews from Argentina, Brazil, everywhere," said Mrs. Nadler. "I think the only tastes I haven't really experienced here are Mexican and Japanese."

But Jews who are "frum for life" (born Orthodox) are less adventuresome. "When I am catering I have to be careful to cook conservatively," Mrs. Nadler said. "Traditional Lubavitchers are still a little leery of seaweed. It's not what they are used to, so they are less likely to try it."

2 tablespoons active dry yeast

2 cups warm water

½ teaspoon sugar

5 tablespoons vegetable oil

1 tablespoon salt

⅓ cup honey

3 large eggs

4 to 5 cups bread flour

4 cups whole-wheat flour

Poppy seeds

1. In a small bowl dissolve the yeast in ½ cup warm water, adding the sugar. Let stand for about 10 minutes or until the yeast starts to bubble.

2. In a large bowl mix the remaining water and the oil and stir. Add the salt and honey. Beat in 2 of the eggs and add the yeast. Gradually add 4 cups each of the bread and whole-wheat flours. Turn out onto a floured work surface and knead for 10 minutes or until smooth, adding more bread flour as needed to make a soft, smooth dough.

3. Form the kneaded dough into a ball and place in a greased bowl. Cover with a towel and let rise for about an hour or until doubled.

4. If you like, you can say the following blessing, "Blessed are Thou, Lord our God, King of the Universe, Who has sanctified us with His commandments and commanded us to separate challah." Then remove a small piece, approximately 1 ounce, from the dough. Immediately after separating the challah say, "this is challah." Then burn it separately in a piece of aluminum foil in the oven or broiler.

5. Divide the remaining dough into 2 portions. Roll out each portion into a long rope-like piece about 1 inch in diameter and approximately 18 inches long. One end

should be tapered thinner. (To make six-braided challahs see page 74).

6. Place the thicker end in the center of a baking pan and coil the strip around itself. Tuck the ends under the challah. Place on a greased baking sheet and let rise, covered, for another 45 minutes. Repeat with the other pieces.

7. Brush the loaves with the beaten egg and sprinkle with the poppy seeds. Bake for 10 minutes in a pre-heated 425-degree oven. Lower the heat to 350 degrees and continue baking for 35 to 40 minutes, or until done. Remove from the cookie sheet and cool on a rack.

Yield: 2 loaves (P)

Little Odessa in Brighton Beach, Brooklyn

One of the great curiosities for visitors to Brooklyn these days is the transformation of aging Brighton Beach into a little Odessa. Since the early 1970s Jewish émigrés from Georgia, Lithuania, and especially the Ukraine's Odessa have been gravitating there. The sidewalks are filled with bargains, with hawkers selling Russian nesting dolls as well as caviar. Inside the grocery shops smoked fish, pumpernickel bread, sausage, and pickles are sold with bargains spelled out in Russian. About 30,000 Jews from the former Soviet Union live in the area.

On one visit I headed for Primorski, one of the typical "clubs" along Brighton Beach Avenue. Chef-owner Reuben "Bubba" Khotoveli was waiting for me. A flamboyant character bedecked in Georgian jewels and necklaces, he emigrated from Kotaissa, Georgia, to Israel briefly in 1971, then went to Detroit, where he worked in an American restaurant before settling in Brighton Beach and opening Primorski. Although the restaurant is billed as Russian, it includes many Georgian specialties like the pressed and grilled chicken, the fresh salads I had tasted in Georgia, and the marvelous bread baked in the restaurant's large ovens. The tables were laden with *zakuski,* small appetizers—eggplant in walnut sauce, marinated mushrooms, spinach with walnuts in wine sauce, roasted red peppers, Russian salad, and a large plate laden with pickled watermelon, tomatoes, carrots, cucumbers, and cabbage. Here, diners drink vodka and celebrate with Georgian singers

*Primorski's Bubba out-
side his Brighton Beach
Georgian restaurant*

chanting melancholy melodies and happy happy-birthday songs. I couldn't help
thinking that this was real paradise for these immigrants—tables laden with the
plenty so lacking in their native land and a familiar atmosphere along with music
and melancholy discussions that Russians love so dearly.

Mr. Khotoveli and I went to the back of the restaurant, pausing briefly in the
room where he grills the chickens and the shish kebabs of the Caucasus. We
walked downstairs to the kitchen. Mounds of rising dough awaited us. He showed
me how he makes his white bread, thicker than pita, shaping it into a big ball for
the Sabbath and indenting it with his fingers as a flat everyday bread before sprinkling it with water. For Georgians the only distinction between the challah and
lechem is the shape. As soon as the crusty bread emerged from the oven, Mr. Khotoveli gave me a goody bag that I happily carried home.

Georgian Challah

2 tablespoons yeast

1 teaspoon sugar

2 cups warm water

6 cups all-purpose flour
   (about)

1 tablespoon salt

⅓ cup vegetable oil

1. Dissolve the active dry yeast along with the sugar in the water in a large glass container. Mix and let sit about 10 minutes.

2. In a large bowl mix 5 cups of the flour with the salt. Add the yeast mixture and the vegetable oil. Work the ingredients together with a spoon; when they come together turn out on a floured board, and knead with your hands until the dough becomes a smooth ball. Place in a greased bowl and let rise, covered, for an hour or so or until doubled.

3. Punch down and divide into 4 balls. Cover with a towel and let rise about a half hour.

4. Meanwhile, place 4 empty round baking pans or cookie sheets in a preheated 400-degree oven for about 10 minutes and remove.

5. When the dough has risen, punch down and divide into 4 balls. At this point you can treat this like everyday or Sabbath bread. For weekdays, press down and stretch, using the back of your hand. Grease the baking pans and press the dough down into them. Using your fingers, make big indentations in the center of the dough. For Sabbath bread, keep the shape in a round and make a few slashes in the bread. Sprinkle the dough, whatever the shape, with water and bake in the oven for about 20 minutes or until the loaf sounds hollow when tapped with a spatula.

Yield: 4 loaves (P)

If Wall Street Is the Financial District, Then the Lower East Side Is the Rye Bread District

Hence the importance of rye bread on the lower East Side. It is at once a plate, a spoon and a hearty nourishing food, and it bulks very large in the East Side landscape. It seems to be on sale everywhere in loaves shaped like a millstone and of pretty nearly the same size and weight. Nor does it appear to be handled so much as food, but as such building material—as stone, wood, or iron beams. It is cast about promiscuously in great heaps, at the base of shop windows and in cellarways, and occasionally it stands piled up on the curb while an old man or young girl keeps watch over it with a large knife. This is used to cut it in halves and quarters, for very few loaves are sold entire. Like bread in rustic France and Italy, it will keep for days, and remains comparatively fresh until eaten, so that there is nothing to prevent even a small family buying a whole loaf except the difficulty of lugging it home. It would almost appear that a block and tackle would be necessary to raise it to the upper floor of an East Side tenement.

Montague Glass, "Kosher Restaurants,"
Saturday Evening Post, August 3, 1929

One of the most important elements of a good delicatessen is pumpernickel. Made by a natural sour fermentation using unbolted rye flour for the dark variety and various proportions of rye and wheat flours for the light variety, this rye bread is made darker with molasses or caramel coloring and includes "chop," the shell or grain of the kernel. The same sour fermentation is used in Jewish rye bread with more wheat flour and no chop.

I have always wondered why American Jews call a very heavy and sour rye bread or *Bauernbrot* "corn bread." Somehow the word corn got lost in the translation. In Germany a Jewish rye bread was made with all rye flour. Not here. In this country some wheat is thrown in. In Yiddish corn means grain so a corn bread could be any bread with grain. Some say that the bread got its name because cornmeal is thrown on the baking sheet when it is baked.

Bread window in
Jewish bakery

Rye Pumpernickel

Gerald Donaldson, an avid breadmaker in Chevy Chase, Maryland, and former neighbor, came up with the following rye pumpernickel recipe, which is as good as any I have ever tasted. It is a slowly fermented loaf. The starter takes a few days as does the bread. Don't speed up the waiting time. Savor it.

STARTER

4 cups freshly ground rye grain*

4 cups slightly tepid potato water

1 teaspoon active dry yeast

½ cup blackstrap molasses

3½ to 4 cups water

¼ cup malt powder

DOUGH

5 pounds white-bread flour

2 cups hard whole-wheat flour

1 cup raw wheat germ

2 cups coarsely ground wheat bran

¼ cup malt powder

5 tablespoons salt or to taste

3½ to 4 cups tap water

½ cup caraway seeds (optional)

Cornmeal for dusting

*Gerry recommends using a coffee grinder and grinding the rye kernels in small batches.

1. Mix the rye, water, yeast, and molasses in a very large stainless-steel container. Cover with a plate and let sit 3 days in a cool spot, i.e. about 60 degrees, so that the starter can ferment slowly.

2. Add the water and malt powder to the starter and dissolve using a whisk or an ancient Bavarian wooden spoon, if you're lucky enough to have one!

3. When the starter is ready, place the remaining ingredients in a large bowl. Make a well in the middle and add the starter. Knead in the bowl for at least 10 minutes or until the bread starts forming a nice large ball. If it doesn't seem to come together as quickly as you want, let it rest for a few minutes and you'll be able to knead more easily. The dough should be stiff.

4. Keep the dough in the bowl and place inside a large white garbage bag so that the dough will not dry out. (Mr. Donaldson sometimes blows up the bag and ties a twist around it. This way the bag is inflated and the air keeps it moist.) Leave it to rise for 10 to 12 hours in the winter and 5 to 6 hours in the summer.

5. Punch the dough down, turn it out on a big work surface, and divide into 4 big portions. Shape into circles or place in greased bread pans. Dust with cornmeal and cover with a plastic bag again. Let it rise until doubled.

6. With a paring knife make 6 slashes in any pattern you like.

7. Place in a cold oven with a broiler pan with hot water on the bottom. Turn the oven to 350 degrees and bake for about 1½ hours or until the loaves are done, sounding hollow when tapped with a knife.

Yield: 4 loaves (P)

Note: Walnut Acres in Pennsylvania is a good mail order source for malt powder, rye grain, and wheat bran.

Biscochos or Ka'ak or Crozettes

Baked round rolls with a hole filled with anise or coriander seeds and dipped in sesame seeds date from ancient Egypt. Surely the forerunner of bagels, these *biscochos, ka'ak,* or *crozettes* were brought to this country by various Sephardic immigrants. Sometimes flavored with fennel and fenugreek (Iraqi), anise (Spanish), or coriander (Egyptian), they make a perfect snack food; certainly itinerant Jews would have carried them in their backpacks.

1 package active dry yeast

1½ cups lukewarm water

1 teaspoon sugar

3 cups all-purpose flour

1 teaspoon salt

*2 tablespoons fennel, anise, or
  coriander seeds*

1 large egg

Sesame seeds

1. Dissolve the yeast in 1 cup of the water with the sugar and let sit for about 10 minutes until it starts to bubble. Gradually add the flour, salt, remaining water, and the fennel, anise, or coriander seeds. Knead until smooth.

2. Place in a greased bowl and cover with a cloth. Let rise for about 1 hour or until doubled in bulk. Punch down the dough and knead again for a few minutes.

3. Divide the dough into small balls, about the size of a walnut. Roll into snake-like pieces about 10 inches in length and about ½ inch in diameter and cut with your pinky or a knife. Twist into rings with a wide hole.

4. Combine the egg with a bit of water and dip the rings into the egg mixture. Then dip them into another bowl filled with sesame seeds.

5. Place on a greased baking sheet, leaving about an inch between them. Let rise again for about a half hour and bake in a preheated 375-degree oven for about 25 minutes or until golden. Reduce the oven to 225 degrees and bake for ½ hour on the bottom rack and ½ hour on the top.

Yield: about 3 dozen (P)

The Bagel: Is It More Than Just a Roll with a Hole?

The bagel, a form of Jewish baked goods sometimes described as a doughnut with rigor mortis, will not disappear from New York tables.

The New York Times, February 4, 1956

First Generation: Bagel and lox with a glass of tea.
Second Generation: Bagel and lox with a cup of coffee.
Third Generation: Bagel and Nova Scotia salmon with a cup of espresso.
Fourth Generation: Two croissants, an omelette aux fines herbes, and a glass of skim milk.

Peter Hochstein and Sandy Hoffman, *Up From Seltzer: A Handy Guide to Four Generations of Jews in the United States,* 1981

As a child I lived in Larchmont, New York. Every Sunday, my father would bring back bagels from one of the thirty or so bagel bakers who still practiced their art in the fifties in New York City. Curious to see if the neighbors who lived behind us were Jewish, my German-born father (who only learned about bagels from my New York–born mother) offered them a bagel. If they recognized it, he told us, then they were Jewish. (In those days in Westchester County people did not always admit to their Jewishness.) Our neighbors recognized and ate the bagel. Another Jewish family!

By the mid-1950s my father was part of a growing Jewish Sunday-morning tradition of men who went out to buy bagels, cream cheese, and lox so their wives could sleep in (not unlike the tradition of non-Jewish men making their own bacon, eggs, and pancakes). Today bagels have become such a part of American

Many rolls with holes at
H and H Bagels

culture that Dunkin' Donuts and Burger King carry them, the *QE2* serves them, and most of us include them on weekly shopping lists.

Theories abound as to their origin. The word derives from *beigen,* German for "to bend," and the bagel is a descendant of the pretzel. The first Jewish community in Poland, established by invitation and charter in the thirteenth century, probably brought *biscochos* with them. The boiled and baked roll with a hole dates possibly from the Roman period. In pockets of Haute Savoie, France, today, there is a boiled and baked anise-flavored bread similar to a bagel. Eventually the bread worked its way to Poland and Russia. Today, in Cracow, where some say the present-day form of bagel was born, the bagel is alive and well, sold on many street corners. According to local tradition Jan Sobieski, the famous Polish leader, introduced bagels to Vienna in 1683 when he rescued the city from the Turks.

In Eastern Europe Jews were particularly careful about their meats, fish, and breads, allowing only Jewish bakers to bake for them. The most likely explanation is one that was given me by two Chasidic women of the Beigel family of Cracow, whose family had been bagel bakers (hence their name) for centuries. They told me about the peddlers, who were religious Jewish men, going out into the countryside and not being able to eat their bread because it had not been blessed. According to Jewish dietary laws, this most holy of foods could not be eaten until after hands were washed and a blessing said. But because clean water was rarely available when they were traveling, the men had to go hungry. So they devised a way of boiling the dough rather than baking it, thus putting bagels outside the category of a traditional bread so that they would not require the ritual handwashing before eating.

Although everyone may have made bagels at one time, Jewish bakers became specialists, often using leftover morning roll dough for the evening and snack bagel. Fortunately for us today, many of the bagel bakers came with the mass of Eastern European Jewish immigrants to New York. The hole helped the bagel hawker on the streets of the Lower East Side, as it does today on the streets of Cracow, by enabling him to thread dozens on long sticks.

Until the late fifties bagels were handcrafted in little two- or three-man cellar bakeries sprinkled around New York's Lower East Side. An expression arose, "*Er ligt in der erd un bakt bagel* [He lies in the earth and bakes a bagel]." In these cellars the oven was built so low that a pit two or three feet deep had to be dug in front of it for the man working the oven.

By 1907 the International Beigel Bakers' Union was created, but by the mid-twenties the number of bagel bakeries declined as Jews turned away from their old folk customs. The Yiddish writer I. L. Peretz referred to "those of us who long ago forgot the bagel." Although there still were bagel bakeries the numbers declined.

*The Lender family
enjoying their bagels*

In 1951 a Broadway comedy, *Bagels and Yox,* put the word bagel into such mainstream magazines as *Time;* bagels were distributed at intermission. That same year *Family Circle* included a recipe for bageles (its spelling). The copy read "Stumped for Hors d'oeuvres Ideas? Here's a grand one from Fannie Engle (who later wrote the *Jewish Festival Cookbook*). Split these tender little triumphs in halves and then quarters. Spread with sweet butter and place a small slice of smoked salmon on each. For variations, spread with cream cheese, anchovies or red caviar. (They're also delicious served as breakfast rolls.)" There is mention here of smoked salmon and of cream cheese but not together.

"Even up to the 1950s, you literally could not give a bagel away from Monday to Saturday," said Murray Lender, son of the founder of Lender's bagels. "Most people still thought of it as a Jewish dish." But clearly, if bagels were featured in *Family Circle,* they were on the way to recognition in America. Mr. Lender's father Harry, a baker in Lublin, Poland, came to New Haven in 1927 and bought a small roll and bread bakery. He quickly converted it into a bagel bakery, one of the few at that time outside of New York. "There was no such animal as a bagel bakery per se in those days," said Mr. Lender. In 1955 when he got out of the service and went into his dad's business, Lender's started to expand, packaging their bagels to sell in supermarkets. At the same time they started to experiment with bagels flavored with onions, egg, and made with pumpernickel flour.

In 1962 Lender's bought and made operational the first bagel machine. At the same time they began freezing bagels, which they marketed nationally under the Lender's brand. In 1984 they sold their business to Kraft, which sold it to Kellogg's in 1996. "Today there are about eight hundred bagel bakeries throughout the nation. These were created by an awareness through our frozen bagel," said

Mr. Lender. According to one Food Marketing Institute statistic, next to frozen orange juice, bagels are the second-highest-volume item in the frozen-food section and should soon outnumber doughnuts in the state of California!

The irony of this bagel story is that today bagel bakeries are not necessarily Jewish-owned or run. H and H Bagels in New York is run by a Puerto Rican family, and John Marx, a Cincinnatian of German background, bakes thirty-six different bagel varieties, including Cincinnati Red bagels, tropical fruit, and taco bagels, in three locations. Marx, who likes to surprise his customers in his Bagelman outfit, was chosen to represent bagels at the Smithsonian's bicentennial celebration in Washington in 1976.

Are bagels the same as they used to be? Lamentably for us bagel purists, the answer is no. Today bagels are bigger, softer, and there is less of a hole.

Izzy Cohen's Water Bagels

Eighty-year-old retired baker Izzy Cohen has become quite a legend in the Los Angeles food world. His advice to would-be bagel bakers: "This is not bagels for dummies. But don't be afraid to try. You have a built-in clientele—your spouse and your kids. Nothing beats a fresh bagel, even if it's lousy!" What I like about this recipe is that you can make the dough and form the bagels, refrigerate or freeze them during the week (as many Jewish bakers used to do), and then boil and bake them on the weekends for breakfast.

2 cups water

3 tablespoons sugar

5 tablespoons dry yeast

1 tablespoon salt

2 tablespoons malt powder

6½ to 7 cups high-gluten flour

Kosher salt, sesame seeds, or

poppy seeds

1. Put the water, sugar, and the yeast in an electric mixer fitted with the dough hook; mix on low speed until the yeast dissolves. Add the salt, malt powder, and 2 cups of the flour, and mix well. Gradually add enough of the remaining flour to make a smooth and relatively firm dough. Let the dough rest for 10 minutes, covered with a towel, either in the bowl or poured out onto a lightly floured counter.

2. Shape the dough into an oblong mass and divide in half with a sharp knife or dough cutter, then divide in half once more. Cut each of these pieces into 4 parts. On a dry wooden table or chopping board, flatten each piece and roll it up jelly-roll style until you have a short, stubby cigar about 3 inches long. Repeat with all the balls. Take each piece and roll it again under your palm until it is 5 inches long. Roll out with one palm until the strand or *flechtel* is about 7 inches long. Wrap around 3 or 4 fin-

gers, overlapping the ends by about 1½ inches. Putting pressure on the overlap, roll the *flechtel* on the table until it is sealed and becomes the same thickness as the rest of the bagel. Repeat with the remaining rolls of dough.

3. If you are baking the bagels right away, place them on a board dusted very lightly with cornmeal and let rise, covered with a cloth, for about an hour. If you want to make them in a few days or freeze them, place on 2 jelly-roll pans dusted with cornmeal and wrap in 2 large plastic bags. Refrigerate overnight or freeze them. If frozen, before proceeding to the next step remove from the freezer to the refrigerator overnight. Then take them out of the refrigerator and let them warm up at room temperature for about an hour.

4. Preheat the oven to 450 degrees. Boil 4 quarts of water in a 5-quart pan. Slide 4 bagels into the boiling water, and boil for 20 to 30 seconds, stirring at least once. Remove with a slotted spoon and put them on a cooling rack over a pan to let the water drain. Repeat with the rest. Sprinkle with the desired topping, such as kosher salt or sesame seeds or poppy seeds.

5. Place the bagels, as soon as you can handle them, onto 2 baking sheets covered with parchment or sprinkled with cornmeal, and put them in the oven. Check them after 8 minutes and turn the pans back to front and switch from rack to rack. Continue baking for about 8 minutes more, or until golden brown. Remove from the oven and cool on racks.

Yield: 16 bagels (P)

Mogen David Bagels

Slice the bagels in half with a sharp knife, allowing four halves per serving. Spread cut sides with butter, cream cheese, or a combination of both. Arrange strips of lox (smoked salmon) into crossed triangles, resembling a Jewish star. May be slipped under the broiler flame for 2 to 3 minutes before serving or heated on top shelf of oven at 350 degrees for 5 minutes. A cookie sheet will hold many of these Mogen David bagels and can be handled easily. Strips of pickled herring may be substituted for the lox, without broiling.

Or cut the bagels and butter each cut side generously. Place strips of cheddar cheese on each to form Mogen Davids and slip under the broiler flame for 2 to 3 minutes to melt the cheese slightly. Serve hot, with or without paprika sprinkled over cheese.   *Adapted from the* Jewish Holiday Cook Book, *Leah Leonard, 1955*

To Make a Good Bialy You Still Need That Thumb

Inside the door of Kossar's Bialystocken Kuchen on Grand Street on New York's Lower East Side there are huge paper bags sitting on the floor with orders written in crayon. The lineup reads like a Who's Who of New York bakeries and delis— H and H, Zabar's, Barney Greengrass, the list goes on. The twenty-four–hour bakery is run by Ukrainian-born Morris Kossar and his son-in-law, Daniel Shinin. Puerto Rican bakers work three eight-hour shifts rolling out bialys. Local Chinese and Irish customers come in at all hours to buy a bialy for a nosh.

Made with only salt, water, yeast, and flour, the soft bialy dough is formed into small rounds, which are first patted down. Later, a thumb indents the center, which is filled with diced onions and sometimes poppy seeds before the bialy is quickly baked in a very hot oven.

It is not clear what the origin of the bialy is. Suspiciously similar to a *pletzlach,* sometimes called an onion board in this country (see page 90), it is also akin to an old Middle Eastern filled dough called *sfeeha.* In Central Asia you'll find similar rolls filled with onions. The Georgian bread punched down with the thumb and made in rounds for the Sabbath is exactly the same (see page 79). It is possible that a Jewish baker from Bialystok, Poland (thus bialy), was in the army in Central Asia, tasted an interesting snack bread and brought the idea back to his bakery. Chances are the name bialy stuck in the United States.

Bialys, unlike most bagels today, are still made by hand although a roll-maker, invented in the 1930s, has increased production tremendously.

Although bialys never repeated their New York reception elsewhere in the country, Jewish bakers, such as the late Abraham Kaplan of Kaplan's Bakery in South Providence, Rhode Island, made their own versions. "My father told me that a customer came into the bakery and asked for a bialy, which he said was an overfermented bagel that was flattened and pocketed with onions," said Danny Kaplan, Abraham's grandson and owner of Barney's Bakery in Pawtucket, Rhode Island. "I take risen bagel dough that has been refrigerated for at least twenty-four hours, flatten the center, and put in chopped onions with garlic and poppy seeds." Danny has added his own touches to appeal to an American audience—larger bialys and ones topped with pizza sauce. Kaplan's bialys resemble a bagel without a hole.

Petrofsky's Bakery Products in Maryland Heights, Missouri, is prepackaging frozen bagels and bialys for in-store bakeries nationwide. "You go into different cities and every city makes a bialy different," said David Petrofsky. "We take the boiled bagel dough and flatten it down and market it as bialys. Some markets thaw the dough and put the onions in the center." Like Petrofsky, Mr. Kossar, now in his eighties, ships his pure bialys nationwide but only to individuals. "Bialys are as popular as bagels," he insists. "People come from out of town, and take home dozens of bialys to freeze. But they'll never be like bagels, because you still have to use your fingers to make that special shape, to make that hole."

Bialys

2 cups warm water

2 packages active dry yeast

1 teaspoon sugar

7 to 8 cups flour

2 tablespoons salt

1/2 cup bread crumbs

1 large finely diced onion

1 tablespoon poppy seeds

Kosher salt

1. Pour the water into a bowl. Add the yeast and the sugar and mix. Let sit about 10 minutes until the yeast starts to bubble.

2. Put 7 cups of the flour and the salt in a large bowl. Add the yeast mixture and stir well. Work the ingredients together with a spoon, then turn out, and knead with your hands until the dough becomes a soft smooth ball. Place in a greased bowl and let rise, covered, for an hour or so, or until doubled.

3. Punch down and divide into 16 balls. Place on a board, cover with a towel, and let rise about a half hour.

4. Using a rolling pin, flatten each ball to about a 4-inch-diameter circle. Then, using your fingers, stretch the sides and then, using your thumb, press down in the center, making a large indentation. Sprinkle the bread crumbs, onion and/or poppy seeds, and salt in the center. Repeat with the remaining 15 balls.

5. Place on a greased cookie sheet and bake in a preheated 450-degree oven for 8 to 10 minutes or until done.

Yield: 16 bialys (P)

Tip: You can use an egg wash around the sides if you like, but most New York bialys do not have that.

Woonsocket, Rhode Island's Community Cook Book — From Pita to Pizza to Pletzel

After years of thumbing through Jewish community cookbooks, my favorite is still the 1947 *Community Cook Book* from Woonsocket, Rhode Island. Whenever someone asks me about an old Eastern European Jewish recipe, I go straight to this compendium of edible history.

If you read carefully, cookbooks tell the story of their community. This one is a wonderful example. Russian Jewish immigrants came to Woonsocket at the beginning of the century. Drawn there by the textile industry, the early immigrants prospered. During World War II, when the men of the community were overseas, the women decided to put together a cookbook as a fund-raiser for the local synagogue. The cookbook committee, headed by Mrs. Coleman Falk, interviewed all the older women like Frances Darman, whose grandmother had come from Lithuania and whose grandson Richard would become Director of the Office of Management and Budget under Reagan and Bush.

Unlike most cookbook compilers, these women did not just take down the recipes from the old-time cooks. They stood over them with pencil and paper while they were cooking, never turning their backs. Mrs. Darman's gefilte fish, for example, is quite unusual. It contains green pepper and is stuffed back in the skin. One of my favorite recipes in the book is that for *pletzlach,* a flat pizza-like dough covered with onions and remembered by Rhode Island Jews as something so delicious it was eaten straight from the bakery oven.

Pletzlach with Onions

Pletzel, which rhymes with pretzel, is the foccacia of the Jewish food world. Also called *pletzlach,* onion *zemmel,* onion *pampalik,* or onion board, it looks and tastes very much like the flat bread laden with onions and poppy seeds I recently ate in the marketplace of Izmir. After all, pizza began as pita, sprinkled with olive oil and *za'atar* (a combination of spices), a meal for a poor person. The following is an adaptation of a *pletzlach* recipe from *The Community Cook Book.*

2 teaspoons salt

2 teaspoons sugar

2 tablespoons solid vegetable
*   shortening*

1 cup plus 2 tablespoons hot
*   water*

1 package active dry yeast
*   (1 tablespoon)*

4 cups all-purpose flour
*   (about)*

1 large egg, beaten

4 red, Vidalia, or other sweet
*   onions, peeled and finely*
*   chopped (4 cups)*

1 tablespoon poppy seeds
*   (optional)*

Kosher salt

1. In a large bowl mix together the salt, sugar, vegetable shortening, and the hot water. When cooled to lukewarm, add the yeast, dissolve it, and let it sit for 10 minutes. Gradually add enough flour, stirring, until you have a dough that holds together.

2. Turn out onto a floured work surface and knead, adding as much of the remaining flour as necessary, for about 10 minutes or until the dough is smooth. Return the dough to the greased bowl and allow to rise for 2 hours or until doubled in bulk.

3. Divide the dough into 10 parts. Roll each piece out in a circle ⅜ inch thick, about 4 inches in diameter and place on a greased baking sheet. Press down in the center, leaving about a half-inch rim. Brush with the egg diluted with water. Pierce the dough with a fork leaving an inch border. Sprinkle with the onions, poppy seeds, and the kosher salt and allow to rise a half hour.

4. Bake in a preheated 375-degree oven for 40 minutes or until golden.

Yield: 10 (P)

Tip: You can also divide the dough in two and roll out into two large rectangles. You can also sauté the onions first until very limp and golden in olive oil and then cover the dough with them, making it more like an Italian focaccia.

Bagel Bread — You Take Some Leftover Bagel Dough and Make Something Softer Inside

Ethnic roots run deep in Providence, Rhode Island. That is why Providence takes its Ma-and-Pa bakeries seriously and why first-rate Portuguese sweet bread, Jewish rye, crusty Italian white, Lebanese pita, oversized bagels, and now bagel bread are all available here.

Bagel bread is made with the flour, sugar, yeast, salt, and water used in bagels and made much in the same way. Instead of boiling the loaves, however, the bakers let the braided dough sit in the refrigerator overnight. The next day they roll it in sesame and poppy seeds, onion, garlic, and salt, and bake it. But while bagel bread has the chewy exterior of a bagel, it has the soft interior of fresh-baked bread.

Like many great gastronomic inventions, it happened by chance. Across the street from Alchemy Ovenworks where it began is a home for the elderly. The story goes that the residents loved the bakery's bagels but found them difficult to chew.

When I first mentioned this story in *The New York Times* I received letters from people who insisted that they had invented bagel bread. Then I saw it myself at the Oakville Market in Napa Valley. Good ideas travel quickly!

Bagel Bread

6 to 7 cups bread flour

2 tablespoons active dry yeast

1 teaspoon sugar

2½ cups lukewarm water

2 teaspoons salt

¼ cup honey

¼ cup vegetable oil

Cornmeal or rye flour for
    dusting

6 tablespoons dried or fresh
    onion

6 tablespoons minced garlic

3 tablespoons sesame seeds

3 tablespoons poppy seeds

Kosher salt to taste

1. Place 6 cups of the flour in a bowl or a KitchenAid mixer.

2. In a large glass bowl mix the yeast with the sugar and the water and let sit for 10 minutes. Add to the flour and mix with salt, honey, and vegetable oil. Knead well, for about 20 minutes or until you have a nice smooth dough, adding more flour if necessary. Place in a greased bowl and let sit, covered, until doubled in bulk. Punch down and divide into 6 8-ounce pieces.

3. Braid the loaves, starting with 3 parallel long pieces. Braid from the middle of the dough, starting with the outside over the middle and then the other outside over the middle. Keep braiding and seal at the end. Flip the bread and continue braiding from the inside. Braid loosely. Place on a cookie sheet sprinkled with cornmeal. Sprinkle the loaves with rye flour and let sit out until the dough doubles in size, about an hour. Refrigerate overnight with a damp cloth over the breads.

4. The next morning, remove the loaves and let sit until they reach room temperature.

5. Mix the dried onion, garlic, sesame seeds, poppy seeds, and kosher salt, adding water to rehydrate the onions. Smear generously on the loaves.

6. Place the loaves in a preheated 400-degree oven and spray with water. Bake for 25 to 35 minutes or until golden and the loaves sound hollow when tapped.

Yield: 2 bagel breads (P)

Mark Talisman's Jewish Onion Bread

"There is nothing like the smell of onions cooking and frying. I always loved onion breads, but they never had enough onions for my taste. So I piled in three kinds of onions and it worked," says Mark Talisman, amateur, but master, baker.

2 tablespoons active dry yeast

1½ cups warm water

1 teaspoon sugar

1 large Spanish onion

1 bunch scallions

6 to 8 cups bread flour

2 tablespoons olive oil plus oil for greasing

2 teaspoons salt or to taste*

2 tablespoons dried onions

2 tablespoons poppy seeds

Cornmeal for dusting

*Since Mr. Talisman is on a salt-restricted diet, he uses only ½ teaspoon salt.

1. Put the yeast in the warm water with the sugar in a bowl and let sit for 10 minutes until it starts to bubble.

2. Meanwhile dice the Spanish onion and the scallions, using two thirds of the green part. You can do this in the food processor.

3. Place 6 cups of the flour in the food processor with the onions. Add the yeast mixture, olive oil, salt, dried onions, and poppy seeds. Blend until a smooth dough is formed, adding flour if needed.

4. Place the dough in a ceramic bowl, coated with additional olive oil. Flip the dough to cover all sides. Let rise, covered, until doubled.

5. Punch down the dough, flatten it out into a pancake, and roll it like a jelly roll. Fold it in on itself to form a smooth round shape.

6. Sprinkle a cookie sheet with cornmeal and place the round on top. Score with a single-edge razor. Let rise again until doubled. Preheat the oven to 400 degrees.

7. Brush with water and sprinkle with additional poppy seeds.

8. Reduce the oven to 375 degrees and bake for 40 minutes, brushing with water again half way through baking, or until the bread sounds hollow when tapped with a spatula.

Yield: 1 large loaf (P)
Note: For a shinier loaf, you can brush with egg white.
You can also make one smaller loaf and a dozen rolls, reducing the cooking times.

Schnecken —
The American Sticky Bun

One of the most popular and most plagiarized of the German kuchen was *Schnecken*. Meaning snail in German, it is a yeast dough that is sprinkled with nuts and raisins, rolled up, then sliced and baked, often in a honey and brown-sugar syrup. *Schnecken* eventually became the American pecan rolls, caramel cinnamon rolls, or sticky buns. The almonds, walnuts, and honey were replaced by pecans and brown sugar.

Different editions of the *Settlement Cook Book* show the progression from *Schnecken* to caramel cinnamon rolls made in a heavy skillet to pecan rolls made in a muffin pan. In a few editions the word "*Schnecken*" disappeared altogether, although the same yeast dough was used for caramel cinnamon rolls and pecan rolls in muffin pans.

One of the most popular *Schnecken* recipes came from the German Jewish Bake Shop in Cincinnati, Ohio. Started in 1929 by the United Jewish Social Agencies as a means of providing part-time employment for women, the shop was immediately successful. The *American Israelite* of 1929 reported, "It (the Jewish Bake Shop) takes them out of their homes temporarily and provides employment for which they are particularly fitted. Recipes made locally famous by Cincinnati housewives interested in the bakery are being utilized in the making of cakes, cookies and the like." According to the late Grace Stix (see page 102), chairman of the Tea Room Committee, in an article in the *American Israelite* in 1932, "The Tea Room acts as a laboratory for Bake Shop products. New dainties are tried out on the public's sweet tooth and popular preference is thus ascertained without waste and over-production."

When German Jewish immigrants came to Cincinnati prior to and during World War II, they were able to find work at the Bake Shop, adding their own versions of Old World favorites. Although the Bake Shop has been closed for many years, Cincinnatians still talk fondly of it and its *Schnecken*.

Jewish Bake Shop's Schnecken

The recipe for the Bake Shop Schnecken came to me from *The Cincinnati Cookbook,* published by the Cooperative Society of the Children's Hospital. Newer versions use 1 cup chopped and 1 halved pecans instead of the walnuts and almonds and 2 cups brown sugar instead of the honey and brown sugar. This is my daughter Merissa's favorite breakfast treat, without the currants.

DOUGH

2 tablespoons or 2 packages
  active dry yeast

½ cup lukewarm water

½ cup sugar

2 sticks (1 cup) unsalted butter,
  at room temperature

1 cup milk

3 eggs

6 to 6½ cups unbleached flour

1 teaspoon salt

**FILLING AND
BOTTOM OF PANS**

1 stick (½ cup) unsalted butter

1½ cups dark-brown sugar

¾ cup honey

1 cup blanched almonds

1 cup chopped walnuts

1 cup currants

½ teaspoon cinnamon

1. To make the dough, dissolve the yeast in the lukewarm water with a teaspoon of the sugar. Let sit for 10 minutes.

2. Place the butter in a saucepan with the milk. Stir over low heat until the butter is melted. Cool to lukewarm. Remove to the bowl of an electric mixer. Add the yeast, the remaining sugar, and the eggs. Gradually add the flour and salt, stirring after each addition. The dough will be very sticky. Place in the refrigerator overnight.

3. The next morning, melt the remaining stick of butter and brush the bottom and sides of 36 muffin tins generously. From the filling ingredients add a half teaspoon of brown sugar and then a teaspoon of honey to each tin, and top with 3 blanched almonds in the shape of a triangle.

4. When the yeast dough is ready, divide into 3 portions and roll each into a rectangle, about 7 by 12 inches wide, on a floured board.

5. Brush the dough with melted butter. Sprinkle each rectangle with one third of the remaining brown sugar, walnuts, currants, and cinnamon. Roll up tightly like a jelly roll.

6. Cut into 12 slices and place in the muffin tins, cut side down. Let rise, uncovered, for half an hour. Brush the tops with melted butter.

7. Bake in a preheated 350-degree oven for 15 minutes. Then reduce the oven to 325 degrees and continue cooking for 20 minutes or until golden. Invert onto waxed paper.

Yield: 36 Schnecken (D)
Note: I often make these ahead and freeze half in the muffin tins. Then I defrost and bake for brunch.

Sweet Buns in Boston — Mary Margolis Cohen's Lithuanian Putterkuchen

Here was this poor grocer, conducting his business on the same perilous credit system which had driven my father out of Chelsea and Wheeler Street, supplying us with tea and sugar and strong butter, milk freely splashed from rusty cans, potent yeast, and bananas done to a turn,—with everything, in short, that keeps a poor man's family hearty in spite of what they eat,—and all this for the consideration of part payment, with the faintest prospect of a future settlement in full. Mr. Rosenblum had an intimate knowledge of the financial situation of every family that traded with him, from the gossip of his customers around his herring barrel. He knew without asking that my father had no regular employment and that, consequently, it was risky to give us credit. . . . he even insisted on my mother's taking almonds and raisins for a cake for the holidays.

Mary Antin, *The Promised Land,* 1912

Jewish immigrant women often minded the store while their husbands studied.

Like Mr. Rosenblum in Mary Antin's description, the late Mary Margolis Cohen ran a family grocery store in turn-of-the-century East Boston. Like many first-generation Eastern European immigrants, she tended the store so that her husband could study the Torah. Because her English was better than that of most of the immigrants, she assisted the local doctor when he made house calls. Born in Meretz, Lithuania, Mrs. Cohen brought many recipes with her, including that for *Putterkuchen,* a raisin-laden sweet bun, similar to the German *Schnecken* (see page 94). Served in Boston for breakfast, it was a special afternoon treat with tea in Lithuania. *Putterkuchen* must have been popular in Boston because it appeared in the 1929 edition of *The Center Table,* written by the Sisterhood of Temple Mishkan Tefila.

Putterkuchen (Butter Kuchen)

1 package active dry yeast

¾ cup warm water

½ cup sugar plus 2 tablespoons

5 to 5½ cups all-purpose flour

½ teaspoon salt

3 large eggs

1 cup sour cream

1½ sticks (¾ cup) melted unsalted butter

1 teaspoon cinnamon

½ cup raisins

1. Mix the yeast and the warm water together with a pinch of sugar. Set aside for about 10 minutes or until bubbly.

2. Put the flour and salt in a large mixing bowl. Make a well in the center and add the dissolved yeast, the eggs, ½ cup of the sugar, the sour cream, and ½ cup of the butter.

3. Mix everything together with a fork and continue beating until thick. When the flour mixture becomes too thick for the fork, flour your hands, turn out the dough onto a floured work surface, and knead with your hands or use a dough hook of the KitchenAid mixer.

4. Remove to a greased bowl. Cover with a dry towel and let the dough rise in a fairly warm room until doubled in bulk, about 1½ hours. Since this is a sticky dough, flour your hands, punch down, and then knead in the bowl for a few minutes, adding flour if needed.

5. Divide the dough into 4 pieces and roll one out into a large rectangle about ⅛ inch thick. Brush with 2 tablespoons of the remaining melted butter. Sprinkle with cinnamon, the remaining 2 tablespoons sugar, and

raisins. Roll into a jelly roll, then cut into 1½-inch slices and place them flat on a greased jelly-roll pan, leaving about an inch in between the rolls. Brush again with the remaining butter and let rise another hour or so, covered, until doubled. Repeat with the other 3 pieces of dough.

6. Bake for 20 minutes or until golden in a preheated 350-degree oven.

Yield: about 3 dozen (D)

Injera (Ethiopian Pancake)

One of the oldest breads in the world—and one of the newest of the Jewish immigrant breads in this country—is *injera,* brought here by Jewish and non-Jewish Ethiopian immigrants. Although they would serve this as a dipping bread in their stewy soups and I would recommend dipping it into the Yemenite soup (page 126), it can also be served dribbled with honey as a breakfast food.

1 package active dry yeast

1 cup lukewarm water

1 teaspoon sugar

2½ cups all-purpose flour

½ teaspoon baking powder

1 cup semolina

1 cup cold water

Margarine for frying

1. Mix the yeast with the water and the sugar in a small bowl. Let sit for about 10 minutes.

2. In a larger bowl place the flour, baking powder, and semolina. Add the yeast and the cold water. Mix well, cover, and leave in a warm place to rise for about 3 to 4 hours.

3. Heat a griddle or a frying pan. Smear with margarine and pour in about 4 tablespoons of batter, leaving a hole in the center. Cover and cook a few minutes until the "pancake" has risen and little holes appear on the surface. Cook only on one side without allowing the *injera* to brown. Repeat with the remaining batter.

4. Eat either hot or cold. Tear pieces off with the hands and dip into a thick soup or serve at brunch with jam or honey.

Yield: about 20 (P)

THREE

Jewish Soups and Their Dumplings

On a visit to our (grandparents) in Milwaukee, where they lived, we were served with chicken soup in which the succulent portions of chicken were afloat. I cast questioning glances at my mother, wretched little snob that I was. Eating one's meat out of a soup dish, after the soup! Years later, in Munich, at the excellent Park Resturant I learned that the famous specialite de la maison was Huhn Suppe, which was nothing more than Grandma Ferber's chicken stewed and served in the soup dish. I ate it with appreciation and a considerable feeling of guilt.

Edna Ferber, *A Peculiar Treasure, 1939*

Vegetable "Bunch" Soup from Charleston

(I) bought matzot sufficient to last us for the week. On the first day we had a fine vegetable soup. It was made of a bunch of vegetables which Zeke brought from Charleston containing new onions, parsley, carrots, turnips and a young cauliflower, also a pound and a half of fresh beef, the latter article sells for four dollars per pound in Charleston.

A letter written by Isaac J. Levy, 1862

During the Civil War Isaac J. Levy described Charleston Soup Bunch, a Sabbath and Passover soup, made from bunches of vegetables, sold to this day in Charleston markets. The "soup bunch" varies seasonally but always includes onions, carrots, and turnips. Sometimes rutabaga, cabbage, celery, collards, tomatoes, or cauliflower are added. At Jewish tables matzah balls are often served in it.

3 large (about 3 pounds) beef shank bones with meat

1 white turnip, sliced

¼ white cabbage, shredded

¼ red cabbage, shredded

½ rutabaga, sliced

4 large carrots, cut into chunks

2 large onions, quartered

1 28-ounce can or 2 pounds fresh tomatoes, peeled

1 handful collard greens

1 stalk celery, cut into chunks

2 teaspoons thyme

Salt and freshly ground pepper to taste

1. Cover the shank bones with water and simmer, covered, for about 2 hours or until the meat is tender.

2. Add the remaining ingredients and simmer, covered, for at least 30 minutes, until the vegetables are cooked. Remove the meat, and strain the soup through a vegetable mill. Adjust the seasonings. You can serve the soup two ways. Either return some of the vegetables to the soup with pieces of the meat or use the broth alone, floating matzah balls on top.

Yield: 8 to 10 servings (M)

New Orleans Chicken Soup

"Our food was Creolized early on," said Polly Henderson, whose Sephardic forebears came from Jamaica to New Orleans in the 1860s. "Our chicken soup was really jazzed up—green onions, a clove or two, bay leaves, and a little red pepper. My mother added curry powder to hers. That really did the trick."

1 4-pound stewing hen or
chicken, cut in 8 pieces
14 cups water (about)
2 whole onions, peeled
6 cloves
3 bay leaves
A handful of fresh parsley
1 sprig of thyme
A few needles of rosemary
A few sassafras leaves
(optional)
2 stalks celery, cut in chunks
3 carrots, peeled and cut in
chunks
¼ teaspoon cayenne pepper or
to taste
Salt and coarsely ground black
pepper to taste
¼ teaspoon curry powder
(optional)
½ teaspoon sugar

1. Clean the cut-up chicken and place in a pot. Cover with water and bring to a boil. Skim off the froth that rises to the surface.

2. Stud the onions with the cloves. Tie the bay leaves, the parsley, the thyme, the rosemary, and the sassafras leaves in a cheesecloth bag.

3. Add to the simmering pot the clove-studded onions, spices in the cheesecloth, and the celery, carrots, cayenne pepper, salt and pepper, curry powder, and the sugar.

4. Return to a boil and then simmer, covered, for about 3 hours or until the chicken falls apart. Strain, remove the chicken, cool, and refrigerate overnight. Remove the fat before heating and serve with small pieces of chicken, matzah balls, or noodles floating in the soup.

Yield: about 12 cups (M)

Friday Night at Grandma Stix's in Cincinnati

My late father told of how he went to his grandmother's for dinner each Friday night in Augsburg, Germany, where they ate *berches* followed by sweet and sour carp, chicken soup with noodles, a roast, and a delicious kuchen for dessert. Sunday dinners were also family gatherings with roast goose often served as the main course. German Jews brought these customs with them to this country. Despite assimilation, the pattern of visiting families on Friday night persisted. In many second-generation American German-Jewish homes, a family Friday night dinner was sacred, but by this century many of the Jewish accoutrements had vanished.

Filmmaker Charles Guggenheim and his cousin Judith Rauh Falk remember Friday night dinners at their grandmother Grace Freiberg Stix's apartment in Cincinnati. Like the Stixes, many of the Cincinnati German-Jewish families made their fortunes in the ready-to-wear clothing business after the Civil War. Mrs. Stix was the prime mover behind the Cincinnati Jewish Bake Shop, a bakery which employed and assisted newly arrived German-Jewish refugees before, during, and after the Second World War.

> We went to Grandma Stix's every Friday night with our aunts and uncles, their spouses, and the eight grandchildren. There was no religious sense but being together meant something to every member of the family. It was a joyful time with story telling, jokes, and political arguments.
>
> Grandma Stix was a distinguished woman, very well bred with very high

Friday dinner with filmmaker Charles Guggenheim and Grandma Stix in Cincinnati

standards of manners. The linen was impeccable with her grandmother's initials on it. Everybody was seated with name plates.

Charles Guggenheim

Grandma didn't do the cooking. She only taught other people how to do it. I can still see her tasting with a demitasse spoon to see if a soup or a sauce needed more salt or whatever. All these German Jewish ladies competed in the kitchen and didn't want to give anyone their recipes. The cooks, always of German descent, worked for maybe 30 to 40 years. Sometimes you stole the cook and sometimes the recipe. If someone gave you a recipe you put attribution. If you stole the recipe you never told anyone where you got it from.

Judith Rauh Falk

Certain foods were always there. The first course was a dark vegetable based soup with very thin noodles and a few carrots. The only person who made noodles that thin was a Jewish woman in Saint Louis, probably a refugee who was trying to make money and sent them to my grandmother. The second course was roast beef and vegetables with salad on the side. The menu didn't change very much. I always remember the gravy over the scalloped potatoes. The butter was always prepared with a design. The cook used a wooden mold or something to give it striation. We held the corn on the cob with silver corn cob holders. It was always a big thing who would carve the meat. It was usually my father. Fifty percent of the time the dessert was my grandmother's chocolate roll.

Charles Guggenheim

We often started off with soup with a rich reduced stock floating with barley or Saint Louis–style thin noodles. The main course would be chicken, fillet, roast beef, or a lamb roast with a glorious dessert. It's amazing we weren't five hundred pounds overweight. The food was a real celebration of life.

Judith Rauh Falk

I felt cheated when we had the barley soup instead of the noodle one. I don't remember having the barley soup until later years, when the woman in Saint Louis died. Someone asked where are the noodles? My grandmother answered, "The woman in Saint Louis died." I never knew her name.

Charles Guggenheim

Grandma Stix's Friday Night Beef Vegetable Soup

Thanks to two compilations of family recipes, including *The Way to Your Man's Heart*, written by Grace Stix Rauh, the daughter of Grace Stix, many of these favorite dishes have been preserved. One example is this rich beef and vegetable (and sometimes chicken-based) clear soup made with either barley or St. Louis noodles.

2 pounds stew veal and/or beef bones plus 1 pound neck meat

3 quarts water

Salt and freshly ground pepper to taste

1 stalk celery with leaves, chopped roughly

¼ cup roughly chopped fresh parsley

1 onion, chopped

¼ head cabbage, shredded

2 medium turnips, quartered

2 cups tomato puree

1 cup whole tomatoes

¼ teaspoon ground ginger

4 carrots, peeled and roughly chopped

2 cups thin noodles

1. Place the bones and water in a large soup pot of at least 6 quarts. Bring to a boil and skim off the foam as it rises to the top.

2. Add all the remaining ingredients except half the carrots and the noodles and bring to a boil again. Simmer, covered, for about 3 hours.

3. Cool to room temperature. Put the soup through a food mill into a bowl.

4. Refrigerate overnight, covered. Before reheating, remove the fat that forms on the top and adjust the seasoning. Bring to a boil. Add the carrots and noodles and cook, about 10 minutes or until done.

Yield: 8 servings (M)

Note: Some German-Jewish families serve soup meat after the soup before the main course, again a carryover from their Germanic roots.

Chicken Soup with Matzah Balls—A Tradition at the MGM Commissary in Hollywood

It is anyone's guess who started the story about chicken soup being the Jewish mother's penicillin, but we all know that it works. Even in Hollywood. But how many people know that in the private dining room at the Metro-Goldwyn-Mayer Commissary chicken soup with matzah balls was served every day? The original recipe, so the story goes, came from the mother of Louis B. Mayer himself.

"Here the joy of eating grandfather's matzah balls was exposed to the gentile world and even some of the Jewish world," recalled Daniel Selznick, grandson of Mr. Mayer. "I often went to the executive dining room to have lunch with my grandfather. He would send back the soup if it didn't include fresh killed chicken. He had a very developed palate about certain kinds of foods, maybe it was because his father-in-law was a kosher butcher and much attention was paid to the preparation of food in his home. The chicken soup at the commissary had a dark, brown color to it, as opposed to the soup that my grandmother served at home, which was a classic lemon-colored broth. At the commissary the chef put the matzah balls under the broiler until they got totally brown and crisp. I've never had them that way anywhere else."

Of course, anyone who knows about the art of making chicken soup realizes that the dark broth came from one of two sources: either the chef put the onion skins in or added a piece of beef, both of which give chicken soup a richer flavor; or perhaps he did both.

Like other Hollywood moguls Mayer also ate at the prestigious Jewish Hillcrest Country Club in western Los Angeles. "At the club he ordered the freshest marinated herring and sour cream, the freshest chicken livers, the best in the entire community, but he didn't order chicken soup there," said Mr. Selznick. "Gentiles used to ask their Jewish friends to bring home the Hillcrest herring, pastrami, and chopped chicken livers." Opinionated on most things, Mr. Mayer did not approve of oversized corned-beef sandwiches. He advised anyone eating with him to have boiled chicken instead.

Louis B. Mayer with his grandson Daniel Selznick

Chicken Soup with Loads of Vegetables

Jewish chicken soup is usually served with thin egg noodles or with matzah balls. The zucchini is my, not MGM's, addition.

4 quarts water

1 large cut-up chicken, preferably stewing or large roaster

Marrow bones (optional)

2 whole onions, unpeeled

4 parsnips, peeled and left whole

1 parsley root (optional)

½ cup chopped celery leaves plus 2 stalks celery and their leaves

1 rutabaga, peeled and quartered

1 large turnip, peeled and quartered

1 kohlrabi, quartered (optional)

6 carrots, peeled and left whole

6 tablespoons chopped fresh parsley

6 tablespoons snipped dill

1 tablespoon salt

¼ teaspoon pepper

1 zucchini

1. Put the water and the chicken in a large pot and bring the water to a boil. Skim off the froth.

2. Add the marrow bones, onions, parsnips, parsley root, celery, ¾ of the rutabaga, turnip, kohlrabi, 4 of the carrots, the parsley, 4 tablespoons of the dill, and the salt and pepper. Cover and simmer for 2½ hours, adjusting the seasoning to taste.

3. Strain, remove the chicken, discard the vegetables and refrigerate the liquid to solidify. Remove the skin and bones from the chicken and cut the meat into bite-size chunks. Refrigerate. Remove the fat from the soup.

4. Just before serving, reheat the soup. Bring to a boil. Cut the zucchini and the remaining 2 carrots into thin strips and add to the soup along with the remaining rutabaga cut into thin strips as well as a few pieces of chicken. Simmer about 15 minutes or until the vegetables are cooked, but still firm. Serve with the remaining snipped dill. You can also add noodles, marrow (see page 108), or clos (matzah) balls (see pages 110-112).

Yield: about 10 servings (M)

Tip: Make a chicken salad with the remaining chicken pieces or use it in the bastilla on page 55. If you want a lighter-colored soup, peel the onions and remove the chicken as soon as the water boils. Throw out the water, put in new water, add the chicken again with the remaining ingredients, and proceed as above.

"Feather Balls Alsatian Style"
Matzah Balls
By Any Other Name

A classic Passover dish that has undergone a metamorphosis in this country is the venerable matzah ball. In the early nineteen hundreds, before commercial matzah meal was available, these matzah dumplings were made with soaked or ground-up matzah, onions, eggs, chicken fat, and spices. They were also called "*klose,*" "*kneidel,*" "*kleis,*" or "*kneidlach.*" Florence Kreisler Greenbaum in her *Jewish Cook Book* in the twenties included an early recipe for what she called "matzah meal kleis." Soon after, the B. Manischewitz Company, in its *Tempting Kosher Dishes Cookbook* of 1930, called them "feather balls, Alsatian style," a matzah ball made from processed matzah meal with one whole cup of chicken fat (!). The term "matzah balls" rose to prominence in the 1930s—accompanied by all the Jewish mother jokes.

The matzah business was started by families like Goodman, Manischewitz, and Horowitz, all baked by Manischewitz today. In January 1883, Jacob Horowitz arrived in New York from Hungary. He rented a bakery and made it ritually fit for the production of unleavened bread. The first year he produced a small amount, and, after his four sons, daughter, and son-in-law arrived in January, 1884, his business grew. Five years later he bought his own bakery.

In 1886, an enterprising Orthodox Lithuanian Jew named Dov Behr Manischewitz arrived in Cincinnati. He began as a part-time peddler and *schochet* for the Orthodox community, which had paid passage for him and his family. In 1887 he started a small matzah bakery, which gradually became B. Manischewitz Baking Company, the largest concern of its kind, with subsidiaries in all parts of the world. By the turn of the century Mr. Manischewitz was shipping his product to England, Japan, France, Africa, Hungary, New Zealand, and Egypt. The matzah-manufacturing pioneer owed his success to the invention of a machine that produced fifty thousand pounds of matzah a day.

The publication of Passover recipes almost kept pace with the volume of matzah production. Recipes were printed in company-sponsored cookbooks, such as Manischewitz's Yiddish-English cookbook and, later, on the backs of matzah packages. Other recipes evolved naturally as Jews adapted local dishes for Passover use.

Marrow Balls for Soup

". . . the American cook has taken this sauce from France, this stew from Hungary, this soup with marrow balls from the Jewish cookery, this chicken dish from Germany, this pastry from Denmark, and, combining them with the best of the native dishes, has evolved a cookery which is on the way to being the most delicious and varied in the world,—a piquant and fascinating mixture of all the nations," wrote Edna Ferber in the foreword to her sister Fannie Ferber Fox's cookbook published in 1928. The novelist goes on to tell us that marrow balls, a tiny matzah dumpling made with beef marrow rather than chicken fat, was considered the Jewish dish given to the rest of the world.

Twenty years after Edna Ferber wrote the above, Edith Green demonstrated a recipe for marrow balls on the first San Francisco television cooking program: "Your Home Kitchen," and later "Menus for Millions." Mrs. Green, who just turned ninety, traces her recipe back in her family for generations in this country and Europe: on one side to the first Sephardic families and on the other to a German family that went to San Francisco in 1854 at about the time of the Gold Rush. In those days marrow was often used instead of chicken fat in matzah or liver dumplings.

4 tablespoons beef marrow
  (from about 1½ pounds
  marrow bones)
3 large eggs, well beaten
1 teaspoon salt or to taste
Dash of grated nutmeg
1 tablespoon chopped parsley
½ cup matzah meal

1. To remove the marrow, place the bones on a paper towel or plate in a microwave for 40 seconds. Using a spoon or a table knife, remove the marrow from the bones (it should just pop out). If you don't have a microwave just take a long, thin knife and try to cut out the marrow.

2. In a bowl cream the marrow with a fork until perfectly smooth. Mix in the eggs, salt, nutmeg, and chopped parsley. Mix in enough matzah meal to make a soft dough. Cover the bowl with plastic wrap and set aside for several hours in the refrigerator.

3. Using your hands, roll the dough into balls the diameter of a quarter. Meanwhile, bring 8 cups of the chicken soup (see page 106) to a simmer. Fill a separate saucepan with water and bring it to a boil. Drop 1 marrow ball into the boiling water as a test; if it doesn't hold together, add more matzah meal to the dough.

4. Test again. When the test ball holds together, drop the remaining balls into the simmering soup and cook 10 to 15 minutes, covered, or until light and cooked through.

Yield: About 20 marrow balls (M)

Television's first cooking lady,
Edith Green of San Francisco

Macaroons for Soup

These crisp soup dumplings look like tiny macaroons and include almonds—thus the name. Although this recipe calls for matzah meal, other versions use cracker crumbs. Deep-frying seems to have been a common way of cooking dumplings in the nineteenth century, even matzah balls. This recipe comes from the *Stockton Community Cookbook,* compiled and published by Temple Israel in Stockton, California, in 1924. Try the macaroons in any chicken soup, even the tortilla soup on page 126.

2 large eggs, separated

½ teaspoon sugar

½ teaspoon grated lemon rind

2 tablespoons matzah meal

1 tablespoon finely chopped almonds

1. Beat the egg yolks with the sugar and lemon rind. When light, add the matzah meal and the chopped almonds.
2. Beat the whites until they are stiff, but not dry. Then fold into the almond mixture. Heat 1 inch of oil in a heavy pot to 375 degrees. Drop the macaroon mixture by teaspoonfuls into the hot oil. Cook a minute or so until crisp. Drain and then add to whatever hot soup you are serving them in.

Yield: 30 (P)

Fluffy Matzah Balls

If you like light, airy matzah balls, you'll like this recipe. It's my son David's favorite, especially when his grandmother makes the matzah balls.

4 large eggs

2 tablespoons chicken fat or
    vegetable oil

½ cup seltzer, club soda, or
    chicken broth

1 cup matzah meal

Salt and freshly ground pepper
    to taste

1. Mix the eggs well with a fork. Add the chicken fat or oil, soda water, matzah meal, and salt and pepper and mix well. Cover and refrigerate for several hours.

2. Dip your hands in cold water and make about 12 balls slightly smaller than Ping-Pong balls.

3. Bring water to a boil in a large pot. Add salt and place the matzah balls in the water. Cover and simmer about 30 minutes or until soft.

Yield: about 12 large, soft matzah balls (M)

Tip: I often make chicken soup and matzah balls ahead. After cooking the matzah balls I just place them in the warm soup, which I then freeze. The liquid keeps them fluffy. I defrost the soup, reheat, and serve. If you like them more al dente, *use large eggs and cook a shorter time.*

Note: To reduce the cholesterol in this recipe, use 2 egg whites and 2 whole eggs as well as canola oil.

Mississippi Baked Stuffed Matzah Balls

Macie Fain Silver grew up in Hattiesburg, Mississippi, where her father ran Fine's, the local clothing store. One of her fondest Jewish memories was of her mother's matzah balls baked in a muffin tin. "My mother baked them in a wooden stove. She took a piece of paper and put it in the oven to calculate how hot it was by the amount of time it took to scorch the paper." These large stuffed matzah balls originated in Lithuania and were connected to the Chasidic religious tradition. The cinnamon stuffing represents the secret sweetness within the spice box at the Havdalah service ending the Sabbath and a wish to stretch the Sabbath as long as possible. I thought of these huge matzah balls recently when we were hiking in the Alps of Austria and stopped for lunch at a mountain hut where they were serving "*knodel suppe,*" a giant bread dumpling floating in broth.

MATZAH BALLS

4 eggs, slightly beaten

2 tablespoons chicken fat or vegetable shortening

1 cup matzah meal

2 teaspoons salt

2 tablespoons chopped parsley

6 tablespoons chicken soup or water

4 quarts salted water

Oil for greasing

FILLING

1 onion, chopped extra fine

2 tablespoons vegetable oil or chicken fat

2 tablespoons matzah meal

1 egg yolk

Salt and freshly ground pepper to taste

Dash of cinnamon

12 cups chicken soup (see page 106)

1. In a medium bowl beat the eggs and the fat together. Stir in the matzah meal, salt, and parsley. Add the chicken soup or water. Refrigerate 1 hour or more, to permit the meal to absorb the liquids.

2. Meanwhile, make the filling. Fry the finely chopped onion in the oil or the fat over a medium heat until it is very crisp. Mix in 2 tablespoons of matzah meal and the egg yolk. Season with salt, pepper, and cinnamon to taste.

3. Dip the palms of your hands in cold water. Form the matzah balls from the refrigerated mixture, making them a little larger than usual, about the diameter of a fifty-cent piece, wetting your hands again as needed. Spoon a heaping teaspoon of filling in the middle of the matzah ball and close well.

4. In a 6-quart pot with a lid bring the salted water to a boil. Reduce the water to a simmer and drop in the matzah balls. Cover the pot and cook just at a simmer for 30 minutes or until plump.

5. Remove the balls with a slotted spoon and put them in greased muffin pans. Coat each matzah ball with a little oil.

6. Bake in a preheated 350-degree oven for about 30 minutes or until the matzah balls are golden brown. To serve, place one matzah ball in the center of a soup bowl and spoon the chicken soup over all.

Yield: 12 baked stuffed matzah balls (P or M)

Tip: You can heat the basting oil with onion to give it flavor. (The original recipe called for a layer of chicken skin in each muffin tin to create oil for the basting.)

Macie Fain Silver (right) and her sister, Reba, in Hattiesburg, Mississippi, in the twenties

This Fowl Is My Substitute, This Is My Surrogate, This Is My Atonement: Kapparot on the Lower East Side

Poultry dealers on the east side of the city, in anticipation of the Day of Atonement, procured a large supply of live chickens so that their customers might have them for killing today, according to their custom. Chickens were to be found everywhere on the lower east side of the city and the chief inspector reported that 29 men under his direction were not enough to prevent the wholesale violation of the law against the sales of live chickens.

The New York Times, September 27, 1895

It must have been quite a scene on the Lower East Side before Yom Kippur in the late nineties. On the morning prior to the fast, each member of the family would swing a live fowl around his head three times repeating the following words in Hebrew, "This fowl is my substitute, this is my surrogate, this is my atonement." The custom of *kapparot* replaces the Temple Yom Kippur sacrifice in which a goat, bearing the sins of the nation, was sent out into the wilderness to die. Like so many other traditions, *kapparot* came to replace a tradition lost with the destruction of the Temple. Some of the chickens were roasted for the family; others were given to the poor. It is a custom continued to this day in many Orthodox communities.

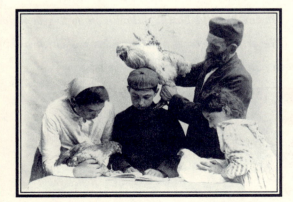

Kapparot — swinging chickens to get rid of sins before Yom Kippur

Dallas Matzah Balls with Pecans

The matzah balls you get in delis have no character at all. In Dallas we like our matzah balls smaller than those and dark, not white. We also make ours southern Jewish, with pecans in them.

Emme Sue Frank, seventy-six, born in Memphis, living in Dallas

2 matzahs

½ medium onion, diced

2 tablespoons chicken fat or vegetable oil

½ cup matzah meal

1 teaspoon salt or to taste

2 tablespoons chicken broth

2 large eggs, beaten

1 tablespoon chopped parsley

½ cup pecans, coarsely chopped

10 cups chicken soup (see page 106)

1. Crumble the matzahs and soak in warm water. Drain well in a colander.

2. Sauté the onion in the chicken fat in a skillet. Turn off the heat and add the soaked matzah, matzah meal, salt, chicken broth, and the eggs. Mix well and fold in the parsley and the pecans.

3. Place in a mixing bowl, cover, and refrigerate a few hours. Then roll into small balls the diameter of a nickel. At this point you can refrigerate the balls until ready to serve or freeze them uncooked on a baking pan. When frozen, put in a plastic freezer bag. Thaw a half hour before using.

4. When ready to serve, simmer in the chicken soup, uncovered, for about 15 to 20 minutes.

Yield: about 20 matzah balls (M)

Kreplach (Jewish Wonton or Tortellini)

The traditional kreplach is similar to a wonton and was brought either by the Khazars to Polish lands or by Jews trading in China, who learned to make them there. Kreplachs are traditionally served floating in chicken soup (page 106) at the meal before Yom Kippur, at Purim, and Simhat Torah. They can also be fried and served with gravy as a side dish with meat. You can use brisket leftovers for the filling rather than the fresh meat called for in this recipe. Recently a Russian immigrant brought a casserole of square kreplach, which she called *pelmeni,* to my home. She served them with sautéed onions, margarine, and white vinegar. She had never heard of kreplach or *pelmeni* in soup.

MEAT FILLING

2 pounds boneless chuck or
   brisket of beef
Salt and freshly ground pepper
   to taste
1 clove garlic
1 carrot
1 piece of celery
3 medium onions
2 tablespoons vegetable oil

KREPLACH DOUGH

¼ cup vegetable oil
2 teaspoons salt
1 cup lukewarm water
4 cups all-purpose flour
   (approximately)

1. Season the meat with salt and pepper and rub with the garlic. Place in a heavy pot and surround with the carrot, celery, and 1 onion. Cook until lightly browned, then add water to cover and simmer for an hour and a half.

2. While the meat is cooking, slice the remaining 2 onions and sauté slowly in the oil until brown.

3. Remove the meat from the heat and let cool. Drain and coarsely grind with all the onions, adding a little broth from the meat if needed to make it moist enough to handle.

4. To make the dough, mix the oil, salt, and water in a bowl. Gradually stir in the flour until a medium-soft dough is formed. Place on a floured board. Knead until the dough is smooth and soft. A food processor works well for this.

5. Cut the dough into 3 portions. Roll out each piece of dough into a rectangle about ⅛ inch thick. Cut into 2-inch squares. Fill each square with about a teaspoon of the meat mixture. Dipping your fingers in flour, fold over into a triangle, and then crimp closed. Join the 2 ends together like a little ring, as you would a tortellini or a wonton. Repeat with the rest of the kreplach. If you like, you can freeze the kreplach at this point. To do so, place them on a cookie sheet in the freezer and, when frozen, transfer them to plastic freezer bags. Otherwise, refrigerate until ready to use.

6. To cook the kreplach, bring about 10 cups of water to a boil in a big pot. Add the salt and about 20 kreplach at a time. When the kreplach have risen to the top, cook for another 5 minutes or until they are *al dente*. Remove with a strainer to a bowl filled with chicken soup, serving about 3 kreplach per person.

Yield: about 5 dozen (M)

Zingerman's Ann Arbor Mushroom and Barley Soup

When I first heard about Ari Weinzweig's delicatessen in Ann Arbor, Michigan, I couldn't believe it. A deli in the home of my alma mater. It's not really a deli but more of an international food emporium like New York's Zabar's with a definite Jewish touch. Mr. Weinzweig, a drop-out Ph.D. candidate, has taken an academic and appetizing interest in updating Jewish recipes like mushroom and barley soup, going back in history to the nineteenth-century Eastern European version similar to that served at New York's Second Avenue Deli.

2 tablespoons dried porcini mushrooms

2 tablespoons margarine

1 large onion, thinly sliced

2 ribs celery with leaves, diced

¼ cup parsley

1 carrot, peeled and sliced

3 cloves garlic, chopped

1 pound fresh porcini or other mushrooms

1 tablespoon flour

2 quarts beef broth or water

1 cup whole barley

2 teaspoons salt

1. Soak the mushrooms in enough hot water to cover for a half hour. Strain through a filter. Reserve the water.

2. Coarsely chop the dried mushrooms.

3. Melt the margarine in a stockpot and sauté the onion, celery, 2 tablespoons of the parsley, carrot, garlic, and fresh mushrooms until soft, about 5 minutes.

4. Lower the heat and add the flour, stirring every 30 seconds for about 5 minutes or until thick.

5. In a soup pot heat the broth or water. Add a cup at a time of the sautéed vegetables and the chopped dried mushrooms to the pot, stirring.

6. Turn the heat to high, and add the reserved mushroom water and barley. Stir well and add salt to taste.

7. Simmer, covered, for about an hour or until the barley is tender and the soup is thickened, stirring often.

8. Add additional chopped parsley, mix thoroughly, and adjust seasonings.

Yield: 6 to 8 servings (P) or (M)

Zingerman's Deli Emporium, Ann Arbor, Michigan

"What Is This Blood-red Compound Called Borscht?"

"What is this?" we asked, almost at random pointing to something which we translated as possibly having some faint relationship to beets.

"Beet soup," said the waiter, with a Cockney accent.

"Beet soup let it be then," we replied. . . . In a twinkling a bowl of this compound—blood red, was put before us.

"What—what," we asked, "is the nationality of this dish—who invented it?"

"It's Polish, sir, and quite a favorite 'ere, Sir," he replied. . . . Boldly we plunged in the spoon and gave it a determined stir; then our courage failed us. Of course there was nothing very repugnant in this innocent beet as a vegetable; but mostly associated with the idea of vinegar, to take a mouthful of it, set our teeth on edge. But try it we must. Slowly we brought the spoon to our mouth, then furtively looked around to see if anybody was looking, and perceiving we were unheeded, bolted it. Rather to our surprise, it was palatable; we tried it again. Perhaps it could only be appreciated by an acquired taste, and we have not the least doubt that had we kept on trying persistently we might in the process of time, by degrees, say in six months or so, providing we had no other source of nourishment, have got to like it."

"A New Cuisine. The Jewish Restaurant—Peculiar Food Experiences of a Seeker after Novel Dishes," *The New York Times,* January 21, 1872

Borscht, a soup that uses fermented or fresh red beet juice as the foundation, often includes meat, cabbage, onions, parsnips, and potatoes and is served hot or cold. Sour cream or sour milk are added to a vegetable-based soup and for a meat-based one a *farweissen,* eggs whipped in at the last minute, is added to whiten it. Eugeniusz Wirkowski, the author of *Cooking the Polish-Jewish Way,* thinks that the main Jewish contribution to Polish cuisine is *russel:* the method of making borscht from beet roots that have been fermented in an earthenware pot with salt, sugar, garlic, bay leaf, and allspice for several days. Borscht itself, however, is not Jewish but Polish. In the restaurant review cited above we can see that borscht was introduced to the American public by Jewish restaurants.

Cold Summer Borscht

I first learned to make this recipe from Esther Lipman, the wife of the late rabbi-gardener Eugene Lipman, who was president of the Central Conference of American Rabbis. While we were filming in California, we asked Mollie Katzen, the high priestess of vegetarianism, to make this borscht with her own additions of dill and garnishes of grated cucumber, scallions, and dill pickles.

4 large beets, washed, peeled, and chopped in large chunks

1 medium onion, peeled and chopped

5 cups cold water

1 teaspoon salt

1½ tablespoons sugar

Juice of ½ lemon

Sour cream, buttermilk, or yoghurt

Chopped chives

1. Put the chopped beets and onion in a 3-quart pot with the water. Bring to a boil and simmer for about 15 minutes, skimming the foam as it rises. Turn off the heat.

2. Add the salt, sugar, and lemon juice. Adjust the seasonings to taste. Puree in a food processor.

3. Cool and refrigerate for several hours. Serve borscht very cold with a dollop of sour cream, buttermilk, or yogurt and, if you wish, a sprinkling of fresh chives. You can also serve the borscht hot, without the sour cream, adding diced, boiled, or steamed potatoes.

Yield: 4 to 6 servings (D)
Tip: Canned beets work very well, too.

Living on a Farm in Connecticut Was a Tough, Rough Life

In 1907 my father came from Kiev and my mother from Poland. At Ellis Island somebody directed them to Newtown, Connecticut, where they lived on a dairy farm. There were six of us, three boys and three girls. Mother cooked on a wood stove. We raised our own chickens. A rabbi from Bridgeport came through once a week and killed the ducks and chicken and geese. She made chicken soup for Friday and we'd eat the chicken from the soup as a meal. We ate wheat berries, garden grown sorrel and rhubarb picked in the fields . . . grew potatoes and onions and dug up the beets, carrots and parsnips and put them in dirt in the cellar. Toward the weekend a truck delivered big chunks of ice for the ice box. Summertime we'd go out in the woods and pick blackberries and huckleberries. My mother made jam but didn't make pies. We sold the milk to a dairy and made our own sour cream and cottage cheese. Mother put a pot of milk almost to a boil, skimmed off

Resting after a hard day on a farm in Connecticut

the top and put the whey in a cloth bag. My father drove into Bridgeport once a week for groceries—he bought sugar in forty-pound bags, and kosher meat. Bridgeport had kosher delis, butchers and a dozen bakery shops. My father couldn't get out of there fast enough. We had summer roomers who did their own cooking. They would play poker, gambling away all afternoon. They had cream cheese and egg for a dairy supper. My mother baked challah on Friday. The guests bought our day old bread and rolls, sour cream, cottage cheese, berries and coffee. 50 cents was enough for bread for a week. We were poor but didn't realize we were poor. It was a tough, rough life.

Sylvia Kirschblum, Newtown, Connecticut

Although there were immigrant farming communities in many parts of the United States, not many succeeded as well as that in Newtown. Mrs. Kirschblum is one of the few remaining descendants of the pioneer dairy farmers in Newtown.

Spinach-Rhubarb Soup

It was natural for these immigrants from Poland and the Ukraine to prefer the sour tastes they knew at home, such as rye bread, pickles, and *tschav* or sorrel soup. Spinach-rhubarb soup, sometimes called borscht by the immigrants, is an example of taste adaptation in this country. This tangy dish may have started out as sorrel or sorrel and rhubarb soup in Poland. On the farm they may have used wild sorrel, which grows everywhere here. Other immigrants, living in cities, could not buy sorrel as easily as in the old country, so they substituted spinach. I found this recipe in early twentieth-century Jewish cookbooks across the country. It is so refreshing on a hot summer day.

³⁄₄ pound rhubarb

1 10-ounce package fresh spinach or sorrel, well rinsed

1 tablespoon salt

4 cups water

1 large egg (optional)

¹⁄₂ cup sour cream or yoghurt

2 sliced scallions

1 peeled and diced cucumber

4 sliced radishes

1. Clean the rhubarb, cut in 1-inch pieces, and simmer, covered with water, about 20 minutes or until tender. Drain.
2. Place the spinach or sorrel, rhubarb, salt, and the water in a pot. Bring the water to a boil, and simmer, covered, for about 5 minutes. Cool slightly. Beat the egg and fold in. Although the egg is traditional, I often omit it. Refrigerate several hours and serve with a dollop of sour cream, scallions, cucumbers, and radishes.

Yield: 4 to 6 servings (P); (D) if served with sour cream or yoghurt

Vegetable Soup at a Kosher Boardinghouse in Atlantic City

"We are the last of the Mohicans," said Rose Zawid as she spooned out more of her delicious applesauce. Zawid's kosher boardinghouse in Atlantic City, New Jersey, a block from the boardwalk, is a welcome relic of the past within walking distance of Donald Trump's post-modern Taj Mahal.

From the age of eight, Mrs. Zawid helped her mother in her native Poland. "If somebody's an artist, it comes naturally," she said in a Yiddish accent. "I went to no school. I grew up with cooking. I love it. It was times I used to sew day and night. I got over this. Now I love to cook day and night."

The Holocaust changed her feelings about food forever. "For eight months I lived in water in a basement in Poland," said Mrs. Zawid, who is in her late sixties.

*Chicken farming in New Jersey
was a good life for immigrants
after World War II.*

"I was hungry so all I thought about was food. I was skin and bones when I was liberated. Now I love to feed people. I always think about that time. It's a thing you can't forget."

With about fifty other survivors of the Holocaust, the Zawids went to Vineland, New Jersey, to become Jewish chicken farmers, raising hens for eggs. "Life was good, a wonderful place to bring up children," said her husband Jack. "Our home was always full of people."

Although they made little money from the eggs, Rose's reputation as a cook spread quickly. One thing led to another and in 1966 she and her husband started a kosher catering service and boardinghouse in Atlantic City. Her family-style dinners read like a what's what of Eastern European cuisine: thick vegetable soup, *tzimmes, kugel,* gefilte fish, challah, potato latkes, potato knishes, flanken. "I cook different," she said. "Everything is fresh. It's a different taste."

Her never-ending basement and two kitchens are filled with the preserves and applesauce that she puts up seasonally. In the fall she makes applesauce with cranberries and preserves from oranges, lemons, grapefruit, and etrogs, the symbolic fruit used at Sukkot. At other times she makes pumpkin preserves and cherry, prune, strawberry, or raspberry preserves, which she folds into her homemade strudels.

Like all good cooks, Mrs. Zawid has strong feelings about food. "Bought challah is like chewing gum," she said. "When I make two thousand gefilte fish patties or potato latkes, I stop counting." Several years ago she and her husband journeyed to Philadelphia, where they prepared their challah and gefilte fish at a highly successful Eastern European dinner at the Museum of the American Jewish Experience for the Book and the Cook, an annual event that attracts food lovers from around the country.

The secret of her success: "I love people and I love my business. If you take away my cooking, you take away my life."

Tschav *(Cream of Sorrel Soup)*

Benjamin Kaplan, Harvard Law School professor emeritus and former State Supreme Court Justice of Massachusetts, likes the sour tastes he remembers from his childhood growing up the son of immigrants living in the Bronx. His poet-wife, Felicia Lamport, feeds his fancy throughout the summer from her Martha's Vineyard garden. For lunch each day the judge eats pureed sorrel with fresh herbs, cottage cheese, and milk. Felicia serves a more dressed-up, hot or cold, cream of sorrel soup for dinner parties.

1 medium onion, chopped fine

2 tablespoons unsalted butter or margarine

10 cups fresh sorrel, stems removed and julienned

2 tablespoons fresh basil

2 tablespoons fresh dill

2 tablespoons fresh parsley

4 cups vegetable broth

1/4 cup white wine

1 cup heavy cream or skim milk

Salt and freshly ground pepper to taste

1/2 cup sour cream or yoghurt

1. Sauté the onion in the butter in a large, heavy stockpot. Add the sorrel and cook a few minutes with most of the basil, dill, and parsley, reserving a few tablespoons for garnish.
2. Add the vegetable broth and the wine. Bring to a boil and simmer briefly, about 10 minutes, uncovered.
3. Add the cream or milk, salt and pepper, and heat briefly. Either leave as is or puree in a food processor. Serve hot or cold garnished with the reserved herbs and, if you like, a dollop of sour cream.

Yield: 6 servings (D)

Rose Zawid's Vegetable Soup

This is a nice, hearty, winter recipe made from vegetables Mrs. Zawid puts up in summer. Mrs. Zawid uses oatmeal as a thickener.

2 parsnips, finely chopped

1 stalk celery, diced

3 onions, peeled and diced

1 15-ounce can plum tomatoes

5 carrots, peeled and chopped

7 cups water

1 cup beef broth

Salt and freshly ground pepper
    to taste

½ cup quick oatmeal
    (optional)

2 cups fresh or frozen peas

1. Put the parsnips, celery, onions, tomatoes, and carrots in a pot with the water and broth and bring to a boil. Add salt and pepper and simmer, covered, for 1 hour.

2. Add the oatmeal and the peas, mix well, and simmer for a few minutes more or until the vegetables are cooked. Serve immediately.

Yield: about 12 servings (M)

Garvanzos (Chick-pea Soup)

Susan Barocas, originally from Denver, Colorado, learned about Turkish cooking from her father, whose family came to this country at the turn of the century. Chick-pea soup is probably one of the oldest soups, dating to the biblical period. For the Sabbath it became the first course of the *chamim*. (See *adafina*, page 164.) The paprika was added in Turkey. The freshness and flavor of the paprika make all the difference in this recipe. My preference is a hot paprika.

1 pound dried chick-peas

1 large onion, chopped

2 tablespoons olive oil

3 to 4 cloves garlic, minced

10 cups cold water

2 tablespoons or more fresh,
    finely ground hot paprika

1. Soak the chick-peas overnight in cold water. Remove any blemished ones, rinse well, and drain. You should have about 4½ cups of chick-peas.

2. In a 4-quart pot, sauté the onion in oil until almost browned. Add the garlic and sauté for 2 to 3 more minutes.

3. Add the chick-peas to the pot and cover with the water. Add paprika and salt and pepper.

Salt and freshly ground pepper
   to taste

4. Simmer, covered, for 1½ hours or until the chickpeas are soft but not mushy.

Yield: about 10 to 12 servings (P)
Tip: You can also add beef or lamb to this soup. With the onions, brown a soup bone or chuck or other meat cut into stewing sizes. Proceed the same as in the above recipe.

Spring Vegetable Soup

One of my family's all-year favorite soups is a fresh potato, carrot, and leek soup. When I learned that in Poland this same soup with kohlrabi and freshly shelled peas was a sign of spring, I added them to the soup. I serve it with homemade bread and a big salad.

1 bunch leeks
2 tablespoons butter or
   margarine
3 carrots, peeled and diced
6 new potatoes, peeled and
   diced
1 kohlrabi, diced
6 cups water
Salt and freshly ground pepper
   to taste
1 cup fresh or frozen peas
1 cup cream or low-fat milk
2 tablespoons fresh snipped dill

1. Clean the leeks by cutting lengthwise, running under water, and removing any grit. Then dice the white and a little bit of the green.
2. In a 3-quart heavy saucepan with a cover heat the butter and add the leeks. Sauté for about 5 minutes or until soft. Add the carrots, potatoes, and kohlrabi. Cover with the water, add the salt and pepper, and bring to a boil. Simmer, covered, for about 10 minutes or until the vegetables are tender. Add the peas and cook 5 minutes more. Add the cream or milk. Heat through, add the dill, and serve.

Yield: 6 servings (D)

Albondigas de Pescado
(Vegetable Soup with Fish Dumplings)

Although some Sephardic Jewish families have had a long history of wandering from country to country, few people look for a continuous gastronomic thread. Danielle Schneider does. "I can trace my roots to Majorca and Barcelona," said Mrs. Schneider, a communications consultant living in Mount Vernon, New York. "One ancestor became the second in

Albondigas, cont.

command of the Jesuit order in Spain—in fact, he founded it with Ignatius of Loyola and translated the scriptures from Greek and Hebrew into Spanish. There is a street in Majorca named Nadal after him." During the Inquisition other members of her family went to Puerto Rico and Cuba, where they were in the sugar business. She, herself, lived in Venezuela and Curaçao.

"This fish soup for Friday night is a combination of fish balls and South American *calabaza*," she said. Instead of the carp and whitefish used in Eastern Europe or other fish from Spain, in Venezuela they made it with snapper or grouper. Mrs. Schneider uses butternut squash here. She also adds another American touch—ketchup and Worcestershire sauce at the end.

2 pounds snapper or grouper, with bones, heads, and skin

3 large onions

11 cloves garlic

Salt and dried hot red pepper flakes to taste

2 large eggs

½ to 1 cup matzah meal or bread crumbs

1 tomato

1 red pepper

2 tablespoons olive oil

2 tablespoons parsley

2 tablespoons fresh coriander

1 tablespoon fresh oregano

4 carrots, peeled and diced

1 pound calabaza or butternut squash, diced

1 tablespoon ketchup

1 tablespoon Worcestershire sauce

1. Place the head, bones, and skin of the fish in a heavy stockpot with water to cover. Add 1 of the onions, quartered, and 4 of the garlic cloves, peeled. Simmer, uncovered, while you are preparing the fish.

2. Grind the fish with a second onion, 4 more cloves of garlic, salt and red pepper, the eggs, and enough matzah meal to hold the mixture together. Make fish patties the size of gefilte fish.

3. Dice a third onion, the remaining 3 cloves of garlic, the tomato, and the red pepper and sauté in a large frying pan in the olive oil until the onion is soft. Add the parsley, coriander, and oregano as well as the carrots and the squash, continue sautéing for another few minutes.

4. Strain the broth and pour some of it into the frying pan, stirring to deglaze the pan. Transfer the strained broth and the vegetables to the pot. Add the fish patties and simmer, covered, for about 20 minutes or until the fish balls are cooked. Combine the ketchup and the Worcestershire sauce and add at the last minute. Serve in a soup bowl.

Yield: 8 servings (P)

Cuban Black Bean Soup and Stuffed Derma

A Jewish-Cuban Thanksgiving meal is American in the real melting-pot sense. It includes a roasted turkey as the centerpiece surrounded by cranberry sauce, plantains, rice, black beans, and stuffed *derma,* with pumpkin pie for dessert. "For Thanksgiving we become Cuban-American," said Sara Kapustin, one of the fifteen thousand Cuban Jews now living in Miami, Florida.

"Cuban-Jewish food is a little Eastern European or Sephardic Jewish and a little Cuban," added Miriam Salazar, also of Miami, who went there from Cuba. Many Eastern Europeans waited in Havana for their visas to the United States between the two world wars, staying on until Fidel Castro came to power, then coming here. "For Friday night we might have chicken soup with *kneidlach* followed by Cuban chicken and rice. We mix things," she said.

In many families Cuban food seems to be reserved for Sunday dinner when they have *arroz con pollo* (chicken with rice), or *picadillo* and plantains. The meal almost always begins with the following Cuban black bean soup.

Cuban Black Bean Soup

I always thought that beans should be soaked before using. Maricel Presilla, consultant to Victor's Cuban Restaurant in New York, showed me how black her unsoaked beans stayed.

1 pound dried black beans

6 cups water

½ teaspoon dried oregano or to taste

Salt to taste

1 onion, peeled and left whole, plus 1 diced onion

2 cloves garlic, diced

2 tablespoons vegetable oil

1 green pepper, diced

1 tomato, diced

Garnish, ½ cup onion, chopped

1. Wash the beans well with water and drain.
2. Place the beans in a 4-quart pot with the 6 cups water. Bring to a boil and add the oregano, salt, the whole onion, and the garlic. Simmer, covered, for about 1½ hours or until the beans are tender.
3. Meanwhile sauté the diced onion in the vegetable oil with the green pepper and tomato for about 5 minutes. Add to the soup and cook 30 minutes longer or until the beans are soft. Serve as a soup or as a sauce on top of rice sprinkled with chopped raw onions.

Yield: 8 servings (P)

Chicken, Lime, and Tortilla Soup

To satisfy Southwestern taste buds, Lenard Rubin, while *chef de cuisine* of the Phoenician Resort in Scottsdale, Arizona, traded in the Massachusetts chicken soup he grew up with for this Mexican-inspired version. At Passover he substitutes matzah balls for the tortilla chips and, of course, omits the corn oil and the hominy.

6 cups chicken stock

¼ cup fresh lime juice

½ cup tomato juice

1 small jalapeño pepper, stemmed, seeded, and diced

1 cup chopped fresh coriander leaves

2 scallions, chopped

Salt and freshly ground pepper to taste

2 fresh chicken breasts, boned, skinned, and grilled

6 6-inch yellow, blue, or red corn tortillas

2 cups corn oil for frying

½ cup cooked hominy

1 fresh avocado

1. Place the stock, lime juice, and tomato juice in a saucepan and bring to a simmer over medium heat.
2. Add the jalapeño, half the coriander, and the scallions. Season with salt and pepper. Simmer, covered, for 45 minutes. Strain and reserve.
3. Dice the grilled chicken and reserve.
4. Julienne the tortillas; fry in hot corn oil (360 degrees) until crispy. Drain and reserve.
5. Heat the hominy in a small saucepan with water to cover over low heat for a few minutes. Drain.
6. To serve, place the chicken and the hominy in small bowls. Pour the soup over, and sprinkle with the reserved tortilla strips. Peel and dice the avocado and add.

Yield: 6 to 8 servings (M)

Yemenite Chicken Soup

Yemenite restaurants in Israel have always served soup with oxtails, brains, even lungs. On New York's West Side Yemenite-Israeli artist Benjamin Levy and his wife, Hanna, serve the tamer version of Yemenite chicken soup every Friday night for dinner with *hilbe* (a fenugreek sauce); *zhug* (a hot sauce); and pita bread. It is a nourishing meal in itself. Hanna, an Israeli of Dutch ancestry, has become the family *zhug* maker. *Zhug* is the Yemenite spicy sauce that she makes three times a year in jars and freezes. Because hers is so good, her niece, who is an El Al flight attendant, flies it to Israel to her Yemenite mother! Hanna has intensified the tastes of the Yemenite soup by varying the cooking time of the ingredients. "I tasted the soup without tomatoes at a Yemenite home," she said. "It tasted better and more authentic to me so I gave it up." Unlike her Yemenite husband's family, who merely breaks up matzah in the soup for Passover, Hanna makes her family's matzah balls for Jewish holidays. With them she always adds *hilbe* (see page 1 2 8) and *zhug,* (below) so essential to Yemenite Jewish cooking . Make them when you have time, and use them for this and other dishes calling for a hot sauce.

1 2 cups water

1 4-pound chicken, skinned or unskinned, and cut into at least 8 pieces

2 teaspoons salt or to taste

1½ tablespoons hawayij (see page 1 2 8) or to taste

3 large onions, peeled and quartered

8 to 9 cloves of garlic, peeled and left whole

3 medium potatoes

2 carrots, peeled and cut into 2-inch chunks

1 cup hilbe

1 cup fresh chopped coriander

1. Bring the water to a boil and add the chicken with the salt and the *hawayij*. Return the soup to a boil, add the onions, and simmer, uncovered, for 1 5 minutes.

2. Skim off any foam that rises and add the garlic. Simmer 1 0 more minutes.

3. Peel the potatoes and cut into quarters. Add with the carrots, and simmer, covered, for another half hour.

4. Serve each person a bowl of soup. Place the *hilbe* and coriander in separate bowls. Let the guests add them to their own taste.

Yield: *1 2 as a first course and 8 as a main course (M)*

Yemenite Zhug *(Yemenite Hot Sauce)*

1 pound serrano peppers

5 whole heads garlic, peeled

1 bunch coriander (about 1 cup), well rinsed

1 teaspoon dried hot red pepper flakes or to taste

½ teaspoon cumin

Salt to taste

Olive oil to cover

1. Place the peppers, garlic, and coriander in the bowl of a food processor and chop fine.

2. Add the hot pepper, cumin, and salt and mix well.

3. Place in a 2-cup glass jar and cover with olive oil.

Yield: *about 2 cups (P)*

Tip: *Use a teaspoon of this whenever you need a hot sauce.*

Yemenite Hilbe *(Fenugreek Sauce)*

3 tablespoons fenugreek

½ cup water

1 heaping teaspoon zhug

Juice of ½ lemon

Salt to taste

1. Soak the fenugreek seeds in the water for at least 3 hours.

2. Drain the water from the fenugreek seeds, leaving a moist paste. Beat with an electric mixer until smooth. Add a heaping teaspoon of *zhug,* the lemon juice, and salt. Adjust seasonings to taste. The sauce should be very spicy.

Yield: about ⅓ cup (P)

Hawayij *(Yemenite Spice Combination)*

2 tablespoons whole black peppercorns

1 tablespoon black caraway seeds

1 teaspoon whole cumin

1 teaspoon cardamom seeds

1 teaspoon saffron

2 teaspoons turmeric

1. Pound all the ingredients together in a mortar and pestle, or use a coffee grinder reserved for grinding spices, or a blender.

Yield: about ¼ cup (P)

Moroccan Pumpkin Soup with Chick-peas in Massachusetts

When Batsheva Levy Salzman was a child in Morocco and then in Israel, her mother would make pumpkin soup for Sukkot. As a child, she watched her mother cook and helped her. Later, when Batsheva married an American and moved to Boston, she began cooking Moroccan for her family and friends. "My American-Jewish family likes the pumpkin soup for Thanksgiving," she said. And so does Caraways, a gourmet shop in Wayland, Massachusetts, where she lives. Word spread about her Moroccan cooking. At a fund-raiser for Temple Shira Tikvah in Wayland, ten people paid about $250,000 for a Moroccan feast of ten different hors d'oeuvres, baked fish, stuffed chicken, couscous, and dessert. "I cook exactly the way my mother taught me," she said. "I cook with my eyes and not for the measurement."

1 12-ounce can chick-peas

2 pounds pumpkin, or butter-
*   nut or calabaza squash,*
*   peeled and cut in chunks*

1 onion, peeled and quartered

½ pound stewing beef, cut into
*   2-inch chunks*

8 cups water or to cover

2 teaspoons cinnamon or to
*   taste*

2 cups chicken soup (see page
*   106)*

2 tablespoons sugar or to taste

1. Drain the chick-peas and peel off the outer skin.
2. In a soup pot mix the squash, chick-peas, onion, and beef and cover with the water. Simmer, covered, for 2 hours or until the meat is soft enough to eat.
3. Add the cinnamon, chicken soup, and sugar. Blend, but do not puree, all the ingredients in a food processor. Adjust the seasoning to taste. Reheat and serve. If the soup is too thick, add more water when reheating.

Yield: 8 to 12 servings (M)

Gundi, A Persian Chick-pea and Chicken Dumpling

Gundi is to Iranian-Jewish cooking what matzah balls are to Eastern and Central European Jewish food. "We make it every Friday evening," said Azizeh Koshki, who has been in the United States for about one year. When I joined a *gundi*-making session in her town house in Rockville, Maryland, to my surprise we went straight to the kitchen floor, where we sat cross-legged as she turned on her new food processor to make the dish.

Gundi, a large chicken dumpling with cardamom and turmeric, is cooked in chicken soup and served as an appetizer for Friday night dinner. A different *gundi* comes from Isfahan and is made from vegetables, rice, and lentils. "You might say that each Jewish woman has her own *gundi* recipe," said Mrs. Koshki through an interpreter. "The more onion, the tastier and softer the *gundi* gets." After Mrs. Koshki added the chick-pea flour, one of the oldest thickeners known to mankind, and mixed and poached her dumplings, we sat down to taste them at the dining room table. It was only then that I realized that the two women had removed their shoes. When I asked her why her shoes were off, she said, "We eat at the table only with Americans. If we were alone we would eat on the floor the way that we cooked on the floor."

SOUP

1 3-pound chicken cut in 8
pieces

2 onions, peeled and quartered

2 green peppers, sliced

Salt and freshly ground pepper
to taste

¼ teaspoon turmeric or to taste

1 clove garlic, crushed

DUMPLINGS

4 medium onions

½ pound chick-pea flour*

½ pound ground turkey or
chicken

1 teaspoon salt

1 teaspoon freshly ground
pepper or to taste

¼ teaspoon turmeric

½ teaspoon cardamon or to
taste

¼ cup water (about)

10 cups chicken broth from
above

½ cup cooked chick-peas

*Available at Middle Eastern food
markets

1. Place the chicken in a pot and cover with water. Bring to a boil and remove any froth that accumulates.

2. Add the onions, green peppers, salt, pepper, turmeric, and the garlic. Simmer, covered, for 45 minutes or until the chicken is cooked. Cool and strain the soup, reserving the chicken and about 10 cups of the broth.

3. Remove the skin and the bones from the chicken and cut the meat into bite-size pieces. Set aside.

4. To make the dumplings, cut the onions in quarters and grate in a food processor.

5. Add to the chick-pea flour and mix well. Add the ground turkey or chicken, the salt, pepper, and the turmeric, and cardamom. Mix well, using your hands. Add enough water to make a sticky dough, about the consistency of meatballs. You should be able to stick your finger through it. Refrigerate a few hours.

6. Dip your hands in cold water, and form the mixture into dumplings 2 inches in diameter.

7. Pour the chicken soup into a soup pot and bring to a boil. Correct the seasoning, add the dumplings, and simmer them, covered, for 15 to 20 minutes. Add the chick-peas and the chicken pieces and simmer, covered, about 5 minutes more.

8. Serve gundi in a bowl with the soup, chicken pieces, and chick-peas, or as an appetizer alone sprinkled with fresh herbs and mint and served with flat bread and pickled vegetables.

Yield: 8 servings, about 16 gundis (M)

FOUR

Fish—From Gefilte to Grouper

You wrote me some time agoe (sic) you was asked at my brother Asher's to a fish dinner but you did not go. I desire you will never eat anything with him unless it be bread and butter nor noe where else where there is the last doubt of things not done after our strict Judia-call method.

A letter from Abigail Franks of Philadelphia
to her son Naphtali in London, 1733.

It is so odd to reflect that with Jews and Catholics, fish is almost traditional for Friday. Is it because in Biblical times the fishermen came to the city with their catch? I think the Sabbath was a very real day of rest after the week's toil and strain, and the remembrance makes me understand dimly the spirit of the old ghetto, when the people lived humbly despised and persecuted, but somehow, rose to spiritual heights with the sinking of the sun on Friday.

Jennie Gerstley,"Reminiscences, Chicago, Illinois,
1859–1934," American Jewish Archives

Jewish Sole Food—Fish Fried in Olive Oil

"Bring us some fish."

"Ah," replied the waiter. "'ow will you 'ave it? There is yellow stew, and red stew, and fried." . . . In a moment "fried fish" was before us, the waiter saying, "all right, now, Sir . . . . Variety is the spice of life, excepting in the eating line, and never . . . do you eat nothing again as wasn't used to be cooked in your mother's house, and you'll never go wrong, axing your parding, Sir, for the advice."

"How is this cooked?" we asked, still rather suspicious.

"Just a mere roughing over with batter, and fried in the best of sweet oil, Portuguese fashion. Christians can't cook fish, Sir; it ain't in 'em. You see fish is a part of Jewish food, just as much as it is for Catholics, not that there is any religious belief belonging to it; but no good Jew can get along at all on a Friday without his fish. You can see it's most as much a ceremony as that of the seven-branched candlestick on a Friday night. . . ."

We must acknowledge, notwithstanding the fervor of the waiter, we took up a fragment on our fork in a suspicious and gingerly like manner . . . we found the morsel delicious. At last we had come to a culinary anchor, after having been tossed about in a sea of hungry uncertainties. The more we ate the better we liked it. As we ate in silence . . . we moralized over our fish. Might not the children of 'Israel, as they passed through the Red Sea—might they not have tarried by the shore, and prepared fish exactly in this way? Undoubtedly we were eating something which could only have been arrived at, in its present perfection, through a long series of traditional art. Your Russian sterletz, fresh from the Volga, at the table of some Bozar; your whitebait at Greenwich, for a ministerial banquet; your sole a la Normande at Phillippes, could not compare with this fried fish.

"A New Cuisine. The Jewish Restaurant—Peculiar Food Experiences of a Seeker after Novel Dishes," *The New York Times,* January 21, 1872

This restaurant reviewer was not the only non-Jew to prefer the taste of fish fried in olive oil to lard. Sometimes fried fish is served warm as it was in the above restaurant and sometimes, on the Sabbath, it is fried the day before and eaten cold. The following recipe comes from the manuscript of Thomas Jefferson's granddaughter, Virginia Jefferson Randolph Trist, around 1800. I have left the recipe as it appeared in the nineteenth century because I love the comments.

Cut 1 or 2 pounds halibut in one piece, lay it in a dish, cover the top with a little salt, put some water in the dish, but not to cover the fish; let it remain thus for one hour. The water being below, causes the salt to penetrate into the fish. Take it out and dry it; cut out the bone, and the fins off; it is then in 2 pieces. Lay the pieces on the side, and divide them into slices half an inch then put into a frying pan, with ¼ pound fat, lard or dripping, (the Jews use oil); then put 2 ounces flour in a soup plate, or basin, which mix with water, an egg is an improvement to form a smooth batter, not too thick. Dip the fish in it, that the pieces are well covered, then have the fat, not too hot, put the pieces in it, & fry till a nice color, turning them over. When done, take it out with a slice, let it drain, dish up, & serve. Any kind of sauce may be used with it; but plain, with a little salt and lemon is excellent. Other fish may be done this way.

—Soyer

Deep-fried Fish English Style

Mynetta Christie was brought up in Cardiff, Wales, where her family made fried fish twice a week. "Cold fried fish is probably the biggest difference in the way people eat fish there and here. My friends in Michigan are also aghast when I talk about fried gefilte fish, which we had for the Sabbath," said Mrs. Christie. "Here you can't get hake so we make fried fish less frequently. Also, everyone is worried about cholesterol. My mother used to put the fish in matzah meal first and then in egg. I do the reverse." In Birmingham, Michigan, where Mrs. Christie has lived for the past seventeen years, she uses haddock, perch, or cod fillets.

2 pounds haddock, perch, or
*   cod fillets*
Salt and freshly ground pepper
*   to taste*
2 large eggs
1 cup matzah meal
4 cups canola or other light
*   vegetable oil (for frying)*

1. Wash and dry the fish and then sprinkle with the salt and pepper. Cut into serving portions if too large.
2. Place the eggs, well beaten, in 1 large soup bowl and the matzah meal in another. Dip the fish first in the egg and then the matzah meal.
3. Heat the canola or vegetable oil to 375 degrees in a heavy pot like a Dutch oven, preferably with a wire basket. Then add the fish, a few pieces at a time. Fry a few minutes on one side until golden and then the other. Remove, drain on paper towels, and continue frying the remaining fish. Serve warm or cold with chips or salads.

Yield: 4 to 6 servings (P)

To Pot Shad, Herring, or Other Fish —
The Jew's Way of Preserving All Sorts of Fish

Sometimes a vinegar sauce was used to make an *escabeche,* which the English author Hannah Glasse, in her *Art of Cookery* (1796), called "The Jews way of preserving Salmon, and all Sorts of Fish." Although *escabeche* was both an Arabic and a Jewish custom, the Jews brought it with them to the New World. In Mary Randolph's *The Virginia Housewife* in 1824 a recipe appears for *caveach* with fried fish pickled with strong vinegar, onions, pounded mace, and pepper.

Escabeche may have originated in the Middle East, but it traveled far. In different countries Jews and non-Jews adapted the pickling process as a way of preserving fish. In Eastern Europe it was used for herring, and in Germanic lands it included sugar and was used for sweet and sour carp. In the Colonies soused salmon, potted shad, and sweet and sour shad were typical Jewish dishes as we see in this recipe from 1871 in *The Jewish Cookery Book,* by Esther Levy. (For more on Esther Levy see page 242.)

Let the fish be well scraped and washed, then lay it for three or four hours in salt; take a good sized jar, and cut the fish in pieces to fit; season it with salt, pepper, cinnamon, cloves, mace, and ginger; put in the jar a layer of fish, one of spices, strewed over smoothly, then sprinkle a little flour over, and pieces of good butter, and so on alternately until the jar is full; pack it down tightly, then fill the jar with vinegar and a little water, cover the jar with a crust made of flour and water, press close to the jar that the steam may not escape; bake it in a gentle oven for five or six hours. Do not remove it from the jar until it is cold. Slice it thin and serve with lemon sauce.

Abigail Franks, the eighteenth-century Jewish woman who wrote to her son to please keep kosher

Salmon Pickle with Fennel

In 1905 the *Ladies' Home Journal* published this absolutely delicious and thoroughly modern pickled salmon recipe with fennel seed in an article on Jewish cookery. Fennel had been associated with Jewish cooking for centuries in Europe. I have embellished the recipe with some fresh fennel.

3 pounds salmon fillet

2 cups plus 1 tablespoon white-wine vinegar

2 bay leaves

¼ teaspoon fennel seed

1 teaspoon salt

Dash of cayenne or to taste

Slices of fresh fennel

1. Place the salmon in a fish poacher with boiling water to cover. Add 1 tablespoon of the vinegar and simmer gently, covered, for 10 to 15 minutes or until just cooked. Drain, taking care not to break the fillet.
2. Put the remaining 2 cups of vinegar, bay leaves, fennel seed, salt, and cayenne into a non-stainless-steel or aluminum saucepan and bring to a boil.
3. Place the salmon in a plastic or ceramic bowl large enough to hold it without breaking. Strain the hot vinegar through cheesecloth over the fish. Marinate overnight or about 12 hours in the refrigerator, spooning vinegar on occasionally. Serve sliced with a garnish of fresh fennel.

Yield: 6 to 8 servings as a first course (P)

Emily Nathan's Baked Fish with Fresh Herbs and Vegetables

Emily Solis Nathan traces her American lineage back to Spanish and Portuguese Jews who arrived in Dutch New Amsterdam in the 1650s. Although most of the original "Pilgrim" Jewish line no longer exists, there are a few descendants like Miss Nathan (no kin of mine, by the way) who represent a cultural, and culinary, link to the past.

Although there was a Luceina on the Pilgrim boat that arrived in New Amsterdam in 1654, it is thought that Miss Nathan's ancestor, the butcher Simon de Luceina, came the following year. From the 1650s on, there have always been members of Miss Nathan's family in New York. A calmly independent woman of great charm, Miss Nathan lives in an apartment overlooking New York's Central Park. An etching of Supreme Court Justice Benjamin Nathan Cardozo, a first cousin once removed, looks down on this petite person as she tells the story of the flight of her ancestor, Isaac Gomez, who left Madrid to escape the Inquisition. "He was close to King Philip IV," she says. "To warn Isaac in case he was about to be arrested, the king set up a code. If he said, 'the onions are beginning to smell,' it was time to leave. Well, they did. And he left."

Like this tale, traditional recipes have been passed down orally in the Nathan family for over three hundred years.

2 onions, sliced

1 rib celery, sliced

1 carrot, peeled and cut in rounds

2 tablespoons olive oil

1 5-pound striped bass, rockfish, pickerel, yellow pike, or any firm fish, gutted and split down the center

2 plum tomatoes, sliced

1 bay leaf

½ cup chopped fresh parsley

1 teaspoon cayenne pepper or to taste

Salt to taste

2 tablespoons lemon juice or to taste

1. In a frying pan sauté the onion, celery, and carrot in the olive oil until the onion is transparent.

2. Put the onion mixture in a baking dish and lay the fish on top. Cover the fish with the tomatoes, bay leaf, parsley, and cayenne pepper. Bake in a preheated 400-degree oven for 20 minutes or until the fish is done, allowing 10 minutes per inch of thickness of fish.

3. Remove from the oven and season with salt. Discard the bay leaf and serve immediately or let cool and serve later, cold. Sprinkle with lemon juice before serving.

Yield: 6 to 8 servings (P)

Alsatian Jews Bring Carpe à la Juive

We had no good carp in our waters. From time to time a few wretched fish, called carp through courtesy, were caught in the Hudson, which no one would eat. These certainly owed their origin to the gold fish. In time these fish had even lost their ornamental characteristics, and were worthless as food. From some of these having been eaten, there arose an idea that all carp were as poor in flavor and as tasteless as those degenerate fish. . . . Now, what can be a more dainty feeder than a carp; his favorite food is salad leaves. Think of a fine fish, fattened to perfection, which has been reared on lettuce and celery!

The New York Times, 1 8 8 0

According to the above article the United States Fish Commissioner imported carp into this country in 1876, probably for the German immigrants who liked carp in their fatherland. Little did the commissioner know that within a year the demand for this carp would increase tremendously with the influx of gefilte fish–loving Eastern European Jews arriving in Manhattan!

Eveline and Guy Weyl of Lexington, Massachusetts, born in France, often serve *carpe à la juive;* for Rosh Hashanah and the Sabbath the dish has a red sweet and sour sauce made from gingersnaps and red-wine vinegar, and for Passover, a green sauce made with parsley. Like the Weyls, other Jews in Europe served *carpe à la juive,* even in Poland where it was often accompanied by almonds and raisins in a cold jelly or with thin carp steaks stuffed with a forcemeat of gefilte fish filling also in jelly. In every case, the fish is served cold, a perfect make-ahead fish for the Sabbath lunch meal. Since carp is still not very popular in the United States, the Weyls often use salmon or pike instead. Ironically, to this day in Poland, a country nearly bereft of Jews, Jewish-style carp is featured on almost every restaurant menu and is served in most homes as one of the twelve dishes on Christmas eve.

Stewed Fish à la Juive

On July 20, 1879, *The New York Times* Household Hints column contained this Alsatian recipe for stewed fish *à la juive* to show readers how to utilize the unfamiliar fish.

½ cup chopped parsley

3 small onions, sliced in rounds

2 cups water

1 teaspoon ground white pepper

½ teaspoon grated nutmeg

1 tablespoon matzah meal

1 sprig saffron

Juice of 3 lemons

3 egg yolks

1 3-pound carp, pike, or salmon, cut into 1-inch steaks (reserve the head and tail)

1. In a large pot bring the parsley, the onions, and the water to a boil, then reduce the heat, and simmer until tender, about 5 minutes. Add the white pepper, nutmeg, matzah meal, saffron, and the lemon juice.

2. Put all the fish pieces (the head and tail as well as the steaks) into the water, adding more water to cover if necessary. Cover and poach for 10 to 15 minutes or until the fish is cooked. Remove the steaks to a platter, arranging them in the original form of the fish. Leave the head and tail in the broth.

3. Reduce the broth by half over a high heat, cooking about 15 minutes, then adjust the seasoning, and strain. Return the broth to the pot, add the 3 yolks, whisking well, and bring just to a boil. When cool, chill overnight.

4. Remove the head and tail from the broth and arrange them with the fish steaks to make the original shape of the fish. Refrigerate overnight. Garnish with the onions and the parsley and some of the reduced broth. Serve the fish at room temperature with any remaining broth in a separate bowl.

Yield: 6 servings (P)

Sweet and Sour Fish

By the 1920s so many American ingredients had been incorporated into German and Alsatian dishes that it was sometimes hard to recognize the original recipe. In the *Stockton Community Cook Book* in Stockton, California, which came out in 1924, a recipe appeared for fish à la Alsace, which used striped bass rather than carp. The original gingersnaps had been replaced by ketchup, Worcestershire sauce, and Kitchen Bouquet! Here is the original recipe, one I often serve at the break-the-fast.

1 3½-pound carp, pike, striped bass, or salmon

Salt

2 large onions, sliced in rings

1 tablespoon olive oil

1 lemon, sliced and seeded

1 bay leaf

1 teaspoon whole peppercorns

½ cup raisins

1 tablespoon salt

5 whole cloves

4 cups water or enough to cover the fish

½ cup red-wine vinegar

½ cup brown sugar

4 to 5 gingersnaps or Lebkuchen

1. Clean and wash the fish thoroughly. Cut in finger-wide strips, but do not cut through the lower skin; also, leave on the head so that the fish can be presented whole. Salt well and keep on ice until the following sauce is prepared.

2. Sauté the onions in the olive oil until golden. Then add the lemon, bay leaf, peppercorns, raisins, salt, cloves, water, and vinegar and bring to a boil. Add the brown sugar and gingersnaps, which will add color to the sauce.

3. Add the fish to the liquid and let simmer, covered, for about 15 minutes or until the fish is done.

4. When cooked, discard the bay leaf and peppercorns. Remove to a large serving dish and pour the sauce over the fish. Garnish with the onions and raisins. This is good either hot or cold. When cold, the sauce forms a jelly coating over the fish.

Yield: 8 to 10 servings (P)

From Gefilte Fish on the Hudson to Mother's Gefilte Fish

My father was selling live carp when the immigrants from Russia and Poland were coming here (about 1910). He used to go up the Hudson and haul live fish down to the city in barrels of water so they could stay alive on the boats. Of course, this was before the Hudson was contaminated. He used horses and wagons to transport them to the stores. They dumped all the fish in the stores in tanks, water being poured on them all. If the fish died, which was very often, the average Jewish woman looked at

it very askance. She wanted live fish. They sold dead fish to others. It was just a matter of taste in those days. Live fish was a big deal. Many people made gefilte fish out of carp alone. Later they became more sophisticated and made it with whitefish and pike.

Eventually my grandfather had a store on Rivington Street, three blocks from the drug store of Armand Hammer's father. This went on for years until World War II. Some guy from Minnesota or Wisconsin decided to can gefilte fish out of carp. It was a miserable product, it wasn't tasty enough but the government was lax and was buying almost anything canned or frozen. When the War started the Jewish boys were smart enough. They wouldn't eat the canned gefilte fish. It was junk. "Why can't we make a real gefilte fish like mother makes," said my nephews. My sister was experimenting with homemade gefilte fish. That's where they got the name "Mother's Gefilte Fish." During the war you couldn't get glass so they put it up in cans. It was very hard for a Jewish woman to buy anything out of a can. It was something they didn't go for. Jars was a barrier you had to break down with Jewish women too. It's a success story. Mother's Gefilte Fish became a staple which it is today.

Sidney Leibner, eighty-three, Deerfield Beach, Florida

Gefilte fish, basically a poached fish ball with filler (bread crumbs or matzah meal), was served for the Sabbath and holidays by Eastern European Jews; it is traditionally made from whitefish, pike, and carp. A fourth fish, called "buffel" by gefilte fish mavens, is buffalo fish, similar to carp in taste and texture.

Like Mr. Leibner's father, first-generation immigrants tried to catch live fish. The late Jack Bloom, one of the founders of the Jewish community in Albuquerque, New Mexico, fished carp until his death at eighty-one. He traveled regularly to the irrigation ditches of the Rio Grande, near the Isleta Pueblo, requested a fishing permit from the Indians, and fished for fresh carp for the "bubbies and zaydes," who, he said, needed it for the Jewish holidays.

My mother-in-law does not insist on live fish, but she is a very demanding customer; she would never accept the first fish offered by a fishmonger. She has even been very reluctant to use my food processor for grinding the fish and is aghast when I suggest poaching the patties for less than 2 hours. (Gefilte fish cooks in less than 20 minutes.) Until I married into this "start-from-scratch" gefilte fish family, we graced our Passover table with the jarred variety. What a difference homemade makes! Now gefilte fish–making has become a welcome twice-yearly ritual in our house—at Rosh Hashanah and Passover. At our Passover seder, we all wait with baited breath for my husband's opinion. "*Peshke,* your gefilte fish is better than ever!" gets a broad grin from his Jewish mother.

The gefilte fish recipe we use today came with my husband's family from the DP camps.

Classic Gefilte Fish

Gefilte fish is one of those recipes where touch and taste are essential ingredients. A basic recipe goes this way: "You put in this and add that." If you don't want to taste the raw fish, add a bit more seasoning than you normally would. What makes this recipe Galicianer (southern Polish) is the addition of sugar. For some reason the farther south in Poland, the more sugar would be added. A Lithuanian Jew would never sweeten with sugar but might add beets to the stock. I have added ground carrot and parsnip to the fish, something that is done in the Ukraine, because I like the slightly sweet taste and rougher texture. If you want a darker broth, do not peel the onions and leave them whole.

7 to 7½ pounds whole carp,
  whitefish, and pike, filleted
  and ground*

4 quarts cold water or to just
  cover

3 teaspoons salt or to taste

3 onions, peeled

4 medium carrots, peeled

2 tablespoons sugar or to taste

1 small parsnip, chopped
  (optional)

3 to 4 large eggs

Freshly ground pepper to taste

½ cup cold water
  (approximately)

⅓ cup matzah meal
  (approximately

*Ask your fishmonger to grind the fish. Ask him to reserve the tails, fins, heads, and bones. Be sure he gives you the bones and trimmings. The more whitefish you add, the softer your gefilte fish will be.

1. Place the reserved bones, skin, and fish heads in a wide, very large saucepan with a cover. Add the water and 2 teaspoons of the salt and bring to a boil. Remove the foam that accumulates.

2. Slice 1 onion in rounds and add along with 3 of the carrots. Add the sugar and bring to a boil. Cover and simmer for about 20 minutes while the fish mixture is being prepared.

3. Place the ground fish in a bowl. In a food processor finely chop the remaining onions, the remaining carrot, and the parsnip; or mince them by hand. Add the chopped vegetables to the ground fish.

4. Add the eggs, one at a time, the remaining teaspoon of salt, pepper, and the cold water, and mix thoroughly. Stir in enough matzah meal to make a light, soft mixture that will hold its shape. Wet your hands with cold water, and scooping up about ¼ cup of fish form the mixture into oval shapes, about 3 inches long. Take the last fish head and stuff the cavity with the ground fish mixture.

5. Remove from the saucepan the onions, skins, head, and bones and return the stock to a simmer. Gently place the fish patties in the simmering fish stock. Cover loosely and simmer for 20 to 30 minutes. Taste the liquid while the fish is cooking and add seasoning to taste. Shake the pot periodically so the fish patties won't stick. When gefilte fish is cooked, remove from the water and allow to cool for at least 15 minutes.

6. Using a slotted spoon carefully remove the gefilte fish and arrange on a platter. Strain some of the stock over the fish, saving the rest in a bowl.

7. Slice the cooked carrots into rounds cut on a diagonal about ¼ inch thick. Place a carrot round on top of each gefilte fish patty. Put the fish head in the center and decorate the eyes with carrots. Chill until ready to serve. Serve with a sprig of parsley and horseradish (see page 397).

Yield: about 26 patties (P)

From Halibut to Shad—
Gefilte Fish Goes American

"Some people in the Midwest make gefilte fish only of whitefish," said Dora Solganik, an octogenarian who lives in Cleveland, Ohio. "I use pike, mullet, perch, and whitefish. I don't like carp. I buy twenty pounds of fish for Passover. Once I tried bluefish but it tasted so bad I threw it right in the sink. I taste the fish too to see if there is enough salt and pepper—if you don't want to swallow it you can spit it out. I make them in the palm of my hand—a nice size. It costs me close to $100 for the fish. This is just the taste. Not just the whole meal. I make it in my apartment and bring it to my grandson in Dayton."

Like many first-generation Jewish cooks, Mrs. Solganik, who was born in Kiev, in the Ukraine, learned to make gefilte fish at her mother's apron string. When she came to the United States in 1922, she discovered different types of fish so she adjusted the recipe. "Fish is so expensive. A lot of people buy the canned fish and doctor it up," she said. "Very few people make their own fish. It's just as good if you buy canned gefilte fish, believe me. But my grandchildren would disown me if I wouldn't make gefilte fish for *Pesach*. They love it."

Like Mrs. Sogalnik's, other gefilte fish recipes vary regionally. "My grand-mother brought her gefilte fish recipe from Lithuania to the eastern shore of Virginia," said Michael Schuchat, a lawyer in Washington, D.C. "In Lithuania she probably used carp, whitefish, and pike. We had gefilte fish every Friday night but, in the spring it was shad because shad was cheap then."

In Alaska, greyling or Mackinaw trout are used; in the northwest, salmon; in Maine, haddock or halibut and mackerel; in Florida, red snapper; in Hawaii, mahimahi and butterfish; in the Southwest, tilapia; and in the Midwest, whitefish with lake trout and pickerel.

First-generation Jewish immigrants coast to coast have adapted their traditional gefilte fish recipe to the local fish available in order to maintain culinary traditions, especially at family gatherings. Second-generation Americans, in the rush to assimilate and with readily available packaged products, often lose sight of this. Some serve canned or jarred gefilte fish, occasionally doctored up with carrots and onions and even tomato juice. In many instances it is the third generation, like the grandchildren of Mrs. Sogalnik, who insist on the traditional recipes.

Maryland Spicy Gefilte Fish with Shad

The other fish complained to God that shad was so sweet so He gave the shad all those bones to make up for it.   The late Simon Schuchat of Baltimore

This recipe originated in Lithuania (notice there is no sugar in it) and is accented by the spices loved by Simon Schuchat's descendants in Maryland.

10 pounds whole shad, heads and tails removed and the shad boned (reserve heads, tails, and frames)

16 cups water or to cover fish bones

4 onions, peeled and left whole*

1 stalk celery, left whole

Salt to taste

8 peppercorns

4 teaspoons Old Bay Seasoning or to taste†

1 pound boned perch or other firm white fish (optional)

3 large eggs

⅓ cup water

½ to 1 cup matzah meal

Red horseradish

Pickled beets

Carrot slivers

Parsley for garnish

*If you like a darker broth leave the skin on the onions.

†See box for substitutes.

1. Wash the shad heads and tails, and place with the bones along with the water in a large pot.

2. Add to the pot 2 of the onions, the celery, 1 teaspoon salt, the peppercorns, and 3 teaspoons Old Bay Seasoning. Bring to a boil and skim the foam off the top. Simmer, partially covered, while preparing the fish, about an hour.

3. Grind the remaining onions in a food processor. Add the fish and continue to process, pulsing on and off, but not to a mush. If you want a firmer fish ball, add the perch or other firm fish.

4. Add salt, the remaining 1 teaspoon Old Bay Seasoning or to taste, the eggs, and the water and process briefly. Add a half cup of matzah meal and process, then continue adding more until the mixture feels tacky, not mushy. Let sit in the refrigerator for 15 to 20 minutes or until the fish mixture is stiff enough to handle.

5. Strain the broth, discarding the fish bones. Return the broth to the pot and bring to a boil.

6. Keep a bowl of cold water nearby, dip your hands in cold water, and mold the fish mixture into rounds the size of a squash ball, about 2 inches in diameter.

7. Place the fish balls in the broth and simmer, covered, for 1 hour, adding more water if needed. Let the fish cool in the broth, then, with a slotted spoon, remove to a platter. Reduce the liquid by half, cool, and then refrigerate the fish and the stock separately. Serve covered with the jellied sauce, red horseradish (see page 397), pickled beets, carrot slivers, and a sprig of fresh parsley.

Yield: about 36 (P)

Old Bay Seasoning's German-Jewish Origin

Old Bay Seasoning was created in Baltimore by a German-Jewish refugee named Gustav C. Brunn in 1939. In Frankfurt, Mr. Brunn had ground spices for pickling. When he came to Baltimore, he started selling pickling spices to German meat packers and pickle-makers. Soon he noticed that cooks in local restaurants would come in and ask him to grind a few pounds of this spice and a few of that for their steamed crabs. He took note of what they wanted and developed a combination of about eleven different spices to come up with his own "Old Bay Seasoning."

Since Old Bay Seasoning is not certified kosher, you can make your own combination of spicy ingredients. Just grind up equal amounts of celery salt, pepper, mustard, pimiento, cloves, bay leaves, mace, cardamom, ginger, cassia, and paprika.

Southwestern Gefilte Fish with Salsa

This recipe found its way to the Southwest with a Polish-Jewish family. Any mild fish would be delicious baked in this salsa. This has been adapted by Clara Yudovich Burak.

2 medium onions, sliced

2 tablespoons vegetable oil

2 cups canned tomato sauce

1 teaspoon sugar

½ cup green olives, pitted

1 serrano pepper, whole

1 bay leaf

Freshly ground pepper to taste

½ cup water

Vegetable oil for frying

6 gefilte fish patties (see page 140)

1. Sauté the onions slowly in the oil until soft and golden.
2. Add the tomato sauce, sugar, green olives, serrano pepper, bay leaf, pepper, and water. Simmer, uncovered, for about 5 minutes.
3. Put about ¼ inch oil in a medium frying pan and heat. Add the fish patties, fry until golden on both sides. Drain and add the patties to the sauce. Simmer, uncovered, about 10 minutes or until the sauce penetrates the fish. Serve hot or cold.

Yield: 6 servings (P)

Tip: You can also omit the frying step and merely heat the gefilte fish in the sauce.

Elegant and Easy Gourmet Gefilte Fish Pâté

The following recipe comes from Monica Fanaberia Protzel of Woodbury, New York. This recipe gives you the traditional gefilte fish taste with a smoother, more elegant texture—and you don't have to make a fish stock or patties.

Marty Freed, chef at Ossie's Table Restaurant at 1314 50th Street, Boro Park, Brooklyn, uses all salmon in this recipe. He also makes an alternate version using the traditional blend of whitefish and pike spiked with Cajun spices, almonds, raisins, lemon dill, jalapeño, and horseradish.

3 pounds fish fillets (whitefish and pike, 1½ pounds each)

4 medium Bermuda onions, peeled and diced (about 2 pounds)

3 tablespoons vegetable or canola oil

4 large eggs

2 cups cold water

6 tablespoons matzah meal

1 tablespoon salt or to taste

2 teaspoons ground white pepper

2 tablespoons sugar

2 large carrots, peeled

Parsley for garnish

1. Have your fish store grind the fillets or grind them yourself in a food processor or meat grinder. Do not puree, but grind fine.

2. Sauté the diced onions in the oil until soft and transparent but not brown. Cool.

3. In the bowl of an electric mixer place the fish, onions, eggs, water, matzah meal, salt, white pepper, and sugar. Beat at medium speed for 15 minutes. Grate in the carrots and mix well.

4. Pour the mixture into a greased 12-cup bundt pan. Smooth the top with a spatula and bake in a preheated 325-degree oven for 1 hour in a larger pan filled with 2 inches water.

5. Cover with aluminum foil and continue baking for 1 hour or until the center is solid. Cool for 5 minutes and then invert onto a flat serving plate.

6. Refrigerate for several hours or overnight. Slice as you would a torte and serve as an appetizer, garnished with parsley and served with red horseradish sauce (see page 397). Leftovers keep for up to five days.

Yield: about 20 appetizer portions (P)

Tip: The mold can be made up to two days in advance.

Si Goldman's Herring Fry

In the fifties and the sixties, there weren't very many Jewish people here; we would get these schmaltz herrings and they were shipped to us out of Denver. Then we'd wrap them in the Yiddish Jewish newspapers, *The Jewish Forward* or the *Tageblatt,* we would wet down the newspaper a little. Then we'd build a fire in the ground and we'd put the newspapers on the fire and we'd bake the her-

Herring Fry, cont.

ring on both sides. Then we'd eat delicious herring. We'd have the whole mountain to ourselves because other people didn't understand the smell. It was delicious. We had good schnapps before we started eating, chairs and tables and picnicked all day long. If somebody did something nice for the UJA drive, then we would invite them to come on the picnic, we started out we had 8 or 10 couples with children, we grew to 30 or 40 people on these picnics.

Si Goldman, Albuquerque, New Mexico

Mr. Goldman was born in Russia, raised in Denver, and settled in 1939 in Albuquerque, where he ran a saddle, work clothes, and uniform manufacturing business. The herring fry on Jemez Mountain was an annual picnic event for him for years.

Here's how he does it.

6 schmaltz herring
Yiddish or other newspapers
Water

1. Wrap the herring in the newspaper and sprinkle with water.
2. Place the herring in the embers of a fire and watch. When the paper is burnt, the herring is done. You can also put the herring in the ashes of an old coal stove to cook. Serve with hash brown potatoes and a shot of whiskey.

Yield: 6 servings (P)

Mark Siegel's Whitefish Salad

I particularly like this version of whitefish salad, because there is no filler in it. Mark, a political consultant who served in the Carter White House, makes it for break-the-fast as well as during the year brunches.

1 4-pound smoked whitefish
5 stalks celery, strings removed
2 cups sour cream
 (approximately)
3 heaping tablespoons
 mayonnaise
Freshly ground pepper to taste
2 tablespoons snipped fresh dill
2 tablespoons chopped parsley
Garnish: sprigs of fresh dill
 and/or parsley

1. Keeping the skin of the whitefish intact and the head still attached, carefully remove the bones from the whitefish and place the meat in a mixing bowl.
2. Dice the celery and combine with the whitefish, along with 1 cup of the sour cream, the mayonnaise, and the pepper. Add the dill and parsley and as much more sour cream as is wanted.
3. Stuff the mixture back into the skin of the whitefish, remaking the shape of a fish. Garnish with additional dill and parsley.

Yield: enough for at least 10 people (D)

Break-the-Fast Meal—A Source of Psychological Bonding

One of the institutions that has definitely changed in this country is the break-the-fast meal of Yom Kippur, the holiest day in the Jewish year. Traditionally the break-the-fast was not a time for celebration but rather a family meal at the end of a day of reflection. In Europe the sound of the shofar both ended the traditional day of fasting and announced to the women that the men were coming home. A piece of honey cake and tea or perhaps herring in cream sauce and a glass of sweet wine ended the fast before the family would sit down to a meal and then go out to the backyard to hammer the first nail in the Sukkah.

But it was not thus for all American Jews. "Earlier in this century anarchists held Yom Kippur balls as part of an anti–Yom Kippur ritual," said Jacob Rader Marcus, professor of American Jewish History at the Hebrew Union College in Cincinnati. The food writer Barbara Kafka tells the story that her grandfather would purposefully go shopping on Yom Kippur. These radical assaults on religion turned into an anti–Yom Kippur ritual in the labor movements as well as *treif* balls at Purim.

For the most part, however, families and extended families still gather together. "Until recently a family was a much larger multi-generational entity," said Rabbi Jeffrey Wohlberg of Adas Israel Synagogue in Washington, D.C. "But with families spread apart in America, nuclear families have sought ways of sharing events. The break fast at Yom Kippur serves not as a religious celebration but as a source for psychological bonding."

This psychological bonding takes many forms. In the fall of 1978 Elizabeth Kennan, the president of Mount Holyoke College, who was married to a Jew, decided to hold an impromptu Yom Kippur service with a break-the-fast at her college-owned president's home. To her surprise about fifty students and a dozen faculty members came. "The Jewish students were boggled that the president would do this in her home and she was surprised that so many of them showed up," recalled Jonathan Lipman, professor of Chinese studies at Mount Holyoke and the leader of the service.

In other cities the break-the-fast has become a major party. For three generations the Ransohoff family of Cincinnati has held a famous break-the-fast with every notable in Cincinnati attending. "Fifty percent of the people were gentiles who came and half of the Jews who came had not been to synagogue. This break-the-fast kept them within the periphery of Jewry," said Dr. Marcus, one of the attendees. "Everybody brings hors d'oeuvres, whatever their specialty is. These appetizers include herring, whitefish salad, devilled eggs, chopped liver, and *hummus,* something they wouldn't have eaten twenty-five years ago," added Mrs. Ransohoff.

Fish Molds with Gelatin—
Scientific Discoveries and the Laws of Kashrut

Until the latter part of the nineteenth century, Americans made natural gelatin, a glutinous material obtained from animal tissues and then boiled for a long time. This was the way Jews made *petcha,* or calves'-foot jelly. The calves' feet were cleaned by first singeing off the hair. Then they were made kosher and stewed with onions and salt and pepper. The meat that was left was freed from the bone. Hard-boiled eggs and vinegar were added, and the whole was allowed to congeal. This formed a sort of firm aspic, which was served cold. Today few people make *petcha* and most buy manufactured gelatin.

Some Jews did not question the kashrut of new scientific products like gelatin. Others did. Gelatin, made from the prepared bladder of the non-kosher sturgeon or from non-kosher animals, fell into a gray area. For some, the amount of gelatin was so minuscule and the chemical change so great that it did not matter. For others, no matter the amount of non-kosher meat, gelatin was still not kosher. Until the 1980s when *kojel,* a vegetarian kosher gelatin, came on the market, many Orthodox Jews would not use any gelatin product, including the popular Jell-O (see page 364).

For those conservative and Reform Jews who used commercial gelatin, they quickly forgot the more labor-intensive baked fish molds made with heavy cream and served with cream sauce. In the recipes that follow I give the old and the new ways.

New England Halibut Mold

This is one of many early-twentieth-century pre-gelatin old-style fish mold recipes in the private collection of Helene Bernhardt, of Providence, Rhode Island. I have sometimes substituted leftover bluefish for the halibut. Add more fresh herbs if you like.

2½ pounds cooked halibut

1 tablespoon chopped chives

1 tablespoon chopped parsley

½ teaspoon curry powder or to taste

1. Shred the halibut and combine with the chives, the parsley, the curry powder, and salt and pepper. Add the heavy cream.
2. Beat the egg whites until stiff and fold in.
3. Turn into a well-greased fish mold and place in an ovenproof pan with hot water which comes to 1 inch from the top of the mold.

*Salt and freshly ground pepper
   to taste*

1 cup heavy cream

4 large egg whites

4. Place in a preheated 350-degree oven and bake about 45 minutes or until done. Unmold, decorate with fresh herbs, and serve hot or cold as an hors d'oeuvre or main course.

Yield: about 12 servings (D)

Barbara Burtoff's Salmon Mousse

This recipe comes from Barbara Burtoff, formerly the food editor of the *Boston Herald*. So many of my friends have requested the recipe from her that I keep tasting it at other people's houses. You can use any leftover fish instead of the salmon.

*1 envelope unflavored pareve
   gelatin*

½ cup boiling water

2 tablespoons diced onion

2 tablespoons lemon juice

½ cup mayonnaise

1 teaspoon dill

1 teaspoon brandy

½ teaspoon salt

½ teaspoon white pepper

*2 cups cooked salmon or 2
   7½-ounce cans red salmon,
   drained*

1 cup heavy cream

½ cup sour cream

1. Dissolve the gelatin in the boiling water in a small bowl.

2. In a larger bowl mix the remaining ingredients and fold in the dissolved gelatin. Pour into a greased 1-quart mold.

3. Refrigerate, at least 6 hours, unmold, decorate with fresh herbs, and serve.

Yield: at least 12 servings (D)

Barney Greengrass's Lox, Eggs, and Onions

As a child, when I visited my grandparents in New York City, my grandmother made lox wings, onions, and hard-boiled eggs for breakfast. Lox wings, which are not as fatty as belly lox and more difficult to remove from the fish, are noticeably cheaper.

I know of no better place to eat lox, onions, and scrambled eggs than Barney Greengrass on the Upper West Side, a New York institution for over sixty years. When I visited the tiny dairy restaurant on a quiet Tuesday morning, two Baltimore ladies were sitting at a Formica table beneath the wallpaper, faded and stained with onion. They had hiked up from their downtown hotel for the Nova Scotia lox heads and wings, broiled with Spanish onions and eggs. Moe Greengrass, son of the founder, was seated at the counter across from the turn-of-the-century ice box. In the old days you could see through the mirror door cakes of ice, which would drip down and cool the butter, cheese, and eggs inside.

Mr. Greengrass took me into the back room to the black Vulcan stove. There in a huge skillet Spanish onions were cooking ever so slowly. You could just smell the sweetness leaching out of the onions. "It's a good thing you didn't come here on a Sunday," he said. "I don't know why people do it, but they wait for hours on line outside with their *New York Times*. They talk and become friends." Later they eat his lox, onions, and eggs.

3 Spanish onions, sliced in
    rounds
3 tablespoons vegetable oil
8 large eggs
½ cup diced lox wings and
    heads*

*You can buy these ends at any
good deli or kosher supermarket
for a fraction of the price of sliced
salmon. When you purchase a pre-
sliced salmon, the end and the
wings are usually not sliced. Save
that part for this dish.

1. Sauté the onions slowly in the oil in a frying pan with a cover. When the onions start to soften, cover, reduce the heat to low, and cook about a half hour, until the onions are very soft. Remove the cover and continue cooking until golden. This way you do not need lots of oil.

2. Beat the eggs well in a bowl. Pour over the onions. Cook slowly, stirring well. Cover for about 10 minutes. Just before the eggs have set, add the lox, and cook until just set.

Yield: 4 to 6 servings (P)

Maine Mock Lobster Salad

If you really want this to taste like a mock Maine lobster salad, serve it in a toasted hot-dog roll.

2½ pounds of a white fish like
    haddock
1 16-ounce can stewed
    tomatoes, broken up
2 stalks celery
Salt and freshly ground pepper
    to taste
¼ cup mayonnaise or to taste
Paprika

1. Place the fish and tomatoes with their juice in a saucepan and simmer for 10 minutes, covered, or until done. Drain in a colander and cool.

2. Dice the celery. Break the fish into bite-size pieces and mix with the celery, salt, pepper, and mayonnaise. Sprinkle with the paprika.

3. Serve on a lettuce leaf garnished with fresh cut-up tomatoes or in the Down East fashion in a toasted hot-dog roll with mayonnaise.

Yield: 4 to 6 servings (P)

Down East Maine Mock Lobster Salad

When the late sculptress Louise B. Nevelson was waiting for the ship to immigrate to the United States in 1904, her mother noticed an attractive young Russian, who was escaping from the tsar's army. Thinking that he might be an appropriate match for one of her nieces, she offered to sell him an extra ticket on the boat on which she and her three children were traveling. (She had an extra ticket because her brother decided not to come.) The young man accepted and went, with the family, to Rockland, Maine, a center of New England Jewish peddlers, rag dealers, and small businessmen. Years later William Smallyrenky, whose name eventually was shortened to Small, married the niece. During the week he peddled clothing, household goods, and pots and pans throughout the state and the nearby islands. Along with the rest of the Jewish community this young man prayed at Temple Adas Yeshurun, established in 1912.

Barbara Small Fishman, a fourth-generation Mainer and his granddaughter, is one of the authors of *Down East Jewish Cooking,* published by the Hadassah chapter in Rockland. Although only one woman in Rockland keeps kosher today, the book is kosher. Hailing from the lobster state, they made sure to include a family recipe for "Mock Lobster Salad."

Even before mock lobster products came on the market, Jews of Maine who kept kosher homes were trying to approximate the taste of the prohibited lobster with the abundant saltwater fish available to them. Instead of the pollock used in "I-can't-believe-it's-not-lobster," they used the local haddock cooked in tomatoes, which made the fish look like lobster. After the tomatoes colored the fish, they were discarded.

William and Rose Evall Small, early Rockland, Maine, settlers

Alaskan-style Sweet and Sour Salmon

Break-the-fast menus go regional, too. Here's a recipe from Seattle's Diamond Jubilee Recipe Collection of the Bikur Cholim Machzikay Hadath Sisterhood, adapted from Adele Steinberg.

2 pounds White King or other
   salmon steaks, 1¼ inches
   thick with 2 salmon heads
2 teaspoons coarse salt (about)
2 cups water
2 large onions, sliced in rounds
2 large fresh tomatoes, sliced
Vinegar to taste
Sugar to taste
2 8-ounce cans tomato sauce
Juice of 6 lemons
1½ teaspoons whole allspice
About 15 bay leaves

1. Cut the salmon into 4 pieces. Rinse and generously sprinkle each piece and the 2 heads with coarse salt. Cover completely with waxed paper to prevent drying and leave overnight in the refrigerator.
2. Bring the water to a boil in a heavy pot. Add the onions, tomatoes, vinegar, sugar, tomato sauce, and lemon juice. Then add the fish. Reduce heat to medium and simmer, covered, for about 10 minutes or until the fish flakes with a fork. Leave the fish in the cooking kettle until cold. This prevents slices breaking when removed. When cold, remove the fish. Strain the broth and pour it over the fish. Then add the allspice and the bay leaves. (Adding spices last avoids bitterness.) Cover and let the fish marinate for at least 3 days. Remove the bay leaves and serve at room temperature. This dish can be kept in the refrigerator for 3 weeks.

Yield: 6 to 8 servings (P)

Pescado con Ruibarbo *(Turkish Fish in Rhubarb Sauce)*

Rhubarb, a harbinger of spring, makes an unusual sweet and sour sauce for fish.

1 pound young rhubarb (4 to 5
   stalks)
3 cups water
½ cup tomato sauce
2 teaspoons sugar or to taste
½ teaspoon salt or to taste
¼ cup vegetable oil
2 pounds fish steaks (salmon or
   halibut) or whole fillet

1. Wash the rhubarb. Cut into 1-inch cubes. Place the water and the rhubarb in a large saucepan, and cook until very soft, about 15 to 20 minutes.
2. Add the tomato sauce, sugar, salt, and oil. Cook over low heat for 5 minutes. Add the fish and cook gently until tender, about 15 minutes. Taste the sauce and adjust the seasoning, if necessary. Add water if the sauce is too thick. Serve hot or cold.

Yield: 4 to 6 as a first course (P)

Turkish Food Comes to Seattle, Washington

"There was nothing on the table but roast chicken I recognized the first time I went to my inlaws," said Gilda Angel. "I wasn't prepared for their foods. No gefilte fish but salmon and rhubarb. No canned peas and carrots but stuffed tomatoes. I had never seen okra before. My Turkish husband had the opposite culture shock with Ashkenazic food. Chopped liver. He had never eaten that before." Some people's palates are awakened by a visit to a foreign country, some by taking a cooking class, some by tasting a dish at a restaurant. Gilda Angel developed her interest in Sephardic cooking during her courtship with Marc Angel, rabbi of the Shearith Israel synagogue in New York City. She became so interested in this cooking that she wrote *Sephardic Holiday Cooking.*

Rabbi Angel comes from the Turkish community of Seattle, Washington. Today there are about four to five thousand of Sephardic descent in Seattle, with two synagogues. The older Bikur Holim congregation is from Marmara and Fikirdaya; the newer, from the island of Rhodes. The first Jewish settlers were fishermen, looking for a new livelihood, at the turn of the century. Rabbi Angel's grandparents came from Turkey and the island of Rhodes.

Mrs. Angel especially likes the following Turkish fish in rhubarb sauce, served at holidays in her husband's home.

Rabbi Marc Angel as a young boy in the Turkish Jewish community of Seattle

Jodi Kassorla's Moroccan Fish

"Fish is a symbol of the week-end, of the pride of Shabbat," says an old Moroccan symbol. Kosher caterer Jodi Kassorla, married to a Sephardic rabbi (see page 406), tries to include fish dishes whenever possible. This Moroccan dish is one of her favorites.

3 tablespoons light olive oil

2 tablespoons chopped parsley

1 onion, chopped

8 garlic cloves, minced

2 tablespoons tomato paste

2 tablespoons lemon juice

1 teaspoon cumin

1 teaspoon coriander

1/2 teaspoon salt

1 teaspoon paprika

1/2 teaspoon dried hot red pepper flakes

1 1/2 cups water

2 pounds orange roughy or grouper fillets

1. Heat the olive oil in a skillet and sauté the parsley, onion, and garlic until the onion is transparent.
2. Add the onion mixture to the tomato paste, lemon juice, cumin, coriander, salt, paprika, red pepper, and water and heat.
3. Put the fish in a shallow baking dish and pour the sauce over it. Bake, covered, in a preheated 350-degree oven for 30 minutes or until the fish flakes.

Yield: 4 to 6 servings (P)

Yemenite Whitefish with Red Pepper and Spices

I love the taste of these simple Oriental fish dishes cooked with fresh vegetables and spices. How in tune with modern taste buds these old recipes are! Make this a day ahead so that the flavors will meld. The recipe is adapted from Aharoni Shinyder.

8 to 12 cloves whole garlic,
peeled

2 fresh red peppers sliced in
chunks

1 heaping teaspoon cumin or to
taste

½ teaspoon turmeric or to taste

Salt and freshly ground pepper
to taste

¼ cup vegetable oil

1 cup water

3 pounds whitefish, whiting,
sea bass, or trout fillets

Paprika to taste

1. Put the garlic, fresh red pepper, cumin, turmeric, salt, pepper, oil, and water in a saucepan and simmer very slowly, covered, for about 1½ hours. Be careful not to let the sauce burn, adding water if necessary.

2. Pour some of the sauce in a baking pan and place the fish on top. Spoon the rest of the sauce around the fish. Cover and simmer on top of the stove for 15 to 20 minutes or until the fish flakes.

3. Serve the next day reheated as an appetizer. You can serve it alone or with roasted pepper salad (see page 277).

Yield: 6 to 8 servings (P)

Sunday Night Cantonese Is Now Dressed-up Hunan

Jews always look for Chinese restaurants, but how often have you heard of a Chinese looking for gefilte fish?

An American-Jewish joke

When I was a child, my mother and father went out alone Saturday night and took the children to the local Chinese restaurant every Sunday night. Chinese food in those days was Cantonese—*egg foo yong,* chop suey, and *moo goo gai pan.* For dessert there were melt-in-your-mouth Chinese almond cookies with an entire almond inside.

Chinese food is a natural for Jews for many reasons. Sunday, when Chinese restaurants are open and Christians are having Sunday dinner, is the night to go out. The food, within the budget of many families, is served family style, which is more relaxing than a multi-course French meal. Wontons are akin to kreplach, and, indeed, many people think that the Khazars brought wontons to Russia, where the Jews learned how to make them. The Chinese use chicken broth, do not mix meat and milk, and disguise pork by cutting it up very small or omit it entirely. Not only was embracing another ethnic group a means of being more American, eating out, in the days before fast foods, reflected on the husband's ability to succeed.

Today Chinese kosher restaurants are crisscrossing the country and are often the first kosher restaurant to appear in a community. In the entire Washington, D.C., area, for example, two of the half-dozen kosher restaurants are Chinese with one operated by Iranian Jews. (Wednesday nights there is an Iranian kosher buffet.)

According to the Kosher Club, a guide to kosher dining facilities for Jewish travelers that has been in existence for four years, two of the most distinctive kosher Chinese restaurants are the Lotus Garden in San Francisco and Vegetarian Heaven in Manhattan, both run by Chinese Buddhists. "This is the only place where Orthodox Jews can comfortably eat 'eel,' 'shrimp,' and 'pork,' " said Stephen Ostrow, president of the Kosher Club. "They are all made out of vegetables and vegetarian spices."

Kosher Club's Chinese Ginger Fish

As a ginger lover, I add more to this dish. An easy way to grate it is to peel first, combine with a little water, and then puree it in your food processor.

1 teaspoon extra-virgin olive
    oil
1½ pounds fillets of grouper,
    flounder, or sole
Salt and freshly ground pepper
    to taste
1 tablespoon fresh ginger,
    peeled and grated
4 fresh scallions, chopped
1 cup water or vegetable broth
Soy sauce to taste
Pinch of sugar

1. Coat a flat baking dish with the olive oil.
2. Clean the fillets and season with salt and pepper. Place the fillets in the oiled dish and cover with the ginger and chopped scallions.
3. Boil the water or broth. Add a dash of soy sauce and sugar, and pour the mixture over the fillets.
4. Bake, covered, in a preheated 350-degree oven for about 10 minutes.

    Serve with white or brown rice and steamed broccoli or other green vegetable.

Yield: 4 servings (P)

Manna Catering's Trout Wrapped in Grape Leaves

Instead of drawing on recipes from old-time Jewish cookbooks, Dan Lenchner and his wife, Joni Greenspan, owners of Manna Catering in Manhattan, take their inspiration from the latest food magazines and cookbooks. They also taste dishes at avant-garde New York restaurants and convert them for life-cycle events for their strictly kosher clientele.

    As a result, Manna Catering prepares dishes using fresh mesquite-grilled tuna, goat cheese, shiitake mushrooms, sun-dried tomatoes, miniature vegetables, and Maida Heatter–rich chocolate desserts.

4 sprigs fresh rosemary
8 sprigs fresh thyme
8 to 12 leaves fresh basil
4 brook trout, gutted with head
    and tail left on

1. Stuff the herbs in the cavities of the fish.
2. Drain the grape leaves and rinse, separating them as you do so. Put the leaves in a bowl and pour boiling water over them. Drain and rinse. Snip off the stems. Using as many leaves as necessary, cover the fish with overlapping leaves, keeping the head and tail exposed.

½-*pound jar grape leaves*
    (you'll need about a dozen)
Salt and freshly ground pepper
    to taste
½ *cup dry white wine*
½ *stick (¼ cup) unsalted butter*

3. Place in a shallow baking dish, add salt and pepper, and enough wine to cover the bottom. Dot with butter, cover with aluminum foil, and bake in a preheated 400-degree oven for 10 minutes per one-inch thickness of fish.

Yield: 4 servings (P)

Anne Rosenzweig's Mustard Crisped Salmon Cakes

Anne Rosenzweig, chef-owner of Arcadia and consultant to the "21" Club, fell into cooking naturally—well, almost naturally. "My grandmother who came from Russia went to White Lake and opened the White Lake Maples," said Ms. Rosenzweig. "While she cooked and cleaned, my grandfather went to *schul* all day. I grew up hearing all these stories about my grandmother's life. As a kid I tasted the food."

Ms. Rosenzweig's dishes often have a Jewish feeling to them. "I am always tasting dishes in my head before I try them," she said. Some of them, such as her roast chicken with latkes, quail with sautéed cabbage and kasha, or fresh mustard crisped salmon cakes with tomatoes and herbs, remind her of her grandmother.

Salmon cakes were a typical Thursday-night dinner specialty in many Jewish homes. When the salmon population decreased, white albacore tuna fish took its place for everyday cooking. Soon tuna fish casseroles replaced canned salmon cakes. One Jewish cookbook of the 1950s called salmon cakes and tuna casserole perfect recipes after a shopping spree! Luckily we are back to fresh. This is a great recipe after any event, even a shopping spree.

Is being a good cook genetic? Chef Anne Rosenzweig's grandmother Anna Resnick (middle) was a cook in the Catskills.

Salmon Cakes, cont.

1 pound fresh Atlantic salmon

2 cups chopped fresh tomato
   (in small dice)

3 whole eggs

1/2 cup finely minced shallots

3 cups fresh bread crumbs
   (preferably from brioche or
   challah)

2 tablespoons Dijon mustard

1/4 cup chopped chives

1/4 cup chopped parsley

Salt and freshly ground pepper
   to taste

1 tablespoon sieved dry
   mustard

1/2 cup vegetable oil

1. Put the salmon in boiling water to cover. Simmer, about 5 minutes, covered, or until it is poached and let turn to room temperature.

2. Remove the salmon from the poaching liquid. Pat dry. Break up into medium pieces.

3. In a large bowl mix the salmon with the tomato, eggs, shallots, 1 cup of bread crumbs, Dijon mustard, chives, and the parsley. Season with salt and pepper.

4. Mix the remaining 2 cups of bread crumbs with the dry mustard. Place in a flat dish. Form the salmon mixture into 8 cakes the size of a hamburger and dust lightly on all sides with the bread crumb mixture.

5. Pour the oil onto a baking sheet, large enough to accommodate the cakes, and heat for a few minutes in a preheated 450-degree oven.

6. Place the cakes on the sheet and bake for 5 to 7 minutes or until golden. Flip and continue to cook for 3 to 5 minutes or until heated through and crispy.

7. Serve with Syrian rice (see page 292) and a green salad.

Yield: 4 portions or 8 cakes (P)

FIVE

בשר

Meat: Cholent, Briskets, and Albondigas

"THE EAST SIDE MEAT RIOTS, THE KOSHER BUTCHER
DOESN'T ROLL IN LUXURY"

Of course, the strike was precipitated by a rise in the price of kosher meat.
Now, kosher meat is generally considered the worst part of the cow, and in
other communities outside of New York, it is the cheapest part of the cow. In
New York, however, where there is a large demand for it, the prices for this
class of meat are far higher than in other cities. In December, chuck steak, as
it is called, was selling around 16 cents a pound, and soup meats and other
kosher meats, proportionately lower. There has been a gradual rise in this
price to the consumer until chuck steak now sells around 20 and 22 cents a
pound, and soup meats around 18 cents a pound. This was a rise in price that
the poor of the East Side and elsewhere, who are compelled to shave their
kosher meat or none at all, could not possibly stand, particularly as the cost
of living has risen in all other directions. The "strike" was inevitable; one has
always occurred when kosher meat rises to such prohibitive figures.

The American Hebrew, April 15, 1910

You could smell the roast all over the house, it had so much garlic in it. A
roast like that, with fresh warm twist, is a delicacy from heaven.

Sholem Aleichem

161

The Jews' "Sunday" Dinner Is Made of Peas Baked in an Oven for Nearly Twenty-four Hours

The Jews' Sunday begins on Friday evening at sunset, after which time no Jew can even light a candle or lamp, or kindle a fire, or cook anything until Saturday night, at the same hour, so that they heat their ovens on Friday; put in their provisions before night, for their next day's meals, and let it stand in the ovens until Saturday noon, when it is taken out, and set on the table, or on the floor, by Moors, whom they contrive to hire for that purpose . . . Their principal and standing Sunday dinner, is called "skanah"; it is made of peas baked in an oven for nearly twenty-four hours, with a quantity of Beeves' marrow bones (having very little meat on them) broken to pieces over them; it is a very luscious and fattening dish and by no means a bad one: this, with a few vegetables, and sometimes a plum-pudding, good bread, and Jews' brandy, distilled from figs and aniseed, and bittered with wormwood, makes up the repast of the Jews who call themselves rich. The poor can only afford "skanah" and barley-bread on their Sunday, and live the rest of the week as they can.

Captain James Riley, *An Authentic Narrative of the Loss of the American Brig* Commerce, 1815

Cholent *pot*

Call it *chamim, cholent, sk'eena,* or *adafina,* this Jewish Sabbath luncheon stew, described above, is one of those dishes that has always distinguished Jewish cooking since at least the fourth century A.D. It was at this time that rabbis, in their written doctrine called the Mishnah, explained how they created *chamim*, a hot food. On late Friday (when it is prohibited to light fires because one must rest on the Sabbath) afternoon the dish was to be covered and put in the hot oven.

When the Jews left the Iberian Peninsula, they brought with them the tradition of these Sabbath stews slowly simmered in embers in the fire. For centuries on Friday mornings they would assemble a combination of fava beans or chick-peas, onions, garlic, and meat, sometimes marrow bones, in a pot with water. The dish was covered with a cloth or a mixture of flour and water to form a crust. It started cooking on Friday before sunset and left to warm all night over coals in a hot oven, which was often sealed with lime to preserve heat. The next day they opened the pot in time for lunch after synagogue.

Every wave of Jewish immigration to the Americas has its own form of *chamim*. In addition, American sailors before Captain James Riley and his crew, enslaved by Barbary pirates, may have brought the dish back with them, substituting native kidney beans for the Old World chick-peas and fava beans, and pork fat for the beef marrow bones, and adding the popular molasses.

Haricot Stew with Beans

This version of *chamim* comes from the nineteenth-century handwritten Gomez family cookbook (see page 8) and is surely one of the oldest recipes for the dish in this country.

6 pounds brisket of beef

2 cloves garlic, peeled and split

Salt to taste

Cayenne pepper to taste

3 tablespoons olive oil

3 onions, peeled and sliced
   thickly

2 cups dried lima, fava,
   kidney, or other beans,
   washed and drained

4 cups water or to cover

1 tablespoon flour

1. Rub the brisket with the garlic, salt, and cayenne pepper. Sear in a heavy casserole in the olive oil.

2. Surround with the garlic, onions, beans, and salt. Add water. Cover and bake in a preheated 250-degree oven for 8 hours.

3. Just before serving, mix the flour with ¼ cup of the gravy, stirring briskly. Then, stirring constantly, pour the paste into the gravy.

Yield: 12 servings (M)

Tip: You can also cook this dish ahead of time, refrigerate overnight, skim off the fat, slice the brisket, and reheat.

Boston Baked Beans and Brisket Jewish Style

An adaptation of *chamim*—showing the American preference for sweetness as opposed to garlic and onions—appeared in numerous Jewish cookbooks at the turn of the century. I make this dish a day ahead, refrigerate it, skim off the fat, and reheat. It is a winter favorite with my family.

1 pound navy or kidney beans

3 pounds brisket of beef

1 sliced onion

1 tablespoon mustard

1 tablespoon salt

¼ cup brown sugar

¼ cup molasses

2 cups boiling water (or to cover)

1. Wash, pick beans over, discard any stones, cover with cold water, and let soak overnight.
2. In the morning drain the beans, put them in a saucepan, and cover with fresh water. Heat slowly and cook just below the boiling point until the skins burst, about a half hour. (This is best determined by taking a few beans on the tip of a spoon and blowing over them; if done, the skins will burst.)
3. When done, drain the beans and put them in a large 6-quart casserole with a lid. Add the brisket of beef and the onion.
4. Mix the mustard, salt, brown sugar, molasses, and water and pour over the beans. Cover and bake slowly in a preheated 225-degree oven for 8 hours, uncovering the casserole the last hour so that the meat and beans will brown.

Yield: 6 to 8 servings (M)

Adafina (Moroccan Style Chamim or Sabbath Stew)

Adafina is similar to a present-day *cocido Madrileño,* served in Spain. Every Jewish cook has his or her own version. Although Moroccan Jews in America serve this for lunch at Rosh Hashanah or the Sabbath, I have made it for dinner parties, placing it in the oven the morning of the day I plan to serve it. This particular recipe started out in Casablanca. I have added my own touches. Serve it with a fresh fruit salad for dessert.

1 cup dried chick-peas

Salt and pepper to taste

¼ teaspoon turmeric

½ teaspoon allspice

1. Soak the chick-peas in water to cover overnight or bring 3 cups water to a boil, add the dried chick-peas, boil for 2 minutes, and let stand 15 minutes.
2. Drain the chick-peas and place on the bottom of a large greased 9-quart or larger casserole with a tight-

1 whole head garlic, broken
into cloves and peeled

1 onion, sliced

1 4-pound top rib of beef, left
whole

MEAT LOAF

1 pound ground beef, lamb,
or veal

Salt and freshly ground pepper
to taste

¼ cup finely chopped onion

1 tablespoon chopped parsley

1 tablespoon honey

1 teaspoon cinnamon

¼ teaspoon ground cloves

2 eggs

3 tablespoons matzah meal
(about)

1 fresh 3-pound beef tongue
(optional)

2 cups rice, uncooked

½ cup vegetable oil

A few threads of saffron

¼ cup sugar

2 tablespoons water

6 to 7 yams or sweet potatoes,
peeled and quartered, or 1
hubbard squash, quartered,
seeds removed, or 2 ruta-
bagas, peeled and quartered

10 to 12 whole small new
potatoes, left whole

4 to 6 dates, pitted

8 eggs in their shells

fitting lid. Sprinkle with salt and pepper and add the turmeric and allspice.

3. Put the garlic cloves, onion, and top rib on top of the chick-peas. Sprinkle again with salt and pepper.

4. To make the meat loaf, mix the ground meat, salt and pepper, onion, parsley, honey, cinnamon, ground cloves, eggs, and matzah meal and form into a loaf. Wrap entirely in aluminum foil and place next to the meat in the casserole.

5. If using tongue, place that in with the rest of the meat.

6. Place the rice in a piece of cheesecloth and close loosely. Place on top of the meat. Pour the oil over the rice.

7. Add water to cover and a dash of saffron. Bring to a boil and simmer, covered, for 1 hour.

8. Mix the sugar and water, place in a saucepan, and cook over low heat, stirring constantly, until the sugar starts to brown. Remove and pour over the meat.

9. Surround the rice with the vegetables, the dates, and the 8 eggs in their shells. Sprinkle again with salt and pepper.

10. Add water up to the top of the vegetables, about three-fourths full. Bring to a boil, cover, and place the *adafina* in a preheated 250-degree oven. Leave to cook slowly overnight or for at least 10 hours. Do not open until ready to serve.

11. You can serve this several ways. Traditionally you would eat the eggs for breakfast, carefully removing them from the pot. Then you would use the broth with the chick-peas as a soup for the first course followed by the *adafina*. Moroccans today in this country would start the meal with salads (see page 276), omitting the soup. To serve the *adafina,* slice the meat and cut the vegetables. Arrange on one large platter, placing the meat in the center surrounded by the vegetables on one side and the rice on the other, or place on several platters in the middle of the table. Decorate with the eggs in their shells.

Yield: 8 to 10 servings (M)

Cholent

Adapted from Sara Brizdle Dickman and Dassi Stern

1 cup mixed dried beans
  (cranberry, kidney, large
  and small navy beans,
  black, and lentils)

2 large onions, chopped, plus 1
  whole onion with skin

¼ cup olive or vegetable oil

3 pounds flanken (short ribs)
  or chuck in one piece

2 tablespoons honey

¾ cup barley

6 potatoes, peeled and left
  whole

2 cloves to ½ head garlic,
  peeled and left whole

2 teaspoons salt

½ teaspoon pepper

2 teaspoons paprika

Water to cover

Neck bones or marrow bones
  (about 1 pound)

1 egg per person (optional)

1. The day before cooking the *cholent,* soak the beans for 6 hours in water to cover. Rinse and drain.
2. Sauté the chopped onions in the oil and brown the meat.
3. Place the honey on the bottom of an 8-quart casserole and heat a few minutes until caramelized. Then add the beans, the barley, potatoes, and meat. Scatter the garlic around the meat. Dissolve the salt, pepper, and paprika in water and pour over, adding water just to cover.
4. Then place the meat bones, whole onion (the skin adds color), and unshelled eggs in the pot. Before Shabbat starts, cover with water and bring to a boil. Then cover with aluminum foil and the lid and simmer for 15 minutes. Remove to a preheated 225-degree oven and cook overnight.
5. In the morning remove the lid and check the water. If the water covers the meat, uncover, and leave for another 2 hours so that the water evaporates to make a thick sauce. If there is no water, you can add a little bit.
6. Serve each ingredient separately on serving plates or on a very large platter with the ingredients separated.

Yield: at least 10 servings (M)
Variations:

Alsatian Cholent: Use lima beans instead of other beans.
Vegetarian Cholent: Omit the meat and add a 15-ounce can of tomatoes.
Indian Vegetarian Cholent: Omit the canned tomatoes and add 2 teaspoons each cumin, tarragon, and turmeric and ½ teaspoon each ground ginger, cinnamon, and curry powder.
General tips: Be adventuresome with this recipe. Use as many different kinds of beans as you want. You can add chestnuts, prunes, sausage, even more bones. If your children have tastes like mine, add more potatoes and reduce

*the number of beans. Never stir the **cholent**, something
you cannot do on the Sabbath anyway. Eat slowly, with
light red wine, beer, or schnapps. Serve with sour pickles,
a large green salad, and a compote for dessert.*
Eli Zabar's tip: Use just white breast meat in the soup.
*Jean-Louis Palladin's Southwest French Cholent: Use white
beans with smoked duck or goose breast as well as kosher
sausages and, if you can make it, add duck confit.*

A Cholent Burn-off in Cleveland

At the turn of the century on New York's Lower East Side, young Jewish boys took
their mother's freshly assembled *cholent* to a nearby bakery to be cooked overnight
if their own oven was too small. Each Friday, Meyer Lansky's mother would give
him a nickel to pay the baker for this task. His route went by Delancey Street,
where crap games were being played. When he was about twelve, he decided to

*Orchard Street on New York's
Lower East Side, 1898*

toss in his mother's nickel and play the game. He lost and returned with an uncooked *cholent* for the Sabbath. The next week he played again and won. He returned with a cooked *cholent*—and began his gambling career.

Fortunately, there are not too many stories like Meyer Lansky's. However, *cholent* is enjoying a rebirth, not only for the religious but for the non-religious as well. Sara Brizdle Dickman of Cleveland, Ohio, makes this Jewish soul food on Saturday throughout the winter as well as for birthdays. "In the Orthodox community," she said, "*cholent* is an easy, inexpensive, and halachically correct (follows the Jewish law that you cannot cook on the Sabbath) dish. When you walk in from synagogue you've got ten guests with you anxious to celebrate the joyous Sabbath meal, and you want something warm. What else can you serve? You just take the *cholent* out of the oven and bring it to the table and it's there."

"In Cleveland," continued Mrs. Dickman, "there are so many kinds of *cholent* that we should have a *cholent* burn-off like they have rib burn-offs." Mrs. Dickman's *cholent* recipe—like many others—has a long history. She got it from a friend in Buffalo, New York, whose ancestors came from Bialystok. And, like every Jewish cook, she has added her own imprint.

Today there are *cholent* purists who think that only meat, onions, and beans will do. Others make chicken *cholents*, vegetarian *cholents*, Crock-Pot ones, and *cholents* with Indian spices in them. Both *salsa* and ketchup have been added as flavorings, and leftovers are great for tortilla fillings! In some areas that are heavily populated with Orthodox Jews, local kosher supermarkets try to offer a *cholent* meat special every Friday.

Cholent is also a midwinter excuse for a secular party. Recently we received a phone call to come for lunch one Sunday. "I feel like making *cholent*," my friend said. The *cholent* was an easy centerpiece for a spontaneous gathering of about fifteen friends.

Chili *(or Cholent)*

When Chaim Reisner decided to become kosher, he refused to give up his palate for good food. Today, he treats cooking kosher as a positive challenge. One of his favorite events is the annual Jewish Renaissance Festival in Morristown, New Jersey, sponsored by the Rabbinical College of America. There he makes his vegetarian and non-vegetarian chili for four hundred people. He tells his takers that he also uses leftover chili as *cholent* for the Sabbath, keeping it warm overnight. After all, what is *cholent* anyway—a mixture of beans, meat, and onions. Add some tomatoes and spices and you have chili.

¼ cup vegetable oil

1 pound ground beef

1 cup onion, chopped

¼ cup chopped jalapeño
   peppers (optional)

1 tablespoon cinnamon

1 tablespoon oregano

1 tablespoon cumin

3 tablespoons chili powder

½ cup fresh or 2 to 3
   tablespoons dried dill, basil,
   or chopped parsley

¼ cup chopped fresh garlic

3 cups tomato sauce

3 cups water

2 cups freshly cooked kidney
   beans or 2 15-ounce cans of
   red kidney beans, drained
   and rinsed

4 to 6 small potatoes, peeled
   (optional)

2 tablespoons red-wine vinegar

Salt and freshly ground pepper
   to taste

1 cup fresh mushrooms,
   quartered

1. Heat 2 tablespoons of the oil in a frying pan. Break up the beef, brown, and drain off the oil.

2. In a stockpot heat the remaining 2 tablespoons of oil. Add the onion, optional peppers, spices, and the garlic. Cook over a medium heat for 3 minutes.

3. Add the beef, tomato sauce, water, beans, potatoes, vinegar, and salt and pepper. Simmer, partially covered, for 45 minutes. Add the mushrooms, continue cooking for another 10 minutes, and serve.

Yield: 4 to 6 servings (M)

Note: You can also treat this as **cholent,** *and put it in a* **Crock-Pot.** *Simmer on a stove for 15 minutes. Leave it on low, adding more water if needed. Mr. Reisner sometimes adds matzah balls or gnocchi to his chili-***cholent.**

Aunt Babette's Fleisch (Meat) Kugel

How different meat loaf sounds from *fleisch kugel* (meat pudding)! And yet, a Jewish meat loaf evolved from a Central and Eastern European Jewish *kugel*. *Kugel*, meaning pudding, is the Sabbath "extra" food that goes along with a stew or *cholent*, sometimes sitting alongside it in the oven, warming overnight. *Kugels* can be made from bread crumbs and flour, potatoes, vegetables, noodles, and other ingredients. Today the typical potato (see page 244) or noodle *kugel* (see page 281) is cooked in a separate casserole from the main meat dish. Sometimes, as in the *Jewish Encyclopedia* of 1903, *kugel* meant the Sabbath meat stew itself. The following meat *kugel* comes from *Aunt Babette's Cook Book*.

Aunt Babette's Recipe

2 pounds of beef, chopped extremely fine (the round is best); have half a pound of suet chopped with it and get your butcher to chop two onions in with the meat, as it will be mixed better. Season with salt, pepper, and half a loaf of grated stale bread half soaked in water and then pressed well and dried in hot fat before adding to the meat. Break in two eggs and mix thoroughly then mold into a huge ball and put into a deep iron *kugel* form or spider that has been well greased and heated before putting in the *kugel*. Dip a spoon in cold water to smooth the top of the *kugel*, put flakes of fat on the top, and bake about two hours, basting often.

My Mother's Meat Loaf

My mother's Jewish-American meat loaf came two generations after Aunt Babette's *kugel*. This was a weekly standard in our house.

1 onion, diced

½ green pepper, diced

1 stalk celery, diced

1 tablespoon vegetable oil

1½ pounds ground beef

½ pound ground veal

½ cup matzah meal, or a slice of challah soaked in water and drained

2 large eggs

1 tablespoon ketchup

1 teaspoon Worcestershire sauce

Salt and freshly ground pepper to taste

2 hard-boiled eggs, shelled (optional)

1 8-ounce can of tomato sauce

1. Sauté the onion, green pepper, and celery in the oil until the vegetables are soft. Drain and mix with the meats, matzah meal or challah, eggs, ketchup, Worcestershire sauce, and salt and pepper. Work well with your hands.

2. Form the meat into a long rectangular loaf, placing the hard-boiled eggs in the middle and put in a loaf pan or shallow casserole, large enough to hold the loaf comfortably. Cover and let sit in the refrigerator several hours.

3. Bake in a preheated 350-degree oven for 1 hour. After 45 minutes, pour off the accumulated fat and cover with the tomato sauce and continue baking 15 minutes more.

Yield: 6 servings (M)

Albondigas, Olmendigas—Meatballs by Any Other Name

Gershom Mendes Seixas, the American patriot and *chazzan* or spiritual leader of the Shearith Israel Synagogue in New York City during the Revolution, closed the synagogue rather than worship under British rule. He rescued the Torah and carried it in his arms to Philadelphia. Eventually, after organizing Mikveh Israel Synagogue there, he returned to New York.

This Revolutionary lay rabbi certainly liked to cook and eat rich food, and he suffered from gout. He had the odd habit of shelling peas while listening to boys prepare their bar mitzvah portions. His letters to his children were chatty missives full of notations about food.

"On my way home supplied myself with some turnips, potatoes, 2 cabbages, celery, beets, thyme, parsley, etc. and one half peck of apples for the children," he wrote. "Ma's own cookery, in addition a large bread fritter as large as a plate with Madeira sauce . . . nothin but alibut and asparagus for dinner and some stew and olmendigas for Shabbas. . . ." He continued, however, with "good appetite."

The *olmendigas* were meatballs, known as *albondigas* in Spanish and Sephardic cookbooks. Non-Jewish versions are usually larger and often made with pork. Old recipes call for a tamarind vinegar sauce, sometimes a pomegranate sauce as in the Persian *fesenjan*, or a Syrian lemon sauce with a cream of rice filling. All predate the more popular tomato sauces, which came to Europe after Columbus.

Albondigas *(Meatballs)*

The following recipe is a modern way to make an old dish. Before the use of tomato sauce, water, vinegar, and flour would have been mixed together to create a sauce.

1 pound ground beef

1 large egg

3 tablespoons matzah meal

2 tablespoons pine nuts

Salt and freshly ground pepper to taste

4 cloves finely chopped garlic

1. Mix together the meat, egg, matzah meal, pine nuts, salt, pepper, half the garlic, half the parsley, and the cumin. Form into meatballs the size of a walnut. Heat the olive oil in a large, heavy skillet and brown the meatballs on all sides. Set aside.

2. Remove all but 2 tablespoons of the fat. Sauté the onion and remaining 2 cloves garlic in the oil until the onions are golden. Add the tomatoes with their juice, cinnamon, honey, and salt and pepper to taste. Simmer,

¼ cup chopped parsley

½ teaspoon cumin

2 tablespoons olive oil

1 small onion, finely chopped

2 cups canned plum tomatoes

½ teaspoon cinnamon

1 tablespoon honey

½ cup water

uncovered, for about 15 minutes or until the tomatoes reduce to a sauce. Add the water and the meatballs and simmer over low heat, covered, for 30 minutes. Sprinkle with the remaining chopped parsley before serving.

Yield: about 20 meatballs (M)

My Mother's Sweet And Sour Meatballs

"Koteletten oder hamburger" appears in a cookbook entitled *Ler-bukh vi azoy tsu kokhn un bakhn* (Manual for how to cook and bake) of 1901. This cookbook, written by Hinde Amchanitzki in Yiddish or (better) "Yenglish" for the immigrant, includes American words transcribed in Hebrew characters. "Buckwheats," "Strawberry Short Cake," "French compote," "Lemon Pie," and "Cheese Cake" all show that this woman was born in Eastern Europe but lived many years in New York. In the introduction she claims that "the best guarantee for good cooking are the long years I ran a restaurant for customers' bad stomachs (dyspepsia and other stomach ailments) and everybody was happy with my cooking." Her recipes came from Russia, Galicia, Hungary, France, and America.

Although my mother did not grow up on the Lower East Side, her parents did. Who knows? Perhaps they ate *koteletten* in Mrs. Amchanitzki's restaurant. But, by the time my mother learned to cook, she had already become Americanized enough to give us straight hamburgers rather than *koteletten* or a more "gourmetized" sweet and sour meatballs, a Jewish standard of the fifties and sixties.

1 pound lean ground beef

⅓ cup matzah meal

½ grated onion

1 large egg

Salt and freshly ground pepper to taste

1 28-ounce can tomato puree

1 ten-ounce jar chili sauce

¼ cup brown sugar or to taste

Juice of 1 lemon

1. Mix the ground meat in a bowl with the matzah meal, onion, egg, and salt and pepper. Roll about a tablespoon of meat mixture into small balls and set aside.
2. Combine the tomato puree, chili sauce, brown sugar, and lemon juice in a heavy saucepan. Adjust seasonings. Bring to a boil and simmer, then gently add the meatballs, one at a time. Simmer, covered, about 20 minutes.
3. Serve with toothpicks in a chafing dish or pass the meatballs on a plate with a bowl for dipping.

Yield: about 40 meatballs, serving 8 to 10 as an hors d'oeuvre (M)

Kibbe Hamda (Syrian Stuffed Meatballs with Lemony Vegetable Stew)

If you like lemony tasting dishes, you'll love these meatballs, shared by Sarina Roffe of the Brooklyn Syrian community. They are delicate and delicious. Serve them with Syrian rice on page 292.

MEATBALLS

¾ pound very lean ground beef
  or lamb

⅓ cup ground rice or cream
  of rice

2½ teaspoons kosher salt

2 tablespoons chopped celery
  leaves

½ teaspoon allspice

3 tablespoons vegetable oil

VEGETABLE STEW

1½ quarts water

1 large potato

2 stalks diced celery

2 carrots, peeled and diced

6 cloves garlic, peeled and
  crushed

1 tablespoon coarse kosher salt

Juice of 1½ lemons or more

½ teaspoon sugar

1 tablespoon crushed dried
  mint leaves

1. Grind twice in a meat grinder ½ pound of the ground beef, rice, and 1½ teaspoons of the salt or process for about 2 minutes in a food processor.

2. To make the filling, mix the remaining ground beef, teaspoon salt, celery leaves, and allspice.

3. Place the vegetable oil in a small bowl.

4. Roll the twice-ground meat mixture into 1-inch round balls. Dip your finger into the oil and then hollow out each ball with your finger. Put ½ teaspoon of the meat filling into the hollow and close the opening. Continue until all are done and then refrigerate or freeze.

5. To make the stew bring the water to a boil in a heavy pot with a cover. Peel the potato, cube, and add with the celery and carrots and simmer for about 20 minutes. Add the crushed garlic and the kosher salt, lemon juice, sugar, and the mint leaves. Simmer, covered, for another 20 minutes. Before serving, bring to a boil and add the kibbe to the pot. Boil another 10 minutes. Taste the sauce. It should have a lemon flavor—you may need to add 2 more tablespoons of lemon juice. Syrian Jews like this thin soupy sauce over rice; it is usually placed in a bowl on the table and everyone ladles some on.

Yield: 6 to 8 servings (M)

Sarina Roffe's Edja *(Syrian Hamburgers)*

These thin hamburger-omelets with vegetables are great stuffed in pita with lettuce, diced cucumber, and tomato and served American style with ketchup or mayonnaise, or Middle Eastern style with hot sauce. Freeze any leftovers for last-minute dinners.

½ pound ground beef

½ onion, finely chopped

1 stalk celery, finely chopped

2 tablespoons finely chopped
*   parsley leaves*

1 to 2 tablespoons matzah meal

½ tablespoon kosher salt

6 large eggs

¼ teaspoon pepper

½ teaspoon allspice

Vegetable oil for frying

Pita bread

Lettuce, cucumber, and tomato
*   for stuffing*

1. In a large bowl mix the meat, onion, celery, parsley, matzah meal, salt, eggs, pepper, and allspice. The mixture will be runny.

2. Pour enough oil into a 6-inch skillet to cover the bottom and heat to medium. Using a serving spoon, pour the meat mixture by spoonfuls into the skillet and form round, thin patties about 3 to 4 inches in diameter. When the edges are browned, turn over with a metal spatula. Cook on the other side and drain on brown paper.

3. At this point the patties can be cooled and frozen or eaten wedged inside one half pita with sliced lettuce, cucumber, tomato and spiced with mayonnaise, ketchup, or *zhug* hot sauce (see page 127).

Yield: about 15 patties (M)

My Favorite Brisket *(Not Too Gedempte Fleysch)*

Gedempte Fleysch—well-stewed—that's how Eastern European Jews prefer their meat. Slow cooking, of course, became a practical necessity with grainy cuts of forequarter meat.

Because a brisket stretched into many meals, it was an economical cut for large families in Europe. Leftovers were ground up to stuff knishes or kreplach. The meaty gravy became the base for a midweek cabbage or potato soup or a sauce to cover *pompushki*, Ukrainian baked dumplings, which resemble Pepperidge Farm's rolls. In this country it became particularly popular.

Brisket comes from the front quarters of the steer, the chest area. The whole piece of meat, from three to ten pounds, is potted (hence the term pot roast) and cooked slowly by braising in liquid. It should be covered and simmered in a 325-degree oven for several hours. Brisket needs to be simmered slowly to transform it into the succulent morsels I remember as a child. It is a dish I serve frequently—on Friday night, at holidays, and at dinner parties.

Brisket, cont.

2 teaspoons salt

Freshly ground pepper to taste

1 5-pound brisket of beef,
*   shoulder roast of beef, chuck*
*   roast, or end of steak*

1 garlic clove, peeled

2 tablespoons vegetable oil

3 onions, peeled and diced

1 10-ounce can tomatoes

2 cups red wine

2 stalks celery with the leaves,
*   chopped*

1 bay leaf

1 sprig fresh thyme

1 sprig fresh rosemary

¼ cup chopped parsley

6 to 8 carrots, peeled and
*   sliced on the diagonal*

1. Sprinkle the salt and pepper over the brisket and rub with the garlic. Sear the brisket in the oil and then place, fat side up, on top of the onions in a large casserole. Cover with the tomatoes, red wine, celery, bay leaf, thyme, and rosemary.

2. Cover and bake in a preheated 325-degree oven for about 3 hours, basting often with pan juices.

3. Add the parsley and carrots and bake, uncovered, for 30 minutes more or until the carrots are cooked. To test for doneness, stick a fork in the flat (thinner or leaner end of the brisket). When there is a light pull on the fork as it is removed from the meat, it is "fork tender."

4. This dish is best prepared in advance and refrigerated so that the fat can be easily skimmed from the surface of the gravy. Trim off all the visible fat from the cold brisket. Then place the brisket, on what was the fat side down, on a cutting board. Look for the grain—that is, the muscle lines of the brisket—and with a sharp knife, cut across the grain.

5. When ready to serve, reheat the gravy.

6. Put the sliced brisket in a roasting pan. Pour the hot gravy on the meat, cover, and reheat in a preheated 350-degree oven for 45 minutes. Some people like to strain the gravy, but I prefer to keep the onions because they are so delicious.

   Serve with farfel (boiled egg barley noodles), noodle *kugel* (see page 281), or potato pancakes. A colorful winter salad goes well with this.

Yield: 8 to 10 servings (M)
Tip: Try adding a jar of sun-dried tomatoes to the canned tomatoes. They add a more intense flavor to the brisket.

Coca-Cola Is the Secret Ingredient for Cleveland's Mr. Brisket

The quintessential brisket maven is Cleveland Heights' Mr. Brisket. Sanford Herskovitz, who is six feet four inches tall and weighs 270 pounds, can usually be found, telephone in hand and Cleveland Browns hat on head, at the front of the store taking telephone orders.

When he was a Ph.D. candidate in clinical psychology at Case Western Reserve University, Mr. Herskovitz earned money delivering meat to restaurants. Now a meat purveyor, he sends his fabled brisket to private customers and carefully selected better restaurants.

The fatter side is the "point"; the leaner side the "flat." When brisket is roasting, the point should be up; when reheating the point should be down. "Use a choice, whole brisket, at least eight to ten pounds," advises Mr. Herskovitz. "Prime is too fat. Never use only the first cut, because the butcher separates the point and flat, making the meat too dry. You can always refrigerate, defat, and reheat the meat."

Mr. Brisket's favorite recipe includes brisket with chili sauce, an envelope of onion-soup mix and a can of sugar-laden Coca-Cola! "The sugar, caramel color, and the Coke make a sweet sauce," he tells his customers. By the way, Coca-Cola was one of the earliest products to be made kosher in this country, having been tested in 1931. But like most Jewish decisions there was some disagreement on its kashrut. It was retested. By 1935 it was declared kosher during the year and for Passover and has been so ever since. So why not put it in your next brisket!

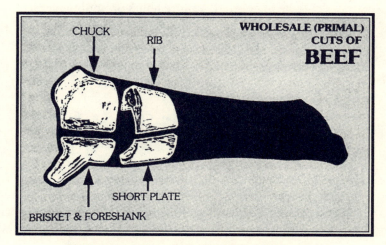

Kosher cuts of meat commonly used in America

Texas Barbecue Brisket as Served to Lyndon Johnson

Typical of many nineteenth-century Texas Jewish families were the Marcuses of Dallas who together with the Neimans founded Neiman-Marcus. The Marcus family came to Dallas from Königsberg, Prussia, via Kentucky. Even though they were assimilated in Texas, some of their Jewish culinary traditions endured. Stanley Marcus, now in his late eighties, whose father along with his sister and brother-in-law started Neiman-Marcus, grew up on Texas steak, fried chicken, and barbecue.

When Mr. Marcus went on buying trips East he always gravitated to the kosher delis in the garment and fur districts. "I learned about the Eastern European Jewish food my grandmother made in New York," said Mr. Marcus. "I used to eat in kosher dairy luncheon places and in some Rumanian restaurants on the Lower East Side like Moscowitz and Leibowitz. All I remember is they had goose fat on the table and bicarbonate of soda. I remember boiled beef and corned beef. I started investigating and found there were 19 different cuts of brisket. Until then I thought a brisket was one place on the cow. I love it."

One of his favorite ways of eating brisket is Texas style as prepared by his daughter Wendy Marcus Raymont. Not only does her father like her version, but one Texas barbecue maven, the late President Lyndon Johnson, raved about it at a dinner at Wendy's home.

1 5-pound brisket of beef

*1 teaspoon salt and freshly
    ground pepper to taste*

1 large chopped onion

2 stalks celery

1 cup chili sauce

1 cup water

¼ cup chopped parsley

1 10-ounce bottle beer

1. Remove most of the fat from the brisket and wash and dry. Sprinkle with salt and pepper.
2. Place the meat, fat side up, in a heavy casserole and cover with the onion, celery, chili sauce, water, and parsley. Bake, uncovered, in a preheated 325-degree oven for 1 hour. Pour the beer over the beef and bake, covered, 3 more hours or until tender.
3. Cool to room temperature, refrigerate, skim off the fat, slice and reheat in the sauce.

Yield: 10 servings (M)

Kansas City Barbecued Brisket

This recipe, which comes from Marsha Pinson, is similar to the only two briskets mentioned in *The Cook Book*, published by The National Council of Jewish Women, in her native Kansas. Braised brisket was one of those dishes that became Americanized early on. Not only were processed ingredients like ketchup and chili sauce added but the liquid the meat was cooked in varied according to the region. In New England the liquid was cider rather than water, in the South smoky barbecue flavors were introduced, and in California corn, peppers, and tomatoes were added. The following barbecued brisket includes liquid smoke as well as a whole bottle of ketchup. The sauce is very American, guaranteed to satisfy barbecue lovers.

1 5- to 6-pound brisket of beef

¼ cup liquid smoke

3 medium chopped onions

1 garlic clove, peeled and
*   halved*

Salt and freshly ground pepper
*   to taste*

3 tablespoons brown sugar

1 16-ounce bottle ketchup

½ cup water

2 tablespoons Worcestershire
*   sauce*

1 tablespoon dry mustard or
*   1½ tablespoons Dijon*
*   mustard*

2 teaspoons celery seasoning
*   (optional)*

6 tablespoons pareve
*   margarine*

1. Wash and dry the brisket and sprinkle with 2 tablespoons of the liquid smoke. Wrap in heavy duty aluminum foil and marinate overnight.

2. The next day open the foil, sprinkle on the chopped onions, garlic, and pepper. Rewrap everything in the foil and bake in a preheated 325-degree oven for 5 hours.

3. Meanwhile combine the remaining 2 tablespoons liquid smoke, the brown sugar, ketchup, water, Worcestershire sauce, mustard, celery seasoning, margarine, and salt and pepper. Simmer, uncovered, for about 30 minutes.

4. Remove the foil, slice the brisket thinly, and pour the sauce over all. Raise the oven to 350 degrees and reheat, covered, for 30 minutes.

Yield: 10 servings (M)

Kansas City family celebrating
Hanukkah

Moroccan Brisket with Olives

> If you don't eat meat for the Sabbath, it's like you're sitting shiva.
> An old Moroccan Jewish saying

In Morocco, this dish would be made with lamb, but immigrants to this country have started using brisket, cooking it like roast lamb. Ordinarily, Moroccan Jews will make a *tagine,* a stew with cut-up lamb, rather than a whole beef brisket.

1 5- to 6-pound brisket of beef

Salt and freshly ground pepper to taste

2 cloves garlic, peeled and halved

¼ cup olive oil

¼ teaspoon turmeric or a few strands of saffron

1 teaspoon fresh grated ginger

2 large Spanish onions, diced

¼ cup chopped celery with leaves

1 small carrot, peeled and sliced in paper-thin rounds

2 large fresh tomatoes, peeled and diced, or a 1-pound can of stewed tomatoes

1 pound green olives*

½ cup water (if needed)

Juice of 1 lemon

*Obtainable at Greek specialty stores

1. Sprinkle the brisket with salt and pepper and rub in the garlic. Sear the meat on all sides in a little bit of the olive oil in a heavy roasting pan with a cover. Remove.

2. To the same pan, add the remaining olive oil, turmeric or saffron, and ginger and sauté the onions until limp. Then add the celery and carrots and sauté a few minutes more. Add the tomatoes and mix. Remove a third of the onion mixture and place the brisket in the onions in the pan. Cover with the remaining onions and bake, covered, in a preheated 350-degree oven for about 3 hours or until the fork goes in and out easily. Remove and refrigerate.

3. Meanwhile, pit the olives. Put them in a pot, cover with water, and boil a minute or two. Drain the olives and cover again with water. Drain again. (This is done to remove some of the saltiness.)

4. Take the brisket out of the refrigerator, remove any fat that has congealed, and slice against the grain. Return to the heavy pan with the reserved onion mixture. Add the olives and sprinkle over the sliced brisket. Add water and lemon. Reheat in a 350-degree oven for a half hour and serve.

Yield: 10 to 12 servings (M)

Brisket in Tahina Sauce—An Israeli-American Dish

After eating a brisket in coconut milk in a Malay restaurant in New York, Israeli-born Dalia Carmel thought of the idea of creating a Middle Eastern–style brisket. "It is a way to tie in the real Jewish cuisine with its geographical locale and cook it with tahina as Arabs do ground beef with tahina in Haifa," said Ms. Carmel, an avid cookbook collector; she is also, as her husband calls her, a "freelance free food consultant."

1 package onion-soup mix

1 cup pineapple juice

1 cup beef broth

1 cup tahina

2 cloves garlic, mashed

Salt and freshly ground pepper
  to taste

½ cup lemon juice

¼ cup water

1 4-pound brisket of beef

1 large onion, finely sliced

1. Mix the onion-soup mix, the pineapple juice, the beef broth, tahina, garlic, salt, pepper, lemon juice, and water.
2. Trim the brisket of most of the fat. Place in a shallow baking pan with a cover and rub with the onion-tahina mixture, making sure that there is at least 2 inches of liquid beneath the meat. If not enough, add more water.
3. Scatter the sliced onions on top.
4. Bake, covered in foil, in a preheated 350-degree oven for 2 to 3 hours or until the meat is fork tender. If too dry after an hour, add broth or pineapple juice.
5. When done, remove the meat from the sauce and cool. Refrigerate the sauce so that the fat can be removed. Slice the meat and place in a pan. Cover with the sauce. If it is too thick, blend in again some pineapple juice or water to thin it out. Cover and reheat in a preheated 350-degree oven for 30 to 35 minutes and serve.

Yield: 8 to 10 servings (M)

Lenard Rubin's Southwestern Blackened and Braised Brisket of Beef

As a child in Bethel, Connecticut, Lenard Rubin grew up eating typical Eastern European Jewish food. Then he worked as a chef at the Phoenician Resort in Scottsdale, Arizona, where he became accustomed to Southwestern chili-based cuisine. There he rethought traditional foods. "A lot of the Jewish food is straightforward, basic good food," he said. "But as people's tastes become more creative and demanding, you have to add a little more excitement to the dishes." His brisket is encrusted with fourteen different spices. "I didn't see Jewish food very much in Arizona," Mr. Rubin said. "Now that I cook, I would like to experiment and integrate these dishes with the kind of cuisine I specialize in and like to cook." Soon he may go back to his cooking roots as he is working as a chef in St. Petersburg, Russia.

¼ cup vegetable oil

1 6-pound brisket of beef (trimmed of fat)

¼ cup Southwestern seasoning blend*

3 medium onions, chopped

2 large carrots, chopped

2 stalks celery, chopped

3 cloves garlic, chopped

2 bay leaves

6 cups chicken stock (or use enough to cover)

1 tablespoon pareve margarine at room temperature

*Mr. Rubin uses a combination of spices that you can mix yourself— ginger, cayenne pepper, cinnamon, cardamom, thyme, garlic powder, onion powder, paprika, coarsely ground black pepper, cumin, kosher salt, basil, oregano, white pepper, and chili powder, using more chili powder and cumin than the others.

1. Heat the vegetable oil in a 6-quart pan or dutch oven.
2. Coat one side of the beef with half the seasoning blend, patting down well. Place the beef in hot oil and cook until brown and crispy on the first side. Put the remaining half of the seasoning on the other side. Then turn over and cook until brown on the other side. This process will take several minutes on each side. Remove from the pan.
3. Add the onions, carrots, and celery to the pan and cook until the onions are golden brown. Add the garlic and cook for one minute. Add the bay leaves, brisket, and chicken stock.
4. Cover with a tight-fitting lid and turn down the heat to a simmer. Cook until very tender (about 2½ to 3 hours).
5. Remove the beef from the pan and set aside. Skim any excess fat from the surface and strain the remaining liquid. An easy way to do this is to make the brisket a day in advance. Refrigerate and then remove the congealed fat. Slice. Reduce the sauce to about half its original volume. Slowly whisk in the slightly softened margarine. Season with salt and pepper to taste. Return the brisket to the pan and reheat.

Yield: 10 to 12 servings (M)

Jim Cohen's Sephardic Brisket

2 dried pasilla *chiles*

I 4-pound brisket

Salt and freshly ground pepper
  to taste

Flour for dredging

¼ cup olive oil

2 onions, diced

2 tablespoons fresh ginger,
  chopped

I cup orange juice

4 cups chicken or beef stock or
  water

I cinnamon stick

I bay leaf

I teaspoon peppercorns

4 tea bags of strong black tea

2 cups dried pitted prunes

2 cups dried apricots

1. Soak the peppers in lukewarm water for 30 minutes. Seed, remove the stems, and chop into tiny pieces.

2. Season the brisket with the salt and pepper and dredge with flour. Heat the olive oil in a large heavy roasting pan and brown the brisket on all sides. Remove from the pan.

3. Preheat the oven to 400 degrees.

4. In the same pan, over medium heat, sauté the onions and ginger until the onions are transparent. Add the pepper and deglaze with the orange juice. Reduce for a few minutes. Add the brisket and enough stock or water to cover. Add the cinnamon stick, bay leaf, and pepper-corns. Cook, uncovered, until the brisket is tender, about 3 hours, turning at 30-minute intervals. Remove the cinnamon stick and bay leaf. Puree the sauce in a food processor or blender.

5. Cool and refrigerate a few hours or overnight. Remove the congealed fat that floats on the top of the liquid.

6. About 30 minutes before serving, bring 4 cups water to a boil. Steep the tea bags in the water to make a strong tea. Discard the tea bags. Put the prunes and apricots in the tea to plump for about half an hour. Then drain them. Reheat with the brisket and the plumped fruit. Serve with saffron rice, mashed potatoes, or cous-cous.

Yield: 8 servings (M)

Delicatessens, The Jewish Eating Experience in America

The first delicatessens here had a strong German accent, and their eats were confined to various kinds of kuchen, kraut, kase, fisch, brot, wurst, und so weiter. . . . Within the memory of man, their very name was exotic. To visit them and breathe their unfamiliar good odors had the tang of an adventure in foreign parts. New Yorkers used to do it just for the thrill. Modest little shops they were, family enterprises, mainly. When you opened the door a bell tinkled somewhere in the room and someone who said "Ja?" came forward to wait on you. Behind the scene in quarters half domestic, half industrial, most of the good things on the shelves front were prepared after recipes and, the homelike manner, handed down in the old country from generation to generation of hausfrau.

The New York Times Magazine, August 15, 1937

Until the late nineteenth century, delicatessens were primarily run by Germans and Alsatians in this country. The word itself derives from German and means delicacies, but is used not only to describe a shop, but also is the word for the products sold in a shop. Eventually Jews, too, went into the business.

"My father opened Reuben's as a delicatessen in 1915 on Broadway and Seventy-third Street," said Arnold Reuben, Jr. "Then we went into the restaurant business in 1920 on Broadway and Eighty-second. We had a restaurant open twenty-four hours a day. By 1918 my father started making big sandwiches. One day a famous actress came in and asked for a big sandwich. He took turkey, ham, Swiss cheese, coleslaw and Russian dressing—which later became the Reuben's special sandwich." Or, as a restaurant guide in 1929 told the story, "Reuben's restaurant (the advertisements will tell you it grew from a sandwich to an institution) laid its foundation the night that Arnold Reuben, proprietor of a tiny uptown delicatessen store, got a telephone order to deliver half-a-dozen pastrami sandwiches to an after-theater party! That gave him an idea. He took off his white apron, came around in front of his delicatessen counter, carted a dozen cases of canned goods into a back room, and set up two lonesome little tables." The Reuben's Sandwich came later. "Our German chef in 1929, when we opened our second restaurant on Madison and Fifty-ninth Street, made it for me because I only ate hamburgers while I was managing the restaurant," said Mr. Reuben, eighty-five. "It was corned beef, toasted on very black Russian pumpernickel with sauerkraut and imported melted Swiss cheese. We never put it on the menu, just sold it to friends and customers. When we got into the restaurant business we started naming sandwiches after actors. We had every kind. Al Jolson, Eddie Cantor, you name them."

Delis were especially attractive for the observant as the stores were open on Sundays, selling canned and packaged goods, often duplicating the services of grocery stores.

More than anything else the delicatessen became the "Jewish eating experience" in this country. "A deli was a little restaurant with a counter, a few stools and smoked beef, pastrami, frankfurters, potato knishes, rye bread, club bread, mustard, and pickles," recalled Norman Podhoretz, editor of *Commentary Magazine,* who grew up in Brownsville, Brooklyn. "Then they branched out and began serving other things including fish as well as bagels, bialys, rye bread, corn bread and dark pumpernickel. Every deli had a 'special.' It was a big, fat knockwurst with beans or fried potatoes. There aren't many of that kind of deli left." In these delis

during World War II, signs appeared like "a nickel a shtickel" for the ends of salami or garlic wurst, or, "Have a Nosh—10 cents."

As Jews became more affluent, two distinct types of delicatessens emerged. "An offshoot of the kosher restaurant is the kosher delicatessen and lunchroom, of which there must be many hundreds in Greater New York," wrote Montague Glass in the *Saturday Evening Post* in 1929. "If you take a glance into the plate-glass window you will see such a display of food, tastefully decorated with strips of vari-colored paper, as Rabelais might have catalogued for one of Gargantua's heartier meals." These kosher delis have always closed on the Sabbath and serve strictly meat meals.

The other type of delicatessen that emerged as Jews became assimilated and moved uptown or to Brooklyn or suburbia was the carry-out or "kosher style" deli. It looked and smelled like a kosher delicatessen, but coffee was served with cream. The overstuffed pastrami and corned beef sandwiches were followed by a piece of New York cheesecake. The three-decker rye-bread sandwich, made famous at Reuben's Restaurant in New York, is a takeoff on the ordinary three-decker American club sandwich. The American three-layer club is served with a toothpick; at the Jewish deli the all-meat-three-decker is served with a knife and fork. Meals in this kind of deli are mockingly called "glatt treif," because they are "very unkosher." But the "Jewish" understated atmosphere often exists with Cel-Ray tonic, Formica tables, and surly waiters. And as far as I am concerned a good deli has at least three or four pages of printed menu containing comments such as "Delicious home cooked meals, kosher-style, like mother used to make."

The quintessential Jewish "kosher style" delicatessen today is the Carnegie on Fifty-fifth and Seventh Avenue in New York, as seen in *Broadway Danny Rose*. It was here that my grandfather took me as a child, and it was here that the deli became known nationwide when *New York* magazine rated its pastrami number one in New York in 1975.

Eight years later, in 1983, when American food was showcased at the Reagan Administration's Williamsburg Summit, Leo Steiner, the late owner, brought the Carnegie's overstuffed sandwiches to the Colonial capital. Here deli food made its national debut along with the desserts of Maida Heatter and the entrees of superstar chefs Wolfgang Puck and Paul Prudhomme. The Carnegie, as noisy as a deli can possibly be, greets each customer with its perfume of intermingled smells of pastrami, corned beef, and pickles. In the front window, strings of garlic, bagels, and salamis hang above jars of bright red peppers. Everything is larger than life. Even the noise. Even the matzah balls. Carnegie has all the right ingredients: a deli counter that resembles a war zone, almost a pound of meat per sandwich, hours from 6:30 a.m. to 3:45 a.m., and proximity to Broadway with regulars like Henny Youngman, Warren Beatty, Dustin Hoffman, Burt Lancaster, and Milton Berle dropping in. For forty years until his death, Leo Steiner was the soul of this restaurant. A schmoozer, it was like him to quip after a robbery, "Idiots! They took the money and left the pastrami!"

Unlike many delicatessens today, Carnegie pickles its own corned beef and pastrami in a solution of salt, pureed garlic, allspice, thyme, mustard seed, and coriander. In a downtown commissary it makes its rich cheesecakes. "Nobody comes here for health food and nobody comes here on a diet so forget the calories and be off a diet," said Milton Parker, Leo Steiner's partner and present owner. It is no wonder, then, that Bob Simon, the CBS reporter held captive during the Gulf War, asked for one thing upon his release. "I want a Carnegie Deli corned beef sandwich . . . with a pickle!" And the Carnegie Deli, never missing a beat, sent one to him on the next airplane.

Choucroute à l'Alsacienne (Braised Sauerkraut)

An early deli "special" was *choucroute à l'alsacienne,* a perfect dish for a winter's dinner with friends.

2 pounds sauerkraut

2 carrots, peeled and diced

*2 medium onions, peeled and
    diced*

*¼ cup rendered chicken fat or
    vegetable oil*

¼ cup chopped parsley

1 bay leaf

6 peppercorns

10 juniper berries

1 meat bone (optional)

1 cup dry white wine

2 cups chicken or beef stock

8 new potatoes, peeled

*1 dozen or so mixed sausages,
    such as veal bratwurst,
    frankfurters, etc.*

*1 corned beef (optional) (see
    page 195)*

Parsley for garnish

1. Drain the sauerkraut and soak it in cold water for a half hour, changing the water once. Drain well, squeezing the sauerkraut with your hands.

2. Sauté the carrots and onions in the chicken fat or oil until the onions are golden. Add the sauerkraut, mix well, cover, and simmer slowly for about 15 minutes.

3. Tie the parsley, bay leaf, peppercorns, and juniper berries in a cheesecloth bag and bury in the sauerkraut, along with a meat bone if you have one. Add the wine and enough chicken or beef stock to cover. Bring to a boil on top of the stove, cover, and bake in a 325-degree oven for 1½ to 2 hours or until the liquid is absorbed by the sauerkraut.

4. About a half hour before serving bring the potatoes to a boil in water to cover.

5. About 10 minutes before serving add sausages and slices of corned beef, if using, to the sauerkraut. To serve, drain the potatoes, sprinkle with chopped parsley, and arrange the potatoes, sausages, sauerkraut, and corned beef on a large platter. Serve with lots of different kinds of mustards.

Yield: 6 to 8 servings (M)

Kosher Hot Dogs Answer to a Higher Authority

But our greatest delight in all seasons was "delicatessen"—hot spiced corned beef, pastrami, rolled beef, hard salami, soft salami, chicken salami, bologna, frankfurter specials and the thinner, wrinkled hot dogs always taken with mustard and relish and sauerkraut, and whenever possible, to make the treat fully real, with potato salad, baked beans, and french fries which had been bubbling in the black wire fryer deep in the iron pot. At Saturday twilight, as soon as the delicatessen store reopened after the Sabbath rest, we raced into it panting for the hot dogs sizzling on the gas plate just inside the window. The look of that blackened empty gas plate had driven us wild all through the wearisome Sabbath day. And now, as the electric sign blazed up again, lighting up the words JEWISH NATIONAL DELICATESSEN, it was as if we had entered into our rightful heritage.

Alfred Kazin, A Walker in the City, 1951

Although beef and pork sausages have been around for over a thousand years, Frankfurt am Main is credited with originating the frankfurter. Whether or not this is really where the hot dog came from will probably always be disputed, but it is a coincidence that Frankfurt dates 1484 as the birth date of the frankfurter, which is a few years before the Jews fled Spain with their *choriza,* a beef sausage that they eventually brought with them to the New World.

On this side of the Atlantic the story goes that a Jewish Bavarian concessionaire, Anton Feuchtwanger, introduced today's hot dog on a bun during the St. Louis "Louisiana Purchase Exposition" in 1903. As the fair opened, Mr. Feuchtwanger was lending white gloves to his patrons to keep their fingers clean while eating piping hot sausages. But most of the gloves were not returned, and the supply began running low. So Mr. Feuchtwanger asked his brother-in-law, a baker, for help. The baker improvised long soft rolls that fit the meat—thus inventing the hot-dog bun.

In 1916 Ida and Nathan Handwerker founded Nathan's Famous, a Coney Island hot-dog stand that grew into a chain of more than fifty establishments. By 1939 Nathan's specialty, spiced hot dogs, had become so popular that Mrs. Handwerker boasted that President and Mrs. Franklin D. Roosevelt served Nathan's hot dogs to King George VI and Queen Elizabeth. In fact, Nathan's became such a well-known place that Nelson A. Rockefeller once remarked, "No one can hope to be elected to public office in New York without having his picture taken eating a hot dog at Nathan's."

While Nathan's was becoming famous with non-kosher but distinctly Jewish beef hot dogs, Isadore Pinckowitz, a Rumanian butcher, who peddled meat from the back of a horse-drawn wagon, started making kosher sausages and hot dogs in a sixth floor walk-up on the Lower East Side in 1928. In the late 1940s Isadore's son Leonard Pines was selling kosher hot dogs to Waldbaum's, the only Jewish national food chain, when it expanded to the suburbs. In those days national supermarket chains did not carry Jewish products. Mr. Pines built the company into a $15.3 million operation by supplying mainly small kosher delicatessens and restaurants with a high-quality, premium-priced line.

In 1965 Pines took his hot dog to advertising copywriter Ed McCabe, who came up with the brilliant "We answer to a higher authority" ad campaign that appealed to Jew and non-Jew alike. "The challenge was to make Hebrew National hot dogs relevant to a national audience that did not know what kosher was," said Mr. McCabe. "Levy's bread had done it with 'you don't have to be Jewish to like Levy's.' We used a quality standard which we juxtaposed with another standard which was government. It worked." Through this ad "kosher" took on a special meaning for the entire country—kosher was cleaner, more carefully prepared. Today Hebrew National, a multimillion-dollar company, maintains that only about 20 percent of its clientele is Jewish. And today, you certainly don't have to be Jewish to eat the latest Hebrew National Franks-in-a-Blanket.

My Grandmother's Franks and Sauerkraut

A staple family dish I have always liked is hot dogs with sauerkraut, a recipe my grandmother brought over from Europe. When our family gathered for the Thanksgiving weekend, Friday lunch was always leftover turkey and franks and sauerkraut.

4 cups sauerkraut

2 cups canned tomatoes

½ cup brown sugar or to taste

1 pound kosher hot dogs, cut up in 1-inch pieces, or cocktail franks

1. Mix all the ingredients together in a heavy saucepan. Simmer, covered, for 1 hour.
2. Adjust the seasoning and serve.

Yield: about 6 servings (M)

Hot Dogs Hungarian Style

Like most assimilated American-Hungarian Jews, Linda Radke of Scottsdale, Arizona, has learned to adapt Hungarian recipes to American tastes. She featured family recipes in *That Hungarian's in My Kitchen,* Five Star Publications. Her recipes show the hodgepodge of what has become American ethnic cuisine. Barbecued hot dogs are sautéed in margarine and simmered in a mock *letcho,* the Hungarian national sauce of tomatoes, peppers, and onions of which there are as many variations as there are Hungarians. Mrs. Radke's recipe includes an American addition: a can of tomato soup. She also includes chili powder and ketchup in her otherwise Hungarian *cholent.* With these recipes she includes traditional Hungarian cucumber salads, savory stuffed cabbage, and chicken paprikash and dumplings, all served Jewish style without the sour cream.

In *The Haimishe Kitchen,* published in 1977 by the Ladies Auxiliary of Nitra, a group of Orthodox people living in Mount Kisco, New York, many of whom came from Hungary and Czechoslovakia, there are four recipes for *letcho,* accompanied by eggs, salami, or rice. This tomato sauce is similar to the Israeli "shakshouka," used in similar ways.

2 medium onions, chopped

2 tablespoons vegetable oil

2 large green peppers, chopped

1 tablespoon paprika or to taste

3 large ripe tomatoes, chopped, or 1 16-ounce can tomatoes with the juice

1. In a large frying pan sauté the onions in the vegetable oil until limp.
2. Add the peppers and sauté, mixing well until limp and the onions are slightly brown.
3. Add the paprika and stir for a few minutes. Add the tomatoes and bring the mixture to a boil. Reduce the heat and simmer, covered, for about 10 minutes. Add the salt and pepper plus the caraway seeds.
4. In a saucepan boil the hot dogs in water to cover for 5

Salt and freshly ground pepper
   to taste

½ teaspoon caraway seeds
   (optional)

4 kosher hot dogs or 6 slices
   kosher salami, diced

2 large eggs (optional)

minutes. Cool under cold water, slice to ¼-inch rounds, and add to the vegetable mixture. Return to a simmer and mix well, cooking for about 5 minutes more. You can do this ahead of time.

5. Beat the eggs well. Bring the *letcho* to a simmer and add the eggs, stirring constantly so that the eggs do not curdle.

Yield: 6 to 8 servings as an appetizer or a main course (M)

Pastrami from Mississippi?

In American cities, where there were large concentrations of Jewish immigrants, pastrami was cured in the delicatessens. Small-town Jews, who wanted to continue their old customs, often had to do the curing themselves. The late Edward Millstein, born in Rumania, immigrated to Natchez, Mississippi, where he cured his own. Try it yourself. It will make a big hit with your family and friends. I do not use saltpeter, thus making a gray, rather than pink color to the meat. For more about pastrami, see Box, page 194.

1 5- to 6-pound piece of
   boneless chuck, brisket, or
   crossrib

2 tablespoons black
   peppercorns

½ cup mixed pickling spices

1 tablespoon saltpeter
   (optional)*

½ pound coarse kosher salt

1 teaspoon brown sugar

8 to 10 cloves garlic, mashed

*Saltpeter is available in some apothecaries and pharmacies.

1. Wash the meat and prick well with an ice pick or cooking fork, so that the seasonings can penetrate it.

2. Mix the spices, mash them together, and rub them with the saltpeter, salt, and sugar into the meat on all sides.

3. Put the spices that are left with half the garlic in a large plastic bag. Set the seasoned meat on top. Sprinkle any spices with the rest of the garlic over the meat. Close the bag and place in the refrigerator. Allow the meat to remain in the brine for two weeks, turning it every few days. Drain.

4. At the conclusion of the two-week pickling period, take the meat from the refrigerator. Remove the meat from the marinade, wash in cold water to remove excess salt and spices, and pat dry. Put 2 pieces of string through the pastrami.

5. Place in the middle rack of a smoker at 190 degrees and smoke for an hour to dry the meat. Apply a light

smoke and leave another 2 to 3 hours or until the meat reaches an internal temperature of 175 to 180 degrees. Remove it before it becomes dry.

6. Steam the meat in water for 30 minutes or until warm. Slice, and serve it with some good Jewish rye bread, mustard and, of course, a pickle!

Yield: 12 to 14 servings (M)

The Millstein family of Mississippi

Pickled Tongue or Beef for Jewish Special Occasions

Fancy brisket is the piece most generally preferred for corned beef. To boil a piece of corned beef wash it thoroughly to take away salt, put it in sufficient cold water to cover, and let it simmer several hours, or until a fork runs in easily. Skim it occasionally. To place it in boiling water and allow it to cook wildly will ruin the best piece ever corned.   *The American Jewess,* 1895

Flora Atkin of Chevy Chase, Maryland, has been continuing a tradition brought to this country with the first of her Dutch and German ancestors in the middle of the nineteenth century. Each Rosh Hashanah and Passover her mother and grandmother pickled a tongue and a corned beef in two large earthen crocks. Mrs. Atkin uses a Pyrex baking dish instead. Chances are the recipe is similar to that used by the early Jews, such as Aaron Lopez of Newport who pickled tongues for export. My mother-in-law remembers how in Poland they would pickle or corn tongue and beef for the two holidays and for weddings, including her own.

1 4-pound tongue or brisket
of beef

1/4 cup large-grained kosher salt

1 teaspoon freshly ground
pepper

2 teaspoons ground ginger

1/2 teaspoon ground cloves

2 bay leaves, crumbled

1 tablespoon brown sugar

1/8 teaspoon nutmeg

1/8 teaspoon paprika

3 cloves garlic, minced

1 tablespoon saltpeter
(optional) *

1/2 cup warm water

*Saltpeter is available in pharmacies
or apothecaries.

1. Wash and remove most of the fat from the tongue or brisket. Mix together all the spices and the garlic and rub well into the tongue or brisket.

2. Dissolve the saltpeter in the warm water and pour over the meat. Place in a large, nonmetal container. Weight the meat down with a stone or brick and cover it with plastic wrap or aluminum foil. (You can also place the ingredients in a plastic bag and weight it down.) Refrigerate for 10 days to 2 weeks. Turn the meat every 2 to 3 days.

3. Place the meat in a large pot of cold water. Bring to a boil and throw away the water. Repeat 3 times.

4. Cover with cold water again, bring to a boil, and cook over low heat, covered, for about 2 hours or until tender. If cooking tongue, peel off the skin while still warm. Cool, slice thin, and place on a platter. Serve with mustard, horseradish, or Segerman Horseradish Special (see page 397).

Yield: 8 to 10 servings (M)

Awaiting the pickled tongue and corned beef at Flora Atkin's seder

Goose Pastrami and Rumanian Delis

In those days little Rumania had more restaurants than the Russian quarter—establishments with signs in English and Rumanian, and platters of
liver paste, chopped eggplant, and other distinctive edibles in the windows.
On Rivington Street and on Allen Street the Rumanian delicatessen was
making its appearance, with its goose-pastrama and kegs of ripe olives and
tubs of salted vine-leaves (which, when wrapped around ground meat, make
a most delicious dish), and the moon-shaped cash caval (kashkeval) cheese
made of sheep's milk, and, most important of all, the figure of an impossible
American version of a Rumanian shepherd in holiday costume, with a flute
at his waxen lips standing erect in the window.

M. E. Ravage, An American in the Making, 1917

Goose pastrami came here with Rumanian immigrants in the late nineteenth century. With the decline in popularity of geese and the rise of the beef industry,
goose was replaced by a fatty cut of brisket. Thus American pastrami was born,
even though to this day it is called "Rumanian pastrami."

The word *pastrami* comes from the Turkish *basturma,* a meat that is sliced, wind
dried, and pickled with dried spices, then pressed together again. It was originally
used as army rations for the Turkish Jannissari corps, the first organized military
force in Europe since Roman times. Jewish peddlers in Rumania (and elsewhere
certainly) quickly learned how the Turks cured their meat and began curing
kosher meat in this same way, no doubt adding more garlic, black pepper, and lots
of paprika. They used it on their long journeys away from a kosher kitchen. It was
the Rumanians who brought the process to New York.

"Pastrami can be made from anything," said Mark Landau, owner of the Pastrami King, a delicatessen specializing in pastrami in Queens, originally started by
Rumanians in Williamsburg. "I make mine from deckel (the neck and shoulder),
not the top of the rib that other people promote. It's not the cut. It is the flavor."
Today most commercial pastrami curers inject spices with saltpeter. The Pastrami
King is one of the few places that dry cure in the old-fashioned way: by rubbing the
meat with kosher salt, garlic, and ground black pepper; covering it with spices;
and pressing it down with a stone, leaving the pastrami in fifty-five–gallon steel
vats where they are weighted down for about a week. Then more spices are added
and the meat is cured for three more days. Finally, the meat is covered with black
pepper, smoked for six to seven hours in a smoker with cedar sawdust, and then
steamed.

Glazed Corned Beef

Glazed corned beef is the American Jewish rendition of glazed ham, sometimes called "faux ham." To satisfy their desires to assimilate into the Christian culture where glazed ham was always a centerpiece at holiday buffets, and to avoid serving the forbidden pork themselves, Jews would coat a cooked corned beef with dark corn syrup; score it with cloves; decorate it with pineapple rings, a maraschino cherry, and sometimes canned apricot halves; and then bake it as they would a ham. The recipe probably originated in the South, perhaps in a community like Savannah, Georgia, where ham was an important buffet item and where glazed corned beef appears in *Jewish Eating is Appealing,* published by the B'nai B'rith Girls and the Daughters of Zion in 1954.

This is Chef Jean Louis Palladin's take on a recipe from *Thoughts for Buffets,* published as a fund-raiser by the Jewish Community Center of Chicago in 1950.

4 to 5 pounds corned beef
   brisket

3 onions, sliced

1 bay leaf

3 cloves garlic

½ teaspoon rosemary

3 carrots, peeled and chopped

1 stalk celery, diced

1 turnip, sliced

2 tablespoons olive oil

8 cloves

1 tablespoon prepared mustard

5 tablespoons ketchup

3 tablespoons balsamic vinegar

2 tablespoons molasses

⅓ cup brown sugar

1 pineapple, peeled and cut in
   circles, centers removed

1 mango, peeled and sliced

1. Cover the meat with water; add the onions, bay leaf, garlic, rosemary, carrots, celery, turnips, and a few cloves. Bring to a boil, then simmer slowly, covered, for about 3 hours or until tender.

2. To make the glaze, place the olive oil, mustard, ketchup, vinegar, molasses, and brown sugar in a saucepan. Bring all the ingredients to a boil. Add the pineapple and mango to some of the sauce in the pan and cook for a few minutes, turning occasionally.

3. Drain the corned beef and put it in a roasting pan. Pour the glaze with the fruits and remaining cloves over the corned beef. Bake it in a preheated 350-degree oven, basting occasionally, for 30 minutes. Slice and serve.

Yield: 8 to 10 servings (M)

Pico Kosher Deli, Los Angeles

Alsatian Sweet and Sour Tongue with Gingersnap Sauce

This typically Alsatian and southern German method of preparing tongue always includes gingersnaps or *Lebkuchen* (see page 348) for the sweet and sour taste. A spicy and sweet sauce was often used for pickled meats because sugar was first used as a condiment rather than as a dessert sweetener. In addition, by the time the meat had been pickled, salt removed, and then cooked, it had lost much of its flavor. With trepidation, because not everybody likes tongue, I brought this dish to a potluck dinner at my children's school. To my surprise everybody, including my husband, not a great fan of tongue, loved it.

MEAT

1 4-pound pickled beef tongue
*   or 2 small veal tongues*

6 bay leaves

3 teaspoons whole peppercorns

1 teaspoon whole cloves

1 onion, peeled and sliced

SAUCE

Salt and freshly ground pepper
*   to taste*

½ teaspoon mace

½ teaspoon ground cloves

½ teaspoon allspice

1½ cups water

10 gingersnaps

2 to 3 tablespoons cider
*   vinegar*

½ cup raisins

¼ cup blanched slivered
*   almonds*

4 to 5 thin lemon slices

Parsley for garnish

1. Place the tongue in a pot of cold water to cover. Add the bay leaves, peppercorns, cloves, and onion. Bring to a boil and then cover. Simmer slowly until tender, allowing about 20 minutes per pound. Remove the tongue(s) from the pot, skin, and trim off any fat.

2. To make the sauce add salt, pepper, mace, ground cloves, and allspice to the water. Crumble up the gingersnaps and place in the water with the vinegar, and heat. The sauce will thicken as it heats. Add the raisins, almonds, and lemon slices. If the sauce stands or is kept for another meal, it will thicken. Thin with water to desired consistency. Adjust seasonings and serve the sauce with the boiled hot tongue sprinkled with the parsley.

Yield: 6 to 8 servings (M)

Stuffed Cabbage with Cranberry Sauce

I am glad you were kind enough to find an excuse for me and kept the Tabernacle celebration, in scenes so naturally appropriate to the season. For my own part I was only once under the shelter of its roof, and partook no further of the feast spread before me than a little bread & salt, tho' I enjoyed the sight of goodly fruit & wine distributed in plenty and listened to a hymn of thanksgiving that we were permitted to meet at the sanctification of this festival & view the emblems of former rejoicing. The palm & branches of goodly trees, mentioned in scripture as taken by the youths & damsels as they went out after the ingathering of the blessings of the year, to dwell in booths and rejoice before the Lord, has always had a great charm in my imagination.

Rebecca Gratz to Maria Gist Gratz, November 5, 1 8 3 7

Rebecca Gratz, considered one of the most beautiful and cultured women during the Federalist period, may have eaten stuffed vegetables at the Sukkot celebration described above. Grape leaves, zucchini, and cabbage, filled with rice or kasha and meat, all symbolize the desire for plenty during the harvest period. While in Europe barley or buckwheat groats were often used as a filling, rice is the most common grain used here.

The following stuffed cabbage with cranberries comes from Massachusetts.

1 16-ounce can jellied
  cranberry sauce
1 15- or 16-ounce can tomato
  sauce
1½ cups water
Juice of 1 lemon
¼ cup brown sugar or to taste
½ cup raisins
½ cup fresh cranberries
1 apple
1 medium head of cabbage
2 pounds ground beef
½ cup uncooked rice
Salt and freshly ground pepper
1 large egg
1 medium onion, grated
4 tablespoons ketchup

1. Mix the cranberry sauce, tomato sauce, 1 cup water, lemon, and sugar in a saucepan. Bring to a boil; then add the raisins and the fresh cranberries. Peel, core, and dice the apple and add. Simmer for another 5 minutes.

2. Core the cabbage and place in a large pot with water to cover. Bring to a boil and then simmer, covered, about 10 minutes or until wilted. Cover with cold water and drain. (Alternately, you can place the cored cabbage in the freezer for several days. Defrost 24 hours before making the cabbage. It will wilt naturally.)

3. In a large bowl mix the meat, rice, salt and freshly ground pepper to taste, egg, onion, ½ cup water, and ketchup, blending with your fingers until well mixed.

4. Trim the ribs off the cabbage, remove the outside leaves, and line a large flameproof casserole with them. Pull off the inside leaves and place them one by one on a board, outside down. Fill with a heaping tablespoon or two of the filling, depending on the size of the leaf. Fold up like an envelope, top first, then bottom and then the 2 sides. Place seam side down in the lined casserole. Repeat with the rest of the cabbage and the filling.

5. Pour the sauce over the stuffed cabbage and simmer, covered, for 2 hours. Then place the stuffed cabbage in a preheated 300-degree oven and bake, uncovered, for one half hour more.

Yield: at least 15 stuffed cabbages or 6 to 8 servings (M)

Tip: Another American way to make this dish is to make a sauce of ¾ cup ketchup, 1½ to 2 cups tomato juice, ¾ cup brown sugar, the juice of 1 large lemon, and sour salt to taste. Make this dish ahead. It tastes much better the next day. Also, this is a good recipe to double. Freeze one portion for unexpected guests.

Building a Sukkah is a fall family tradition in many American-Jewish homes.

Hungarian Goulash

One of those freethinking Yiddish actresses who ate at the Café Royale on the southeast corner of Second Avenue and Twelfth Street was Fanny Brice. The late Irving Howe described her acting as "Yente Grandeur." Like others she probably sipped tea with a slice of lemon through a sugar cube clenched in her teeth. But unlike many of the others she cooked her own version of Hungarian goulash on the road using a twenty-five-cent alcohol portable stove, which she carried with her wherever she went.

2 medium onions, coarsely chopped

2 tablespoons vegetable oil

2½ pounds beef chuck or veal stew or round, cut into 1-inch cubes

½ pound meat from shank bones

2 tablespoons sweet paprika

2½ cups warm water

1 medium ripe tomato or 1 cup stewed tomatoes

2 green peppers

1 pound potatoes

Salt and freshly ground pepper to taste

Cherry pepper pods

Noodles

1. Peel the onions and chop coarsely. In a 6- to 8-quart heavy pot with a cover, heat the oil, and sauté the onions. Keep the heat low so the onions do not brown.

2. When the onions are transparent, add the beef or veal and the shank bone meat. Sauté with the onions for about 10 minutes.

3. Remove the pot from the heat. Add the paprika, stirring rapidly with a wooden spoon. Immediately after the paprika is absorbed, add the 2½ cups warm water.

4. Return the pot to the heat, cover, and cook over a low to medium heat for about 1 hour.

5. While the mixture is cooking, peel the tomato and cut it into 1-inch pieces. Seed the green peppers and dice. Peel the potatoes and cut into ¾-inch dice and place in cold water.

6. After cooking for about 1 hour, add the peppers, tomato, and potatoes, and enough water to make a soupy stew. Add the salt and pepper. Simmer slowly, covered, for 30 minutes or until the goulash is tender.

7. Serve with hot cherry pepper pods and noodles.

Yield: 6 to 8 servings (M)

Café Royale on the Lower East Side

For years the Café Royale on Second Avenue has been Yiddish Bohemia's lyrical protest against the Machine Age. . . . With the same habituation and fervor with which their fathers had attended their synagogues in the Russian and Polish Ghettos, these intellectuals have been haunting the sacred precincts of the Café, a little island of conviviality in a roaring sea of city loneliness, drinking Pilsner beer and tea with lemon, and raising each other's blood pressure with heated arguments over Toscanini's interpretation of Mozart's "Haffner" symphony, over the superiority of goulash over wiener schnitzel or, whether the Yiddish theatre on Second Avenue has gone caput, is ausgespielte, in short—is at its last gasp. . . . The more affluent of them sit at the tables, gorging themselves on chopped liver and goulash—the less affluent picking daintily at a Greek salad in which little pieces of Maatjes herring peer pensively out of the green shrubbery. Of course many of the actors and actresses are unemployed. They cannot afford to order anything substantial. So they gallantly carry on their pretension at well being, blaming it all on their poor appetite or on an upset stomach, and they order—just tea, waiter, just tea with lemon!

"Art with Tea and Lemon," Works Progress Administration, 1930s

New York's Café Royale was a haven for journalists like
Abraham Cahan (center) of the **Daily Forward.**

Kartofelnyie Kotlety *(Meat-Stuffed Potato Latkes)*

It was a charming café, and it was packed. The Little Russian Café in Denver had bright red walls, hardwood floors, small tables covered with white tablecloths, warm red napkins, Russian tea cozies, and samovars. The fifteen different ice-cold vodkas and the hot Russian tea were served in glasses. The food, strictly from St. Petersburg, included beef stroganoff, *golubtsi* (stuffed cabbage), *pelmeni* (meat-filled dumplings; see page 1 1 3), and *kartofelnyie kotlety* (meat-stuffed potatoes). Eugene Valershteyn and his parents, Rem and Nina, who run a similar restaurant in Boulder, came from St. Petersburg in 1 9 8 0. Because Mrs. Valershteyn was a good cook, people encouraged the family to open a small restaurant. They did and little by little earned enough to open a second one.

2 pounds potatoes

2 eggs

Salt and freshly ground pepper to taste

1 pound leftover boiled beef or brisket with gravy

2 tablespoons vegetable oil

1 medium onion, grated

2 tablespoons fresh parsley

1 tablespoon beef broth if needed

Flour for dredging

Margarine or vegetable oil for frying

1. Peel the potatoes and cover with cold water. Simmer until tender, about 2 0 minutes. Remove, drain well, and mash with a potato masher or put through a grinder. Do not puree. Add the eggs and salt and pepper and mix well.

2. Grind the boiled meat in a food grinder or with the food processor.

3. In the oil sauté the onion until it is golden. Add salt and pepper, parsley, and the ground beef, adding a tablespoon or so of beef broth if it is too dry.

4. Put about a third of a cup of the potato mixture in the cup of your hand. Place 2 tablespoons of the meat filling in the center and completely enclose, first shaping like a ball and then patting down to form a plump hamburger. Dredge in the flour and then fry in the margarine or vegetable oil until golden on each side.

Yield: 8 large potato pancakes (M)

Hamad, Iraqi Braised Lamb with Beets and Tomatoes

Hamad, which means sweet and sour, is often served at Rosh Hashanah. "Iraqi meat dishes are always braised in chopped tomatoes with turmeric," said Shoshanna Sofaer, who prepared this dish at a family gathering in Washington. You can add carrots, turnips, zucchini, and parsnips to it.

3½ to 4 pounds shoulder of lamb, diced in one-inch cubes

1 28-ounce can plum tomatoes, drained and diced, juice reserved

Salt and freshly ground pepper to taste

1 clove garlic, mashed

1 teaspoon turmeric

2 teaspoons sugar

2 pounds beets

Juice of ½ lemon

Cooked rice

1. In a heavy saucepan, mix together the lamb with the tomatoes, salt, pepper, garlic, turmeric, and sugar. Cook on a high flame, stirring, until the meat is brown. Then simmer, covered, on top of the stove for about 2 hours, adding more juice from the tomatoes if necessary.

2. Meanwhile, cook the beets in water to cover for about 20 minutes. When cool enough to handle, peel, and dice.

3. Add the beets to the stew and simmer, covered, about 20 minutes more. Just before serving, add the lemon juice and adjust the seasonings. Serve with white rice.

Yield: 8 servings (M)

Picadillo

In Sara Kittrie's Mexican-American Jewish home, leftover chicken from soup becomes chicken tacos with *salsa,* fried onion, tomatoes, garlic, and chilies; tortillas are filled with *picadillo,* a ground beef dish reminiscent of her childhood in Mexico. After making the blessing over the *challah* on Friday night, she often serves the *picadillo* with rice, tortilla, and guacamole. This is a great family dish.

2 onions, chopped

1 large green pepper, diced

2 tablespoons vegetable oil

1½ pounds ground beef

Salt and freshly ground pepper
    to taste

1 clove garlic, crushed

1 16-ounce can stewed
    tomatoes

2 bay leaves

Pinch of cumin

2 tablespoons raisins

2 tablespoons almond slivers

2 tablespoons red wine vinegar

2 large potatoes, peeled and
    diced

3 carrots, peeled and diced

1. In a heavy frying pan with a cover sauté the onions and green pepper over medium heat in the vegetable oil until the onion is soft. Add the meat, break with a fork, and cook until the meat is browned.

2. Add the salt, pepper, garlic, tomatoes, bay leaves, cumin, raisins, almonds, vinegar, potatoes, and carrots to the meat. Mix well, cover, and simmer for about a half hour. Serve with the rice or in a tortilla with the guacamole.

Yield: 6 servings (M)

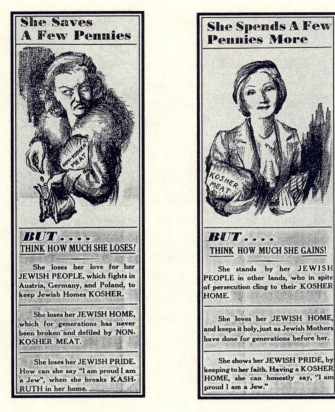

She Saves A Few Pennies

BUT....
THINK HOW MUCH SHE LOSES!

She loses her love for her JEWISH PEOPLE, which fights in Austria, Germany, and Poland, to keep Jewish Homes KOSHER.

She loses her JEWISH HOME, which for generations has never been broken and defiled by NON-KOSHER MEAT.

She loses her JEWISH PRIDE. How can she say "I am proud I am a Jew", when she breaks KASHRUTH in her home.

She Spends A Few Pennies More

BUT....
THINK HOW MUCH SHE GAINS!

She stands by her JEWISH PEOPLE in other lands, who in spite of persecution cling to their KOSHER HOME.

She loves her JEWISH HOME, and keeps it holy, just as Jewish Mothers have done for generations before her.

She shows her JEWISH PRIDE, by keeping to her faith. Having a KOSHER HOME, she can honestly say, "I am proud I am a Jew."

Bialystok Tsimmes with Sweet Potatoes, Carrots, Prunes, and Apricots

Charlotte Rudel of Johnstown, Pennsylvania, has been making her mother's Bialystok *tsimmes* her entire life. In a letter to the editor of the *Pittsburgh Jewish Chronicle* she wrote, "Isn't it silly that the shape and size of the carrots can cause more stress than whether your child graduates college as scheduled, and isn't it absurd that I get all riled up because five times someone says, 'You use prunes in your tsimmes?' (Yes. I use prunes . . . despite the apricot fans.)

"Wow! To be so concerned that the potatoes are not cut in thirds but are whole! . . . The stress of trying to duplicate 'Tsimmes' to please all generations and the memories of their childhood 'Tsimmes' is no easy task."

Tsimmes is a Yiddish word meaning fuss and comes from the German "*zum essen*," to eat. Because it takes time to make *tsimmes,* the word came to mean making a big deal over something. *Tsimmes* may make Mrs. Rudel nervous, but her recipe is delicious!

3 pounds short ribs (flanken) or chuck, cut into 2-inch cubes

1. Sprinkle the meat with the salt and pepper and brown, with the sliced onions, in the chicken fat or oil.

Salt and freshly ground pepper
   to taste

3 medium onions, sliced

2 tablespoons chicken fat or
   vegetable oil

6 cups water or beef bouillon to
   cover

3 large sweet potatoes, peeled
   and quartered

5 large carrots, peeled and
   quartered

3 large white potatoes, peeled
   and quartered

¾ pound dried prunes, pitted

¾ pound dried apricots

¼ cup brown sugar

¼ cup apricot jam (optional)

Dash of nutmeg

½ teaspoon cinnamon

Juice of 1 lemon

Slivered rind and juice of
   1 orange

**HALKIE OR POTATO
KUGEL TOPPING**

1 large peeled and grated
   white potato (about 2 cups)

2 cups matzah meal

2 eggs

2 tablespoons fresh parsley

1 onion, coarsely grated

1 tablespoon chicken fat or
   vegetable oil

Salt and freshly ground pepper
   to taste

½ cup water

2. Place the meat, onions, and juices in a 4-quart casserole and cover it with the water or beef bouillon. Bake in a preheated 350-degree oven, covered, for 2 hours. If you want to remove the fat, refrigerate overnight and remove the congealed fat.

3. Add the quartered vegetables with the prunes, apricots, brown sugar, apricot jam, nutmeg, cinnamon, lemon juice, and orange rind and juice to the meat. Add more water if too thick.

4. To make the topping, mix the grated potato with the matzah meal, eggs, parsley, onion, chicken fat or oil, and salt and pepper and up to ½ cup water, as needed, to make a sticky dough. Flouring your hands, spread the potato dough and press very thinly over the *tsimmes* and bake, covered, for 45 minutes.

5. Uncover, season with salt and pepper, and cook an additional 30 minutes or until the liquid disappears and the top turns crusty. Bring the pot to the table and serve.

Yield: at least *10* servings (M)

Tsimmes with Beets, Turnips, and Beef

The following *tsimmes* with beets, turnips, carrots, and meat came from Vilna to Brooklyn earlier in this century. When I make this for my family I do not tell the children that it includes beets and turnips. For some unknown reason they never ask me how the dish became so red. They love it.

3 teaspoons salt

½ teaspoon pepper

3 pounds flanken, chuck, or brisket of beef

2 onions, chopped

2 tablespoons flour

3 cups boiling water

¼ cup honey or to taste

8 carrots, coarsely grated

1 turnip, coarsely grated

1 beet, coarsely grated

1 sweet potato, peeled and quartered (optional)

1. Mix 2 teaspoons of the salt and pepper and rub it into the beef. Place in a Dutch oven or heavy pot with the onions and brown slowly over a medium heat. Add the flour, mixing well. Add the water, stirring, until it reaches the boiling point. Cover and simmer slowly for about 1 hour.

2. Mix the honey in with the meat, then add the vegetables and remaining salt. Cover and bake in a preheated 375-degree oven for an hour and a half, removing the cover for the last 15 to 20 minutes. Taste and adjust seasonings, if necessary.

Yield: 6 to 8 servings (M)

Argentinian Carbonada Criolla, Tsimmes by Any Other Name

When I first tasted Argentinian *carbonada criolla* in Jerusalem, the flavors reminded me of *tsimmes*. The two dishes have many of the same components: sweet potatoes, carrots, meat, and, if you like, prunes. "First-generation Jews in Argentina make *tsimmes* and second and third who want to be more assimilated make *carbonada criolla*," said Marta Wassertzug, now of Rockville, Maryland.

Many Argentinian Jews came to this country in the 1970s, leaving a military dictatorship of which they did not approve. Their ancestors had gone to Argentina in the nineteenth century under the auspices of Baron de Hirsch, a philanthropist, who wanted to develop his land in the Pampas region.

Like other Jews from Argentina, the beef capital of the world, Ms. Wassertzug makes many beef dishes, including *carbonada criolla*. This is a showstopper—a perfect harvest one-pot meal for a party.

1 10-pound large round
  squash, such as pumpkin or
  calabaza
¼ cup margarine
Salt and freshly ground pepper
  to taste
4 pounds beef chuck, cubed
2 tablespoons olive oil
1 cup coarsely chopped onion
4 cloves garlic, peeled and
  chopped
4 cups water or beef stock
1 12-ounce can Italian plum
  tomatoes, drained and
  chopped
1 teaspoon fresh oregano
3 large sweet potatoes, peeled
  and cubed (about 2 pounds)
3 large white potatoes (about 2
  pounds) (optional)
3 carrots, peeled and sliced in
  large chunks
1 10-ounce package frozen corn
  kernels
8 pitted prunes
8 peach halves (canned)

1. Scrub the outside of the squash with a vegetable brush and trim the bottom so that it will sit flat. Cut out a lid 6 inches in diameter and remove the pits and fiber from inside.

2. Smear the inside of the pumpkin with margarine and sprinkle with salt, pepper, and water. Bake the pumpkin in a large, shallow roasting pan in a preheated 375-degree oven for 45 minutes or until tender but still firm. (You do not want the pumpkin to collapse.)

3. Meanwhile, brown the meat in the oil in a heavy pot with the onion and garlic.

4. Add the water or stock, tomatoes, and oregano and simmer, covered, for 15 minutes. Add the sweet potatoes, peel and dice the white potatoes, and add with the carrots and simmer for another 15 minutes. Add the corn, prunes, and peaches and simmer for 5 minutes more.

5. Fill the pumpkin carefully with the meat and vegetable mixture. Replace the lid and continue baking in the 375-degree oven another 15 minutes.

Yield: 10 to 12 servings (M)

Pastel de Papa *(Argentinian Potato Meat Pie)*

Ms. Wassertzug also makes *pastel de papa,* the following Argentinian meat pie that I first tasted many years ago at the home of Argentinian Jews in Israel.

Ms. Wassertzug's daughter, Deborah, a student at the University of Maryland, was watching some Irish students cook shepherd's pie for international night. "Wait a minute," she said. "That's not shepherd's pie! It's *pastel de papa.*"

The only difference between the Jewish and non-Jewish Argentinian versions of *pastel de papa* is the elimination of milk from the potatoes and the use of kosher beef instead of the mixture of beef and pork in the Jewish version. This is one of my husband's favorite weekday dishes. It lends itself to creative additions and subtractions of vegetables, depending on what your family likes to eat.

6 large potatoes

2 tablespoons vegetable oil

1 large onion

2 cloves garlic

1 green pepper, chopped

1 large tomato, peeled and
  diced

2 pounds ground beef

Oregano to taste

Salt and freshly ground pepper
  to taste

½ teaspoon cumin or to taste

6 tablespoons pareve
  margarine

2 hard-boiled eggs, diced
  (optional)

½ cup pitted olives (optional)

½ cup raisins (optional)

Paprika to taste

1. Peel the potatoes and boil them, covered, for about 25 minutes or until soft.

2. Meanwhile, heat the oil and sauté the onion, garlic, and green pepper in a frying pan until the onion is soft and transparent. Add the tomato, the ground beef, oregano, salt and pepper, and cumin and cook, breaking up the beef with a fork, for a few minutes until the meat is brown. Drain off any fat.

3. Drain the potatoes and mash them with 4 tablespoons of the margarine and salt. Beat the potatoes until they are creamy.

4. Stir the eggs, olives, and raisins into the meat; blend well. Place the meat mixture in a 6-cup casserole and cover with the mashed potatoes, sprinkle with paprika and dot with the remaining margarine.

5. Bake, uncovered, in a preheated 375-degree oven for about 20 minutes or until the crust is golden.

Yield: 6 to 8 servings (M)

SIX

עורף

Chicken, Goose, Quail, and Their Stuffings

Few persons are aware of the injury they sustain, by eating the flesh of diseased animals. None but the Jewish butchers, who are paid exclusively for it, attend to this important circumstance.

Mary Randolph, *Virginia Housewife,* 1824

In those days everybody kept kosher in Rockland, Maine. The fulltime rabbi was also the schochet who would slaughter chickens for twenty five cents. My great uncle told me the story that every Friday morning his mother took a chicken out of the yard and gave him the chicken and a quarter and told him to go to the rabbi's house to slaughter the chicken and pay the rabbi. One day he decided he didn't need to pay the rabbi the quarter; he could do it himself. So he took the chicken down to the wharf and slit its throat and put the quarter in his pocket. He did this for several weeks until his mother caught him. It had not occurred to him that a rabbi had a license to kosher an animal.

Barbara Small Fishman, Rockland, Maine, 1991

Lewis Lewisson's Annual Thanksgiving Aid in Providence

Each year at Thanksgiving Lewis Lewisson, a Jewish dry-goods merchant who came to Providence from Prussian Poland in the late 1840s, ran an ad in the *Providence Journal* offering his clientele Thanksgiving dinner. Mr. Lewisson operated a clothing bazaar that catered to sailors and other poorer peoples right near the harbor.

The first year he distributed twelve hundred pounds of bread and five hundred pounds of turkey. Not only was this good advertising, it was Mr. Lewisson's way of telling Governor Phillip Allen of Rhode Island that Jews and other minorities were also Americans.

Turkey traditions die hard in America but not the stuffings within. Mr. Lewisson may very well have eaten the following chestnut stuffing, which comes from a private collection of recipes from Harriet Meyer of San Francisco. (For more on Mrs. Meyer, see page 243.)

Chestnut Stuffing for Turkey

Adapted from Harriet Meyer's private recipes, 1913

3 dozen chestnuts

3 tablespoons pareve
    margarine

1 large shallot

1 koshered chicken liver,
    chopped fine*

10 finely chopped mushrooms

Salt and freshly ground pepper
    to taste

1/2 teaspoon thyme

1 teaspoon chopped parsley

1/2 cup fresh bread crumbs

*To kosher a liver you must remove all the blood, which means broiling it over an open flame before using.

1. Cut an x-shaped gash in each chestnut shell. In an ovenproof skillet place 2 tablespoons of the margarine, heat, and add the chestnuts, shaking until covered with the margarine. Set in a preheated 350-degree oven for 5 to 10 minutes. Remove the shells and inner skin and cook until tender in boiling, salted water to cover for about 5 minutes or until tender.

2. Remove 12 chestnuts from the water. Drain and press them through a ricer. Drain the rest and leave whole.

3. Dice the shallot and sauté with 1 more tablespoon of the margarine. Add the liver and sauté for 5 minutes. Then add the mushrooms and the riced chestnuts. Season with salt, pepper, thyme, and parsley. Fold in the bread crumbs and the remaining chestnuts, being careful to keep the chestnuts intact. Cool, and stuff the turkey.

Yield: 4 cups, enough for an 8- to 10-pound turkey (M)

Corn-Bread Stuffing from Virginia

When Sheldon Cohen assembled his typewritten *Chef Shell's Favorite Recipes in 1991, A collection of Traditional Jewish and Personal Delights*, his children asked him to include his Thanksgiving corn-bread stuffing, which he makes with leftover corn bread or kosher corn-bread stuffing mix.

¾ pound chestnuts

1 large onion

2 stalks celery

2 tablespoons vegetable oil

½ pound mushrooms

2 cups corn-bread stuffing mix

1 stick (½ cup) pareve
  margarine

2 large eggs, beaten

½ cup chopped parsley

¼ teaspoon marjoram

¼ teaspoon thyme

1 teaspoon sage

Salt and freshly ground pepper
  to taste

1. Score the chestnut shells and boil in water to cover for about 10 minutes. Peel the shells from the chestnuts and quarter.

2. Dice and sauté the onion and celery in the vegetable oil. Quarter the mushrooms, add them when the onions are soft, and sauté until the onions are golden.

3. Use leftover corn bread or prepare the stuffing mix according to the directions on the package. Melt the margarine and add with the eggs to the stuffing. Add the chestnuts, the sautéed onions, the herbs, and seasonings and mix well.

4. Do not stuff ahead of time as harmful bacteria growth could spoil the uncooked fowl. Just before roasting, stuff the body and the neck of the turkey, but do not pack in as the stuffing will expand. If packed in too tightly it will be very dense instead of light. Sew the abdomen and neck closed and sew the legs together close to the body so that the stuffing cooks evenly.

Yield: enough stuffing for an 8-pound turkey (P)

A Good Aroma of Melted Goose Fat Filled the Jewish Home

Where did the Jews first learn their passionate fondness for the "Jewish eagle?" Was it in France that they were taught their appreciation for "paté de foie gras?" or was it in southern Germany? Did the expulsion of the Jews from France spread the noble art of goose-fattening, with that pernicious taste for cracklins which peoples Karlsbad with Jews? Or was it the need of having a substitute for lard which has enthroned the goose in our affections?

The Owl: Official Organ of The Young Men's Hebrew Association,
New Orleans, February 1902

Until the arrival of vegetable-based fats like Crisco, Jews in America were using olive oil, shipped from Italy, chicken and goose fat, or products like Swift's coto-suet vegetable oil, which had "every quality of olive oil, thickened with prime beef suet" as stated in the magazine the *American Jewess* in 1895. Unfortunately Swift's cotosuet vegetable oil included non-kosher beef suet.

In an 1850 letter to the editor published in *The Occident,* a Jewish newspaper in Philadelphia, a reader complained that olive oil was being mixed with lard before bottling. Regardless of the proportions, olive oil was now contaminated for all Jews. In the absence of an American Jewish juridical court to determine olive-oil purity, *The Occident* suggested asking the Grand Rabbi of England to settle the controversy over lard oil. Mordecai Noah, who was concerned about dietary laws in his own home, decided to conduct a chemical test of the so-called lard oil. He discovered that there was no lard in imported olive oil and that, in fact, lard oil would be more expensive for the Bordeaux, Leghorn, and Lucca olive oil producers to export than pure olive oil.

Schmaltz *(Rendered Poultry Fat)* with Gribenes *(Cracklings)*

Today few Americans use cholesterol-laden schmaltz. It was a surprise for me, then, to go to Crown Heights, Brooklyn, to a Lubavitcher home to see a huge vat of chicken fat being rendered on someone's stove.

1 goose or chicken

¼ cup sliced onion

Kosher salt to taste

¼ cup water

1. Remove the fat and the fatty skin from a goose or chicken. Wash, dry well, and cut up into 2-inch square pieces, measuring 1 cup.
2. Place in a heavy skillet, add the sliced onion, sprinkle with salt, and add the water. Heat, uncovered, over a very low heat, letting the fat melt slowly, until it is completely melted, for about a half hour. When the onion and the skin begin to brown, remove the *gribenes* with a slotted spoon to a container and refrigerate. Remove the fat to a separate container and refrigerate or freeze.
3. Use the *gribenes* for snacks or cook along with kasha *varnishkes,* noodle pudding, mashed potatoes, or chicken livers over potatoes. The fat can be used for cooking and is especially good for making chopped liver, potato pancakes, and *matzah brei* (fried matzah).

Yield: about 1 cup (M)

Chicken Livers with Gribenes and Potatoes

2 teaspoons goose or chicken fat

1 tablespoon gribenes

1 boiled potato, sliced

2 prepared chicken livers or

   1 goose liver*

1. In a small skillet heat the fat with the *gribenes.*
2. Add the sliced potato and sauté until golden. Add the liver and sauté about 5 minutes or until thoroughly cooked.

Yield: 1 serving (M)

*To kosher the liver it must be cut open across its length and width and placed with the cut part facing downward over the fire, so that the fire will draw out all of the blood. Before broiling, it is washed and lightly salted. Finally, the broiled liver must be washed 3 times to remove any blood. After it is koshered, the liver can be sautéed.

Gribenes and Schmaltz
Spread on Pumpernickel . . .
Ummm, Good!

I was close to "my grandmother" because I loved her but also because she lived just around the corner. Our two houses on Lexington Avenue were separated in the rear by an areaway. From my bedroom window I could look out and down and see her living-room window. That was more fun than the telephone. . . .

Friday visits, morning and afternoon, to her house were the best. In the morning I would walk right into her kitchen full of confusion. The whole room was a mixture of dough drying for noodles, pots boiling, and the wooden kitchen table sprinkled all over with flour. It was like a rehearsal in a theater. The stage was being set, the props arranged, and the acts run through for this Friday night supper that was ten or eleven hours away and would be the finished performance. The only thing in the whole kitchen that wasn't in a mess was Bubeshu (her grandmother).

Gertrude Berg, *Molly and Me,* 1961

For many Jewish adults today childhood memories include savory aromas from their grandparents' neighboring apartment, a snack of a slice of pumpernickel with schmaltz and a radish, and cooking lessons at a grandparent's knee that were partly entertaining stories of the old country.

Jill Jaffe, from Lawrence, Massachusetts, lived in an old Victorian one-family home with an apartment for her grandparents upstairs. "My grandparents were strictly kosher. My favorite dish was my grandmother's *petcha* (calves' foot jelly), which she made with chicken feet and lima beans. My grandmother made *gribenes* and rendered her chicken fat on top of the stove. What a big boon it was when Oleo came out! We had a flavor other than chicken fat to lubricate the potatoes, which we always had with chicken livers and onions."

Grandma Lina's Roast Goose Stuffed with Chestnuts and Apples

"In Germany, even the poorest Jews served goose to start the New Year," my grandmother Lina would remind me as we sat down to our traditional holiday turkey, "that rich people's food would bring a poor man luck."

Grandmother Lina always served a fresh young goose at Sukkot. Later, the fatter geese would provide her with goose fat throughout the long winter. Grandpa Rudolph looked forward most of all to this time of year. After eating lightly during the summer months, he could once again grow fat, snacking on *gribenes,* which Grandma Lina always kept in a jar next to his chair along with his ever-present cigar.

In the United States, roast goose appears on the holiday table less and less often. Except for very special occasions, chicken, beef, lamb, and turkey are substituted. How my grandfather would have moaned over all this!

1 8- to 10-pound goose

4 apples

2 cups cooked, peeled
  chestnuts, quartered

½ cup raisins

1 cup prunes

Salt to taste

1. Remove the excess fat from the cavity and giblets. Render the fat and save to use in cooking.

2. Peel, core, and dice the apples. Mix them with the chestnuts, raisins, and prunes, and stuff the cavity about three-fourths full. After stuffing the goose, truss it and place the bird, breast side up, on a rack in a roasting pan. Rub with salt.

3. Roast for 1 hour in a preheated 400-degree oven. Prick the skin with a fork at ½-inch intervals to let the fat escape. Reduce the temperature to 350 degrees and roast for another hour. As the fat accumulates, remove it with a bulb baster. To test for doneness, prick the thigh with a fork; the juices should be yellowish. If they are tinged with pink and further cooking is necessary, reduce the oven to 325 degrees and continue roasting until the goose is cooked.

4. Remove more drippings with a bulb baster and let the bird rest for 15 minutes before carving. Meanwhile, put the pan on top of the stove and bring to a simmer. Using a spoon try to break up the bottom crust, stirring constantly until dissolved. Use the bulb baster to remove the pan juices to a bowl for gravy. Serve with a light salad.

Yield: 8 servings (M)

Tip: This stuffing can also be used for holiday turkey.

Go to Gansemayer's for Goose

Gansemayer, a familiar name to every German in Manhattan, is a gentleman who, seventy years and more ago, established himself as a specialist in geese. Nearly seventy years ago, the original Simon Mayer was a butcher, with three daughters. One of them married a little fellow named Goldman. Riding home one evening on a Madison Avenue car, little Herr Goldman heard a precocious youth chirrup, merrily: "There's old man Gansemayer, and his son and daughter." And the name stuck. Gansemayer, which merely meant "goose-Mayer" then, now means Manhattan's headquarters for rare, delectable concoctions in which there figures every imaginable part of a goose, save only its honk!

You go to Gansemayer's—still located on Manhattan's Thirteenth Street, where it's been for half a century—for everything in the way of goose. Here there will be roast goose, broiled goose, with delectable red cabbage, potatoes, and applesauce; stuffed goose; potted goose; "gansgrieben," which, unless you're up on your German, you won't know means the skin of the goose, thoroughly rendered and served crisp and crackly; goose neck; goose giblets (called by an unpronounceable name); and goose livers.

River James, *Dining in New York,* 1930

Judah Benjamin's Friday Night Chicken with Peppers

Judah P. Benjamin, Secretary of State for the Confederacy, was known as a gourmet. His great friend, Varina Davis, wife of President of the Confederacy Jefferson Davis, wrote in a letter to a friend that Benjamin liked McHenry sherry, anchovy toast, and beefsteak pie. "Benjamin broke through the crust," she wrote, "breathed in the aroma deeply, then, with the care of one of the great chefs of Paris, forked the morsels into his mouth with his eyes closed, savoring every nuance of the spices, saying, 'I have only eaten it in this perfection on the Cunard steamers and I shall enjoy the memory of the scream of the sea birds, the lashing of the sea, and the blue above and the blue below.' "

After she offered him some hot bread with flour from a noted mill in Virginia and watched him spread a walnut paste on it derived from a huge tree on the White House grounds, Benjamin sighed, "Ah, with bread made of Crenshaw's flour, spread with paste made of English walnuts and a glass of McHenry's sherry a man's patriotism becomes rampant."

Mr. Benjamin, who also liked broiled chickens, came from a Sephardic background. His mother had lived in the West Indies and England before coming to the United States in 1811.

Dr. Benjamin Strong of Potomac, Maryland, who claims to be Mr. Benjamin's great-great-grandson out of wedlock, sent me a family recipe for chicken. In his letter he wrote, "This recipe was given to Varina Davis, the wife of the President of the Confederacy. It was noted on the recipe card that Mrs. Davis considered this recipe the finest, and it was served at the State functions in Richmond and Biloxi, Mississippi."

Although I could find no reference to this particular recipe in Mrs. Davis's correspondence, this old Navarran dish with chicken, tomatoes, olives, and peppers, called *pollo a la chilindron,* could well have been served in Benjamin's mother's kosher home in Fayetteville, North Carolina. Chances are the dish started out in Spain as a chicken with olives, similar to that eaten today in Morocco. The tomato and the peppers were added during his mother's family's travels this side of the Atlantic.

Judah Benjamin was a known gourmet.

Chicken with Peppers, cont.

*1 2- to 3-pound chicken, cut
    into 8 pieces*

*Salt and freshly ground pepper
    to taste*

¼ cup olive oil

2 large onions, quartered

*1 teaspoon finely chopped
    garlic*

*1 red pepper, seeded, deribbed,
    and cut lengthwise in ¼-inch
    strips*

*1 green pepper, seeded,
    deribbed, and cut lengthwise
    in ¼-inch strips*

*1 yellow pepper, seeded,
    deribbed, and cut lengthwise
    in ¼-inch strips*

*½ cup diced smoked turkey
    pastrami*

*6 medium tomatoes, peeled,
    seeded, and finely chopped,
    or 1 20-ounce can plum
    tomatoes with liquid*

*12 black olives, pitted and cut
    in half*

1. Pat the chicken pieces dry with paper towels and sprinkle them with salt and pepper. In a heavy skillet heat the oil over moderate heat until a light haze forms above it. Brown a few pieces of the chicken at a time, starting them skin side down and turning them with tongs. Regulate the heat so that the chicken colors quickly and evenly without burning. As the pieces become brown, transfer them to a plate.

2. Add the onions, garlic, peppers, and pastrami to the fat remaining in the skillet. Stirring frequently, cook 8 to 10 minutes over a moderate heat until the vegetables are soft but not brown. Add the tomatoes, raise the heat to medium high, and cook briskly until most of the liquid in the pan evaporates and the mixture is thick enough to hold its shape in a spoon. Return the chicken to the skillet, turning the pieces about with a spoon to coat them evenly with the sauce. Cover tightly and simmer over a low heat for 25 to 30 minutes or until the chicken is tender but not falling apart. Stir in the olives and taste for seasoning. Transfer the entire contents of the skillet to a heated serving bowl or deep platter and serve at once with rice or orzo.

Yield: 6 servings (M)

Gallina a la Vinagreta (Chicken with Vinegar Sauce, Olives, Raisins, and Garlic)

Myths abound concerning the cooking of Jewish food. It is true that Jews have always been garlic and onion eaters. A letter from a simple curate in the fifteenth century about the "abominable" new Christian goes as follows, ". . . for you must know that before the Inquisition their ways were just those of the filthy Jews, owing to their constant intercourse with them: thus they were gluttons and big eaters, and never lost their Jewish tastes in eating . . . stew of onions and garlic, and fried in oil, and the meat cooked in oil . . . to avoid lard, and oil with meat is a thing which gives an ill smell to the breath; and their doors smelt foul owing to stews and they themselves had the same smell as the Jews owing to their stews and to their not being baptised."

In the ancient world, garlic was known as an aphrodisiac. Since a Jewish husband is supposed to fulfill his marital obligation to his wife at least on Friday night, rabbis have suggested that garlic be used in dishes at the Sabbath eve meal. This old Sephardic chicken dish with lots of garlic comes from Danielle Schneider of Mount Vernon, New York (see page 1 2 3 for more on her). This is a perfect chicken for a Friday night dinner; it would be put on the stove before the Sabbath began and simmered for a few hours until the family was ready to eat. Mrs. Schneider's mother used to cut the garlic in half once it was cooked, squeeze out the cloves and put them in the sauce. "By the time they were cooked they were so sweet," said Mrs. Schneider.

*1 4-pound chicken, cut in
    8 pieces*

½ lemon

*2 cloves garlic plus 1 whole
    head*

Salt to taste

½ cup olive oil

*1 pound little white
    onions*

¼ cup green olives

¼ cup raisins

2 cloves

1 cinnamon stick

2 bay leaves

1 tablespoon peppercorns

¼ cup vinegar

*¼ cup Marsala or other sweet
    wine*

4 potatoes (optional)

1 . Clean the chicken with the lemon. Rub with the garlic cloves and sprinkle with salt.

2 . Heat the olive oil in a large sauté pan or pot with a cover over medium heat. Brown the chicken on all sides.

3 . When the chicken is brown, surround with the white onions, olives, and raisins. Slice off the top of the whole head of garlic and place in the center with a clove on each side and add the cinnamon stick, the bay leaves, and the peppercorns. Sprinkle with the vinegar and the wine. (You might want to tie the cloves and the peppercorns in a cheesecloth.)

4 . Cover and simmer over a very low heat for about 2 hours. You can add the peeled and diced potatoes to this dish for the last 1 5 to 2 0 minutes of cooking if you like or serve it with cooked rice. Discard the bay leaves and serve. Delicious!

Yield: 6 to 8 servings (M)

Jennie June's Brown Fricassee Chicken

The first American Jewish recipe I found for fricassee, a kind of ragout—usually made with chicken, browned lightly with onions in fat and then simmered in the drippings—came from a section on Jewish recipes in Jennie June's *American Cookery Book* of 1866. Jennie June Croley was one of the first American newspaper women and founder of the Sorosis Club. In her only cookbook she included a chapter on Jewish "receipts," which probably came to her from her Jewish friend, Genie H. Rosenfeld. "These are all original and reliable,—the contribution of a superior Jewish housekeeper in New York," she wrote. Mrs. Rosenfeld was the wife of the dramatist, Sydney Rosenfeld, who was also the first editor of *Puck*.

This nineteenth-century recipe cooks well today. The slow sautéing of the onions along with the nutmeg, mace, and thyme enhances the taste of the chicken. Serve it with rice.

1 4-pound frying chicken, cut up into 8 pieces

6 tablespoons olive oil

6 medium onions, sliced in rings

1 clove garlic, minced

2 tomatoes, peeled, or 1 16-ounce can stewing tomatoes with liquid

1 sprig fresh thyme

Salt and freshly ground pepper to taste

1/2 teaspoon allspice

Dash of mace

1/2 cup water

1. Brown the chicken in 2 tablespoons of the oil in a heavy sauté pan and set aside.

2. Drain the pan, add the remaining oil, and simmer the onions very slowly, covered, for about 15 minutes or until soft. Remove the cover, add the garlic, and sauté until the onions are golden.

3. Add the tomatoes and simmer a few minutes. Then add the chicken, the thyme, salt, pepper, allspice, mace, and water. Cover and cook for a half hour or until the chicken is tender, adding water if sauce is too thick.

Yield: 6 servings (M)

Ess Ess Mein Kind — Eat That Chicken

The peddlers also sold chickens and geese hung from carts by the neck. A housewife bought a half or a quarter of a chicken, and many of those who could not afford a whole one bought smaller pieces for the Sabbath meal.

Hutchins Hapgood, *The Spirit of the Ghetto,* 1902

I'll never forget the day my grandmother told me about the "poo-pek." This was the kidney of the chicken entrails. That too, I relished and always waited for it to be cooked so I could gobble it down. The "poo-pek" was not to be confused with the "pipik." The "pipik" was my child's belly-button on which she put the "hamdela and the hemdela" (I think that meant undershirt). Whenever I cook, I like to feel I am part of my grandmother's legacy. The most Jewish part of her was her love. And her love went into her cooking as it did into my heart.   Roberta E. Sherry, Alhambra, California

Every part of the chicken was important to the poor immigrant family. The mother kept saying to her children, "Eat, eat, my child." Weight and food were connected to survival because an early symptom of feared tuberculosis was loss of appetite and loss of weight. The Eastern European immigrants either bought smaller pieces as described above or tried to stretch one whole chicken, using the breast for cutlets or gefilte chicken, the carcass for soup, and the giblets and wings for fricassee, adding some tiny ground meatballs. A beloved part was the feet for fricassee and for soup.

Molly Picon in the film
Mamele *(Poland, 1938)*

Chicken Fricassee with Meatballs

According to the food writer Mimi Sheraton, who loved her mother's chicken fricassee dearly, meatballs were a Jewish addition to the dish. This may be, but meatballs, a sign of abundance, may have been included in America in the same way that Italians added meatballs to their pasta dishes.

The following chicken fricassee with meatballs came to Queens from Rumania three generations ago. A favorite sight was to watch the chicken feet being singed before being thrown into the pot. The late May Aledort added Chinese noodles to her mother's dish and insisted, according to her handwriting on the tomato-blotched recipe, that the tomato sauce must be Hunt's.

1 3-pound chicken, cut into 8 pieces with giblets (except the liver)

1 package extra giblets

6 wings (about 2 pounds)

Salt and freshly ground pepper to taste

¼ cup vegetable oil

4 medium onions, peeled and finely chopped plus ½ onion, grated

2 cloves garlic, peeled

3 cups tomato sauce (or to taste)

1 cup water

2 pounds ground beef

2 medium eggs

¼ cup bread crumbs or matzah meal

1. Season the chicken, giblets, and extra wings with salt and pepper and sauté in oil over a medium heat in a Dutch oven or other large casserole. Remove from the pan and set aside.

2. Add the chopped onions to the pan and cook until golden. Drain. Add the chicken, garlic, the giblets, the extra wings, tomato sauce, water, and, if necessary, additional tomato sauce so that the liquid comes two thirds up the side of the chicken. Cover and simmer gently for 20 minutes.

3. In the meantime, make the meatballs by mixing together the ground beef, the remaining half grated onion, eggs, bread crumbs or matzah meal and salt and pepper. Form into tiny meatballs, slightly smaller than the size of a walnut. Add carefully to the chicken, pouring in a little more water or tomato sauce if the sauce has evaporated. Simmer, covered, for 20 to 30 minutes or until the meatballs are done. Serve with rice, noodles, or crisp Chinese noodles.

Yield: 8 servings (M)

Note: Other recipes have sliced carrots and peppers in the sauce as well as tomato paste and vermouth instead of tomato sauce . . . and, if you want, a few raisins and apricot pieces.

Gefilte Chicken

"This is a dish my grandmother used to make," said Lynn Gerber of Chevy Chase, Maryland. Her grandmother Fanny Levine came to Brownsville, Brooklyn, from Vilna in 1903. "We sat around one day and asked her to show us how she made it. I am glad we did. Now we have the recipe."

2 pounds ground chicken or
*　turkey*

1 medium onion, chopped

1 grated carrot

½ cup matzah meal

1 teaspoon peanut or vegetable
*　oil*

Kosher salt to taste

1 teaspoon sugar

2 large eggs, beaten

½ cup cold water

2 red peppers, sliced in rings

2 Spanish onions, sliced in
*　rings*

1. Mix the ground chicken or turkey, onion, carrot, matzah meal, oil, salt, sugar, eggs, and water. Grease the bottom of a 9- by 13-inch glass baking dish or use non-stick cooking spray.

2. Place in the pan 1 large red pepper ring and smaller onion rings within the pepper. Take ⅓ to ½ cup of the chicken mixture and form into a round patty. Place the patty over the pepper and the onions. Repeat until all the mixture is used up.

3. Bake for 45 minutes in a preheated 350-degree oven. Serve hot or warm.

Yield: makes about 12 patties, serving 6 to 8 people (M)

Kosher Grits, Gumbo, and Jambalaya at a Jewish Nursing Home in New Orleans

When you think of a kosher nursing home, you think of very mild chicken soup and boiled meat. Not in New Orleans. At the Jewish Community Center's Willow Wood Nursing Home, Audry Edmonds makes sure that her Louisiana clientele have enough spice in their food. Every once in a while she prepares a Cajun feast with kosher jambalaya, gumbo and red beans and rice. "Kosher Cajun's not hard," she said. "You just don't spice it up much for the older people. I use all the spices I would at home with garlic salt, onion, bell pepper, Season-All but not the hot jambalaya spices like cayenne pepper," she explained. "We use turkey and kosher sausage for the gumbo and red beans and rice with kosher sausage. On the milk side it's all Jewish—quiches, lox, bagels and cream cheese. We stick to Cajun when it comes to meat." The cook must be doing something right with these potentially fiery dishes because there is always a waiting list at the hundred-bed home.

West Hartford's Crown Supermarket— New England's Largest Kosher Supermarket

The Crown Supermarket in West Hartford, Connecticut, is more than a market. Open since 1940, it is the meeting place of the Jewish community, kosher or not, and is the largest kosher grocery store in New England. "On Sunday mornings it is a real social scene. The aisles are filled not with madly rushing people and carriages, but with friends kibbitzing and catching up with one another," said Amy Warner, who grew up in West Hartford. Modern and streamlined, the full-service store has an enormous deli department as well as meat, fish, and the Five O'Clock Shop with prepared food to go. In the basement two in-house kitchens—one dairy and the other meat—make everything from scratch, even the cream cheese spreads, the poached salmon, the meat loaves, and the sesame noodle salad with snap beans. On any given day there are forty items for families on the go, such as fresh chicken pot pies, homemade knishes, pasta dinners, and turkey cutlets.

In the 1950s the Crown challenged the Blue Laws, which forces Sunday closings, because as a kosher supermarket, it had always been closed on Saturday. Eventually the law was reversed. Today the market teems with people and new tastes on Sundays.

Chicken Jambalaya

This recipe is adapted from the *Kosher Cajun Cookbook* by Mildred L. Covert and Sylvia P. Gerson, two New Orleans women who have written several kosher Cajun cookbooks. It is not far from the Jewish version of Spanish rice, which consists of chicken, rice, and tomatoes as described by Mrs. Rorer in 1902. See page 240 for more on Mrs. Rorer.

1 large onion

2 shallots

1 green pepper

1 stalk celery

2 cloves garlic, peeled

*1 3-pound frying chicken, cut
   into 8 pieces*

1 tablespoon paprika

¼ cup olive oil

*½ cup diced veal sausage,
   sliced*

*1 28-ounce can stewed
   tomatoes*

1⅓ cups chicken broth

1 cup uncooked rice

1 teaspoon minced parsley

½ teaspoon thyme

½ teaspoon salt

½ teaspoon black pepper

*¼ teaspoon Tabasco sauce or
   to taste*

1. In a food processor fitted with a metal blade process the onion, shallots, green pepper, celery, and garlic with on and off pulses until they are minced, or chop by hand. Set aside.

2. Rub the chicken with paprika. Brown the chicken in olive oil in a large skillet. Remove the chicken from the pan and set aside.

3. Add the chopped vegetables to the pan. Sauté until the onion is transparent, about 10 minutes. Stir in the diced sausage, tomatoes, chicken broth, rice, herbs, and the seasonings. Return the chicken to the pan and spoon the sauce over it. Heat to boiling; then reduce the heat, cover, and simmer for 30 minutes or until the chicken is tender. Adjust seasonings and serve.

Yield: 6 servings (M)

Tip: Vary this dish depending on what is in your refrigerator. A nice menu would be to start with Chicken, Lime, and Tortilla Soup (see page 126), followed by this jambalaya and a green salad with the almond pecan torte for dessert.

Give Me My Southern Fried Chicken with Matzah Meal

My life growing up in Albany, Georgia, was similar to that in *Driving Miss Daisy*. And so were the relationships. In my own house the cooking was done by a black cook trained by my grandmother. When the cook became ill, my mother cooked for the cook. Many of the usual Jewish traditions were mixed with southern ones with a black influence. We had, for example, good southern pit barbecue and Brunswick stew with kreplach in it. We'd also eat things that my grandfather remembered from Rumania and that my grandmother tried to reconstruct. It was a delightful mixture. We didn't have a kosher house. We'd have Jewish homemade gefilte fish and matzah balls with southern vegetables and fried chicken. At Passover we'd go to Temple B'nai Israel, founded in 1840, for a communal seder with most of the one hundred Jewish families. It was very pleasant. The dinner was usually prepared by the women of the sisterhood. We had very good matzah ball soup with a beef base soup with tomatoes. One of the reasons I can't give recipes is my grandmother taught our cook how to cook and she didn't read so she cooked with "a right smart of this and a little bit of that" and you cooked until it was done. How did you know it was done? You looked. The fried chicken was delicious, very tasty, peppery, quite crisp and not heavy.

Ellen Rollins, born in Albany, Georgia

For many Southern Jews like Ellen Rollins, in whose home the cook was black, Jewish food became all mixed up—green tomatoes with kippers and grits, black-eyed peas served with kishka and schmaltz, and red beans and rice and matzah meal–breaded Southern fried chicken.

Georgian-Jewish Southern Fried Chicken

In addition to the matzah meal, Southern chicken became "Jewish" when the lard was replaced with vegetable shortening and the chicken was dipped in egg instead of milk.

1 teaspoon salt

1 clove garlic, mashed

2 teaspoons sweet paprika

*2 frying chickens, cut into
    8 pieces each*

1 teaspoon bitters

1 teaspoon lemon juice

1 teaspoon bourbon

¼ cup water

2 large eggs, well beaten

1½ cups matzah meal

*Vegetable oil or shortening for
    frying*

1. Mix the salt, garlic, and paprika in a small container. Place the chicken in a bowl and sprinkle with the spices.

2. In a saucepan bring to a boil the bitters, lemon juice, bourbon, and water and pour over the chickens. Let marinate for several hours.

3. Drain the chicken and put on a plate. Beat the eggs and add to the remaining marinade in a separate bowl. Place the matzah meal in another bowl. Roll the chicken pieces in the matzah meal, then in the egg mixture, and finally in the matzah meal again.

4. Heat about 4 inches of oil to 375 degrees in a heavy pot. Gently add several pieces of the chicken and let it brown well, for about 6 minutes. Turn over and brown for another 6 minutes on the second side. Then turn down the heat to low and let it cook slowly for another 10 minutes until the chicken is well cooked inside. Repeat until all the chicken is cooked.

Yield: at least 8 servings (M)

Tip: I use an electric wok for frying. It uses less oil because of the sloping sides.

North Carolina Variation: Instead of marinating the chicken, merely combine salt, pepper, and Accent to taste in a bag with the matzah meal and dip the chicken first in the egg mixture and then shake in the matzah meal before frying.

South Louisiana Stewed Chicken

This spicy chicken stew is served Cajun style with rice, or Jewish style with matzah balls (see page 110). Adapted from Carol Anne Blitzer.

1 cup flour

Salt to taste

1 teaspoon black pepper

1 teaspoon cayenne pepper

1 large stewing chicken, cut
*   into 8 pieces*

Vegetable oil for frying

1 large onion, finely chopped

4 ribs celery, finely chopped

1 bunch chopped parsley

1 bunch green onions
*   (scallions), finely chopped*

1 bell pepper, finely chopped

1. Mix the flour, salt, black pepper, and cayenne pepper in a paper bag. Toss the chicken pieces in the bag one at a time until they are coated. You may need more seasoned flour if you run out.

2. Fry the chicken pieces in 2 inches of hot oil until golden brown. A black iron pot works beautifully for this. Remove from the oil and drain on a paper towel or brown bag.

3. Pour off some of the fat, leaving about ½ cup in the pot. Add some of the leftover flour and cook over a medium heat, stirring constantly, until browned to a dark roux. Do not let it burn.

4. Turn off the heat and add the chopped vegetables to the roux, stirring until they are soft.

5. Add hot water to the roux, stirring to make it smooth; you need about 1½ inches of liquid in the pot.

6. Return the chicken pieces to the pot, making sure that they are almost covered, adding more water if necessary.

7. Cover and cook slowly for about 2 hours, or until the chicken falls away from the bone.

8. Add more salt, black pepper, and cayenne pepper if needed. This needs to be well seasoned.

Serve hot with rice or Cajun matzah balls (see page 394).

Yield: 8 servings (M)

Iraqi Chamim with Chicken and Rice

Unlike the beans and meat *chamim* of the Sephardic Jews, Iraqi and Indian Jews often make a Sabbath stew of chicken and rice. Once heavily seasoned with cardamom, cloves, turmeric, and cinnamon and scattered with rose petals, it often included whole eggs in the shell and turnips or beets. Everything was steamed together in a wide-bottomed copper pot, covered with quilts, and put over slow-burning coals. "I remember the hard-boiled eggs very clearly," said David Sofaer of San Francisco. "I looked forward to eating them. They were cooked by the steam of the *chamim*." These same eggs, preserved by long cooking, were food for merchants and itinerant rabbis as they voyaged during the week. Today the dish rarely contains eggs, turnips, and potatoes, and it is cooked in a hot oven for 1½ hours. Nevertheless, the modern version is delicious. The crust of rice that forms inside the casserole is still the prized portion as it has been for hundreds of years in the Sofaer family.

2 cups basmati rice

4 cups water

Salt and freshly ground pepper to taste

4 large carrots, peeled and chopped

2 medium tomatoes, peeled, chopped, and seeded, or 2 cups canned plum tomatoes, drained and chopped

1 teaspoon turmeric

½ teaspoon ground ginger

1 cardamom pod or ⅛ teaspoon ground cardamom

1 4-pound chicken, fat removed but not skin

1. Mix all the ingredients except the chicken in a large greased casserole. Place the chicken in the middle.

2. Cover and bake in a preheated 350-degree oven for 1½ hours or until most of the liquid has been absorbed. The rice and chicken should be slightly moist. Serve with fresh coriander chutney (see page 266) and a green salad.

Yield: 6 to 8 servings (M)

Bukharan Chicken Pilau

According to food historian Karen Hess, pilau came to this country by way of the Jews who fled Persia and went to Provence. There the dish became so much a part of the regional cuisine that pickled pork was added to it. This version, eaten by Bukharan Jews for the Sabbath and, unlike Ashkenazic Jews, for Passover, came from Bukhara to Palestine to Los Angeles.

⅓ cup vegetable oil

4 medium onions, diced

3- to 4-pound frying chicken,
   cut into 8 pieces

5 to 6 large carrots

2 cups white rice

Salt and pepper to taste

½ teaspoon cinnamon

¼ cup raisins (optional)

3 cups water

¼ cup toasted pine nuts
   (optional)

1. In a large pot heat the oil, then add onions, and cook them, stirring occasionally, until they are barely golden.

2. While the onions are cooking, thoroughly clean the chicken, removing as much fat as possible. Add the chicken pieces to the pot and cook, uncovered, over medium heat for 15 minutes, mixing occasionally.

3. While the chicken is cooking, peel the carrots, then make them into shavings using a vegetable peeler or use the julienne blade of a food processor.

4. Remove the chicken and onions and place a handful of rice and handful of carrots in the bottom of the pot. (Don't worry if there doesn't seem to be much oil in the pot.) Replace the chicken and onions, top with the remaining carrots, salt, pepper, cinnamon, and raisins. Cook, covered, over low to medium heat for 10 minutes.

5. Sprinkle the remaining rice over the chicken, add the water, and cook, uncovered, over high heat until it boils vigorously. Stir the rice, being careful not to disturb the chicken. Cover and reduce the heat to low. Cook for one-half to one hour or until the rice is done. After 20 minutes, wrap the cover of the pot in a thin kitchen towel to absorb excess moisture. Then put the cover back on. Serve piping hot, garnished with pine nuts if desired.

Yield: 4 to 6 servings (M)
Tip: To make a vegetarian version, omit the chicken and substitute fresh mushrooms and red pepper. For crisper vegetables, stir in lightly sautéed vegetables just before serving the pilau.

Syrian-American Chicken with Tomato Sauce and Spaghetti

"This chicken dish started with sliced potatoes," said Sarina Roffe of the Brooklyn Syrian community. "The trick was to make the potatoes crusty on the bottom—we love that crispness in our household. Because we all liked spaghetti with tomato sauce, we replaced the potatoes." The tomato sauce is still doctored-up Syrian style with allspice and cinnamon and the chicken rubbed with paprika in the Middle Eastern tradition.

1 3½-pound chicken
Kosher salt to taste
Freshly ground pepper to taste
1 teaspoon paprika
¼ cup vegetable oil
1 6-ounce can tomato paste
1 cup tomato sauce
1 tablespoon cinnamon or to taste
1 tablespoon allspice or to taste
½ teaspoon white pepper
1 pound thin spaghetti

1. Season the chicken with salt, pepper, and paprika and sprinkle with 2 tablespoons of the oil or spray with vegetable spray. Place the chicken in a roaster and bake, covered, in a preheated 350-degree oven for 1 hour.
2. Remove the chicken from the oven and pour 2 tablespoons of the drippings into a saucepan. (You can add all but I wanted a less fatty sauce.) Add the tomato paste and sauce, cinnamon, allspice, and the white pepper. Stir over a low heat to mix thoroughly.
3. Meanwhile, cook the spaghetti according to the directions on the package. Drain and mix with the sauce.
4. Pour the remaining 2 tablespoons of the oil into the bottom of the roaster, swirling it around the sides and reheat until very hot. Remove from the heat and add the spaghetti to cover the bottom and sides of the pan. Place the chicken in the center, breast up, and bake, covered, for 30 minutes. Remove the cover and brown for 15 more minutes. Remove the chicken to a serving platter and surround with the spaghetti.

Yield: 6 to 8 servings (M)

A Nineties Twist to a Grandmother's Roast Chicken

My grandmother made a great Friday night dinner in her two-story limestone in Crown Heights, Brooklyn. She might as well have run a restaurant. There was lots and lots and lots of stuff—kreplach, *gribenes*, gefilte fish, blintzes, homemade noodles, roast chicken, glazed carrots, egg barley with dried Polish mushrooms. In 1918 during an influenza epidemic my grandmother was 20 years old with two children. First her husband died and two days later her mother died. With eight younger siblings and two of her own she took care of ten kids in the family. Then an aunt caught the flu and died leaving 8 or 9 children. My grandmother then married her uncle and raised 18 kids.

The secret to her roast chicken was to cook it long enough to render the fat from the chicken and make it crispy.

Eddie Schoenfeld, New York restaurateur

4 cloves garlic or to taste

1 4-pound chicken, cut into halves or eighths

Juice of 1 lemon

Salt and freshly ground pepper to taste

Sprigs of fresh rosemary, thyme, and sage

¼ cup vegetable or olive oil

1. Smash the garlic slightly with a knife and rub into the chicken well along with the lemon. Salt and pepper the chicken and cover with the herbs. Dribble with a little of the vegetable or olive oil. Cover and leave in the refrigerator overnight, turning the herbs and chicken once.

2. Remove the herbs from the chicken. Heat a heavy ovenproof skillet large enough to hold all the pieces. Add the remaining tablespoon or 2 of the oil and place the chicken skin side down. Brown the chicken over a medium-high heat for about 5 minutes on one side.

3. Remove the skillet with the chicken to a preheated 350-degree oven and bake for 30 to 40 minutes or until the chicken is crisp and the juices run clear.

Yield: 6 servings (M)

Chicken Fingers—A Friday Night Tradition for Children

Since Friday night dinner in the American Jewish home often means chicken, cooks try to find recipes appealing to children. As a child in the fifties I remember barbecued chicken wings at a neighbor's every Friday; at my home roast chicken alternated with the latest "gourmet" recipe, such as baked fried chicken with corn flakes or in a sauce made from apricot jam and mayonnaise. Today, in a world influenced by McDonald's, I sometimes make these chicken fingers for my children. They love them. This recipe is adapted from Dorothy Regensteiner.

2 whole chicken breasts, skinned and boned

1 large egg, beaten

2 tablespoons warm water

3 tablespoons vegetable oil

Onion salt to taste

Salt and freshly ground pepper to taste

Fresh bread crumbs made from last week's leftover challah

1. Cut the chicken breasts into 3-inch strips.
2. Mix the egg, warm water, oil, onion salt, and salt and pepper in a wide soup bowl.
3. Place the bread crumbs in a second bowl.
4. Dip the chicken strips into the egg mixture and then the bread crumbs. Refrigerate a few hours.
5. Bake in a preheated 350-degree oven for 30 minutes or until golden or fry in a slight amount of additional margarine until golden on each side.

Yield: 4 to 6 servings (M)

Grilled Garlic and Coriander Chicken

This is a recipe with biblical ingredients that my neighbor Cindy Goldman shared with me. It is simple to make and good for a Shabbat dinner in the summer. You can make it several hours ahead and serve it at room temperature with a good tabbouleh salad (see page 292). Coriander was thought to be the biblical manna in the desert.

3 boned and skinned chicken breasts, halved

2 cloves garlic, peeled and diced

Salt and freshly ground pepper to taste

Juice of 1 lime

¼ cup good extra-virgin olive oil

1 cup chopped fresh coriander

1. Place the chicken in a glass Pyrex dish. Rub with the garlic and season with salt and pepper to taste. Dribble the lime juice and the olive oil over the chicken. Sprinkle with the coriander and let sit in the refrigerator covered for several hours.
2. Cook on an outdoor grill several minutes on each side. When browned, serve or let sit until ready to serve at room temperature.

Yield: 6 servings (M)

Anne Rosenzweig's Molasses Roast Quail with Savoy Cabbage and Kasha

Judith Gerber, an Israeli ex-kibbutznik living in upstate New York, started Glatt Game Gourmet. "The Jewish people caught quail when they were wandering in the desert," said Ms. Gerber. "One aspect of my company is bringing the old to the new and to the health conscious, who all want low-in-fat foods. You can eat as much of my quail and venison as you want and don't have to worry about your health. Next we would like to have partridge and bison, also biblical game."

A perfect use of quail is Arcadia chef Anne Rosenzweig's molasses roast quail with Savoy cabbage and kasha.

THE QUAIL

8 5-ounce quail, boned

1½ cups vegetable oil

½ cup molasses

1 head garlic, sliced in half

1 orange, sliced with rind on

1 knob fresh ginger, sliced (about 2 inches)

Small handful cracked black pepper

THE CABBAGE

¼ pound smoked goose breast or ¼ cup vegetable oil

1 tablespoon chopped garlic

1 pound Savoy cabbage, cored and slivered

1 large carrot, peeled and julienned

1 medium zucchini, julienned using only outside half-inch

½ cup lightly toasted pine nuts

Pinch of caraway seeds

Salt and pepper to taste

1. Place the quail in a glass bowl and cover with the oil, molasses, garlic, orange, ginger, and black pepper. Cover and let sit overnight in the refrigerator.

2. Remove the quail from the marinade. Heat a large sauté pan over a moderately high heat. Place the quail in the pan breast-side down. Cook until golden brown, about 5 minutes. Turn, continue cooking for 2 more minutes. Remove from the heat and keep warm.

3. To prepare the cabbage, brown the goose breast until slightly crispy and add the vegetable oil in a large sauté pan. Over a moderately high heat add the garlic, cabbage, carrot, and zucchini and toss quickly. Cook until the cabbage is just barely wilted. Add the pine nuts, caraway seeds, and salt and pepper. Serve hot with kasha (see page 287 for the best way to cook kasha) as a bed for the quail.

Yield: 8 servings (M)

American Jewish chefs like Anne Rosenzweig reinterpret classic Jewish dishes.

Kosher Chicken in the Pot at The Lodge at Vail?

One of the extraordinary trends in the 1990s is Jewish food popping up just about every-where. While skiing on the slopes in Beaver Creek, Colorado, I learned about a Jewish chef who only uses kosher chickens.

"I use kosher chicken because my mother said they taste better," said Jim Cohen, chef at The Lodge at Vail. "I think they taste much better than free-range chickens."

At the Culinary Institute of America, Chef Cohen was taught the classic *mirepoix,* which is two parts onion to one part celery and one part carrot. "My classic training just didn't work for my mother's chicken soup. She put in three parts carrot to one part parsnip, celery, and onion with a little parsley. By listening to my mother, I now make good chicken soup."

Besides his chicken soup, similar to the one on page 106, Chef Cohen makes a great chicken in the pot, one of the most popular dishes on his menu. "You can put anything in it that's seasonal," he said. "If fresh peas are available throw them in at the last minute. I've put in cauliflower or broccoli."

1 4-pound kosher chicken, cut in 8 pieces

Kosher salt and freshly ground pepper to taste

1/4 cup extra-virgin olive oil

12 ounces dark beer

8 white boiling onions about the size of a quarter, peeled (about 1 pound)

8 whole garlic cloves, peeled

4 wedges of green cabbage from a medium head (2 1/2 pounds)

3 large carrots, peeled and cut in 1-inch-long chunks

4 medium yellow potatoes, quartered, or 12 new potatoes whole (about 2 pounds)

2 cups chicken stock

1/2 cup chopped flat-leaf parsley

1. Season the chicken with kosher salt and pepper. Sear the chicken in 2 tablespoons olive oil in a sauté pan. Place in a clay pot or casserole with a cover.

2. Deglaze the pan that the chicken was seared in with the beer.

3. Place the beer, the vegetables, and the stock in the pot with the chicken. Cover and cook in a preheated 400-degree oven for about 1 hour or until the chicken and the vegetables are tender. Remove from the oven, add the remaining olive oil and parsley, and check for seasoning.

   Serve in soup bowls.

Yield: 4 to 6 servings (M)
My tip: Add cooked matzah balls at the last minute—delicious!

Chicken Pandora with Sun-dried Tomatoes and Artichoke Hearts

This is a good recipe, especially for a buffet dinner because you don't need knives. It was inspired by the popular chicken Marbella in the *Silver Palate Cookbook* and is typical of the kind of colorful and tasteful food in the Crown Supermarket's prepared food case. Adapted from Joy Stern of Washington.

½ cup good quality red-wine vinegar

½ cup plus 1 tablespoon light olive oil

½ cup fresh oregano

¼ cup fresh parsley, chopped

1 head fresh garlic, peeled and pureed

Kosher salt and freshly ground pepper to taste

3 bay leaves

1 cup ripe pitted olives, halved

5 pounds of boneless and skinned chicken breasts, halved

¾ cup brown sugar

1 cup good red wine

8 shallots, chopped

1 tablespoon margarine

1 cup sun-dried tomatoes, halved

2 16-ounce cans artichoke hearts, drained

1. In a 9- by 12-inch or similar size baking dish, mix the wine vinegar, ½ cup of the olive oil, the oregano, parsley, garlic, kosher salt, pepper, bay leaves, and olives. Add the chicken breasts and marinate, covered with foil, in the refrigerator overnight.

2. The next day sprinkle with the brown sugar and red wine. Bake for 1 hour, covered, in a preheated 350-degree oven. Cool.

3. Remove the chicken breasts and cut into bite-size chunks and return to the baking dish.

4. In a frying pan sauté the shallots in the margarine and remaining tablespoon olive oil over a medium-high heat. Add the sun-dried tomatoes and artichoke hearts.

5. Pour the sun-dried tomato mixture over the chicken and reheat in the 350-oven for about 15 minutes. Discard the bay leaves and serve with a large green salad, saffron rice, and a good bottle of red wine.

Yield: 12 servings (M)

SEVEN

יְרָקוֹת

Vegetables and Salads—From Leeks to Latkes

The things she brought back from market! Eggplant in midwinter, and tomatoes, and a yellow fruit which had the shape of a cucumber and the taste of a muskmelon. I had never seen such huge eggplants in all my life. And there was another thing which was entirely strange, but which inquiry revealed was cauliflower—an article father had once eaten at the home of my cousin, the doctor, in Bucharest and had never ceased talking about.

M. E. Ravage, *An American in the Making,* 1917

An onion must be cut across the top that sticks out of the earth, not the bottom that rests in the soil. This way you are not shortening yours or anybody else's life. I lost my mother in October 1978 and would never cut any growing vegetable or fruit any other way. I guess Jewish mothers from Europe got through to their children—even in America.

Elaine R. Parnes, Bell Canyon, California

Prasa (Turkish Leeks with Tomatoes)

Leeks were one of the earliest Jewish vegetables, first eaten in captivity in Egypt. "We remember the leeks, onions and garlic," moaned the Israelites in the desert (Numbers 11:6). This dish, best prepared in advance, can be served cold, at room temperature, or heated and has been adapted from a recipe by Susan Barocas.

1 to 2 tablespoons olive oil

1 16-ounce can whole tomatoes with the juice or

4 to 6 over-ripe tomatoes, seeded and roughly chopped, reserving 1½ cups juice

2 cloves garlic, diced fine or crushed

4 large leeks, cut lengthwise, thoroughly cleaned, and cut into 1-inch pieces, using the tender green and white parts

Juice of 1 small lemon

Salt and freshly ground pepper to taste

1. To make the *sofrito,* which is the basis of dishes like this, heat the olive oil in a saucepan. When just hot, carefully add the tomatoes without any juice, mashing them roughly. (Watch out for splattering oil.) Stir to blend and simmer for 3 to 5 minutes.

2. Add the garlic to the *sofrito* and simmer for 3 to 5 minutes more.

3. Add the leeks and 1 cup of the juice saved from the tomatoes. Slowly simmer the mixture, covered, for a minimum of 1 hour until the leeks are really soft and the flavors have blended, adding more juice or water if the leeks become too dry.

4. Add the lemon juice and the salt and pepper. Stir and simmer, covered, for 10 to 15 minutes longer just to blend the flavors. Serve hot, cold, or at room temperature. The dish will keep several days in the refrigerator.

Yield: at least 6 servings (P)

Tip: Vary the garlic and the amount of lemon to your taste. If you are not a garlic lover substitute a tablespoon of brown sugar for the garlic.

Tip: An easy way to clean leeks is to trim them, chop them, put them in a strainer inside a bowl of cold water and swish them around several times to remove the grit and separate the pieces.

Tomatoes and a Jewish Doctor in Colonial Williamsburg

When the explorers brought tomatoes to Europe from Peru and Mexico, European physicians tested them first to see if they were edible. This relative of the nightshade family was thought to be poisonous, with bitter fruits containing toxins and/or hallucinogenic compounds. The Germans called it "wolf-peach" because they thought the juices could be used to evoke werewolves. It was the British who brought the tomatoes to the United States as ornamental plants, not as food.

At the same time that tomatoes were being discovered here, Jews in Eastern Europe associated them with the color of blood. Since blood is taboo in Jewish cooking, Jews either avoided eating tomatoes or cooked them to death as they did meat.

Thomas Jefferson credited Dr. John de Sequeyra (pronounced *Siccary*), a Sephardic doctor in Colonial Williamsburg, as the first to introduce the tomato as a food plant to Virginia. The doctor believed that daily consumption of the tomato not only maintained good health but prolonged life. At the time he was taking care of the third president's father. According to one account, Jefferson created some commotion in the late 1700s when he made a display of eating a tomato in public in Lynchburg, Virginia.

With the Jewish doctor's blessing—and possibly that of other doctors—people began using tomatoes in cooking. Dr. Sequeyra may very well have eaten a variation of this leek and tomato dish.

Of Green Beans and Judia

Of all the New World beans integrated into the diet with the Columbus exchange, one was different. *Judia,* string bean in Spanish, means both Jew and green bean. There are a number of theories as to why this bean—native to India, Bengal, and Central and South America—should be called *judia* (pronounced *hudia*). It is possible that a Jewish merchant was the first to bring to Spain string beans from South or Central America or from India. Some called the bean *"faba judea,"* meaning bean from the East. Or perhaps merchants knew that Jews bought beans for the Sabbath dish and started calling these new beans *judia.* Another theory is quite extraordinary. Just as Jews are different from everyone else, green beans are unlike other beans because they are not soaked in water or "baptized" before being used! Some say that green beans resemble the horns that the Jews were rumored to have, or the color of the green beans resembles the olive skin of the Jews. This is one gastronomic puzzle that will probably never be solved.* Although *judia* originally meant green beans, it has come to mean all beans in Spanish.

*Many of these theories come from various editions of Juan Corominas's *Diccionario Critico Stimologico Castellano E Hispanico,* Madrid Gredos.

Old Sephardic String Bean and Beef Stew

An old Jewish recipe that was brought to this country with the earliest Sephardic immigrants is for a tomato-less beef and string bean stew. The recipe came to the New World before tomatoes went to the old. Because it was a traditional family recipe, passed down from generation to generation, it has remained in its original form.

3 pounds lean brisket of beef, chuck, shoulder steak, or breast deckel (second cut of brisket)

1 clove garlic

Salt and freshly ground pepper to taste

2 tablespoons olive oil

12 tiny whole or 3 large onions, sliced

4 whole black peppercorns

½ teaspoon whole allspice or to taste

2 cups water or tomato juice (about)

2 pounds fresh string beans

1. Rub the brisket with garlic and season well with salt and pepper. Brown in the oil in a heavy pan. Remove.
2. Spread the onions on the bottom of the pan, then place the brisket on top. Put the peppercorns and allspice in a cheesecloth bag and add.
3. Add enough water or tomato juice to cover the meat and simmer, covered, for 2 hours. Let stand until cool and then refrigerate several hours or overnight. Skim off the fat and slice thin.
4. Remove the tip ends and string the beans if desired. Add to the meat and simmer slowly, covered, ½ hour more or until the beans are tender. Adjust seasoning and serve.

Yield: 6 to 8 servings (M)
Tip: A later version of this "Jewish" recipe from Mrs. Rorer's **New Cook Book** *of 1902 includes a tablespoon of sugar and 2 tablespoons of vinegar added 15 minutes before serving. The proportions of sugar and vinegar depend on the strength of the vinegar. The more sugar needed the stronger the vinegar is.*

The First Kosher Cookbook in America

Having undertaken the present work with the view of proving that, without violating the precepts of our religion, a table can be spread, which will satisfy the appetites of the most fastidious. Some have, from ignorance, been led to believe that a repast, to be sumptuous, must unavoidably admit of forbidden food. We do not venture too much when we assert that our writing clearly refutes that false notion. . . . The want of a work of this description has long been felt in our domestic circles.

Esther Levy, *Jewish Cookery Book,* 1871

Esther Jacobs Levy, author of the *Jewish Cookery Book,* the first American kosher cookbook, written in 1871, was probably an English Jew living in Philadelphia. Little is known about her except that she registered the book herself at the Library of Congress. According to the Philadelphia census of 1870, an English-born Esther Levy lived in the home of Judah Isaacs, a Dutch physician, and was a clerk in a store. By the census of 1880 there was no Esther Levy. She may have remarried or died.

Mrs. Levy's recipes come from the different backgrounds of Jewry—English, German, Sephardic, and American. Local dandelion greens are used in salads, and corn is cooked in a fritter resembling oysters, a popular nineteenth-century dish. In the 1870s *The New York Times* published one of the book's recipes for *wosht,* or sausage and rice, without acknowledging the source.

Mrs. Levy suggests the main dinner meal for Sunday, to accommodate the work week of the Jewish shopkeeper. According to custom, preparation for this Sabbath meal was carried out on Friday—it was enjoyed, however, on Sunday, when "husbands are at home, then something good must be prepared in honor of the lords of the household."

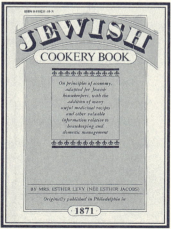

Esther Levy wrote the first kosher cookbook in America in 1871.

Esther Levy's Pennsylvania Corn "Oysters"

These fritters were a popular vegetable in the eighteenth and nineteenth centuries.

6 ears boiled corn or 3 cups
   frozen corn
Salt and freshly ground pepper
   to taste
3 large eggs, separated
1½ tablespoons flour
Nutmeg to taste
2 tablespoons unsalted butter
   or margarine
2 tablespoons vegetable oil

1. Grate the corn off the cobs and season with salt and pepper.
2. Beat the yolks well until they are thick. Mix the yolks with the corn and add the flour and the nutmeg.
3. Beat the whites until stiff peaks form and fold into the corn mixture.
4. Heat the butter or margarine and oil in a frying pan. Place a heaping tablespoon of the batter in the pan and fry light brown on both sides. Drain and serve immediately.

Yield: 15 to 20 corn "oysters" (D) or (P)

Onions and Chestnuts

The old recipes for this dish included goose fat and veal or chicken gravy added just before serving. Adapted from Harriet Meyer's Cookbook, 1913.

¼ cup chicken fat or vegetable
   oil
4 pounds of onions, peeled and
   sliced in rounds
2 pounds chestnuts
5 cups water (about)
Salt and pepper to taste

1. Heat the chicken fat or oil in a skillet and sauté the onions until golden.
2. Bring 5 cups of water to a boil and add the chestnuts. Simmer for about 10 minutes. Peel and add to the onions.
3. Add a half cup of water to the onions and chestnuts and simmer, very slowly, for about 20 minutes, adding more water if needed. Season with salt and pepper.

Yield: about 8 servings (M) or (P)
Variation: Another Alsatian version adds 1½ pounds of prunes to the chestnuts in step 3, simmering them for half an hour or until soft. This creates a sweet and sour effect.

Onions and Garlic from Alsace to San Francisco

At the time of the Gold Rush and the Revolution of 1848, some French Jews went to San Francisco to establish branches of Rothschild and Lazard Frères, and others, after 1870, came to escape Bismarck's occupation of Alsace. The women arrived with good olive oil, garlic and onion bulbs to reseed, and other delicacies to add to their cooking. There are some who say that the taste for good food in that city stems from this French immigration.

A gem of a private cookbook from San Francisco in 1913 comes from the descendants of Harriet Meyer, the mother of the owner of *The Washington Post* and a kin to the Levi Strauss family. The dishes were Alsatian and they were Jewish with recipes for puff pastries and tarragon chickens as well as Passover sponge cakes and macaroons. I could not help but notice how many dishes included shallots and onions. In the recipe (opposite) for onions and chestnuts, soup fat was used to brown the ten cents' worth of onions.

Turn-of-the-century picnic in San Francisco with relatives of Harriet Meyer

Sweetened Cabbage In Pennsylvania Dutch Style

"In the eighteenth century Jews in Pennsylvania were known for making sugared kraut," said food historian William Woys Weaver. The taste has lingered. At the Country Club Diner and Pastry Shop in Philadelphia, which specializes in Jewish-American food, the coleslaw is sweet and sour in the Pennsylvania Dutch—and Jewish—tradition but is called "health salad" because it contains no mayonnaise.

1 head cabbage (2 pounds)

2 tablespoons salt

1 large Spanish onion

⅓ cup sugar or to taste

¼ cup cider vinegar or to taste

2 tablespoons water (about)

1. Shave the cabbage very fine in a food processor or with a sharp knife.
2. Sprinkle with the salt and let sit about an hour.
3. Shave the onion and add with the sugar, vinegar, and water, adjusting seasonings to taste.

Yield: 12 servings (P)

Note: You can also mix red and white cabbage, but sometimes the colors will run. Add some green pepper, tomatoes, carrots, whatever you have.

Kosher picnic on the frontier

A Jewish Homesteader's Potato Kugel

I was busy in the kitchen, carefully scooping out the eggs encased in layers of hardened coarse salt. I then began peeling pounds of potatoes, which my mother would grate on the fine side of the grater. My mother was making a huge potato kugel, made from fresh potatoes, onions, eggs, a little flour, and baked with plenty of goose fat. It wasn't Friday night, but my mother put a white linen tablecloth over the oilcloth-covered dining table.

Sophie Trupin, *Dakota Diaspora, Memoirs of a Jewish Homesteader,* 1984

On the frontier and in Europe *kugels* were cooked in a clay pudding pot, similar in shape and texture to our flower pots, which housed the fifteen- to twenty-inch-high potato or noodle mixture. In this country *kugels* are more like casseroles baked in flatter, wider pans and are not restricted to potatoes and noodles.

¼ cup rendered chicken fat or
vegetable oil
1 cup chopped onions
1 cup chopped leeks
2 pounds russet potatoes,
peeled and grated coarsely
2 tablespoons fresh parsley,
dill, or basil
4 large eggs, well beaten
Salt and freshly ground pepper
to taste

1. Heat 2 tablespoons of the chicken fat or vegetable oil in an 8-inch skillet. Add the onions and leeks and sauté until golden.

2. Remove, cool slightly, and mix with the potatoes, parsley, and the eggs in a mixing bowl. Season with salt and pepper.

3. Place the remaining 2 tablespoons of chicken fat or oil in the sides and bottom of a 13- by 8-inch oval gratin casserole (or similar size) and bake in the top third of a preheated 400-degree oven for 50 minutes or until golden. You may want to take a pastry brush and occasionally brush the top of the *kugel* with any fat or oil on the sides of the *kugel* during baking.

Yield: 6 to 8 servings (M) with chicken fat; (P) with vegetable oil

Thursday Something New—A Novelty— A Potatonik, a Little Heavier Than a Kugel

Sontag bulbes
Monday potatoes
Tuesday and Wednesday again potatoes
Thursday something new a novelty a potato
Friday on Shabbes potatoes

It is no wonder that Jewish soldiers in the Austro-Hungarian army came home from World War I singing the above Yiddish song. *Bulbes, kartofflanik, mandiburki, gemlock,* and the Yenglish *potatonik* are all Yiddish words for potato, a food eaten every day in Eastern Europe. Some of the ingredients for dishes like fried potato skins were so meager that the dishes were happily abandoned when the Jews arrived at Ellis Island. But some recipes like potatonik, which has the texture of bread and the flavor of potato pancakes, have lingered.

"My mother was a 'galitz,' (from Galicia) and her family ate lots of potatoes in their poverty," wrote Florence Naumoff of Glendale, Arizona. "She made the most wonderful 'potatonik.' It was made with potatoes, onions, yeast, flour, salt and pepper. It came out of the oven crispy, crusty! Sometimes she actually baked in aluminum ice trays, stuck her hand in the oven to 'feel how hot,' and I never ate burnt food! I make a kugel and latkes, of course, but that's different. When I asked her how do you know you have the right consistency, she said, 'a little heavier than latkes' (in lieu of specific ingredient amounts.) And potatonik? 'a little heavier than kugel.' "

Potatonik

Like Mrs. Naumoff, Joseph Hilsenrath, born in Kolomya, Ukraine, and currently of Silver Spring, Maryland, makes *potatonik*. "It is my favorite food. My mother used to make it and now I make it. Where the potatoes are called *bulbes* the bread is called *bulbavnik,* and here we call them potatoes so the bread is *potatonik*."

1 package active dry yeast
   (1 tablespoon)
¼ cup warm water
Pinch of sugar
2½ pounds potatoes
2½ cups all-purpose flour
1½ tablespoons salt or to taste
2 medium onions, sliced thin in
   circles
2 tablespoons vegetable oil
   (about)

1. Place the yeast in a bowl with the water and sugar and let it sit for about 10 minutes or until it starts to bubble slightly.
2. Peel and grate the potatoes and place with the flour in a mixing bowl and add the yeast mixture with the salt. Mix all the ingredients well and let rise, covered, in a greased bowl for 45 minutes.
3. Layer the onions in a 9- by 12-inch or 11- by 17-inch greased baking dish. Cover with the potato flour mixture and flatten out.
4. Bake in a preheated 375-degree oven for about 10 minutes. Brush with the oil and continue baking about 35 more minutes or until golden and crisp.

Yield: about 10 servings (P)
You can serve this as a snack, a starch with your meal, or even as a crispy hors d'oeuvre with drinks. However you serve it, the **potatonik** *will be gone in no time.*

Pioneer Farmers in North Dakota

From a neighbor I learned to make citron and green tomato pickles and cakes and pies, and in turn I taught my neighbors how to make coffee cake, potato salad, cottage cheese, noodles, etc. Canned tomatoes were a great luxury and were used on state occasions. . . . Often on beautiful moonlit nights our neighbors would come to see us, bringing their entire family. When the children grew tired, we put them to bed, and the women would proceed to get up a meal, cooking meat and potatoes, making pies and biscuits. We had no labor saving foods in those days, but we had good jolly times on these occasions. . . .

In winter we killed our meats and froze them. In summer we bought fresh meat from the market and kept it by tying it to a rope and lowering it into the coolness of the well where it kept as though on ice. Fresh fruit of any sort was almost unknown. I still remember the delight my children knew when they received their first barrel of apples, a gift from their Uncle Sam. We used Arbuckle's coffee, paying a dollar for eight pounds. Our fare was meat and potatoes, bread and vegetables. Everyone had good gardens and dried fruits. Syrup and jelly came in large wooden pails.

American Jewish Archives, *The Early Days: The Story of Sarah Thal, Wife of a Pioneer Farmer of Nelson County, North Dakota,* April 1971

Elsewhere other Jewish Dakota homesteaders describe the huge meals they would make for hungry workers at threshing. For the first time some of the non-Jewish farmers tasted porkless feasts—brisket with bean and barley soup or split pea soup with beef as well as potato or noodle *kugels.* One woman tells of how her neighbors taught her how to make a two-crust pumpkin pie, something she did not know in Europe, and another bemoans the fact that in winter there was so little to eat that her family ate bacon.

Homesteaders in North Dakota

Fargo, North Dakota, Carrot Ring

Some homesteaders eventually went into the seed and grain business or ran clothing stores as did Jay Siegel, eighty-three, who lived in Fargo, North Dakota, for fifty years. Making a special attempt to introduce Jewish foods to local people, she baked her Jewish carrot ring, which she served with roast turkey to her children's teacher. Later, the recipe was included in *Favorite Recipes,* put out by the Temple Sisterhood of Fargo.

½ cup margarine

½ cup vegetable shortening

½ cup brown sugar

½ teaspoon baking soda

3 tablespoons warm water

1 large egg, beaten

1 teaspoon lemon juice

Grated rind of 1 lemon

1¼ cups all-purpose flour

½ teaspoon salt

½ teaspoon baking powder

1 cup grated raw carrots
   (about 3 large)

½ teaspoon cinnamon

Nutmeg to taste

2 cups cooked sugar snap or
   other peas for garnish

1. In a food processor or mixer cream the margarine, vegetable shortening, and the sugar.
2. Dissolve the baking soda in the warm water and add to the shortening.
3. Add the egg, lemon juice and rind, flour, salt, baking powder, carrots, and spices to the shortening. Mix well.
4. Place the batter in a greased 8-cup ring mold and bake for 45 minutes in a preheated 350-degree oven. Loosen the edges of the ring mold with a knife. Unmold and fill the center with crisp sugar snap peas or fresh green peas.

Yield: 8 to 10 servings (P)

Apple and Carrot Tsimmes

One day when I was making *tsimmes,* a Jewish historian from Moscow dropped in. He hadn't tasted this tasty combination of carrots and sweet potatoes, prunes and sometimes meat in years. He thought that my version was sweeter than what he remembered as a child in Vilna, but so are most Jewish recipes after they reach this country.

When I visited Poland I noticed that to this day sweet potatoes are not part of the diet. By speaking to Polish Jews, I learned that for them a *tsimmes* includes carrots and sometimes prunes but no meat. (See pages 204–207 for more on *tsimmes.*) Try this Polish *tsimmes* from Rose Zawid of Atlantic City, New Jersey. For more about Rose Zawid, see page 119. This would be a good one for Passover.

6 carrots, peeled and sliced in
   ¼-inch rounds

1 cup hot water

3 tart apples (Granny Smith)

½ cup raisins

¼ cup brown sugar or honey

Salt to taste

⅛ teaspoon white pepper

1 cup orange juice

2 tablespoons potato starch

1 to 2 tablespoons margarine

1. Place the carrots in a saucepan, add the water, and cook, covered, until tender, about 10 minutes. Peel, core, and slice the apples in thick wedges, adding for the last 5 minutes of cooking time. Drain and turn into a lightly greased 2½-quart casserole.

2. Add the raisins, brown sugar, salt, and pepper. In a small bowl mix the orange juice and potato starch until smooth. Pour over the carrot-apple mixture in the casserole. Dot with the margarine and bake in a preheated 350-degree oven for 30 minutes or until the top is golden brown.

Yield: 8 servings (P)

Newish Jewish—Southwestern Tsimmes Stuffed in Chilies

This *tsimmes* created by Chef Lenard Rubin of the Phoenician Club in Phoenix, Arizona, is so good that I sometimes serve it alone without stuffing it into the chilies.

¾ pound pitted prunes

6 medium peeled carrots, cut in
   chunks

3 medium sweet potatoes
   (about 2 pounds), peeled
   and diced

6 tablespoons honey

½ teaspoon nutmeg

½ teaspoon cinnamon

½ teaspoon salt

1 tablespoon lemon juice

¼ cup orange juice

2 tablespoons chopped fresh
   coriander

12 green or red Anaheim chilies

1. Mix all the ingredients except the coriander and the chilies in a greased 3-quart baking dish.

2. Cover and bake in a preheated 250-degree oven, stirring occasionally, until the vegetables are soft, but not mushy, about 2 hours. Let cool.

3. Using a fork or a potato masher mash the mixture coarsely with the chopped coriander to facilitate stuffing into the chilies. This can be prepared a day ahead.

4. Place the chilies on a cookie sheet in a preheated 450-degree oven. Roast for about 20 minutes, turning occasionally, or until the skin is black. Remove to a plastic or paper bag and leave until cool. Peel off the skin.

5. With a sharp knife, make a slit from the bottom of the stem to the point of each chili.

6. Gently scrape out the seeds and rinse the inside of the chili.

7. Pat each chili dry and stuff with chopped *tsimmes* so that each chili is slightly overstuffed, causing the slit in the chili to open, exposing the filling.

Southwestern Tsimmes, cont.

8. Bake in a preheated 350-degree oven for 10 to 15 minutes. Serve with Lenard Rubin's brisket on page 182. Alternately, you can merely put the stuffing mixture in a greased flat casserole, approximately 9- by 13-inch, and bake in a 350-degree oven for about 20 minutes or until it is warm.

Yield: 10 to 12 servings (P)

Cauliflower Kugel

One of the biggest eye-openers for the Eastern European immigrants to this country was the profusion of fresh vegetables. Even in cooking classes sponsored by settlement houses in large cities, where the newcomer learned to cook with the new vegetables, it was hard for them to understand that you did not have to cook vegetables to death to remove harmful germs. Instead of merely boiling cauliflower or broccoli for a few minutes, they often turned vegetables into a *kugel*, which enabled them to make a hot dish for the Sabbath. You can also make this *kugel* with broccoli. Adapted from *Spice and Spirit: The Complete Kosher Jewish Cookbook.*

1 large head cauliflower or
*   1 large bunch broccoli*
4 cups water
Salt to taste
2 large onions, diced
¼ cup vegetable oil plus oil for
*   greasing the pan*
Freshly ground pepper to taste
2 large eggs, beaten
2 tablespoons matzah meal or
*   wheat germ*
2 tablespoons cornflake crumbs

1. Wash the cauliflower and separate into large florets. Bring the water to a boil. Add the salt and the cauliflower and simmer, uncovered, for 15 minutes or until tender. Drain, place in a bowl, and mash.
2. Using a 7-inch skillet, sauté the onions in the vegetable oil until soft and lightly browned.
3. Add the onions to the cauliflower and add the pepper, eggs, and matzah meal or wheat germ. Place in a greased 9-inch square pan or casserole and sprinkle with the cornflake crumbs. Bake in a preheated 350-degree oven for 45 minutes or until golden.

Yield: 8 servings (P)

South Indian Kosher Cauliflower, Potato, and Pea Curry

One of the latest phenomena are kosher ethnic restaurants in large cities like Los Angeles and New York. I tasted the following dish at a now defunct kosher Indian vegetarian restaurant on lower Lexington Avenue, nestled in between several other Indian restaurants in New York City.

1 cauliflower

Vegetable oil for deep frying,
plus 2 tablespoons

2 medium potatoes

1 large onion, chopped roughly

1 large tomato, peeled, seeded,
and chopped

5 cloves garlic, crushed

1-inch fresh gingerroot, peeled
and grated

1 teaspoon garam masala
(obtainable at Indian
grocery stores)

Salt and freshly ground pepper
to taste

½ teaspoon turmeric

Cayenne to taste

1 bay leaf

¾ cup water

½ cup fresh or frozen peas

⅔ cup fresh coriander, chopped

1. Cut the cauliflower into florets. Wash and dry the cauliflower and then heat vegetable oil to 375 degrees in a deep fryer or electric wok. Deep fry the cauliflower for a few minutes until golden. Drain. Peel and dice the potatoes in half-inch chunks and deep fry.

2. In a heavy frying pan or Dutch oven with a top, sauté the onion in the 2 tablespoons oil. Add the tomato, garlic, and spices. Sauté for a few minutes, then add the water.

3. Add the cauliflower and potatoes, cover, and simmer for about 20 minutes or until the potatoes are cooked but not mushy. Finally add the peas, simmering, covered, just a few minutes until cooked through. Sprinkle with coriander and serve with Indian rice or *chapati* (Indian bread).

Yield: 6 servings (P)

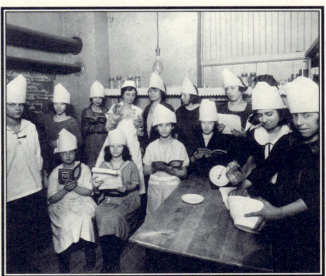

An immigrant cooking school
in Chicago

Sabbath with a Lubavitcher Family in Crown Heights, Brooklyn

Like many Jewish mothers, Cyrel Deitsch spends Thursday and Friday morning in the kitchen preparing for the Sabbath. But unlike most American Jewish mothers she has twelve children to feed, and, with the addition of Sabbath guests, her table stretches to welcome perhaps a dozen more people in her brownstone in Crown Heights, Brooklyn. Mrs. Deitsch is one of the three editors of *Spice and Spirit: The Complete Kosher Jewish Cookbook,* written by the Lubavitch Women's Cookbook Organization. Before the book was published in 1990, she spent three years testing variations of gefilte fish, *tsimmes,* and *kugels,* dishes she serves weekly at her seventeen-foot-long dining-room table.

"I like my table to be full of people," Mrs. Deitsch said during a Sabbath observed at her home. "When I was a student I was alone for holidays. I encourage my children to bring guests, and I like to invite people with no families."

Except for the shiny dark brown *sheitel* (wig) she wears, you could not tell that this middle-aged, serenely beautiful grandmother, whose own children range from ages six to twenty-three, is Orthodox. Her husband, Zalman, is in the textile business. His family, like hers, were refugees during World War II, and followed their rabbi from the Ukraine to this country in 1945.

Her entire life centers on the four-block route from her apartment to the kosher shops on Kingston Avenue, to the cookbook group's office in another edi-

Cyrel Deitsch lighting Sabbath lights in Crown Heights, Brooklyn

tor's basement, and to 770 Eastern Parkway, the international headquarters of the Lubavitcher movement.

For the Sabbath Mrs. Deitsch orders eight pounds of ground pike and whitefish, which she molds into about twenty-eight pieces of gefilte fish. She orders two two-pound loaves of *challah* for each main meal, representing the double portion of manna given to the Hebrews in the wilderness.

Mrs. Deitsch's chicken soup is packed with vegetables like zucchini and rutabaga, and with matzah balls. "I used to make my soup with whole chicken, but my children did not like the soup meat so I ended up throwing it out," she said. Now she makes her soup with chicken bones discarded by her butcher.

She also roasts four chickens and makes two briskets. On Thursday she and two of her daughters make three *kugels,* one of which is made with cauliflower or broccoli.

The last dish she makes each Friday, summer or winter, is *cholent.* It is kept all night on a *blech* (an aluminum sheet placed over a gas or electric burner). Mrs. Deitsch's *cholent* is meatless. "My children like to have pizza on Saturday night after Shabbat is over," she said. "We wait six hours after a meat meal until we can eat a milk product. If I put meat in the cholent they couldn't have the pizza."

As the Sabbath begins with a siren in Crown Heights, Mrs. Deitsch lights the candles with her five daughters. No more cooking, no more telephone calls, no more errands for twenty-four hours. Together the family walks to the synagogue to pray and then returns for dinner. The men say the blessing over the wine, filling the cup to overflowing so that their blessings for good and plenty are fulfilled. Then they all wash their hands ritually in the kitchen. Not a word is said until two of the *challahs* are blessed, cut and passed, dipped in salt, and then eaten. A sweetness continues for one whole day of prayer, rest, and eating until the havdalah candle is lit Saturday after sundown, starting the new week. The day ends with the passing of the spices, thus prolonging the sweetness of the Sabbath before the pressures of the everyday week begin.

Lubavitcher women like Mrs. Deitsch spend a good deal of their spare time praying. And they believe that *mitzvoth* (good deeds) will hasten the arrival of the Messiah.

"I like to go to the synagogue to davan [pray]," Mrs. Deitsch said. "If I wouldn't have the food ready beforehand, I would be stuck in the kitchen. And, by letting people know about the dietary laws through our cookbook, we are doing our part in getting people close to the Messianic period."

For a Rumanian Immigrant an Eggplant Was a Purple Tomato

. . . my first day's peddling made one thing certain: I was a successful business man. . . . And that evening I had the satisfaction of going to a Rumanian restaurant on Allen Street and ordering the first meal I had ever paid for in America. It consisted of a dish of chopped eggplant with olive-oil, and a bit of pot-roast, with mashed potato and gravy. . . . Thenceforth I returned to my restaurant every night. It was a great comfort, after a day spent out in the cold to go into a cozy room, and have a warm meal, and hear my native Rumanian spoken. Now and then a musician would wander in and gladden our hearts with a touching melody of home, and we would all join in until the tears drowned our voices.

M. E. Ravage, *An American in the Making: The Life Story of an Immigrant,* 1917

When Rumanian immigrants like Mr. Ravage came to this country, they made a mishmash of Yiddish, Rumanian, and English, calling a cucumber a "pickle," and an eggplant a "purple tomato." Their wonderful eggplant salads, which they used to cut up with choppers in wooden bowls, distinguished Rumanian immigrants in this country and elsewhere.

1 2-pound eggplant

2 red peppers

2 cloves fresh garlic

2 medium tomatoes

1 small onion

Salt and freshly ground pepper to taste

2 tablespoons olive oil or as needed

1. Prick the eggplant and the red peppers with a fork and put them on a cookie sheet in a preheated 450-degree oven for 20 minutes or until charred. Let the eggplant cool on the pan, but place the peppers immediately in a plastic bag and twist closed. When the eggplant is cool enough, peel it; after the peppers have steeped in the bag 15 minutes, peel them, and remove seeds.

2. Chop the garlic, tomatoes, and onion with the eggplant and pepper. You can use an old-fashioned chopper for this or pulse them in a food processor until the ingredients are chunky, not pureed.

3. Season with salt and pepper and drizzle with olive oil.

Tip: A nice touch is to add a tablespoon of fresh basil and parsley to the salad.

Yield: 6 to 8 servings (P)

Sammy's Famous Rumanian Mashed Potatoes with Gribenes

The more assimilated we Jews become, the more nostalgic we are for the Jewish food of the past. Sammy's Rumanian Steak House, the Jewish Mamma Leone's, is one way of trying to recapture that past in a raucous, cholesterol-laden good-time Charlie kind of way.

Twenty years ago Sammy's opened on Chrystie Street on the Lower East Side in New York. For some, this restaurant was a reminder of the turn-of-the-century Rumanian Jewish restaurants around Second Avenue, of the abundant meals of their childhood, replete with bottles of seltzer and schmaltz on the table and waiters telling loud, Yiddish jokes. One dish, a hit with uptown and downtown Jews, is the mashed potatoes with *gribenes*.

2 pounds russet potatoes

1 large onion, sliced in rings

1/4 cup schmaltz or 1/2 stick (1/4 cup) pareve margarine

1/4 cup gribenes* (optional)

1 large egg

1 teaspoon kosher salt or to taste

Pepper to taste

*See page 213 for gribenes.

1. Peel and quarter the potatoes and place in a saucepan, adding enough water to cover by 1 inch. Bring to a boil, lower the heat, and simmer until the potatoes are soft, about 15 minutes.

2. Meanwhile, sauté the onion in 2 tablespoons of the schmaltz or margarine and cover. Cook slowly over a low heat until the onions are clear, about 15 minutes. Then raise the heat and sauté until golden, adding the *gribenes* to warm through.

3. Drain the potatoes in a colander and return them to the saucepan. Over a very low heat, coarsely mash the potatoes with an old-fashioned masher, adding the egg, the remainder of the schmaltz or margarine, and the salt and pepper. Cover with the onion and *gribenes* and serve.

Yield: 6 to 8 servings (M) or (P)

Stan Zimmerman of Sammy's Rumanian

The Hebrew Race Has Been Waiting 4,000 Years for Crisco

One of the most important prepared products for the Jewish housewife was the invention of Crisco in 1910. Three years after the product was on the market Procter & Gamble was advertising that Crisco, a totally vegetable shortening, was a product for which the "Hebrew Race had been waiting 4,000 years."

Crisco certainly affected the Jewish kitchen. Procter & Gamble advertised in the Jewish press claiming how cheap and kosher Crisco was. Immigrant women were eager to learn how to use new American products. In 1933 Procter & Gamble published a bilingual booklet, *Crisco Recipes for the Jewish Housewife,* in Yiddish and English, which included about sixty dishes such as baked gefilte fish, brown potato soup, *kipfel, mandlach,* etc. Clearly Procter & Gamble had found an author who knew Jewish cooking. Its ads in the Yiddish press showed Brooklyn and Bronx housewives making potato pancakes and strudel with Crisco.

Eggplant Pancakes

This was probably used by the many Rumanian immigrants. I've adapted it from *Crisco Recipes for the Jewish Housewife,* 1933.

1 eggplant (about 1 pound)

2 large eggs

Salt and freshly ground pepper to taste

2 tablespoons finely chopped onion

5 tablespoons bread crumbs or matzah meal

1 tablespoon chopped parsley

Vegetable shortening for frying

1. Peel the eggplant and dice into half-inch pieces. Place in boiling salted water to cover and simmer, uncovered, about 10 minutes or until tender. Drain well.

2. In a mixing bowl combine the eggs, salt and pepper, onion, bread crumbs or matzah meal, and the chopped parsley. Fold in the eggplant, adding more bread crumbs or matzah meal, if needed to hold together.

3. Heat a griddle or nonstick pan, then smear with vegetable shortening. Drop heaping tablespoons of the eggplant batter into the pan and pat down. Fry a few minutes on each side and serve with the following spinach pancakes and a green salad for a vegetarian dinner.

Yield: about 12 pancakes (P)

Spinach Pancakes

I first tasted a version of this recipe in Jerusalem at Bavly, a vegetarian restaurant. You can add any herbs you want to it. Adapted from *Crisco Recipes for the Jewish Housewife*, 1933.

2 pounds fresh spinach

¼ cup water

4 large eggs

1 bunch scallions, chopped (about ½ cup)

½ teaspoon nutmeg

Salt and freshly ground pepper to taste

1 cup bread crumbs or matzah meal

Vegetable shortening

1. Cook the fresh spinach in a saucepan with a little water to cover over a medium heat for about 5 minutes. Then drain well.

2. Beat the eggs and mix with the spinach and the scallions. Add nutmeg, salt and pepper, and enough bread crumbs or matzah meal to hold it all together.

3. Heat a griddle or frying pan. Spread thinly with vegetable shortening. Form spinach patties with about ¼ cup of the mixture and fry a few minutes on each side. Serve with the preceding eggplant pancakes and a mixed green salad.

Yield: about 10 pancakes (P)

Note: This is a nice recipe for Passover.

Market night in the Jewish Quarter of New York

Designer Latkes Are Crisscrossing the Country

When Jeffrey Dworkin was in the Peace Corps in Nepal in the late sixties, he dreamt about potato latkes. The aroma of chicken fat intermingled with onions seemed to waft through the mountain air; he could almost see his grandmother bruising her knuckles grating the potatoes before she combined them with matzah meal and egg. When he returned to Cleveland, he went straight to his grandmother's house.

"I walked into the kitchen and was stunned," said Mr. Dworkin, now a lawyer in Montpelier, Vermont. "I saw her standing there over the frying pan with an empty box of dehydrated latkes next to her on the counter. I knew then that my life had changed forever."

For many Jews the anticipation of Hanukkah opens a storehouse of memories of real potato latkes past, of grandmothers who spent hours lovingly grating and frying potatoes for their families. But that doesn't mean that everyone makes traditional potato pancakes today.

Although some people use shortcuts with dehydrated or frozen latkes, freshly made potato pancakes have become chic. Today, designer latkes are crisscrossing the country. These high-fashion potato fritters are laced with scallions, zucchini, carrots, and apples and sometimes topped with goat cheese. It is not the potatoes that are essential to what latkes, a Yiddish word that comes from the Russian *latka*, symbolize at Hanukkah. "After all it is the oil, not the potatoes which make the latkes," said Dov Noy, professor of Jewish folklore at the Hebrew University of Jerusalem. The oil in which the pancakes are prepared symbolizes the cleansing and rededication of the Temple in Jerusalem after it was defiled by the Syrians some twenty-one centuries ago. The Maccabees found only enough sacred oil to light the menorah for one day. But somehow one day's supply lasted eight.

"The fact is that latkes were cheap and you had oil so you connected it with the miracle of Hanukkah," Professor Noy said. Before potatoes arrived in Poland and Russia, latkes were fritters made most probably from buckwheat groats.

Jason Wolin, an owner and former chef of Mrs. Simpson's Restaurant in Washington, D.C., layers his latkes with his mother's tradition and his own French technique. "These new wave latkes, like a new wave enchilada or new wave pizza, need a historical point of reference," he said. "We can make it new, but like a fine chicken soup the soup must taste like it came from the kitchen of the house. Wringing the potatoes and saving the starch is still the ultimate trick."

Crispy Traditional Potato Pancakes

Ever since I visited a tiny French village in the Ardeche where I tasted a *"craque,"* an extraordinary crisp thin potato pancake as large as a plate, I have changed my view of the taste of potato pancakes. For me they should be thin and crisp. This is only possible if you squeeze out as much water as possible from the grated potato, omit flour or matzah meal as fillers, and gently flatten the pancakes on a very hot skillet. Although the taste of hand-grated potato latkes is superior to that of those grated in the food processor, the difference is definitely marginal. So don't feel guilty if you don't want to use elbow grease and cut your fingers.

2 pounds russet (baking) or
  Yukon Gold potatoes
1 medium onion
½ cup chopped scallions,
  including the green part
1 large egg, beaten
Salt and freshly ground pepper
  to taste
Vegetable oil for frying

1. Peel the potatoes and put in cold water. Using a grater or a food processor coarsely grate the potatoes and onions. Place together in a fine-mesh strainer or tea towel and squeeze out all the water over a bowl. The potato starch will settle to the bottom; reserve that after you have carefully poured off the water.

2. Mix the potato and onion with the potato starch. Add the scallions, egg, and salt and pepper.

3. Heat a griddle or non-stick pan and coat with a thin film of vegetable oil. Take about 2 tablespoons of the potato mixture in the palm of your hand and flatten as best you can. Place the potato mixture on the griddle, flatten with a large spatula, and fry for a few minutes until golden. Flip the pancake over and brown the other side. Remove to paper towels to drain. Serve immediately. You can also freeze the potato pancakes and crisp them up in a 350-degree oven at a later time.

Yield: about 2 dozen pancakes (P)
Variation: If you want a more traditional and thicker pancake, you can add an extra egg plus ⅓ cup of matzah meal to the batter.

Zucchini Parmesan Latkes

At Hanukkah I always made potato pancakes at the last minute so we tried my
recipe but added zucchini to change the color. I wrang out the hand-grated
potatoes in a tea towel and got rid of as much of the liquid as possible but
retained the starch. I always add scallions, onions, and eggs but no filler.

   Rochelle Rose, mother of the proprietors of Mrs. Simpson's Restaurant

This recipe was created at the first of Mrs. Rose's sons' restaurants, 209½, on Capitol Hill
in Washington, D.C. This recipe appeared in the "You Asked for It" column in *Gourmet*
magazine in 1977.

2 pounds zucchini

½ pound russet potatoes,
   peeled

½ tablespoon lemon juice

1 cup chopped scallions

½ cup grated Parmesan cheese

1 teaspoon chopped garlic

¾ cup chopped parsley

1 teaspoon salt

½ tablespoon pepper

2 teaspoons sugar

⅓ cup flour

2 medium eggs

Peanut oil for frying

1. Grate the zucchini and potatoes and toss in the lemon
juice to prevent browning. Squeeze the zucchini and
potatoes through towels or a sieve. It is imperative that
you get almost all the moisture out of the vegetables.
2. Add the scallions, cheese, garlic, ½ cup of the parsley, salt and pepper, sugar, flour, and eggs and toss to
make sure that the ingredients are well mixed.
3. Heat a ½ inch of peanut oil in a pan until hot and add
thin silver dollar–size pancakes, frying over high heat
until golden brown and crispy. When serving, sprinkle
with a little more salt and the remaining chopped
parsley.

Yield: 24 pancakes (D)

*First you light the Hanukkah
candles, then you eat latkes.*

Curried Sweet Potato Latkes

The New Prospect Café, a health-oriented restaurant and catering company in Park Slope, Brooklyn, includes these curried sweet potato fritters on their Hanukkah menu. Add some fresh grated ginger to the pancakes for an Asian touch. Sweet potatoes need the flour to give the pancakes body.

1 pound sweet potatoes, peeled

½ cup all-purpose flour

2 teaspoons sugar

1 teaspoon brown sugar

1 teaspoon baking powder

½ teaspoon cayenne powder

2 teaspoons curry powder

1 teaspoon cumin

Salt and freshly ground pepper
    to taste

2 large eggs, beaten

½ cup milk (approximately)

Peanut oil for frying

1. Grate the sweet potatoes coarsely. In a separate bowl mix the flour, sugar, brown sugar, baking powder, cayenne pepper, curry powder, cumin, and salt and pepper.

2. Add the eggs and just enough milk to the dry ingredients to make a stiff batter. Add the potatoes and mix. The batter should be moist but not runny; if too stiff, add more milk.

3. Heat ¼ inch of peanut oil in a frying pan until it is barely smoking. Drop in the batter by tablespoons and flatten. Fry over medium-high heat several minutes on each side until golden. Drain on paper towels and serve.

Yield: 16 three-inch pancakes (D)

Carrot and Parsnip Latkes

"In our carry-out department we know that our customers will make the basics like brisket for holidays, so we try to create eclectic accompaniments like new kinds of potato pancakes or *kugels*," said Michael Gross, owner of the New Prospect Café. "Root vegetables, like parsnips, are nice in the winter so the recipe just evolved naturally."

2 medium carrots, peeled

5 small parsnips (about 1 pound), peeled

¼ cup all-purpose flour

2 large eggs, beaten

1 teaspoon minced chives or scallion

1 teaspoon chopped parsley

Salt and freshly ground pepper

Peanut oil for frying

1. Grate the carrots and parsnips coarsely. Toss with the flour. Add the eggs, chives, parsley, and salt and pepper to taste. Mix until evenly moistened.

2. Heat ¼ inch of peanut oil in a sauté pan until it is barely smoking. Drop in the batter by tablespoons and flatten. Fry over medium heat until brown on both sides.

Yield: 16 to 18 two-inch pancakes. (P)

Zucchini and Chili Latkes

These have more bite than traditional latkes. The recipe is adapted from Janos Restaurant in Tucson, Arizona.

2 russet potatoes

1 Anaheim chili, peeled, seeded, and finely diced

2 zucchini, grated

½ onion, grated

2 large eggs

¼ cup matzah meal or all-purpose flour

Salt and freshly ground pepper

Vegetable oil or chicken schmaltz for frying

1. Peel and grate the potatoes and place, with the chili, zucchini, potato, onion, eggs, matzah meal, and salt and pepper to taste in a bowl and mix thoroughly.

2. Heat about ½ inch of oil in a non-stick skillet over medium high heat.

3. Add the batter in 3-tablespoon dollops, flattening each pancake with a spatula.

4. Cook about 3 minutes until the first side is brown, then flip the pancakes and cook until the second side is brown.

5. Transfer the pancakes to a cookie sheet and bake in a preheated 350-degree oven until they are cooked through and crisp, about 12 to 15 minutes.

Yield: 12 three-inch pancakes (P) or (M)

Rosh Hashanah in Flatbush, the Syrian-Jewish Community of Brooklyn

In the Aleppo-based Syrian-Jewish community in Brooklyn lives Rae Dayan, a well-known cooking teacher whom I visited just before Rosh Hashanah. "We say blessings over many dishes for the New Year," she said as she offered my friend and me some *ka'ak,* a savory ring-shaped cracker (see page 82). "Our meal is almost like a Passover seder."

Syrian Jews like Mrs. Dayan in this community, believed to be thirty thousand strong, inaugurate the New Year with an apple dipped in sugar and sometimes honey. It symbolizes the hope that man will be judged sweetly. Swiss chard expresses the wish that our enemies may disappear and leeks that our enemies may be destroyed.

Other foods like black-eyed peas, chick-peas, and pomegranates are eaten to show the wish for abundance. Fresh dates and *adjwah,* date crescent cookies, are eaten because the Hebrew words for "an end" and "dates" are similar. This blessing asks that our enemies be brought to an end.

Most important is the cooked head, or part of a head, of a lamb, fish, or calf, such as the tongue or even a chicken neck. The head expresses the hope that the New Year will see the Jewish nation redeemed and at the head of the nations of the world, rather than at the tail as a small, downtrodden people.

A Middle Eastern sweet shop for the Syrian Jewish community in Brooklyn

Lubyeh (Syrian Black-eyed Peas with Veal)

In the South black-eyed peas start the secular New Year. So do they with the Syrian-Jewish community for the Jewish New Year.

1 onion, chopped

2 cloves garlic, minced

2 tablespoons vegetable oil

½ pound veal stew meat, cut into one-inch-square cubes

2 cups water

1 cup black-eyed peas, which have been soaked overnight in water to cover

1 teaspoon salt or to taste

⅛ teaspoon pepper

1 teaspoon allspice

½ teaspoon cinnamon

2 tablespoons tomato paste

1. In a heavy skillet with a cover sauté the onions and garlic lightly in the oil.
2. Add the cubed veal and brown briefly. Add 1½ cups of the water, cover, and simmer slowly for 20 minutes.
3. Meanwhile, drain and simmer the black-eyed peas in water to cover for 20 minutes. Drain and add the peas, salt, pepper, spices, tomato paste, and the remaining ½ cup water to the veal mixture. Cover and cook over low heat for 1 hour or until the peas and veal are tender. If the stew dries out, add a little more water. Serve warm.

Yield: 8 servings (M)

Syrian Swiss Chard and Chick-peas

Another symbolic dish for Rosh Hashanah, this is a nice change as a side dish all year.

1 onion, chopped

2 tablespoons vegetable oil

1 cup chopped celery

1 cup water

1 bunch Swiss chard, washed well and chopped

1 10-ounce can chick-peas, drained

1 teaspoon kosher salt

⅛ teaspoon pepper

1. In a skillet sauté the onion in the oil until soft. Add the celery and continue to sauté about 5 minutes.
2. Add the water, Swiss chard, chick-peas, salt, and pepper to the onion mixture and simmer on low heat, covered, for 30 minutes, adding more water if the vegetables become too dry. Serve hot or cold.

Yield: 4 to 6 servings (P)

Kosher Dill Pickles

Next to rye bread, the pickle which is lavished so generously on the customers of kosher restaurants seems to be in greatest demand. There is one store on Hester Street, facing the little park, which probably contains enough pickles to have exhausted the entire cucumber crop of the Eastern seaboard. Olives, green salted tomatoes, sauerkraut and bell peppers are also dispensed there, and their odor must long since have dried up in the salivary glands of the population for blocks around. If Wall Street be the financial district and the West Thirties the garment district, then the East Side between the Bowery and Ridge Street and from East Broadway to Houston Street ought of right to be called the rye bread and pickle district, if not the sausage district.

Montague Glass, "Kosher Restaurants,"
The Saturday Evening Post, August 3, 1929

Since I was ten years old I have been in the pickle business. My brother-in-law painted old whiskey barrels to age the pickles in. These days they are used as flower pots. We made three kinds of pickles—dill, sweet, and half sour. Half sour are unfermented pickles made daily with garlic, mustard seeds, peppercorns all put at the bottom of a jar in a salt brine to absorb the flavors of the spices for about a week. A garlic pickle has been fermented and then fresh spices added before refrigeration. It makes you pucker up. As it ages the skin turns brown through fermentation.

Jessie Eisenberg, pickle manufacturer, The Bronx, New York

2 cups water

1 tablespoon kosher salt

1 tablespoon white vinegar (optional)

4 to 5 cucumbers (about 5 inches long)

2 heads dill

1 clove garlic, sliced

1 teaspoon mixed pickling spices

1. In a saucepan bring the water to a boil. Add the salt and boil for 2 minutes. Let cool for 5 minutes. Then add the vinegar and let the mixture cool for several hours.
2. Wash the cucumbers and dry with paper towels.
3. Put 1 dill head in the bottom of a sterilized quart jar.
4. Pack the cucumbers into the shoulder of the jar. Add the garlic and the pickling spices. Cover with the remaining dill. Add salt and water to within 1 inch of the top of the jar and keep partially covered for 2 to 3 days.
5. When the jar starts to bubble, let it bubble a day or two, removing the scum daily. Then seal and store in a dry, cool place for about 3 weeks before using. Refrigerate after opening. The pickles should last several weeks after opening in the refrigerator, or indefinitely unopened.

Yield: 1 quart (P)

Syrian Pickled Cauliflower

Pickling is one of the oldest ways of preserving. Americans are mostly familiar with cucumber pickles of the Eastern European Jews, but Syrian Jews preserve other vegetables—cauliflower, turnips, carrots, mushrooms, and artichoke hearts. Rae Dayan (see page 263) brings them out as salads the way most Americans toss together a bowl of fresh lettuce and tomatoes.

1 cauliflower, cut into florets

3 cups water

1 cup white vinegar

2 tablespoons kosher salt

3 cloves garlic, cut in halves

1 fresh beet (peeled and halved)

1. Break the cauliflower into florets.
2. Mix the water, vinegar, and salt in a large glass measuring cup.
3. Put the cauliflower florets into 2 quart jars with the garlic and the beet. Add the vinegar mixture to the jars until the liquid covers the vegetables. Close the jars tightly and refrigerate.

Yield: 2 quarts (P)

Variations: Substitute 2 pounds of turnips, peeled and sliced into rounds, or 1 cabbage, cut into chunks, for the cauliflower.

Fresh Iraqi Coriander and Green Pepper Chutney

This refreshing chutney includes some of my favorite ingredients—coriander, ginger, coconut, and lime juice. It is a traditional accompaniment to the Iraqi *chamim* (see page 229) and goes well with any grilled chicken or fish dish.

¼ cup lime juice

2 small green peppers, cored and chopped roughly

1 bunch coriander, cleaned and stemmed (about 3 cups)

¼ teaspoon salt

½-inch fresh gingerroot, peeled and roughly chopped

1 cup finely shredded sweetened coconut

1. Place lime juice, green peppers, coriander, salt, and gingerroot in a blender or a food processor using a steel blade.
2. With the machine running drop in the coconut gradually until the mixture is somewhat rough.

Yield: about 2 cups (P)

Salonika Sfongato, Lilly Modiano's Spinach and Cheese Casserole

This is one of those marvelous last-minute recipes. I have used the cheeses called for as well as whatever cheese—like ricotta, farmer, or even cottage cheese—I happen to have in my refrigerator. Just make sure that one of your cheeses has some bite to it.

3 pounds fresh or 4 10-ounce packages frozen chopped spinach

2 tablespoons butter or margarine

1 bunch scallions, chopped

1 cup snipped fresh dill

1 cup chopped fresh parsley

1 tablespoon fresh mint

2 tablespoons milk

½ pound feta cheese, crumbled

¼ pound sharp cheddar cheese, grated

3 large eggs

2 tablespoons grated Parmesan cheese

2 tablespoons vegetable oil

1. Cook the spinach over medium heat in a saucepan, uncovered, until very little liquid is left.

2. In a large pan sauté the scallions in butter or margarine until soft but not brown. Add the herbs, mix well for 1 minute, then add the spinach and cook over a medium heat until no liquid is left. Add the milk, the feta, the cheddar, and eggs and mix thoroughly.

3. Lightly oil a 9- by 13-inch Pyrex dish and spread the spinach mixture evenly. Sprinkle with Parmesan cheese and oil. Bake in a preheated 350-degree oven for about 45 minutes or until nicely brown. Serve warm or at room temperature with a big salad. This is also a good dish at Passover.

Yield: 6 to 8 servings (D)

Turkish Double-duty Zucchini— First Kaskarikas (*Zucchini Strips*) . . .

"Turkish Jewish cooking is vegetable-based," said Ida Dana, one of Washington's best Turkish cooks. "Meat plays second stage. And we never waste anything." Mrs. Dana recalled how her mother would divide a bunch of spinach into three piles. "She would fill and roll up the large outer leaves with rice and meat for a typically Turkish *dolma,* she would chop

the small inner leaves for a *burekas* filling, and the stems she would cook into an appetizer."
For Turkish Jews a salad always includes cooked beets, green beans, and celery knobs or
eggplant, dressed with olive oil, garlic, vinegar or lemon juice, and fresh parsley. Mrs.
Dana is just as economical with zucchini. The peels are simmered and marinated for the
kaskarikas and the pulp baked for *kalavasucho,* a zucchini pie.

6 medium zucchini, well
    cleaned
½ cup vegetable oil
¼ cup tomato sauce
Juice of 1 lemon
1 teaspoon salt or to taste
Pepper to taste

1. With a knife peel the zucchini lengthwise leaving
some of the flesh on the peel, about ¹⁄₁₆ inch thick.
Reserve the peel and set 4 cups of the pulp aside for
kalavasucho, the recipe that follows.
2. Cut the peels into one-inch slices. Mix the remaining
ingredients and simmer in a saucepan, covered, for
about 10 minutes or until cooked *al dente.*

Yield: 4 to 6 servings (P)

. . . Then Kalavasucho *(Turkish Zucchini Pie)*

4 cups zucchini pulp (see
    above)
2 large eggs
¼ cup flour or matzah meal
½ cup cottage cheese
1 cup shredded mozzarella or
    Gruyère
1 cup kasseri cheese
1 tablespoon grated cheddar
    cheese
2 tablespoons snipped fresh dill
Salt and freshly ground pepper
    to taste
Grated Parmesan to taste
3 tablespoons vegetable oil

1. Using the grater with large holes on your food processor shred the zucchini pulp or grate by hand. Using
your hands squeeze hard to remove the excess liquid.
2. Add the eggs, flour or matzah meal, cottage cheese,
mozzarella or Gruyère, *kasseri,* cheddar, and dill. Season
with salt and pepper. Place in two greased 8-inch pie
pans or a 9- by 13-inch pan and sprinkle with Parmesan
cheese. Dribble with oil and bake in a preheated 350-
degree oven for 30 minutes. Serve as a dairy main
course with a salad.

Yield: 2 zucchini pies, serving 8 to 10 people (D)

Brighton Beach's Georgian Spinach Salad with Pomegranates

This is one of my favorite salads—it is unusual, easy, and it can be made ahead of time.

2 pounds fresh spinach

2 tablespoons walnut oil

2 tablespoons olive oil

2 cloves garlic, crushed or
   finely chopped

4 scallions, chopped

1 cup fresh coriander

1 cup walnuts

1 tablespoon fresh lemon juice

Salt and freshly ground pepper
   to taste

1 handful pomegranate seeds

1. Steam the spinach in water just to cover for a minute or so. Drain well.

2. Heat the walnut and the olive oil in a frying pan. Add the garlic and the scallions, sautéing briefly. Then add spinach and half the coriander and sauté a minute or 2.

3. Grind the spinach mixture with the remaining coriander and walnuts through a hand meat grinder or in the food processor, pulsing on and off, until chunky, not pureed.

4. Add the lemon juice and salt and pepper. Adjust the taste, adding more walnut or olive oil if desired. Sprinkle with the pomegranate seeds and serve.

Yield: about 2 cups or 4 to 6 servings (P)

Georgian—Or Is It Italian?—Eggplant Bits

Georgian fried eggplant bits remind me of *melanzana alla giudea,* a Jewish-style eggplant dish I had tasted once in Jerusalem. It was prepared by a descendant of the Italian Jewish Finzi Contini family. In Italy eggplant has often been called a Jewish fruit, perhaps because Jewish merchants, who had tasted it in the Middle or Far East, carried a few of the seeds to Italy. The recipe for these fried eggplant bits probably traveled from one Jewish home to another with merchants or with itinerant rabbis who would stop for the Sabbath in homes throughout Europe and Asia. Except for the spice combinations, which varied by region and not by religion, the dish stayed the same, even in Brighton Beach, its new home, with so many immigrants from Georgia.

2 pounds eggplant, unpeeled

1 tablespoon salt (about)

2 garlic cloves, minced

4 scallions, chopped

¼ cup olive oil

1 teaspoon of a combination of coriander, cumin, fenugreek, and cayenne pepper, or to taste

Freshly ground pepper to taste

1 handful pomegranate seeds (optional)

1. Slice the eggplants into 2-inch by 1-inch by ½-inch slices. Sprinkle with the salt and let sit in a colander over a bowl for 30 minutes. Wash off the salt and drain.

2. Sauté the garlic cloves and the scallions with the eggplant bits in the olive oil, stirring occasionally, for about 20 minutes or until the eggplant is chewy and slightly crisp. Drain on paper towels.

3. Sprinkle with the spice combination and salt and pepper to taste. If you like, serve sprinkled with the pomegranate seeds.

Yield: 6 servings as an appetizer (P)

Los Angeles Italian Caponata

When tomatoes and green peppers arrived in Italy, they were added to fried eggplant bits, turning it into caponata. In France it became ratatouille with zucchini. Linda Goldenberg Mayman of Los Angeles, not a traditionalist when it comes to kosher food in her home, serves this dish for the Sabbath and at the Passover seder as a salad.

3 pounds eggplant, unpeeled

1 red or yellow bell pepper, cored

2 medium onions, peeled and sliced into thin rounds

4 medium tomatoes or 2 cups canned plum tomatoes, drained and chopped

6 tablespoons olive oil

1 clove garlic, minced

1 teaspoon salt

½ teaspoon sugar

¼ teaspoon oregano

⅛ teaspoon freshly ground black pepper

2 tablespoons fresh lemon juice

Lettuce leaves

2 tablespoons chopped parsley

2 tablespoons pine nuts

1. Keeping the vegetables separate, slice the eggplant lengthwise and then into half-inch half-moon slices. Cut the pepper into julienne strips. Peel the onions and slice into thin rounds. If using fresh tomatoes, peel them, remove the seeds, core, and cut into small chunks.

2. Place 3 tablespoons of the olive oil in a large skillet. Sauté the sliced onions and pepper until the onions are just wilted, about 5 minutes. Add the garlic and the eggplant. Cover and cook, stirring occasionally, until the eggplant is done, about 10 minutes. Add salt, sugar, oregano, and pepper, stir, and cook about 2 minutes more.

3. Remove from the stove and gently stir in the tomatoes. Transfer the mixture to a large bowl. Mix in the remaining olive oil and the lemon juice. Chill at least 4 hours.

4. Serve on lettuce leaves, sprinkled with parsley and pine nuts.

Yield: 8 servings (P)

Here Comes Paprikas Weiss —
Weiss with the Paprika on His Back

When Isadore Weiss settled in Yorkville, on New York's Upper East Side, at the end of the nineteenth century, he earned a living sweeping floors in a drug store. His wife, like any respectable Hungarian housewife, complained that she couldn't cook properly without paprika. So Mr. Weiss, who loved his Hungarian food dearly, wrote a letter to a friend in Szeged, Hungary, who sent him some paprika. When the shipment arrived, all the neighbors came over and borrowed some. Mr. Weiss wrote for more and started to travel around to the nearby neighborhoods with a backpack selling his paprika. As he walked by, the children would say, "Here comes Paprikas Weiss."

When Mr. Weiss saved enough money to start a shop on Eighty-first Street and Second Avenue, he knew what he would name it. "If the name Paprikas Weiss was good enough for the kids it was good enough for me," he told his grandson Edward. Recently it has closed, but for a long time to many American cooks, Hungarian food meant mail order from Paprikas Weiss.

"Paprikas Weiss carried various spices and herbs that found their way into Mama's soups, stews, and, of course, the apricot cakes and strudels," wrote Marie Jastrow in *A Time to Remember.* "Their specialty was a very strong, very red paprika, which we could not get at the grocer's in our street." Mrs. Jastrow came with her parents from Serbia at the turn of the century. Chances are her mother went to Paprikas Weiss for the *lekva* and the ground poppy seeds she made for *beigli,* the Central European *hamantashen* at Purim. I did also, when I lived in New York over fifty years later.

Paprikas Weiss' Hungarian Cucumber Salad

Hungarian Jewish food is a perfect example of acculturation. Take this piquant cucumber salad, which can be made with one of the three different kinds of paprika—mild, sharp, or sweet. Taken there by the Turks who discovered it in the New World, paprika has been cultivated in Hungary since the sixteenth century.

3 cucumbers

Salt to taste

1 onion

1. Peel the cucumbers and slice into very thin rounds. Sprinkle with salt and let stand for 15 minutes. Squeeze out the liquid from the cucumbers.

Freshly ground pepper to taste

2 tablespoons white vinegar

2 teaspoons water (about)

Fresh sweet paprika to taste

2. Slice the onion very thin and mix with cucumbers. Add the salt, pepper, white vinegar, and water to cover the vegetables. Sprinkle paprika generously on top.

Yield: 6 servings (P)

Growing Up in L.A. with Bukharan Food

Ruth Moussaieff Mason wanted to learn how to write a cookbook about her Bukharan past. I wanted to learn about Bukharan Jewish food. So she invited me for a typical Bukharan Shabbat breakfast in her Riverside Drive home on New York's West Side.

The eggs and potato that we were eating, she explained, were the top layer of their Sabbath dish whether it be *bokla,* a bean-based *chamim* with lamb shanks, chick-peas, and onions, or *osevo,* a rice-based one that includes beef, tomato sauce, and onions. The eggs and potato, separated from the rest of the dish by a layer of waxed paper, constituted breakfast fare for the Sabbath, always with fresh lemon juice as a condiment. Ruth, whose husband is a vegetarian, was trying to make the *osevo* without the meat and was not successful. "It can't do for me," she said.

As we nibbled the roasted eggs and potato with tahina sauce, Ruth told of her childhood, growing up in Los Angeles, where she knew only one other Bukharan family. Her parents came to California from Bukhara by way of Palestine in 1939. Like many Bukharan Jews their name, Moussaieff, meaning son of Moussa, ends in "aieff." "Our food was so different from that of my American friends," said Ms. Mason. "For snacks Americans would have cookies and milk and I'd have avocados mashed with lemon or oriental salad." Ms. Mason's mother added "her" flavorings of salt, lemon, and pepper to the local avocado. "There was a lot of rice around, though; even during the week we might have hamburgers or lamb chops with rice and always a fresh salad, always dressed with lemon, salt, and pepper."

"Whenever I would ask my mother how she made her dishes, she would say 'with love,' " said Ms. Mason. "I think she meant it. When she peels a carrot, she washes it carefully and handles every ingredient lovingly."

Bukharan Salad

My family and I grew up calling this "Bukharan salad," though I later discovered it's a version of chopped Israeli salad. No matter how much my mother made, the bowl got emptied.

Ruth Moussaieff Mason

6 cucumbers

6 juicy red tomatoes

6 scallions

3 or 4 sprigs coriander (optional)

Juice of 1 large lemon

2 to 5 tablespoons vegetable oil or to taste

Salt and pepper to taste

1. Wash all the vegetables; trim the scallions, discarding the green tips. Peel the cucumbers. Chop them, the tomatoes, and the scallions as small as possible, about ¼-inch dice.

2. Wash and dry the coriander. Mince it and stir it into the vegetables. Add the lemon juice, oil to taste, and salt and pepper. Stir well and chill. Serve in small bowls.

Yield: 4 to 6 servings (P)

Mesclun Salad with Nasturtiums and a Champagne Basil Vinaigrette

You can serve this vinaigrette with any greens, but the new mesclun mix is especially good. This is a great way to use that leftover champagne and to display your flowers.

1 tablespoon Dijon mustard

2 tablespoons white-wine vinegar

2 tablespoons dry champagne

2 tablespoons olive oil

⅓ cup vegetable oil

2 tablespoons chopped fresh basil

Salt and freshly ground pepper

4 cups mesclun mix or other greens

1 handful of nasturtiums or other edible flowers

1. Whisk together the mustard, vinegar, and champagne in a small bowl.

2. Slowly add the oil while whisking so that the ingredients do not separate. When all the oil is added, add the fresh basil and salt and pepper to taste. Refrigerate.

3. When ready to serve, arrange the salad leaves on individual plates. Dribble with the vinaigrette and decorate with the flowers.

Yield: 6 to 8 servings (P)

Contemporary Kosher Cuisine at Levana

In the avant-garde of contemporary kosher restaurants in the United States sits Levana, located on New York's West Side. "We were raised Orthodox in Brooklyn," said Abe Kirschenbaum, who owns the restaurant with his brother and his mother. "We went away from kashrut for about fifteen years and then in our early thirties returned. It gave us a different perspective. We couldn't go back to just gefilte fish and chicken in the pot. One of our quests is to educate the customer. Teach them about fresh fish. Cooked rib eyed steak to order." Ten years ago when the family opened Levana, their restaurant took on a life of its own, attracting people like themselves who had tasted rare steaks, venison, quail, and other dishes before they become Orthodox. "We started out as a dairy café and worked our way into meat," continued Mr. Kirschenbaum. "It's like drinking good wine. You work your way into a good Bordeaux." Instead of trying to use unnatural ingredients to approximate cream sauces and butter creams in their meat restaurant, they avoid the use of non-dairy creamer in their sauces. Instead they use vegetable juices and essences. They search for high quality red kosher beef, venison, and quail. Bread is made at the restaurant. For desserts they use fresh fruit and good quality bittersweet chocolate.

Although Levana is closed for the Sabbath, it is open in the winter after sunset on Saturday and will occasionally hold private Friday night dinners with everything prepared ahead of time. Recently I attended such a dinner. The guests proceeded to the wash basin in the center before eating and sat down to a *nouvelle* kosher meal with individual robust *challah,* a cold salmon mousse with tarragon, a mesclun salad with nasturtiums and a champagne basil vinaigrette. The main course was Cornish hens with morels and wild rice, and for dessert fresh berries and a double chocolate mousse cake. Sound Jewish? Sound kosher? It was both.

*Abe Kirschenbaum
goes* nouvelle
*at his Levana
restaurant.*

Moroccan Salads—Perfect for an American Bat Mitzvah

When we planned the lunch for our daughter Daniela's Bat Mitzvah, we chose what we considered the best of Jewish cuisine. Although our appetizers included mini bagels with lox and cream cheese, *hummus* on endives, spinach *burekas,* and whitefish salad on *radicchio,* our main course was Moroccan Jewish couscous with a variety of fresh Moroccan salads. The beauty of these salads, besides their extraordinary flavors, is that they taste better if you make them ahead of time. Perhaps that is why Moroccan cooks serve them at all ceremonial meals from the Sabbath to Passover, varying the vegetables seasonally.

The salads were flavored with *ras el hanout,* a blend of more than a dozen spices, including cardamom, cinnamon, mace, nutmeg, allspice, cinnamon, dried peppers, cloves, turmeric, fresh ginger, black pepper, dried lavender flowers, and dried rosebuds. Obtainable at Middle Eastern stores, it can also be made at home.

Moroccan Eggplant Salad

To my taste this is the king of eggplant salads. Start two days ahead. Charles Suissa, a Moroccan kosher caterer in Washington, D.C., salts the eggplants, not to get rid of the bitter juices as some superstitious people say, but so that when sautéed they will absorb less fat.

2 eggplants (about 2 pounds)

2 tablespoons kosher salt

Vegetable oil for browning

3 tablespoons tomato paste

2 cloves garlic, mashed

Juice of 2 lemons

1 tablespoon cumin or to taste

Harissa or dried red
　　pepperflakes to taste

½ teaspoon ras el hanout (see
　　box above)(optional)

½ cup chopped fresh coriander

1. Score the eggplants in stripes lengthwise with a vegetable peeler. Then slice in ½-inch rounds. Sprinkle with the salt and let sit in a strainer over a bowl overnight.

2. The next day squeeze out the remaining juice from the eggplants using paper towels and heat 1 inch of vegetable oil in a large skillet. Brown on both sides. Drain on paper towels and refrigerate overnight in a covered dish.

3. The next day mix the tomato paste, garlic, lemon juice, and spices in a small bowl. Add to the eggplants, gently coating them. Sprinkle with the fresh coriander. Serve at room temperature.

Yield: 4 to 6 servings (P)

Moroccan Red Pepper Salad

As a fan of roasted red pepper salads, I believe the success in making this easy recipe lies in the quality of the peppers and the marinating time. Make this at least a day in advance.

6 red peppers or a combination
of red, yellow, orange, and
green
3 cloves garlic, pressed
Salt and freshly ground pepper
to taste
⅓ cup olive oil
3 tablespoons lemon juice

1. Place the peppers on a cookie sheet in a preheated 450-degree oven for 20 minutes or until charred outside, turning once. Immediately remove and place in a paper bag sealed tight for 30 minutes. Then peel off the outer skin, remove the seeds and membranes, and slice in long strips, about ½ inch wide.
2. Mix the peppers with the garlic, salt and pepper, and the olive oil. Let marinate overnight. Just before serving add the lemon juice.

Yield: 4 to 6 servings (P)
Note: For a Rumanian-Jewish pepper salad, put the roasted peppers in a jar tucked in with a clove of garlic. Then boil equal parts water and vinegar to which a little sugar, salt, and pepper are added. Pour over the roasted peppers to fill the jar and refrigerate until ready to use.

Carrot Salad

Although Moroccan Jews serve this salad throughout the year, it is particularly popular at Rosh Hashanah when carrots symbolize a sweet New Year. This should also be made a day or so in advance. Adapted from Solange Emsellem.

1 pound carrots, peeled
½ teaspoon salt or to taste
1 clove garlic, minced
Juice of 2 lemons
Freshly ground pepper to taste
1 teaspoon cumin or to taste
½ teaspoon paprika
¼ cup vegetable oil
½ cup parsley, minced

1. Place the carrots in a saucepan with enough cold water to cover. Add salt and bring to a boil. Simmer, uncovered, 15 to 20 minutes or until tender.
2. Drain and slice in rounds ¼ inch thick.
3. Mix the garlic, lemon juice, salt, pepper, cumin, paprika and vegetable oil and pour over the carrots in a bowl. Let sit a day or two in the refrigerator before serving, sprinkled with the parsley, at room temperature.

Yield: 4 to 6 servings (P)

Rosh Hashanah Potluck with Lentil, Chick-pea, Red Pepper, and Broccoli Salad

Rita Michaelson of Providence celebrates the second night of Rosh Hashanah with many Jewish professors from Brown University. This *havurah* or group has a potluck dinner at someone's beach house on Narragansett Bay. Mrs. Michaelson has contributed the following composed salad with chick-peas and lentils, a dish with some ingredients familiar to the Jews in the ancient world yet served today in a very modern setting. Use your imagination with this recipe. You can add mushrooms, asparagus, green beans, olives—whatever you like. You might want to go to an Indian store for different colored lentils to make this especially attractive.

SALAD

1 pound broccoli

2 cups chick-peas (1 12-ounce can)

2 tablespoons fresh lemon juice

2 tablespoons fresh parsley

¼ cup olive oil

1 garlic clove, mashed

Salt and freshly ground pepper to taste

2 cups lentils

2 red peppers

VINAIGRETTE

2 tablespoons balsamic vinegar

1 garlic clove, mashed

Dash of sugar

1 teaspoon French mustard

¼ cup olive oil

¼ cup fresh mint

Fresh lettuce for garnish

1. Cut the broccoli into florets, cook briefly in boiling salted water, and plunge into iced water.

2. Drain the chick-peas and mix with the lemon juice, parsley, ¼ cup olive oil, garlic clove, and salt and pepper. Set aside.

3. Clean the lentils and cook in boiling salted water for about 20 minutes or until *al dente*. Drain.

4. Place the red peppers in a preheated 450-degree oven for 20 minutes. When charred, place immediately in a brown paper bag to cool down for about 30 minutes. Peel, remove seeds and membranes, and slice into thin strips about ½ inch wide.

5. To make the vinaigrette mix the balsamic vinegar, garlic clove, sugar, and mustard in a small bowl. Whisking constantly, pour in ¼ cup of oil. Add the salt and pepper to taste and garnish with diced fresh mint. Set aside in an attractive small bowl.

6. Using a large platter place all the vegetables and grains in individual sections, using lettuce as a garnish. Serve as a salad or first course, with the vinaigrette in a bowl with a spoon on the side.

Yield: at least 12 servings (P)

E I G H T

Grains and Dairy Delights

Three Jewish women were playing mah-jongg and were served *kugel*. One of the women said, "This *kugel* is delicious. It's almost as delicious as mine."

The second said, "What do you mean *kugel*? It's *kigel*." And they debated between *kugel, kigel, kigel, kugel*. Then the second woman turned to the third woman, "Which is correct?"

"I wouldn't know," she replied. "In my house we are Americanized and we say pooding."
A Jewish-American joke

Ours was the last dairy farm in Brooklyn, a half acre on the corner of New Jersey and Family avenues. When we closed in 1972 Bob Teague put us on television. At Passover we didn't put labels on our milk because the rabbis knew the containers were kosher and that we changed the cows' feed during the holiday. My father started it in 1915 when he came over from Austro-Poland. When the boys needed money on Sunday, they would go on the trucks. That's how the kids all survived and made money for college. I still remember moving into the farm. In those days we sold the milk off a horse-and-wagon. It was hard work. We worked six days a week. The only day off was Saturday. We'd get up at four o'clock to milk the cows. God was good to us. Now we are living off the fat of the land.
Sylvia and Nathan Wank, owners of Kahal Dairy Kosher Milk, Brooklyn

Noodle Kugels — The Quintessential American-Jewish Dish

The first to bring noodle *kugels* to this country were probably the Bavarian or Alsatian Jews who called them *schalet*. They would line a pan with noodle dough, which they often then filled with apples. As new immigrants from Central and Eastern Europe brought their own versions, *schalet* turned into *kugel*. Whereas a noodle *kugel* in Poland may have been sweetened with a few raisins and cinnamon—or may not

Don't forget the eggs for **kugel.**

have been sweetened at all—or a noodle dish in Hungary with a little sugar and sour cream, in this land of milk and honey *kugels* include dollops of sour cream, graham-cracker crumbs, cream cheese, cottage cheese, apricot jam, and canned pineapples. Today *kugels,* still served as a savory, rarely a dessert, are made coast to coast.

San Antonio Kugel

In 1992, the Society Hill Playhouse of Philadelphia presented the comedy *Beau Jest,* which focuses on the trials and tribulations of a Jewish family. In the play the Goldmans ate Mrs. Goldman's *kugel* at family get-togethers, a dish served to the guests during intermission. As part of a promotion of the play, the playhouse sponsored a "kugel contest." The finalists appeared at a *kugel* bake-off at the OY! Philadelphia Festival. Over five hundred *kugel* recipes were received from Jewish and non-Jewish *kugel*-makers: *kugels* with kasha, with cabbage, with plums, and with tomato sauce and parmesan cheese. The hundred best— except the winning *kugel* whose creator would not reveal the secret ingredients—were put into a *Kugel Contest Cookbook.*

Philadelphians must like *kugel*. Several years ago a now-defunct Jewish magazine in

Philadelphia sponsored a national *kugel* contest. Two sisters-in-law, one living in Chevy Chase, Maryland, and the other in San Antonio, Texas, entered without telling each other. One won first prize and the other second.

1 1-pound package broad egg noodles

1 stick (½ cup) pareve margarine

¼ cup sugar

2 large eggs, slightly beaten

½ teaspoon cinnamon or to taste

2 Winesap apples

2 pears

½ to 1 cup orange juice

Juice of ½ lemon

½ to 1 cup white raisins

1. Cook the noodles in boiling salted water for 10 minutes. Drain and rinse with cold water.

2. Add the margarine to the noodles and mix until melted.

3. Add the sugar, eggs, and cinnamon. Grate the apples and pears and add with the juices and raisins. Mix gently.

4. Pour into a greased 9- by 13- by 2-inch rectangular casserole. Bake in a preheated 325-degree oven for 1½ hours to 2 hours, depending upon the degree of crustiness desired. Serve warm or cold as a side dish with turkey, chicken, or a brisket.

Yield: 10 to 12 servings (P)

BROOKLYN VARIATION: *This recipe, which originated in Kiev, uses 6 tablespoons orange marmalade and ¼ cup brown sugar in place of the fruit. It also has 6 eggs.*

GALVESTON VARIATION: *This one substitutes raisins, walnuts, and 2 cups of applesauce for the fresh fruit.*

Noodle Kugel Served at the American Embassy in Rome

Whenever Sheila Rabb Weidenfeld, former White House Press Secretary to Betty Ford, makes her mother's noodle pudding, everyone wants the recipe. "There is something about it that makes it just right," said Sheila, who also loves her mother's borscht, blintzes, and brisket. Mrs. Rabb served the *kugel* to dignitaries in Rome while her husband, Maxwell, was United States Ambassador to Italy. "You can't wreck this recipe, no matter what," said Mrs. Rabb. Through the years Mrs. Rabb has learned how to lower the calories by using yoghurt instead of sour cream and sugar substitute for the half cup sugar.

A similar *kugel,* topped with cornflakes, has been served for the past twenty years at the Congregation of the Sons of Zion's break-the-fast at the end of Yom Kippur in Holyoke, Massachusetts. A few days ahead of time volunteers from the sisterhood multiply the recipe thirty times to accommodate the two hundred guests.

½ pound broad noodles

2 cups cottage cheese

2 cups milk

⅓ cup butter or margarine, melted

2 teaspoons cinnamon

½ cup plus 2 tablespoons sugar

3 large eggs

1 teaspoon salt

1 cup sour cream or yoghurt

¼ cup raisins

¼ cup dried apricots or other dried fruit

¼ cup slivered almonds

1. Cook the noodles according to the directions on the package and drain.

2. Combine the cottage cheese, milk, butter or margarine, 1 teaspoon cinnamon, ½ cup sugar, eggs, salt, sour cream or yoghurt, raisins, and apricots. Fold in the noodles.

3. Place in a greased 9- by 12-inch casserole.

4. Sprinkle with the remaining teaspoon of cinnamon and 2 tablespoons sugar. Cover with almonds.

5. Bake in a preheated 350-degree oven for 45 minutes to one hour or until firm. Serve as a side dish with a fish or dairy meal or as a dessert.

Yield: 4 to 6 servings (D)

Jerusalem Kugel

When the Margulis family left Jerusalem to live for a few years in Scarsdale, New York, their son, Shaul, had two big regrets: he would have to leave his great-aunt Miriam and the seventh-generation Jerusalem *kugel* that she sold to others and gave to them for each Sabbath. "Everybody knows her and everybody knows her *kugel* is the best," said Shaul, fourteen, the cook of the family. "We felt uncomfortable asking for the recipe because the secret was her livelihood. When we left we still wanted to eat the *kugel* so we finally asked for it."

Jerusalem *kugel* is like no other. It is made usually with very thin noodles, which are caramelized and combined with freshly ground black pepper. Then it is baked for a long time and cut like a cake. The story goes that this *kugel* came to Jerusalem with the followers of the *gaon* of Vilna. Shaul didn't want to give me the secret so here is my version instead.

Serve this as a peppery sweet accompaniment to a roast, much the way we serve sweet potatoes at Thanksgiving. It is one of my favorites.

2 teaspoons salt or to taste

1 pound capellini (very thin noodles)

½ cup vegetable oil

1. Bring 3 quarts of water to a boil in a large pot. Add 1 teaspoon of the salt and the *capellini* and cook according to the package directions until *al dente*. Drain well and set aside in a bowl.

2. In a medium saucepan heat the oil and ½ cup of the

¾ *cup sugar*

4 eggs

*1½ to 2 teaspoons freshly
ground black pepper*

1 teaspoon cinnamon

sugar. Stir constantly until the sugar turns very dark, almost black (about 10 minutes).

3. Add this hot caramel to the pasta and mix well. Cool slightly.

4. Beat the eggs in a bowl and add the remaining salt, pepper, cinnamon, and the remaining ¼ cup sugar. Pour into the pasta mixture, tossing well. Transfer to a greased tube pan and bake, uncovered, in a preheated 350-degree oven for 1 hour or until golden on top. Remove from the oven, turn upside down on a serving plate, unmold, and serve.

Yield: 8 to 10 servings (P)

Evansville, Indiana's Kugel Fair

Evansville, Indiana, an old river city at the boot tip where Kentucky and Illinois meet, was one of the early German Jewish communities in this country. Every year the Jewish women put together an ethnic food fair as a fund-raiser for Hadassah Hospital in Jerusalem.

"Yesterday was blintz day," said Susan Shovers, one of the organizers of the fair, during a telephone interview. Together the women made over five hundred blintzes and hundreds of *kugels.* In addition, they also made briskets, cabbage, vegetable and matzah ball soup, and cheesecakes. "The women are good cooks and the non-Jewish community loves our food. They freeze it for the Christmas holidays," said Mrs. Shovers. "When you want to be Jewish in a small community you try hard." The following Midwestern *kugels* are especially popular at the fair.

*"Making the kugel"
in the 1940 film*
The Jewish Melody

North Shore Chicago Hadassah's Lick-Your-Fingers Kugel

This is definitely American—with dark brown sugar and pecans! Your guests will love it.

1½ sticks (¾ cup) salted butter
  or margarine, melted

¾ cup dark brown sugar

1 cup pecans, halved

1 pound wide noodles

4 large eggs

1 teaspoon cinnamon

½ cup sugar

2 teaspoons salt

1. Pour half the butter into a 12-cup mold or tube pan. Swirl it around the bottom and up the sides.
2. Press the brown sugar into the bottom and press the pecans into the sugar.
3. Boil the noodles according to the package directions and then drain. Mix with the eggs, the remaining melted butter, cinnamon, sugar, and salt and pour into the mold.
4. Bake in a preheated 350-degree oven for 1 hour and 15 minutes or until the top is brown. Let sit for 15 minutes before unmolding. The top will become slightly hard like a praline. Serve cold or at room temperature.

Yield: 10 to 12 servings (D) or (P)

Noodle Kugel with Fresh Coriander and Corn

Even the new American chefs are making *kugels*. I like this Southwestern one with corn and coriander from Lenard Rubin, who learned this when he was a chef in Arizona.

1½ sticks (¾ cup) butter,
  melted

1 pound medium egg noodles

½ pound cream cheese, slightly
  softened

2 cups sour cream

6 eggs, separated

1 cup corn kernels, cooked

¼ cup chopped coriander

1 cup sugar

5 tablespoons dry bread crumbs

1. Coat a 9×13-inch square baking pan with a small amount of the butter.
2. Cook the noodles in boiling, lightly salted water. Drain and rinse the noodles. Shake out all the excess water. Put the noodles into a bowl and toss with the remaining melted butter, reserving 1 tablespoon.
3. In a blender puree together the cream cheese, sour cream, and the egg yolks. Add this mixture to the noodles and mix well.
4. Toss the corn and coriander with the noodles.
5. Beat the egg whites with the sugar until shiny and stiff. Gently fold the whipped whites into the noodles. Pour the mixture into the buttered baking pan.

6. Heat the remaining 1 tablespoon of butter in a sauté pan and add the bread crumbs, cooking until lightly browned. Sprinkle the crumbs evenly over the top of the noodles. Place in a preheated 350-degree oven for 1 hour or until the top is golden brown. Let chill before cutting into triangular shapes. (Cut squares and then cut in half to form the triangles.) This can be prepared a day ahead and reheated.

Yield: 8 to 10 (D)

Spinach and Three-Cheese Kugel

This savory kugel won first prize in a kugel contest that I judged at the District of Columbia Jewish Community Center. It's adapted from Rosemary Fallon.

8 ounces wide egg noodles

3 tablespoons unsalted butter or margarine

¼ cup onion, finely chopped

2 tablespoons fresh parsley, chopped

1 10-ounce package of frozen spinach, chopped

¾ cup sour cream

1 cup small-curd cottage cheese

2 large eggs, beaten

¼ cup Parmesan cheese, grated

½ cup Swiss cheese, shredded

1 teaspoon salt

½ teaspoon white pepper

½ teaspoon thyme

Dash of nutmeg

1. Cook and drain the noodles according to the package directions and toss with 2 tablespoons of the butter.

2. Using a small frying pan sauté the onion and parsley in the remaining tablespoon butter for about 5 minutes, or until the onion is transparent. Fold into the noodles.

3. Cook the spinach according to the package directions, drain well and fold into the noodles with the sour cream, cottage cheese, eggs, Parmesan and Swiss cheeses, salt, pepper, and thyme.

4. Pour into a greased 2-quart baking dish, sprinkle with nutmeg, and bake, covered with aluminum foil, for 45 minutes, in a preheated 350-degree oven. Remove the foil and cook for 15 minutes more or until the top is bubbly and crusty at the edges.

Yield: 6 to 8 servings (D)

Lasagna Served Hadassah Style — Without the Meat

The Bialik group of Hadassah in Silver Spring, Maryland, has been making large amounts of this lasagna for fund-raising suppers for years. My guess is that the recipe started when there were very few kosher cheeses and thus they used cottage cheese and Muenster instead of mozzarella and ricotta cheese. My cousin, Dorothy Regensteiner, a longtime member of this group, makes it for her—and my—family. You can try it her way, or substitute other cheeses and add spinach or other vegetables. What I especially like about this recipe is that the lasagna cooks right in the dish—it doesn't have to be boiled first.

1 chopped onion

2 cloves garlic, minced

2 tablespoons vegetable oil

1 35-ounce can plum tomatoes

12 ounces tomato paste

½ cup chopped parsley

2 tablespoons chopped fresh basil

¼ teaspoon oregano

Salt and freshly ground pepper to taste

1 teaspoon sugar

1 pound Muenster cheese, cubed

1½ pounds cottage cheese or ricotta cheese

3 eggs, beaten lightly

¾ pound lasagna noodles

1. Sauté the onion and the garlic in the oil. Add the tomatoes, tomato paste, half the parsley, basil, oregano, salt and pepper, and sugar. Simmer, covered, for 40 minutes.

2. Mix the cheeses, eggs, and the remaining parsley in a bowl.

3. Put a small amount of sauce in the bottom of a 13- by 9-inch Pyrex dish. Cover with a layer of uncooked lasagne noodles, then a layer of cheese. Repeat once and pour the sauce over the top. If the sauce as it seeps down does not come half way up the side of the lasagna add a little water.

4. Bake in a preheated 325-degree oven for 1 hour.

Yield: 8 comfortably (D)

Farfel and Mushrooms

Selig's Kosher Delicatessen in Highland Park, Illinois, may look like a turn-of-the-century American deli, but it is not. Its owners, the Spuns, came here as refugees from Poland in 1947. The two met in New York and went to Chicago after they were married in 1957. For years he was in the delicatessen and grocery business and she was a homemaker, cooking for her young family.

One of the most popular dishes served at the delicatessen is farfel and mushrooms. In Yiddish, *farfel* means tiny pieces of egg noodles shaped like pellets or barley. Thus farfel is sometimes called egg barley in this country. "By sautéeing the onions and mushrooms separately and adding in the cooked farfel you get a better flavor," said Mrs. Spun. Instead of the traditional mushrooms try *shiitake* or *porcini* and serve the dish for a special meal. The result is delicious.

3 onions, chopped

3 tablespoons vegetable oil

½ pound mushrooms, sliced

½ pound farfel (barley-shaped egg noodles)

2 cups chicken broth or water

Salt and freshly ground pepper to taste

2 tablespoons chopped parsley

1. Sauté the onions in 2 tablespoons of the vegetable oil until the onions are golden. Remove, add the mushrooms, and cook them over medium high heat, stirring, until they are firm but tender.

2. In a separate 2-quart pot with a cover sauté the *farfel* for a minute or 2 in the remaining tablespoon of oil. Add the chicken broth or water and salt and pepper. Bring to a boil and then simmer, covered, for about 10 minutes or until the farfel is cooked.

3. Drain the farfel and add to the onions and mushrooms. Adjust the seasoning, sprinkle with the parsley, and serve as a side or main dish for a vegetarian meal.

Yield: 4 to 6 servings (M) with chicken broth; (P) with vegetable oil/water

Kasha Varnishkes at Wolff's in New Jersey

In 1925 Wolff Brothers of Paterson, New Jersey, published a Yiddish English cookbook with recipes culled from a kasha cooking contest run in all the Jewish newspapers throughout the country. "Recipes of thousands of Jewish dishes were sent us," they wrote modestly, "but we selected only the very best among them and these are listed here." The recipes included buckwheat blintzes, vegetarian buckwheat cutlets, and "a tasteful grits soup" made from their Health Food (merely unroasted buckwheat groats), green peas, and potatoes. The *varnishke* recipe was basically a kreplach-type noodle stuffed with kasha, buckwheat groats, and *gribenes*.

Packaged bow-tie noodles, large and small, quickly replaced the flat homemade egg noodles in the American version of *kasha varnishkes*. The trick to a good *kasha varnishke* is to toast the whole-grain buckwheat groat well over a high heat for 2 to 4 minutes until you start smelling the aroma of the kasha. This will seal the groats so that there is a nutty, crunchy taste to them, a good foil to the soft taste of the noodles. When I make mine—a favorite in my family—I add fresh parsley and sometimes coriander. Although traditional-ists use bow-tie noodles for this, try rigatoni, shells, or any other kind of noodle you like.

2 large onions, sliced in rounds

2 to 3 tablespoons margarine or chicken fat

1 large egg or egg white, slightly beaten

1 cup medium or coarse kasha

2 cups water or bouillon

Salt and freshly ground pepper to taste

¾ pound large or small bow tie–shaped noodles

2 tablespoons chopped fresh parsley

2 tablespoons chopped fresh coriander (optional)

1. Sauté the onions in 2 tablespoons of the margarine or chicken fat in a heavy frying pan with a cover until golden. Remove to a plate.

2. Beat the egg in a small mixing bowl and stir in the kasha. Mix, making sure all the grains are coated. Put the kasha in the same frying pan, set over a high heat. Flatten, stir, and break up the egg-coated kasha with a fork or wooden spoon for 2 to 4 minutes or until the egg has dried on the kasha and the kernels brown and mostly separate.

3. Add the water or bouillon, salt, and pepper to the frying pan and bring to a boil. Add the onions, cover tightly, and cook over low heat, steaming the kasha for 10 minutes. Remove the cover, stir, and quickly check to see if the kernels are tender and the liquid has been absorbed. If not, cover and continue steaming for 3 to 5 minutes more.

4. Meanwhile, bring a large pot of water to a boil. Cook the bow-tie noodles according to the directions on the package. Drain.

5. When the kasha is ready, combine with the noodles. Adjust the seasoning, sprinkle with the parsley and coriander. If desired, add a bit more margarine or chicken fat. Serve alone with a salad or with a pot roast, the stuffed chicken on page 405, or the Chicken Pandora on page 236.

Yield: 6 to 8 servings (M) with chicken fat/bouillon; (P) with margarine/water

Cabbage and Noodles—A Galicianer American Staple

We ate this dish on Shabbat and special occasions growing up in State College, Pennsylvania. It was my family's alternative to potatoes!

Ann Steinberg, Chevy Chase, Maryland

I have tasted this simple dish at restaurants in France, Hungary, Austria, and the United States.

1 large onion, diced
½ stick (¼ cup) butter or
  margarine
½ head cabbage, shredded
  (about 2 pounds)
Salt and freshly ground pepper
  to taste
1 teaspoon sugar
½ pound wide egg noodles,
  bow-tie pasta, or rigatoni
2 tablespoons poppy or
  caraway seeds

1. Sauté the onion in the butter or margarine until the onion is transparent. Add the cabbage to the onion and cook over a low heat, stirring occasionally, until the cabbage is soft. (This will take about 14 minutes.) Season with salt and pepper. Add sugar if desired.
2. Meanwhile, cook the pasta according to the directions on the package. Drain and mix with the cabbage and the poppy seeds. Serve immediately, adjusting seasoning to taste.

Serve alone or with brisket or salmon croquettes.

Yield: 6 servings (P) with margarine; (D) with butter

Italian-Jewish Food Is In

Although the Italian Lattanzi family of New York is probably the most ambitious of all the kosher Italian restaurateurs—they have two restaurants in Manhattan as well as a third that features Roman-Jewish menus—other Italian restaurateurs nationwide have Italian-Jewish menus. Tragara, in Bethesda, Maryland, for example, makes an Italian Passover menu each year and has even re-created a sixteenth-century Passover feast. Walter's, an Italian restaurant in East Greenwich, Rhode Island, prepares Italian-Jewish menus on demand.

It is no wonder that there is an Italian-Jewish connection—besides the fact that Jews like Italian food. Jews have lived in Italy continuously for the past two thousand years and there have been new waves of immigration from Spain and Central Europe. Cooks and food historians are interested in the food of the Jews of Italy and in particular of the Jews of Rome. As Edda Servi Machlin relates in her fine *The Classic Cuisine of the Italian Jews,* "a well known ancient Italian adage advises one to 'dress like a Turk and eat like a Jew.' "

Rotolo di Pasta con Spinaci

This recipe comes from the notebooks of the late Resy Guetta Luzzatto, whose husband came from one of the oldest Venetian Jewish families. As a young bride she observed many old Jewish ladies while cooking. Her son, Francis, inherited the notebook with this recipe from Trieste. Roberto Donna of Washington's Galileo Restaurant helped me decipher the ingredients. The result is *buonissimo!*

PASTA

1¼ cups all-purpose flour (about)

Pinch of salt

2 medium eggs

1 tablespoon olive oil

SPINACH FILLING

4 pounds fresh spinach, washed

5 tablespoons olive oil

3 cloves garlic, peeled and mashed

1 medium onion, peeled and diced finely (1 cup)

Salt and freshly ground pepper to taste

Pinch of nutmeg

½ cup bread crumbs (about)

½ cup Parmesan cheese

½ stick (¼ cup) unsalted butter

6 sprigs fresh sage

1. To make the pasta, put the flour on a board and sprinkle with the salt. Make a well in the middle and add the eggs, one at a time, with the oil.

2. With a fork beat the eggs and oil well and then gradually incorporate into the flour. As soon as the liquid has been absorbed use your hands and knead until a smooth ball is formed. Flour the dough, cover, and let it rest for at least half an hour.

3. Wash the spinach twice, place in a large pan with the water. Bring to a boil and steam, covered, for a few minutes until limp. Drain, squeeze gently, and with a knife chop it fine.

4. In a large frying pan, heat the olive oil and add the garlic. Let it cook until golden and then remove the garlic. Add the onion and cook until the onion is soft, about 5 minutes.

5. Add the spinach, salt, and pepper. Continue cooking, stirring constantly until the spinach is cooked. Drain and set aside to cool.

6. Return the spinach to the pan with the nutmeg and bread crumbs, and continue cooking over a medium heat. Cook a minute or two until the liquid is absorbed.

7. In the meantime, take the dough and roll out as thinly as possible, about 30 inches by 12 inches.

8. Place the dough on a towel dusted with flour. Spread the spinach mixture over the pasta, leaving a half inch border on the longer side. Taking the longer side, roll slowly with your hand and using the towel into a jelly-roll shape. Cut in 2. Wrap each roll in a towel and tie up each side with twine, as well as in a few places in the middle.

9. Bring a big pot of water to boil with a little salt. Add

the spinach roll, lower the heat, and simmer, uncovered, for about 20 minutes.

10. Remove from the water gently with a strainer. Drain a few minutes, remove the towel, place the roll on a cutting board, and slice with a sharp knife in inch slices.

11. Put the slices of spinach roll in a greased baking dish. Sprinkle on most of the Parmesan cheese and bits of butter, then bake in a preheated 350-degree oven for 5 minutes, just enough to let the butter melt.

12. Place the sage in boiling water for a minute. Drain and sprinkle over the dish with additional cheese and pour on butter resting in the pan.

Yield: 6 to 8 servings with 2 per serving (D)

Juroti, Bukharan Lentils and Rice

Try this refreshing snack. If your family doesn't like garlic, substitute some fresh mint.

1 cup brown lentils

5 cups water (about)

Salt to taste

½ cup white rice

6 to 12 garlic cloves

2 tablespoons vegetable oil (about)

Yoghurt

1. Rinse the lentils thoroughly in cold water.

2. Bring the water to a boil in a pot. Add salt and the lentils, simmering, uncovered, about 15 minutes, or until they are half done. Squeeze a lentil to see if it has softened.

3. Now add the rice, stirring occasionally, adding more water if necessary. Cook, slowly, uncovered, 20 minutes longer.

4. While the lentils and rice are cooking, mash the garlic cloves and sauté in the oil in a frying pan over high heat for a minute or 2 or until golden. Serve the lentils and rice in a bowl topped with the garlic and a few tablespoons of yoghurt.

Yield: 4 to 6 servings (D)

Rae Dayan's Syrian Rice with Orzo

I love the different textures in this dish. It is easy to make and a nice change from an ordinary rice or pasta accompaniment to meat or chicken.

¼ cup vegetable oil

¼ cup orzo

2 cups rice

3½ cups water

2 tablespoons kosher salt

1. In a medium saucepan heat the oil and brown the orzo until it is slightly brown.
2. Wash the rice in a bowl with warm water, rubbing lightly. Drain and repeat 2 more times.
3. Bring the 3½ cups water to a boil, add the rice, orzo, and salt, and let the water return to a boil, stirring thoroughly.
4. Cover the pan tightly and lower the heat. Simmer the rice and orzo for 20 minutes or until the water is absorbed. Then fluff with a fork.

Yield: 4 to 6 servings (P)

Couscous Tabbouleh

Moroccan Jews in this country taught me to use couscous instead of *bulghur* in this tabbouleh dish. Sometimes I mix several different kinds of grains together. I always make it with lots of lemon, mint, and vegetables.

1 cup couscous

2 cups chopped parsley

2 medium tomatoes, coarsely chopped

1 large onion, finely chopped

Salt and freshly ground pepper to taste

Juice of 3 to 4 lemons

½ cup extra-virgin olive oil

½ cup chopped fresh mint leaves

1 cucumber, finely chopped

1 green pepper, finely chopped

1. Soak the couscous in water to cover for one half hour. Squeeze dry.
2. Mix the couscous with the parsley, tomatoes, onion, and salt and pepper. Add the lemon juice, olive oil, and mint and toss together. (Adjust the amount of lemon juice according to your taste for tartness.) Before serving, add finely chopped cucumber and green pepper.

Yield: about 8 servings (P)

German Apple Schmarren

German and Alsatian Jews dearly loved apple pancakes, recipes for which appeared in turn-of-the-century Jewish cookbooks from coast to coast.

"I remember my father's Sunday morning apple pancakes," said Lois Greene of Waterbury, Connecticut. "He combined the eggs and other ingredients in a huge iron frying pan. After a short while, he put the apple slices over the top of the eggs and sprinkled them liberally with sugar, cinnamon, and lemon juice. As the eggs cooked, they puffed up around the apples. The fragrance was divine! When he judged the eggs and apples done, he cut the pancake like a cake."

My daughter Merissa, an expert on pancakes, thinks this is a terrific recipe.

1 cup all-purpose flour

1 teaspoon baking powder

⅛ teaspoon salt

3 large eggs

1 cup milk

2 large apples

2 tablespoons butter

Confectioners' sugar

Juice of ½ lemon

1. Mix the flour, baking powder, and salt. Add the eggs and milk and beat until smooth.

2. Peel, core, and slice the apples in eighths. Gently stir in the apples.

3. Heat a 10-inch ovenproof skillet on the range. Brush with the butter and pour in the batter. Bake in a preheated 350-degree oven for about 15 minutes or until the pancake puffs up at the sides and is crisp and brown. Sprinkle with confectioner's sugar and lemon juice.

Yield: 4 to 6 servings (D)

Purim Fritters, French Toast By Any Other Name

Hebrew balls have ever been the very best of their kind, both in quality and quantity. Always notable for the inexhaustible fund of belles . . . they have become a specialty which the proprietress of the various ball-rooms delight to honor, a feature of Gotham, as inevitable, as Evacuation Day and the 23rd of February. "Long may they wave."

The Jewish Woman, June 31, 1862

The Hebrew Purim ball at the Academy of Music

With the attention given to fund-raising Purim balls in the nineteenth century, it is no wonder that American Jewish and non-Jewish cookbooks include desserts for this holiday of letting go, of celebrating, and of joy at the deliverance of the Jewish people from danger in the ancient Persian empire. During the reign of King Ahasuerus the Jewish queen Esther saved her people from a plot to destroy the Jews, which was led by the king's minister Haman. Today most Americans eat a triangular pastry called *Hamentashen,* but they did not in nineteenth-century America.

The earliest Purim recipe I could find was Purim Fritters in *Jennie June's Cookbook* of 1866. These fritters, known today as French toast, must have been popular during this period. The 1876 *National Cookery Book* called the fritters Queen Esther's toast. The *National Cookery Book,* which included a good sprinkling of Jewish recipes, celebrated the Centennial Exhibition of 1876 in Philadelphia.

Take a loaf of baker's bread, cut off the crust and cut in slices of one-half inch thick; put them in a dish and soak them in cold milk, but not so long as to allow them to mush; when soaked, take them out and drain them. Beat eight eggs very thick, and pour a little of the egg over each slice of bread so as to penetrate them; then take each slice of bread and dip it into the eggs that are beaten, and fry a light brown color, in rendered butter, from which the salt has been extracted; when this is done sprinkle over the fritters a little powdered cinnamon, and serve with a syrup made of white sugar.

(D)

Jewish French Toast

A Sampling from Di Grine Kuizine from Klez Kamp Cooks is a charming pamphlet from the cooking classes at Klez Kamp, a Yiddish annual gathering that takes place in the Catskills each December. One of the amusing recipes is Jewish French Toast made from Uneeda Biscuits, a product that was advertised frequently in the Yiddish press. Tsirl Waletsky of the Bronx, who contributed the recipe, wrote, "My mother made Hanukkah cheese sandwiches by putting in a filling of farmers cheese between two Uneeda biscuits." She also made the Jewish French Toast with leftover *challah*—I recommend the *challah*.

1 egg, slightly beaten

¼ cup milk

½ teaspoon vanilla

2 ½-inch-thick slices challah

2 heaping tablespoons farmer cheese

1 tablespoon raisins

½ teaspoon cinnamon

1 tablespoon coarsely ground walnuts

Oil or butter for frying

1 scant tablespoon honey

Sliced fresh fruit (optional)

1. Whisk together the egg, milk, and vanilla in a bowl. Add challah and soak.

2. In another bowl mash the cheese with a fork and 1 tablespoon of the egg batter. Add the raisins, cinnamon, and nuts.

3. Spread the cheese mixture on 1 slice of the challah. Cover with the other slice.

4. Heat the oil or butter in a medium hot pan. Fry the challah sandwich, turning carefully after one side has browned to brown the other. Dribble honey on top before serving. You can also top with sliced fresh fruit.

Yield: 1 serving (D)

The Governor's Wife's Blintzes

Every grandmother has her specialty. For Dorothy Licht, wife of Frank Licht, the late governor of Rhode Island, it is blintzes. "As a new bride I asked my mother-in-law who came from Russia to teach me her recipe. From then on I had to make them for her when she entertained," said Mrs. Licht. It has been Mrs. Licht's signature dish ever since. She makes batches several times a year and keeps them in the freezer. For brises, for home visits, or just family gatherings, Mrs. Licht prepares them for her family.

Blintzes, which are the thin pancakes filled with cheese traditionally eaten at Shavuoth, are of Russian-Polish origin. Suspiciously like French crepes or Chinese egg-roll wrappers, blintzes, or *blinchiki,* were often filled with shredded leftover brisket to make a complete meal or to serve as an accompaniment to chicken soup. They were also filled with farmer or pot cheese for a dairy meal. In this country many people, like Mrs. Licht, have added the richer cream cheese.

FILLING

1 pound cottage cheese

½ cup farmer cheese

⅛ pound cream cheese

1 large egg

2 tablespoons matzah meal

¼ cup sugar

BLINTZES

2 cups flour

1½ cups water

1 cup milk

7 large eggs

2 tablespoons potato starch

Butter for frying

Sour cream

1. To make the filling, mix together thoroughly the cottage cheese, farmer cheese, cream cheese, egg, matzah meal, and sugar in a bowl. Set aside in the refrigerator at least 1 hour.

2. To make the blintzes, put the flour, water, milk, eggs, and the potato starch in a blender or food processor in 2 batches. Blend each batch, pour into a bowl and then let the batter rest for a half hour.

3. Grease a non-stick 6-inch skillet or omelet pan with butter. Pour in a small ladle of the batter. Tilt the pan so the batter covers the bottom and pour off any excess. Cook until the pancake blisters. Do not turn. Flip the pancake onto waxed paper, cooked side up.

4. Spread 1 heaping tablespoon of cheese filling along one end of the pancake. Turn the opposite sides in and roll up like an envelope.

5. Fry the blintzes in butter or oil or bake them in a preheated 425-degree oven until brown. Serve the blintzes with sour cream.

Yield: about 3 dozen (D)

Alaskan-style Blintz Loaf

If you do not want the chore of cooking each pancake separately, try this quick blintz loaf that I found in the *Diamond Jubilee Recipe Collection* of the Bikur Cholim Mahzikay Hadath Sisterhood in Seattle, Washington. Your guests will love it.

BATTER

¼ cup melted unsalted butter

¼ cup sugar

2 eggs

¾ cup milk

1¼ cups flour

1 teaspoon baking powder

½ teaspoon salt

FILLING

1 pound small-curd cottage cheese

1 large egg

1 teaspoon sugar

Pinch of salt

2 tablespoons melted butter

1. To make the batter, mix the butter, sugar, eggs, milk, flour, baking powder, and salt in a blender or mixer, processing until smooth.

2. Pour half the batter mixture in a greased 9-inch square or round pan.

3. To make the filling, mix the cottage cheese, egg, sugar, salt, and butter and spoon over the batter. Cover with the remainder of the batter mixture. Bake in a preheated 350-degree oven for 1 hour.

Yield: 4 to 6 servings (D)

Tav Bisleh *(Green Onion Omelette)*

The following dish, adapted from *The Persian Jewish Cook Book,* by The Sisterhood of the Persian Hebrew Congregation, Skokie, Illinois, 1987, came with immigrants from Azerbaijan in the twenties.

4 large eggs

2 tablespoons water

1 tablespoon flour

1 whole bunch green onions, diced (about ¾ cup)

½ teaspoon salt

2 tablespoons dill, chopped

1 tablespoon dried peppermint leaves

2 tablespoons unsalted butter

1. Beat the eggs, water, and flour in a mixing bowl. Add the onions, salt, dill, and peppermint and mix well.

2. In a 10-inch frying pan, melt the butter over a medium heat. Add the egg mixture and cover. When the bottom and sides are firm, place a large plate over the top of the frying pan and turn over onto the plate. Slide off of the plate back into the frying pan. If needed, add a little more butter. Brown the other side, remove the same way and serve.

Yield: 4 servings (D)

Alsatian Onion Torte

Onions—the odorous onion where every breath causes the aesthetic maiden to shudder, possesses some very commendable qualities. It is an excellent medicine in case of nervous prostration and useful for coughs and all sorts of colds. And last, but not least, a courageous indulgence wherein every other day will soon clear and whiten the complexion.

American Hebrew Journal, July 1896

Fortunately, Jews like onions and garlic again! I first learned to make this tart from Alsatian-born Andre Soltner, chef at Lutèce. Eaten by Alsatian Jews instead of the ham-and-cheese-studded quiche lorraine, this is the kind of a tart you can make at the last minute. Vary the filling with mushrooms and Swiss cheese, and broccoli or asparagus, if you like.

CRUST

2 cups all-purpose flour

1/3 cup unsalted butter

1/3 cup vegetable shortening

Dash salt

2 tablespoons cold water

Dried beans for weighting the
*   crust*

FILLING

2 tablespoons unsalted butter

1 pound (about 4) onions,
*   peeled and sliced in rounds*

3 large eggs

3 tablespoons heavy cream

Dash nutmeg

Salt and freshly ground pepper
*   to taste*

1. To make the crust, place the flour, butter, vegetable shortening, and salt in a food processor and pulse on and off. Gradually add the water until a dough ball is formed. Remove, cover in plastic wrap, and refrigerate for 30 minutes.

2. On a lightly floured board, roll out the dough to about 10 inches and line a 9-inch pie pan or tart pan with a removable rim. Press into the pan and side. Trim the rim and remove excess dough. Prick the bottom of the tart with a fork. Line the pan with aluminum foil and refrigerate a few hours or overnight.

3. Heat the butter in a frying pan. Add the onions and sauté slowly, covered, for about 30 minutes over a low heat until the onions are golden and soft. Cool the onions and set aside.

4. Fill the foil-lined pie crust with the dried beans. Bake in a preheated 450-degree oven for 10 minutes. Reduce to 375 degrees and cook until the crust is done, about 5 more minutes. Remove the foil and the beans.

5. In a mixing bowl beat together the eggs, heavy cream, nutmeg, and salt and pepper and add the onions. Pour into the pie pan. Return to the oven and bake 30 minutes or until the center is custard-like. Serve immediately.

Yield: 6 servings (D)

Cheese Enchiladas

Harriet Rochlin either makes the enchiladas with the following homemade chili sauce or, when she doesn't have time, she uses Las Palmas piquante or mild enchilada sauce.

SAUCE

4 dried chilies (preferably ancho or red Anaheim)

2 dried chiles de arbol

2 cups water or to cover

2 cloves garlic, pressed

2 tablespoons finely chopped onion

2 whole peppercorns

Pinch of oregano

½ piece of toast

Salt to taste

Vegetable oil for frying

1 dozen fresh corn or flour tortillas

FILLING

1 pound dry, white cheese like queso cotija, sharp cheddar, or Monterey Jack, crumbled or grated

1 medium onion, finely minced

2 to 3 tablespoons green olives, finely minced

1. Open up the chilies and remove the seeds and the veins. Brown the chilies on a lightly oiled griddle for a few minutes until they start to turn color. Watch them carefully. You don't want them to burn.

2. Place the chilies in water to cover in a saucepan and bring to a boil. Simmer for about 2 minutes, just to soften.

3. Using a slotted spoon, remove from the water and put in a blender with the garlic, onion, peppercorns, oregano, toast, and salt to taste. Blend until the sauce becomes the consistency of a thick puree, adding more water if necessary. Return to the saucepan and warm.

4. Heat 2 tablespoons of the vegetable oil in a frying pan. Dip the tortillas, one by one, into the oil to soften, then into the sauce to lightly coat.

5. Put the tortilla on a plate. Across one end spread a heaping tablespoon of cheese and half a tablespoon each of onions and olives. Roll the filled end until the tortilla resembles a tube. If possible, serve immediately, with a light garnish of sauce, crumbled cheese, and a touch of onion. If to be served later, put in a baking dish and reheat in a 350-degree oven until hot, and top with the heated sauce.

Yield: 12 enchiladas (D)

Enchiladas, Tamales, and Cheese Tortillas Jewish Style in Arizona

At first sight, I was struck by the variegated ambience in my mother-in-law's kitchen. On the east wall stood a new (1946) electric range, and in the southwest corner, the old wood stove my mother-in-law favored for baking breads and cakes. Scarred pine drain boards were crowded with mason jars, electrical appliances and draining dishes flanked the sink. Above, tall windows admitted north light and a view of rounded hills bearded with amber Mexican hay. In the center was an oak table big enough for gallons of peaches and plums cut up for compote; corn husks spread for a hundred tamales; a lug of *ugerkes*, cucumbers, for pickling, or a *koldire*, a feather bed, for a sick child. Near the back door was the pantry where were stored beef and tongue corning in tall crocks with rock-secured lids, tin boxes of homemade cookies and cakes, preserved fruits. In days of less money and greater strength, I was told, my mother-in-law kept chickens, turkeys, a cow, and the pantry reeked of newly-laid eggs and curing cheese. . . .

American meals, while served often, were considered a special event. My mother-in-law acquired a yen for Mexican cooking and learned to prepare authentic recipes with minor adjustments for personal taste. It wasn't the hot seasoning that bothered her; I never heard her complain a dish was too *picante* or *chiloso*. What she disliked was pork, omnipresent as tortillas in a Mexican kitchen. Once she left her parents' Orthodox home, her dietary habits were governed by purse and palate. Shellfish and other non-kosher foods, she learned to enjoy; but *hazer*, pig, never. So she substituted chicken and easy-to-shred beef for pork, and Fluffo for lard when preparing enchiladas, tacos, tamales, frijoles, arroz. Most of her five children and twelve grandchildren became passionate aficionados of her style of Mexican cooking. One son tells of a midnight ride on a Nogales-bound bus when he was summoned home from college to visit his desperately ill mother. Bouncing along, tears on his cheeks, he guiltily recalls thinking: If Mama dies, who'll make the enchiladas?

Harriet Rochlin, "My Mother-In-Law's Kitchen," *The Arizona Post*

Mamaliga, Mamaliga, Rumanian Jewish Polenta

My mother made *Mamaliga,* this very thick cornmeal mush and poured it out onto a dinner plate. Pop, using his fork, went back and forth on it, making ridges. It was that thick. Then she put cheese on top of it, and fried chopped onions. This was a favorite—I guess like pizza to most of us! My mother used to use the expression, *"Es Mamaliga licht in punem,"* literally "when you eat Mamaliga it shows in your face" when she met someone who looked Jewish.

Florence Naumoff, Glendale, Arizona

One of the curiosities of culture and cuisine is the appearance of corn-based *mamaliga* as the national dish of Rumania. Corn was brought to the Old World after the discovery of America, but it only took hold as a basic food in Rumania and parts of Italy, where it was turned into *mamaliga* and polenta. Basically a polenta, often served with various kinds of cheese on top, *mamaliga* is the dish that Rumanian Jewish immigrants remember fondly. Along with *kernatsalah,* a kind of *kishke* (stuffed casing with flour, onions, etc.), *mamaliga* is highlighted in a nostalgic Jewish song called "Rumania, Rumania."

Some say that Rumanian Jews started the dairy lunch room, which they called "milky dinners" so that they could serve their beloved *mamaliga.* (Because of the Jewish prohibition against mixing milk and meat, *mamaliga* could not be served at a restaurant that served meat.) *Mamaliga* without cheese can also be served as a side dish with pot roast and tastes great dipped into the gravy.

Mamaliga, Rumanian Cornmeal Mush

Michael Cernea, senior advisor for Sociology and Social Policies at the World Bank, comes from Iasi, Rumania. He showed me the gourmet's version of *mamaliga,* replete with hot melted butter for dipping, four kinds of cheese, and sour cream. Cernea cuts the *mamaliga* into slices with a string, not a knife, and serves it with fresh whole onions that "must" be smashed into rings with the palm of one's hand. According to him, this squeezes out the onion's too strong juices at once.

5 cups boiling water

1 teaspoon salt or to taste

*3½ cups coarse yellow
    cornmeal (about)*

1 stick (½ cup) butter

1 cup grated Swiss cheese

*1 cup Rumanian brinza or
    kashkeval or hard ricotta
    cheese, grated*

*1 cup feta cheese, broken up
    into small pieces*

1 cup pot cheese

1 cup sour cream

1 large onion, cut in rounds

*6 scallions, chopped in two-
    inch lengths*

1. Pour the water into a heavy saucepan and bring it to a rapid boil.

2. Add salt and pour in the cornmeal very slowly, stirring constantly with a long wooden spoon. Then reduce the heat to medium and continue stirring until the cornmeal is very thick and firm, about 15 to 20 minutes. You may need someone to hold the handle of the pan while you stir. When the cornmeal forms a ball and no longer sticks to the side of the pan but comes away cleanly from the side, turn it out onto a wooden board to serve. Press it down and shape it like a loaf or cake.

3. Cut it into 8 pieces on the wooden board. Traditionalists will use a string to cut it.

4. Meanwhile, warm up 6 dinner plates; melt the butter and place in 6 ramekins.

5. On the table provide plates of the Swiss cheese, *brinza,* feta, and pot cheeses, a bowl of sour cream, and a plate of raw onion rings and scallions.
Serve immediately as a main course with a green salad.

Yield: 6 servings (D)
Adam Tihany's Transylvanian variation: After cooking the corn meal, layer it in a 9×13-inch casserole with the butter, cheeses, and sour cream, and heat for a few minutes under the broiler.

Wolfgang Puck's Jewish Pizza

Years ago when I visited superstar chef Wolfgang Puck at his restaurant Spago, in Los Angeles, the chef said that he was going to make me his "Jewish pizza." To this day, this delicious smoked salmon and *crème fraîche* dotted pizza is one of his signature dishes. After our meeting, Wolfgang married Barbara Lazaroff and has been celebrating Passover seders at the restaurant ever since.

PIZZA DOUGH

1 package fresh or active dry
*   yeast*

¼ cup warm water

1 tablespoon honey

1 teaspoon salt

2 tablespoons olive oil plus oil
*   for the bowl*

¾ cup cool water

3 cups all-purpose flour
*   (approximately)*

PIZZA TOPPING

3 to 4 ounces smoked salmon,
*   sliced paper thin*

¼ cup extra-virgin olive oil

½ medium red onion, sliced
*   thin*

¼ cup minced fresh dill

⅓ cup crème fraîche or sour
*   cream*

Freshly ground black pepper to
*   taste*

4 heaping tablespoons domestic
*   golden caviar (optional)*

1 heaping tablespoon black
*   caviar (optional)*

4 sprigs fresh dill for garnish

1. Dissolve the yeast in the warm water; stir in ½ teaspoon of the honey and set aside for 10 minutes.

2. Mix the remaining 2½ teaspoons honey with the salt, olive oil, and cool water and set aside.

3. Put the flour in the bowl of a food processor. With the processor running, slowly pour the honey-oil mixture in through the feed tube. Then pour in the dissolved yeast. Process until the dough forms a ball on the blade. If it is too sticky, sprinkle on a little more flour.

4. Scrape the dough out onto a lightly floured surface and knead until smooth. Transfer to an oiled bowl and let rest, covered, for 30 minutes.

5. Divide the dough into 4 equal parts. Roll each into a smooth, tight ball. Put on a flat sheet or dish, cover with a damp towel and refrigerate for 1 to 3 hours.

6. One hour before baking, remove the dough from the refrigerator and let it come to room temperature before rolling and shaping.

7. Preheat the oven, preferably with a pizza stone inside, to 500 degrees for 30 minutes while getting the pizza ready.

8. Cut the salmon into 2-inch squares and reserve.

9. Roll or stretch each ball of dough into four 9-inch circles. Put the circles on an oiled, floured baking sheet.

10. Brush each pizza with olive oil to within 1 inch of the edge and sprinkle with red onion. Put the pizzas in the oven and bake 8 to 12 minutes, until the crusts are golden brown.

11. While the pizzas are baking, mix the dill with the *crème fraîche* or sour cream and season with pepper.

12. When the pizzas are done, transfer to warm dinner plates and spread with the *crème fraîche* or sour cream mixture. Arrange the pieces of salmon on top and, if desired, put a tablespoon of golden caviar in the center of each and spoon a little black caviar on the golden caviar. Garnish each pizza with a sprig of dill and serve.

Yield: 4 servings (D)

Pomegranates and Pistachio Nuts
for Persians on Pico Boulevard

Several years ago I visited Elat, a large kosher Iranian market on Pico Boulevard in Los Angeles, which later burned down. It overflowed with hundreds of items, including fresh pomegranates, pistachio nuts, dates, roasted chick-peas, raisins, cucumbers, apples, rose waters, and fresh mint leaves, all signs of hospitality, served to visitors at Persian Jewish homes and even during shiva.

About twenty thousand Iranian Jews live in the United States, the bulk of whom came here after Khomeini came to power in 1979. "When we arrived fifteen years ago, there were no Persian foods," said Homa Sarshar, a journalist living in Los Angeles. "We used to ask our families to send us dried vegetables like *shanbelileh* (fenugreek), herbs, and other ingredients. If we couldn't find them we couldn't use them." Iranians substituted spinach or parsley and green onion tops for *shanbelileh* in their dishes and turmeric for the prohibitively expensive saffron. They often had to do without the cumin ground with rose leaves. "We couldn't find dried lime, *zireh orhel,* seeds which gave taste to Jewish cooking, so we imported them. I don't know one Jewish family who didn't bring them in their pockets. Now we can get everything. We can get fresh fenugreek, sweet lemons, Iranian cucumbers, which we eat as fruit, melons, and spices." Today farmers are growing Iranian vegetables and fruits in Fresno. The biggest importer of Iranian spices is a Jewish family named Soofer. In addition to grocery stores there are about a dozen kosher Iranian restaurants with a handful of Iranian kosher caterers.

Like many Iranian Jews, Mrs. Sarshar cooks both Iranian and western foods. "Even in Iran I used to make macaroni for my children," she said. Mrs. Sarshar, like other immigrants, likes to showcase her food for Americans. "They don't like the way Persian food looks but they like the way it tastes."

NINE

Desserts: Cakes and Kuchen

There I found the table set for breakfast, and a magnificent display it was, with its German-silver coffee-urn and pressed glass bowl, and silver plated spoons and white linen . . . I was invited to partake of a cup of coffee with cake. I was amazed. Cake for breakfast! If I had been offered swan's eggs or steak or broiled pigeons, or almost any other thing, I should have kept my self-possession. But the very notion of serving cake for breakfast struck me as an extravagant fancy of which only millionaires were capable.

M. E. Ravage, *An American in the Making,* 1917

A PLEA FOR HOME-MADE ICE CREAM

Ice cream is generally regarded by families of limited means as a luxury only to be indulged in on special occasions, when company is expected or for birthdays and high holidays. The poor children, who never get half enough of this frozen delight, are told that it is very unhealthy, and that to partake too freely thereof is fraught with the most disastrous consequences to their little stomachs. This widely diffused belief, and the expensiveness of cream when ordered from a confectioner's, have relegated this most palatable of dainties to the realm of rarely-to-be-attained desires.

The American Jewess, 1896

As she bent over the wash-tub rubbing the clothes, she visualized the hot, steaming strudel just out of the oven and the exclamations of pleasure as the neighbors tasted it.

Anzia Yezierska, "The Lost Beautifulness," 1921

Levi Strauss and a Popular San Francisco Jewish Dessert

One tribe of Indians, the Cherokee, called peddlers egg eaters because food offered to them was not prepared according to kosher dietary laws. Jewish peddlers had to refuse it so wherever they went they asked for eggs in trade existing on a diet of eggs and vegetables until they returned home to a kosher kitchen.

Elizabeth Van Steenwyk, *Levi Strauss, The Blue Jeans Man,* 1988

After he arrived in this country from Germany in 1851, Levi Strauss traveled across the country carrying denim for tents and landed in San Francisco, where he soon opened a store in 1853. Eggs were neutral foods that Strauss took with him when he went across the country.

A special occasion Bavarian dessert, one popular until a generation ago with descendants of Levi Strauss' siblings (he never married), was *Dampfnudel,* literally a "steamed dumpling." The name does not do justice to this dessert—a rich brioche-like cake, bathed in caramel sauce and served warm topped with a vanilla sauce or ice cream. During Levi Strauss' days it would have been steamed in a Dutch oven on a trivet with a bed of coals underneath and on top. *Dampfnudeln* was so much part of the lives of the Bavarian Jews that children used to sing,

Dampfnudel hamma gestern g'habt,
Dampfnudel hamma heaut,
Dampfnudel hamma alle Dag
Weil's uns halt gefrut!

We had *Dampfnudel* yesterday
Dampfnudeln again today
We have *Dampfnudeln* every day,
We like it fine that way!

Levi Strauss was known as an egg eater as he crossed the country with a pack on his back.

Bavarian Dampfnudel: Dumpling Cake Soaked in Caramel Sauce

Before she passed away, Rhoda Haas Goldman of San Francisco, a descendant of Levi Strauss' brother, shared this recipe with me. "My grandmother made it all the time," said the late Mrs. Goldman. Try it. It is a grand dessert, worthy of your best dinner party.

CAKE

2 packages active dry yeast

1¾ cups lukewarm milk

6 cups all-purpose flour

4 sticks (2 cups) unsalted
 butter

2 egg yolks

¼ cup sugar

1 tablespoon sherry

1 teaspoon salt

1 teaspoon vanilla

CARAMEL SAUCE

2 cups sugar

½ cup warm water

1 tablespoon unsalted butter

½ cup maple syrup

½ cup heavy cream

Dash vanilla

VANILLA SAUCE (OPTIONAL)

2 tablespoons unsalted butter

2 tablespoons flour

1 cup milk or heavy cream

½ cup sugar

Brandy or rum to taste

1 teaspoon vanilla

1. In a bowl dissolve the yeast in ¾ cup of the warm milk. Add it to 2 cups of the flour and mix. Let rise, covered, for 1 hour.

2. After an hour melt 1¾ cups of the butter in a saucepan and add to the flour mixture with the remaining 4 cups of flour, the remaining cup of the milk, egg yolks, sugar, sherry, salt, and vanilla. Beat well with a spoon or an electric mixer and let rise again, covered, in the mixing bowl for another hour. The dough will be very soft. You can also refrigerate the dough for several hours and let it return to room temperature before continuing.

3. Flour a board and roll the dough out 1 inch thick; cut circles with a small biscuit ring or cookie cutter, 2 inches in diameter.

4. Melt the remaining ¼ cup butter in the Dutch oven. Arrange one layer of the biscuit rounds on the bottom, touching, then make two more until you have used up all the dough. Allow to rise 45 minutes, covered, or until the dough has reached the top of the Dutch oven.

5. Meanwhile, make the caramel sauce. In a saucepan mix 2 cups of the sugar with ¼ cup of the water. Very gradually add the remaining water. Boil until smooth. Add the butter, syrup, cream, and vanilla. Continue boiling until thick. Set aside.

6. To make the vanilla sauce, melt the butter in a small saucepan and add the flour, stirring constantly until the mixture bubbles. Then gradually add 1 cup of the milk or cream, stirring until thick. Add the sugar, brandy or rum, and vanilla. Set aside.

7. After dumplings have risen for 45 minutes, bake, covered, on the bottom rack of a preheated 400-degree oven 45 minutes or until golden. Remove from the oven

and keep warm on the back of the stove until needed. Ten minutes before serving, reheat the caramel sauce and pour over the cake. When the sauce has seeped through the dough, flip onto a serving plate. Cut in slices as you would a cake. Serve with the vanilla sauce or vanilla ice cream.

Yield: 12 servings (D)

Kuchen, The Pride of Every German Baker

During the first year or two of our coming to Appleton my mother rather grandly established Friday afternoons At Home. . . . On Friday mornings the house was fragrant with the scent of baking dough; of sugar and spice . . . of fruits bubbling on the bosom of plum, apricot and apple kuchen. The cheese kuchen, made from a recipe in which cottage cheese was smartened by lemon juice and grated lemon peel, was a specialty of the house. At about four o'clock the tantalizing fragrance of coffee would be added to the rest. These Friday afternoons became something of a stampede.

Edna Ferber, *A Peculiar Treasure*, 1939

Kuchen, any of several varieties of coffee cake, were the pride of every nineteenth-century immigrant German baker, both Jewish and non-Jewish. Each cook or housewife had a yeast-based *"kuchen"* dough, which she would shape into rectangular crusts and top either with fruit or cheese, or she would twist with cinnamon and nuts into a streusel or coffee cake, or roll up jelly-roll style into *Schnecken*, snails, or sticky buns (see page 94). By the end of the century, baking powder came into use and replaced yeast in many kuchen. Quick breads and cakes gradually replaced the slower yeast-raised doughs. In May 1906, the *Ladies' Home Journal* ran an article on *kuchen* by Lola D. Wangner. "There seems to be a steadily-growing fondness among us for the German coffee-cakes or 'kuchen,' " Mrs. Wangner wrote. "They are to be found on many of our breakfast-tables on Sunday mornings. These cakes are peculiar to Germany, every part of the Fatherland having its own methods of making them, and there are more than one hundred recipes."

Kuchen North Carolina Style

Kuchen means different things to different people. The basic *kuchen* dough can be formed into a jelly roll, as it is in this version, which has been in Leah Baach Tannenbaum's family in North Carolina for three generations. Like so many of the recipes from old German-Jewish families, it came from Bavaria. "In Greensboro we served kuchen-like coffee cake with coffee or for Sunday brunch the way people eat bagels today," said Mrs. Tannenbaum.

1 package active dry yeast

¼ cup warm water

1½ cups sugar (about)

2 sticks (1 cup) unsalted butter

3 large eggs, separated

½ cup milk

*4 cups all-purpose flour
    (about)*

½ teaspoon salt

1½ teaspoons cinnamon

½ cup raisins

½ cup chopped pecans

1. Dissolve the yeast in the water with a teaspoon of the sugar. Let stand for about 10 minutes or until it bubbles.

2. In the bowl of a mixer or food processor cream the butter with 3½ tablespoons of the sugar, then mix in the egg yolks. Add the milk and the yeast mixture.

3. Gradually add 3 cups of the flour and the salt to the butter and sugar, beating well. The dough will be very sticky. Cover and refrigerate overnight.

4. Next morning, remove from the refrigerator, uncover, and leave at room temperature for about an hour.

5. Dipping your hands in flour, remove the dough from the bowl. Knead, adding more flour as necessary until the dough is smooth and soft. Divide the dough in 3 pieces and roll each third out on a floured pastry cloth to an approximate 8- by 12-inch rectangle, about ⅛ inch thick.

6. Place the egg whites in the bowl of an electric mixer. Start beating, gradually adding ¾ cup of the remaining sugar, and beat on high until the mixture is stiff like a meringue.

7. Spread one-third of the egg-white mixture in the center of one of the three rectangles of dough, leaving at least a 2-inch border.

8. Mix the remaining sugar with the cinnamon, raisins, and nuts. Sprinkle the dough with a third of the cinnamon mixture, and roll up, starting at the long side, jelly-roll style. Repeat with the other 2 rectangles and the filling. Place on a greased jelly-roll pan and bake in a preheated 350-degree oven for 40 minutes or until golden. When cool, slice and serve.

Yield: 3 kuchen (D)

Pflaumen or Zwetschenkuchen, Plum Cake in Kansas City

Tea Stiefel, who came to Kansas City, Missouri, from Dinslaken, Germany, during World War II, brought two basic dessert recipes with her: her *meurbeteig* (cookie dough for tarts) and her *heifeteig* (yeast-based) dough. The following *Pflaumenkuchen* (called *Zwetschenkuchen* in southern Germany and Alsace) is served traditionally at the high holidays and to break the fast of Yom Kippur, when Italian plums are in season. Mrs. Stiefel buys the plums in the fall, freezes them, and then prepares the cake all year round. You can also make this with the *meurbeteig* crust on page 3 1 4.

HEIFETEIG CRUST

1 cup milk

1 tablespoon active dry or
*   1 package yeast*

1 stick (¹⁄₂ cup) unsalted butter,
*   melted*

¹⁄₂ cup sugar

2 whole eggs

4 cups all-purpose flour

Dash salt

FILLING

4 pounds Italian plums

¹⁄₂ cup sugar

Sweetened whipped cream

1. Heat ¹⁄₄ cup of the milk in a saucepan. When luke-warm dissolve the yeast in it.

2. Cream the butter with the sugar. Beat in the eggs and add the yeast mixture. You can use a food processor to prepare this dough.

3. Add the flour and salt in 3 or 4 parts, alternating with the remaining milk. Process for a minute or so to make a stiff dough. Place the dough in the refrigerator overnight. (The well-wrapped dough will keep in the refrigerator up to 2 weeks.)

4. On a floured board using a rolling pin roll out the dough to 1 0 by 1 5 inches. Place on a greased cookie sheet. Let it rise, uncovered, while you are preparing the plums.

5. Wash the plums and cut them in half. Remove the pits and make a slash on top of each half ¹⁄₄ inch deep.

6. Sprinkle the dough with a little flour and place the plums on the dough, standing on end, points up, letting each piece overlap the next.

7. Bake in a preheated 3 5 0-degree oven for 1 hour. Immediately upon removing the kuchen from the oven sprinkle with the sugar. (Mrs. Stiefel sprinkles on the sugar after baking so that the plums will not give up as much juice during baking.) Cut in squares and serve with a dollop of sweetened whipped cream.

Yield: at least 1 2 servings (D)

Poor Man's Purim Cake

In 1879, *The New York Times* ran a recipe for Poor Man's Purim Cake in its household hints section. It was probably called Poor Man's Purim Cake because the ingredients cost just 20 cents or because it called for so little fat and so few eggs. In later cookbooks this same recipe is called "Quick Cake." If you use a food processor, as I did, it can be made very quickly indeed.

1½ cups sugar

½ stick (¼ cup) unsalted butter

2 large eggs

1 cup milk

3 cups all-purpose flour

1 teaspoon baking powder

Grated rind of 1 lemon

Confectioners' sugar (optional)

1. Place the sugar and the butter together in a food processor with the steel blade and process until creamed.

2. Add the eggs and the milk, pulsing after each addition. Then add the flour, baking powder, and the lemon rind, pulsing until a smooth mass is formed.

3. Place the dough in a greased and floured 9- by 9-inch square baking pan. Pat down and bake in a preheated 350-degree oven for 30 minutes. When cool enough to handle, turn out on a rack.

4. Sprinkle with confectioners' sugar, slice, and serve.

Yield: 1 Purim Cake, serving about 8 people (D)

Erwin Stiefel ate his wife's plum kuchen, kissed her, and went off to fight in World War II.

Gesundheitskuchen, Good Health Cake

This good health cake, customarily offered to people who were sick or sitting shiva in Germany, was brought to me by a friend after the death of my father.

2 sticks (1 cup) unsalted butter

2 cups sugar

6 large eggs, separated

3 cups all-purpose flour

4 teaspoons baking powder

1 cup milk

1½ teaspoons vanilla

Grated rind of 1 lemon

Juice of ½ lemon

1 tablespoon light rum

Pinch salt

Confectioners' sugar (optional)

1. In a mixer cream the butter until light. Add the sugar and the egg yolks. Continue to mix at a medium speed for about 8 minutes.

2. In a separate bowl mix the flour and the baking powder.

3. Warm the milk in a saucepan and add it to the butter mixture alternating with the flour and the baking powder. Add the vanilla, lemon rind and juice, and the rum.

4. Beat the egg whites with the salt until the whites are stiff. Fold into the butter-flour mixture.

5. Grease and flour two 8-inch bread pans and divide the batter equally between them. Bake in a preheated 350-degree oven for about 50 minutes or until a toothpick comes out clean when inserted in the cake. Leave in the pans for several minutes. Run a knife along the sides of the cakes and unmold. Serve as is or sprinkle the top with confectioners' sugar.

Yield: 2 cakes (D)

The Way to a Man's Heart — The Settlement Cook Book

The Settlement Cook Book began as a German-Jewish cookbook, created by a woman who sought to help the wave of immigrants that swept into the United States at the turn of the century. First issued in 1901 as a pamphlet containing one hundred German Jewish and turn-of-the-century American recipes, it has proved to be one of the most successful American cookbooks.

Lizzie Black Kander, the daughter of German-Jewish pioneer farmers, was known as the Jane Addams of Milwaukee for her work on behalf of Eastern European immigrants. In 1896, Mrs. Kander, then chairman of the Milwaukee Section of the National Council of Jewish Women of Philanthropy (NCJW), established the Milwaukee Jewish Mission or settlement house in quarters borrowed from two synagogues.

By 1898 the Mission had begun to sponsor cooking classes every Sunday. The Mission women taught the girls, who ranged in age from thirteen to fifteen, how to build a fire, to cook, and to bake. Each girl would prepare her own dish, often with her mother, older sisters, or friends as spectators. Although they were not schooled in "New World" cooking, the young pupils of the Mission kitchen were better versed in the practices of kashrut than their teachers, a problem that led to some uncomfortable moments.

In 1901 Mrs. Kander and co-author Mrs. Henry Schoenfeld took their collection of recipes to a local printer, who published it in book form. In 1940 Kander recalled the genesis of the cookbook: "All our friends, who were outstanding housekeepers, rallied to the cause. With their help we added to this collection a number of more elaborate recipes that for years were used and reused in the families." The one thousand copies of the first edition of *The Settlement Cook Book* were given at a nominal sum to the children, raffled as prizes, and sold in a Milwaukee department store. By 1912 the book had become so successful that the *Milwaukee Free Press* wrote, "*The Settlement Cook Book,* now in its sixth edition and considered the most accurate and simple cook book ever published, is used in many homes in all parts of the country. The proceeds of the sale of the useful volume bought the prestigious site of the building and has since contributed to the support of the domestic science department."

In 1925 Mrs. Kander reported to the cookbook committee that *The Settlement Cook Book* was now being used in China, Hawaii, Palestine, and Australia. The committee raised $50,000 from book sales for a new community center and directed additional money from earnings for its upkeep. In 1929 she reported that five hundred cookbooks were sold by "the Schuster stores." Simon and the same Schuster became Simon & Schuster and bought the rights to the book in 1965.

Mrs. Kander strove to keep pace with current tastes and in a 1924 column in the *Milwaukee Telegram* offered a "Chinese menu" from the cookbook to accompany the latest fad: mah-jongg parties. She attributed the success of *The Settlement Cook Book,* which had sold 500,000 copies by 1940, to the fact that it is a home cookbook. "The recipes are tested in my own kitchen," she said. "They are practical, economical and reliable. The directions are given in simple language and are easy to follow. Because of America's cosmopolitan population, the dishes of all nationalities have been included."

Open-faced Peach Tart with a Meurbeteig Crust

My mother received a copy of *The Settlement Cook Book* when she was married in 1937 and has been cooking from it ever since. From it she learned to make the following open-faced pie with a *muerbeteig* (butter or margarine) crust, a southern German and Alsatian recipe. My mother and I make all our open-faced tarts based on the Settlement recipe. At Rosh Hashanah we fill them with Italian plums, in the summer with peaches, blueberries, even strawberries. I sometimes make a half dozen of these tarts when fresh berries and fruits are in season and freeze them uncooked. When I have a dinner party I bake the pie just before my guests arrive.

MEURBETEIG CRUST

1 cup all-purpose flour

1 tablespoon sugar

*1 stick (½ cup) unsalted butter
    or pareve margarine*

1 egg yolk

Salt to taste

1 teaspoon brandy

FILLING

*⅓ cup peach, raspberry, or
    strawberry jam*

1 tablespoon brandy

2 pounds freestone peaches

⅓ cup sugar

1 teaspoon cinnamon

1 teaspoon grated lemon rind

*¼ cup fresh raspberries,
    blueberries, or blackberries*

1. To make the crust, mix the flour and sugar together. Using your hands or a pastry blender, cut in the butter until the mixture resembles coarse crumbs. Add the egg yolk, a dash of salt, and brandy to moisten the crust. Or mix the dough in the food processor.

2. Turn the dough onto a board and knead briefly. (This step is unnecessary with the food processor.)

3. Place the dough in the center of a 9-inch pie plate and with your fingers pat it out to cover the bottom and up the side. Refrigerate for a half hour.

4. Preheat the oven to 450 degrees and prebake the crust for 10 minutes. Reduce the oven to 375 degrees and bake another 5 minutes. Remove from the oven.

5. To make the filling, mix the jam with a little brandy and spread on the crust. Peel, pit, and cut the peaches in eighths. Place around in a circle so that each overlaps the other and they eventually form a spiral into the center.

6. Sprinkle with the sugar, cinnamon, and lemon rind. Sprinkle with the berries. (You can freeze it at this point.)

7. Reduce the oven to 350 degrees. Return the tart to the oven and bake about 30 minutes or until the crust is golden brown and the peaches juicy.

Yield: 6 to 8 servings (P) or (D)

Paper-thin Dressed-up Vermont Strudel

My mother made two kinds of strudel at Kutsher's. Dressed up strudel was the kind she stretched until you could read through the dough. She made everyday strudel by just rolling out the dough. My friends asked every time they visited Kutsher's, "Is your mother making dressed up or everyday strudel." My friends and I preferred her dressed up variety.

Milton Kutsher, owner of Kutsher's resort in the Catskills

Like the owner of Kutsher's resort, June Salander of Rutland, Vermont, has been making dressed-up apple strudel for most of her eighty plus years. "I usually start in the fall when Cortland apples are in season," said Mrs. Salander during an apple strudel session in her son Jim's kitchen. Born in Ross, Poland, Mrs. Salander came to this country in 1920 with her mother, brother, and sister.

As a bride she moved to Rutland, the Jewish hub of central Vermont, where her husband, Lewis, ran the Combination Store. Jewish peddlers settled in nearby Poultney and later West Rutland in the nineteenth century. As Rutland grew and they became grocers and retailers, they moved to the center of town. In 1983 Mrs. Salander's Rutland Jewish Center produced a *Kosher Yankee Cookbook,* which included a Jewish version of baked beans with short ribs and maple syrup, latkes with maple syrup, and Mrs. Salander's stuffed cabbage with its Vermont touch of apples.

For the last fifty years her kosher home has been a welcome haven to anyone traveling from New York to Montreal. Ever since the kosher butcher died in the late 1940s, however, the Salanders have been journeying to Albany, one hundred miles away, for their meat.

Mrs. Salander's *challah* is her calling card for the main synagogue events and her *cholent* has received high marks in the *cholent* bake-off held at the conservative synagogue. "We used to take the *cholent* on picnics, wrapping it in blankets so that it would stay warm," recalled her son Jim, now a vascular surgeon in Bethesda, Maryland.

Of all the foods Mrs. Salander cooks today, her strudel, which she stretches as easily as other people swing a sheet over a clothes line, is the favorite. "When I went to West Point my mother would send me the strudel," said Jim, who now makes it for his own children. As his mother and he stretch the dough, his children Abraham and Hannah help, eagerly awaiting the final testing—a forkful of strudel.

June Salander's Vermont Apple Strudel

DOUGH

3 to 3½ cups high-gluten flour

1 tablespoon sugar

1 teaspoon salt

½ cup vegetable oil

1 cup lukewarm water

FILLING

12 Cortland, Granny Smith, Rome, or Golden Delicious apples (about 2 quarts)*

1 cup sugar (depending on the tartness of the apples)

2 teaspoons cinnamon

½ to ¾ cup good apricot, strawberry, or other jam, or orange marmalade

3 cups finely ground and dry leftover sweet rolls, challah, or cake

½ cup vegetable oil

*Do not use McIntosh; they are too wet.

1. Preheat the oven to 150 degrees or to its lowest setting and leave the door open. Or make sure your kitchen is very warm.

2. To make the dough mix 3 cups of the flour, the sugar, and the salt on a board. Make a well in the flour and pour into the well the oil and the water. Mix with a fork and then knead well with your hands, sprinkling on more flour as necessary until the dough forms a workable mass. Roll it back and forth to seal it. Using your hands, grasp a fistful of the portion nearest you, then swing your arm and slam it down treating the dough as you would a club. As it hits the board the dough will stretch. Keep taking additional fistfuls until the dough is pliable and does not show any tears. It should be as smooth and elastic as a baby's bottom. Gather the dough together, place it in a well-greased ceramic or wooden bowl, cover, and let rest in a warm place, either in the oven, which you will turn off now, or a warm spot for about 2 to 3 hours. (Although Mrs. Salander does not do this, you can also make the dough in a food processor, pulsing it until it is as smooth as possible.)

Strudel making with June Salander of Rutland, Vermont

3. On a table or other flat surface that is at least 3 feet by 5 feet, spread a clean sheet or old tablecloth so that the edges hang slightly over the sides. Sprinkle the sheet with flour and roll out the dough to form a 9- by 13-inch rectangle. Then with your fingers press the dough out as thin as possible, trying not to make any tears in the dough.

4. (The novice may want to ask a friend to help stretch the dough.) Then, using your hands, start stretching from the center, drawing your fingers over the entire length of the dough, manipulating it from underneath, and gently lifting the dough with your fingertips until you can read a newspaper through it. It should be stretched to the edge of the 5- by 3-foot surface. When you are finished, the dough will cover the entire table's surface. Try to minimize the number of holes, but a few won't matter. Pull off any thickened edge of unstretched dough. Let dough dry for about 5 minutes.

5. Peel and chop the apples. Scatter them along the wide edge of the dough in a long mound about 2 to 3 inches wide and 1 to 2 inches high, leaving about a two-inch border of dough. Sprinkle the apples with the sugar and cinnamon; drop dollops of jam over the apples. Sprinkle the cake crumbs over the rest of the dough—this will keep the layers separate—and drizzle the oil over the same stretched dough.

6. Taking hold of the sheet on the 5-foot side, lift the sheet up and over the apples to start rolling up the dough jelly-roll style. When completely rolled, roll the strudel back and forth gently to seal. It will be about 3 inches in diameter. Take a little oil in your hands and rub on the top and sides of the strudel.

7. Place a greased jelly-roll pan or cookie sheet next to the strudel. Using your hands, gently lift one half of the strudel on the sheet or pan and then carefully transfer the rest onto the cookie sheet. You may have to form the pastry into a large crescent or spiral or you may have to use 2 cookie sheets and break the strudel in half. If you break it in half make sure to seal the ends. (If desired, you can freeze the strudel at this point.)

8. Bake in a preheated 375-degree oven on the top rack

of the oven for 45 minutes or until golden. If the strudel begins to brown too quickly, lower the heat.

9. Remove from the oven and immediately brush the strudel with the apple juices surrounding it. Let it rest on the cookie sheet until lukewarm. Slice and serve.

Yield: about 20 servings (P)

Tip: You can add nuts and raisins if you like. You can also substitute pears for the apples, adding some fresh or ground ginger—delicious. A shortcut dough is Pepperidge Farm's puff pastry. Use the above filling without the cake crumbs and 4 sheets of the pastry. You can also use phyllo dough with the cake crumbs.

Eli Zabar's Tip: Sprinkle the crumbs under and over the apples. Substitute butter for the oil in this recipe.

Ohio Shortcut Strudel

If you like strudel and want a quick recipe try this one that Helen Coplan of Baltimore shared with me. She learned it from a friend in Ohio. Adapted from Helen Coplan, it is similar to the strudel recipe in Marian Burros and Lois Levine's *Elegant but Easy Cookbook*.

2 sticks (1 cup) unsalted butter

2 cups all-purpose flour

Dash of salt

1 cup sour cream

2 cups chunky apricot preserves

1 cup shredded coconut

1 cup slivered almonds

1. Place the butter, flour, salt, and sour cream in a food processor and process until smooth.

2. Divide into 2 balls. Cover with plastic wrap and refrigerate a few hours or overnight.

3. Flour a board and using a rolling pin, roll the pieces out into 2 squares about 12 inches by 12 inches.

4. Smear half the apricot preserves over one piece of the dough. Then sprinkle with half the coconut and half the almonds. Repeat with the second. Roll up and place on 2 greased baking sheets and bake in a preheated 350-degree oven about 45 minutes or until golden. Cool and cut into 1-inch slices.

Yield: 2 strudels (D)

German Apple Torte from Butler, Missouri

Regine B. Harwick, who came to Butler, Missouri, population 6,000, brought this apple torte from Germany after World War II.

CRUST

2 to 2½ cups unsifted all-
   purpose flour

Dash salt

1 stick (½ cup) unsalted butter
   or margarine

2 large tablespoons Crisco or
   other vegetable shortening

2 large eggs

¼ cup sugar

1 teaspoon baking powder

1 teaspoon vanilla

Grated rind of 1 lemon

2 tablespoons ice water

FILLING

6 to 8 large Jonathan apples
   (about 3 pounds)

½ cup sugar

Juice of ½ lemon

½ cup raisins (optional)

¼ cup pecan pieces

TOPPING

½ stick (¼ cup) butter or
   margarine

¼ cup sugar

¼ cup pecan pieces

3 tablespoons water or cream

Dash of cinnamon

Whipped cream or vanilla ice
   cream (optional)

1. Put 2 cups of the flour, salt, the butter or margarine, and Crisco in a food processor. Using the on-off method, process until the dough reaches a crumb-like texture. Add the eggs, sugar, baking powder, vanilla, lemon rind, and ice water, with the motor running, processing until blended, adding more flour if way too sticky. The dough will be very soft.

2. Press two thirds of the dough into the bottom and 2 inches up the side of a greased 9- or 10-inch springform pan. Refrigerate the remaining dough until ready to use.

3. To make the filling, peel and slice the apples in eighths in a bowl with the sugar and the lemon juice. Sprinkle with the raisins and the pecans. Place in the springform pan.

4. Roll out the remaining third dough between 2 pieces of waxed paper, adding a tablespoon or 2 of flour as needed to make it easy to handle. Place the top gently over the apples. Press the dough together with your fingers or a fork as in a 2-crust pie.

5. To make the topping cut up the remaining butter or margarine into small pieces and dot the crust. Sprinkle with the sugar and the pecans. Dribble the water or cream over the top. Sprinkle with cinnamon sparingly.

6. Bake in a preheated 425-degree oven for 15 minutes. Reduce the heat to 350 degrees for 35 minutes or until golden brown. Let cool 10 minutes before removing the springform pan. It is delicious served with a little ice cream or whipped cream.

Yield: 8 to 10 servings (P); or (D) with optional butter, whipped cream, or ice cream

Tip: You can make the apple torte ahead and freeze before baking. Remove from the freezer, let sit a few hours, and then bake as above.

Cincinnati Linzertorte

One of my favorite desserts is *Linzertorte,* which is made with a crust of hazelnuts, walnuts, or almonds and filled with raspberry preserves. It comes from the city of Linz, Austria, close to the southern German border and was a dessert much cherished by German-Jewish immigrants. Jews either used goose fat or butter in the crust for this famous torte. This recipe comes from a German-Jewish bakery in nineteenth-century Cincinnati. It includes baking powder—a turn-of-the-century addition that did not appear in the original recipes. This is a delightfully robust *Linzertorte* with a crunch to the crust adapted from the Joseph family.

2 cups all-purpose flour

Pinch salt

½ teaspoon cinnamon

½ teaspoon cloves

1 teaspoon baking powder

½ pound ground walnuts or almonds

½ cup sugar

2 large eggs, one separated

1¾ sticks (¾ cup plus 2 tablespoons) unsalted butter or margarine

1 tablespoon brandy

1 cup thick raspberry or apricot jam

Confectioners' sugar

1. Sift together the flour, salt, cinnamon, cloves, and baking powder into a bowl. Add the walnuts, sugar, 1 whole egg, and 1 yolk.

2. With a wooden spoon or the tips of your fingers, work in the butter and brandy to make a smooth dough. You can also use a food processor for this. Wrap and refrigerate at least 30 minutes, or until firm. This is a very short crust.

3. Roll out about half of the dough into a circle about ⅓ inch thick. Using a shallow 9-inch pie pan with a removable bottom, line the bottom and side with the dough.

4. Spread the jam on top. Roll out the remaining dough and, using a pastry cutter or sharp knife, cut into strips ½ inch wide. Arrange the strips in a lattice pattern on top of the torte. Brush with the remaining egg white.

5. Bake in a preheated 450-degree oven for 15 minutes. Reduce the oven to 350 degrees and continue baking about a half hour or until the crust is lightly browned. Let cool for 5 minutes and then sprinkle with confectioners' sugar.

Yield: 1 torte (D) or (P)

Note: You can also refrigerate the dough and make Linzer cookies, using two 3-inch cookie cutters, one with a hole and one without. Bake in a preheated 350-degree oven on a greased cookie sheet for about 10 minutes or until slightly brown. Remove to a rack and fill with the raspberry jam. It will make about 30 cookies.

Charlotte à l'Alsacienne *(Alsatian Apple Charlotte)*

The following old recipe is a classic apple charlotte that would have been served warm in a Jewish home in France or southern Germany. It is often made, as is this recipe, with left-over *challah*. Try sprinkling it with kirsch.

2 pounds Granny Smith,
    Cortland, or any good
    cooking apple
1¼ cups sugar
½ teaspoon cinnamon
4 cups boiled milk or water
12 slices challah or other dense
    white bread, crusts removed
2 tablespoons unsalted melted
    butter or margarine
2 tablespoons kirsch
3 large eggs, separated
½ pound chopped almonds
Bread crumbs

1. Peel and core the apples. Dice them and sprinkle ¼ cup of the sugar and the cinnamon over them.

2. Pour boiling milk over the white bread, cover, and let soak a few minutes. Drain off the milk and add the butter, remaining sugar, kirsch, yolks of eggs, chopped almonds, and the apples.

3. Beat the egg whites until stiff and fold in.

4. Grease a 9-inch bundt pan and sprinkle with fine bread crumbs. Pour the mixture into it and bake in a preheated 375-degree oven for 1 hour or until done. Serve immediately or if you let cool, reheat just before serving. Serve as is or with ice cream or the vanilla sauce served with the *Dampfnudel* on page 307. Add a little dash of kirsch to each serving.

Yield: 8 servings (D) or (P)

Bertha Simon Aram's family had a bakery in Cincinnati, with **Linzertorte** *as one of their specialties.*

If You Give Me a Charlotte Russe
I'll Give You Anything You Want

Growing up in Brownsville, Brooklyn, you got charlotte russe at the corner candy store where everyone hung out until a certain age. They were seasonal, arrayed in a glass container on the counter, regarded as a special treat. They were spongecake wrapped with stiff cardboard and whipped cream on top. There were two kinds of bakeries—bakeries that did their own baking pastries and cakes and commissioned bakeries that got their stuff from other bakeries. Brooklyn was a culture, much more positive identity than the Bronx for Jews anyway, a real place with its own distinctive ethos. Bronx was more pretentious.

Norman Podhoretz, editor of *Commentary Magazine*

Charlotte russe was so delicious that Fanny, in *Once Upon a Time in America,* promised that she would dole out sexual favors to anyone who gave her one. Although charlotte russe was by no means Jewish—it was a popular Victorian dessert—it became a winter fixture in city neighborhoods. An early recipe I found for this paper-case variety was in *Miss Parloa's Kitchen Companion,* 1887:

Charlotte russe that is served in paper cases or in the small china souffle dishes can be made without gelatine, and is liked by some people much better than that which is moulded with the aid of gelatine.

Line eight or ten fancy moulds with sponge cake or sponge fingers. Sprinkle into two quarts of whipped and drained cream four table-spoonfuls of sugar and three table-spoonfuls of wine, or, instead of wine, half a teaspoonful of vanilla extract. Fill with this preparation the dishes that have been lined with cake, and put them in the refrigerator for an hour.

At serving time put a candied cherry or a fresh strawberry on top of each dish of cream.

Or, this charlotte russe may be made in one large glass dish. Line the bottom and sides of the dish with cake, and fill with the cream preparation. Let it stand in the refrigerator for an hour. At serving-time dot with fresh strawberries or candied cherries.

If one be in a hurry, this dish may be served as soon as made.

Orange Charlotte

"We were one of the original pioneers in the supermarket industry," said the late William Golub of Schenectady, New York, shortly before his death at eighty-eight. Mr. Golub was a socialist whose father founded Price Chopper Supermarkets. "During the Depression everybody was going broke. As wholesale grocers, we were selling to the little stores. As every-

One of the first Jewish-owned supermarket chains in America, in Schenectady, New York

body began losing their jobs, our customers began falling by the wayside. We started buying things in large quantity and selling them for little more than wholesale." (Waldbaum's, the other early Jewish New York supermarket chain, had dairy stores on Long Island from the turn of the century and went into supermarkets later.)

The following orange charlotte recipe comes from Mr. Golub's late wife, Estelle, one of the first women managers of a supermarket. The recipe was included in *From Generation to Generation, A Celebration of the Senses,* commemorating one hundred years of Agudat Achim of Schenectady, New York.

1 cup orange juice

1 envelope unflavored gelatin

½ cup sugar

½ cup water

1 tablespoon grated orange rind

1 cup heavy cream or non-dairy whipped topping

2 egg whites

20 ladyfingers (about)

Orange sections from one orange, seeds removed

1. Sprinkle the orange juice over the gelatin to soften. Meanwhile, heat the sugar and water together until the sugar dissolves and bubbles break over the surface. Remove from the heat and stir in the softened gelatin until dissolved. Add the grated orange rind and cool in the refrigerator until thick as unbeaten egg whites.

2. Whip the cream until it feels firm. Beat the egg whites until they are stiff. Beat the gelatin mixture until frothy and light. Mix gently or fold all three together carefully.

3. Grease an 8-inch springform pan and line the side with ladyfingers that have been split. Place the orange sections in the bottom of the mold. Spoon in the orange cream mixture very carefully and chill in the refrigerator until firm, about 4 hours or overnight.

4. To serve, loosen the edges of the charlotte with a knife. Invert over a serving plate. If it does not come out easily, dip the mold in warm water for a brief ten seconds.

Yield: 6 to 8 servings (D or P)

Regard Thy Table and Our Treasured Recipes— Two Postwar Fundraising Cookbooks

Just after World War II, during the heyday of fundraising cookbooks, my mother was the chairman of a cookbook project at the Larchmont Temple in Larchmont, New York. In 1950, *Regard thy Table, A Cook Book of Treasured Recipes,* was published.

The typewritten photo offset cookbook with quotations from the Talmud was illustrated with delightful angels by Gertrude Blue, the mother of wine and food writer Anthony Dias Blue. This compendium included, as did so many others of the period, Hawaiian chicken, chop suey, along with gefilte fish and matzah pancakes.

One year later in 1951 Temple Israel in nearby White Plains produced *Our Treasured Recipes,* also a typed cookbook with line drawings and quotations. Temple Israel's innovative idea was to write to famous people, including the President and the Vice President of the United States, for recipes. All the written responses were produced in the cookbook. Vice President Alben Barkley wrote that Mrs. Barkley asked him to send recipes for Hush Puppies and Baked Pork Chops! For obvious reasons only the hush puppy recipe was included.

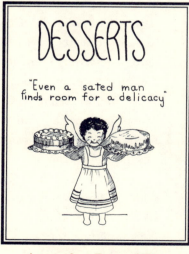

A page from **Regard Thy Table** *cookbook (1950)*

Crustless Apple Crumb Cake

One recipe from the Temple Israel cookbook was a crustless apple crumb cake. An Americanized apple streusel, also known as apple crisp, it was a favorite Friday evening dessert during my childhood. "Fill any size pie plate with apples, depending upon the size of cake desired," were the vague directions.

12 Cortland, McCoun,
    McIntosh, Greening, or
    Granny Smith apples (about
    12 cups)
Rind and juice of 1 lemon
½ cup white sugar or to taste
½ teaspoon cinnamon (about)
2 cups all-purpose flour
    (about)
1 cup dark brown sugar
1½ sticks (¾ cup) unsalted
    butter or margarine
1 cup orange juice

1. Peel, core, and slice the apples. Place in a greased 9-by 13-inch or equivalent rectangle baking dish. Grate the lemon rind and then squeeze the juice over the apples. Sprinkle with the white sugar and about ¼ teaspoon of the cinnamon.

2. In a mixing bowl pinch together the flour, brown sugar, and butter or margarine. Scatter over the apples and then sprinkle with the remaining ¼ teaspoon cinnamon.

3. Pour the orange juice over the crumb topping. It will seep through to the apples.

4. Bake in a preheated 400-degree oven, approximately 30 minutes or until the apples are soft and the top is brown and crusty. Serve warm with whipped cream or vanilla ice cream.

Yield: 10 to 12 servings (P) or (D)

Tip: I often add fresh mint or fresh cranberries to my apples—delicious.

Russian Sour-Cream Cake

In the mid-fifties my husband and I felt it was time for a Jewish influence in the cuisine and we tried it in a diner. I remember my cheese man gave me a sample of five pounds of cottage cheese and I made fifty blintzes and they all sold out. Our customers seemed to love Jewish food . . . borscht, potato latkes, even our sour cream cake. The non-Jews were fascinated by the abundance of food, the size of the portions.

Miriam Perloff, founder of the Country Club
Restaurant and Pastry Diner, Philadelphia, Pennsylvania

Sour Cream Cake, cont.

Ever since I visited Henry's Diner in Burlington, Vermont, owned by the Frank Goldstein family since 1945, I have been intrigued with the idea of Jewish-owned diners. This one in Philadelphia has abundant American and Jewish food. Somehow people think Jewish for sour-cream coffee cakes, perhaps because there is a Russian influence, perhaps because they think brunch.

CAKE

2 sticks (1 cup) unsalted butter

2 cups sugar

4 large eggs

2 teaspoons vanilla

4 cups all-purpose flour

2 teaspoons baking soda

2 teaspoons baking powder

1/4 teaspoon salt

2 cups sour cream

TOPPING

2 tablespoons sugar

1/2 cup chopped walnuts

1/2 cup brown sugar

2 teaspoons cinnamon

1. To make the cake, cream together the butter and the sugar. Add the eggs and the vanilla, beating well.

2. In a separate bowl sift together the flour, baking soda, baking powder, and salt and add to the other ingredients, alternating with the sour cream. Beat well until smooth.

3. To make the topping, mix the sugar, walnuts, brown sugar, and cinnamon.

4. Grease and flour a 10-inch tube pan. Starting with the cake batter, alternate layers of the cake batter and the filling 3 times. You should end up with the filling.

5. Bake in a preheated 350-degree oven for 1 1/2 hours or until a toothpick comes out clean when inserted. Leave in pan about 15 minutes and then, remove, inserting a knife around the sides.

Yield: at least 12 servings (D)

Michael London's Chocolate Brioche-like Babka

Michael London started baking as a little boy in Brooklyn, watching his grandmother and mother. Now, Michael and his wife, Wendy, live in Greenwich, New York, and run Mrs. London's in Saratoga Springs. One day I had the honor of watching Michael make his fabulous chocolate babka during a visit to Washington: while filming for the television series, we returned to watch him in action at his friend Sarabeth Levine's new kitchen in the Chelsea Market. Michael's babka is more elaborate than most. I have tried to be true to his format, except for the use of dry yeast instead of fresh, and the amount of egg yolks. (I use 5 large eggs instead of 1 cup of yolks.) You will need a heavy-duty mixer for this recipe. This extraordinary babka takes time because the dough must chill and rise twice and because there are several fillings. The result is well worth the effort.

CAKE

1 scant tablespoon or 1
   package active dry yeast

1. To make the cake, dissolve the yeast in the milk. Put 2 cups of the flour in the bowl of a large mixer with the heavy-duty stirrer known as the paddle. Add the yeast mixture and mix for about 15 minutes or until well

1 cup lukewarm milk

5½ cups all purpose flour

⅔ cup sugar

1½ teaspoons salt

5 large eggs or 1 cup egg yolks

1½ teaspoons vanilla

Zest of ½ orange

Zest of ½ lemon

1 cup (2 sticks) unsalted butter,
*   melted*

FILLINGS

¾ cup Thompson raisins

5 tablespoons dark rum

4 ounces almond paste*

½ stick unsalted butter

¼ cup sugar

1 large egg

½ teaspoon vanilla

½ cup slivered almonds, toasted

8 ounces good-quality,
*   preferably imported,*
*   bittersweet chocolate*

STREUSEL AND
CINNAMON SUGAR

¼ cup plus 4 teaspoons sugar

½ cup unbleached all-purpose
*   flour*

1 stick unsalted butter, softened

1½ teaspoons cinnamon

1 teaspoon vanilla

1 large egg

1 tablespoon water

*Available at specialty supermarkets

incorporated to make the sponge. Let the sponge rest in the bowl, covered, for about an hour, or until it doubles in volume.

2. To the sponge add the sugar, the remaining flour, salt, eggs or egg yolks, vanilla, and the orange and lemon zests. Using the paddle, work the ingredients for 10 minutes on medium speed until all the ingredients are incorporated. Melt the butter, cool slightly, and add in a very slow stream until it is completely worked into the dough. Continue mixing for another 3 to 4 minutes. The dough will be very soft. Leave the dough in the bowl, covered, until doubled in volume, about another hour.

3. Flour your hands, punch down the dough, divide it into 3 pieces, and place on lightly floured parchment paper on a tray, cover with plastic wrap, and refrigerate overnight or until cold enough to handle.

4. The next day, blanch the raisins in boiling water for a minute or two, drain, then place in a small bowl with 4 tablespoons of the rum or enough to cover, and set aside while preparing the other fillings.

5. To make the almond filling, place the almond paste in a food processor with the steel blade, and soften it by pulsing on and off. Then add the butter, the sugar, the egg, the remaining tablespoon of rum, and the vanilla. Pulse to incorporate. Then add the almonds and process until finely chopped. Set aside in a bowl.

6. Melt the chocolate in a double boiler. Cool slightly.

7. To make the streusel, use your fingers to mix the ¼ cup sugar, the flour, half the butter, ½ teaspoon of the cinnamon, and the vanilla into a crumblike texture. Set aside.

8. Dust the board with flour. Shape 1 piece of the dough with your hands into a rough oblong, adding more flour if needed, and roll out into a rectangle about 13×6 inches, ¼ inch thick.

9. Spoon on one-third of the almond filling, then, using a plastic spatula, spread one-third of the chocolate filling thinly over the dough, leaving about a ½-inch border. Sprinkle on a third of the rum-soaked raisins and finally approximately a third of the remaining 4 teaspoons sugar combined with the remaining 1 teaspoon cinnamon (both listed under Streusel). Brush the top and side border with

Chocolate Brioche-like Babka, cont.

the final egg mixed with the tablespoon water to help seal. Repeat with the other 2 pieces of dough.

10. To assemble the babkas, roll up each piece of dough like a jelly roll, starting from the short end. Twist the rolled-up dough around and around to form a spiral, then place in 3 separate greased loaf or tiny Bundy pans. To form a large circular babka, place 2 pieces of the twisted dough into a greased bundt pan, joining them at the ends. Brush the top with the remaining ½ stick softened butter. Sprinkle two-thirds of the streusel mixture over the loaves. Let the babkas rise until the dough starts to fall over the top of the pan, about 1 hour. Sprinkle again with the remaining streusel.

11. Preheat the oven to 350 degrees and bake the babkas for 45 minutes, or until the streusel is golden brown and the dough slightly hard to the touch.

Yield: 3 babka loaves or 1 large Bundy babka and 1 loaf (D)

Dining Kosher in the White House

When Franklin Delano Roosevelt was governor of New York, he often invited two Jewish guests to lunch at the executive mansion in Albany. It soon came to the attention of the Roosevelts that these men ate only fruit, dessert, and coffee. From then on Eleanor Roosevelt served dairy and vegetable foods in a new set of dishes especially reserved for these two guests. As Jewish consciousness grew in the sixties and the seventies and people in general were less afraid of voicing dietary preferences, the White House would prepare special meals for its kashrut-observing guests. "If they are happy with a fruit or vegetable plate we have separate dishes for that," said Hans Raffert, the executive chef in the White House. "If people request a kosher meal we sometimes order out from a kosher caterer."

State dinners with multiple kosher meals began during the Carter Administration. "It really started with Menachem Begin," recalled Henry Haller, then White House chef. At the Camp David Peace Treaty dinner in 1978, there were 1,300 for dinner with 50 kosher portions brought in. Later, a kosher state dinner for 180 guests was served to Prime Minister Menachem Begin on April 15, 1980. The menu included cold Columbia River salmon with sauce *verte* and golden twists, roast duckling with glazed peaches, wild rice, fresh asparagus, and mixed green salad. The kosher California wines were Kedem Seyval Blanc, Kedem Chaunac, and Kedem Champagne.

Although the White House chefs usually serve butter-rich petit fours, a non-dairy frozen orange sherbet cake with Grand Marnier sauce and pareve pastries were prepared for this dinner.

Ann Amernick, probably the first Jewish woman to cook in the White House, was an assistant pastry chef for presidents Carter and Reagan. "The entire White House kitchen had to be kosherized at the last minute," she recalled. "The *mashgiachs* came with blowtorches as big as they were. They spent all day burning and covering surfaces with aluminum foil. The kitchen was unbearably hot. I felt it was a historical moment and at the same time it was comical. Roland Mesnier, the pastry chef, was desperately trying to get the sorbets made and one of the *mashgiachs* was following him around with the blowtorch. Every time Roland turned around the *mashgiach* was there. While some of the cooks had a partial understanding of kashrut from past experience in hotels and lessons in cooking school, the reality in the White House was another story."

The Story of Häagen-Dazs—American Ice Cream with a Danish Name

Probably the most famous Jewish ice-cream concern is Häagen-Dazs. Reuben Mattus, a Polish immigrant, started in the ice-cream business in the 1920s as a child of ten just after he and his widowed mother, Leah, stepped off the boat. Since his uncle was in the Italian lemon-ice business in Brooklyn, they joined him. Reuben helped his mother squeeze lemons for the ices they sold first in Brooklyn and then in the South Bronx.

"In those days we bought the ice from the Great Lakes in the winter and buried it with sawdust in pits in the ground until summer," he said. Until 1927, before the first refrigerator was manufactured, ice cream was seasonal. By the late twenties the Mattus family began making ice pops, and by 1929 chocolate-covered ice-cream bars and sandwiches.

"We had a problem making good ice cream so we hired an ice-cream maker. People wouldn't buy our ice cream. I said to myself, 'Why can't we make good ice cream so people will buy it?' Then I got a hold of some books and I studied how to make ice cream. The first thing I told my mother was to fire our ice-cream maker. The most important thing is to make it taste good."

Mattus's new kind of ice cream went against the rules and was so heavy that he had to change his equipment. "I prided myself on being a marketing man. If you're the same like everybody else you're lost. The number one thing was to get a foreign sounding name. The only country which saved the Jews during World War II was Denmark, so I put together a totally fictitious Danish name and had it registered. Häagen-Dazs doesn't mean anything. It would attract attention, especially with the umlaut. If I made good ice cream I wanted my people to get it, so I made it kosher. The first place we marketed it was Manhattan, in pint containers at gourmet stores. Schrafft's cost fifty-two cents a pint. Ours was seventy-five cents a pint. I didn't believe in selling it for fifty-nine cents. I made a special ice cream for people who wanted a special taste. That was my attempt and it worked. It sold by word of mouth." Now, at age eighty, Mr. Mattus has just started a new business, low-calorie Mattus ice cream.

Ann Amernick's Chocolate Torte

Today, Ms. Amernick is one of Washington's premier pastry chefs. This cake, like her other desserts, is light and rich.

CAKE

9 ounces semisweet Lindt or
Caillebaut chocolate

5 tablespoons milk

1³/4 sticks (³/4 cup plus 2
tablespoons) unsalted butter,
softened

5 large eggs, separated

³/4 cup sugar

³/4 cup cake flour

2 tablespoons rum

¹/2 cup apricot preserves

CHOCOLATE GLAZE

8 ounces semisweet Lindt or
Caillebaut chocolate

1 stick (¹/2 cup) unsalted butter

1. To make the cake, melt the chocolate with the milk over low heat in a 2-quart saucepan, stirring constantly. Add the butter and stir well. Add the egg yolks, ¹/4 cup of the sugar, and the cake flour. Set aside.

2. Beat the egg whites until they form soft peaks. Then beat in the remaining ¹/2 cup sugar, a tablespoon at a time. Continue to beat until the meringue is glossy and forms stiff peaks.

3. Whip the chocolate mixture until fluffy.

4. Fold the meringue into the chocolate mixture and mix until no streaks show. Pour into 2 buttered and floured 8-inch cake pans and bake in a preheated 350-degree oven for about 30 minutes or until a few crumbs adhere to a toothpick inserted in the middle. The tops of the cakes will probably crack. Let the cakes cool for 10 minutes and turn onto a cake rack. When cool, brush 1 cake with the rum and then cover the layer with a thin glaze of apricot preserves. Cover with the second layer, its smooth surface face up.

5. To make the chocolate glaze, melt the chocolate with the butter, stirring well. Cool a few minutes at room temperature and pour enough over the top of the cake to cover. Let the chocolate cool further and beat just until it becomes thick and fluffy. Spread the glaze around the side of the cake.

Yield: 6 to 8 servings (D)

My Family's Favorite Ice-Cream Cake

You can make this cake with traditional or unusual flavors. Frozen yoghurt is a good change, too. The fudge sauce is adapted from Mickey Bazelon.

CRUST

*24 cream-filled chocolate
    sandwich cookies (about 2
    cups crumbs)*

*³⁄₄ stick (6 tablespoons)
    unsalted butter*

*1 pint chocolate ice cream or
    frozen yoghurt*

*1 pint raspberry sherbet or
    frozen yoghurt*

*1 pint vanilla ice cream or
    frozen yoghurt*

FUDGE SAUCE

1 stick (¹⁄₂ cup) unsalted butter

*2 8-ounce packages bittersweet
    chocolate*

2 ounces semisweet chocolate

¹⁄₂ cup cream or lowfat milk

1 teaspoon vanilla

1 cup heavy cream

Fresh raspberries for garnish

1. To make the crust, whirl the cookies in a food processor to make a powder.

2. Melt the butter and mix with the cookies. Using your fingers, press three inches up the side and on the bottom of a 9-inch springform pan.

3. Remove the ice cream or frozen yoghurt from the freezer and let it soften slightly. Starting with the chocolate spoon the ice cream or frozen yoghurt into the springform pan, pressing down until smooth. Repeat with the raspberry and finally the vanilla. Refreeze, wrapped well. You can do this at least a week ahead.

4. To make the fudge sauce, melt the butter and the chocolate in a saucepan over low heat. Add the cream and beat until shiny. Cool slightly and add the vanilla.

5. Just before serving, whip the cream and pipe it around the mold. Garnish with fresh raspberries and serve with the sauce on the side.

Yield: at least 12 servings (D)

Note: You can also line the pan with ladyfingers and use any kind of ice cream or frozen yoghurt that suits your fancy.

Cheesecake Memories with Immortal Flavors

Why, I can dream away a half-hour on the immortal flavor of those thick cheese cakes we used to have on Saturday night. . . . I am no cook, so I cannot tell you how to make such cake. I might borrow the recipe from my mother, but I would rather you should take my word for the excellence of Polotzk cheese cakes. . . .

Do you think all your imported spices, all your scientific blending and manipulating, could produce so fragrant a morsel as that which I have on my tongue as I write? Glad am I that my mother, in her assiduous imitation of everything American, has forgotten the secrets of Polotzk cookery. At any rate, she does not practice it, and I am the richer in memories for her omission. Polotzk cheese cake, as I now know it, has in it the flavor of daisies and clover picked on the Vall; the sweetness of Dvina water; the richness of newly turned earth which I molded with bare feet and hands; the ripeness of red cherries bought by the dipperful in the market place; the fragrance of all my childhood's summers.

Mary Antin, The Promised Land, 1912

The cheesecake Mary Antin describes was most likely a pressed cottage- or farmer-cheese cake with a yeast dough or perhaps a short crust. A decade or so after Ms. Antin wrote this nostalgic description of cheesecake from her native Russia, Fannie Ferber Fox, who lived in Boston in the 1920s, gave a recipe for a cottage-cheese cheesecake in her *Fannie Fox's Cook Book* (see page 108). Although not a Jewish cookbook per se, there are many German-Jewish recipes in it. In the foreword her sister Edna Ferber wrote, "Some of the recipes herein are culled from the finest of the Jewish cookery, which, for delicacy and flavor, cannot be excelled. The crumbling and toothsome torte made from the humble cottage cheese and the commonplace zwieback is one of these. It is called Zwieback Cheese Torte and is usually eaten to the accompaniment of choked murmurs of rapture." The same recipe appeared in the 1930 edition of *The Settlement Cook Book.*

Zwieback Cottage-Cheese Torte

In most kitchens today, the zwieback crust has been replaced by a graham-cracker crust. Cottage cheese no longer has to be sieved. We have food processors to puree it and, of course, cream cheese has replaced cottage cheese in most cheesecake recipes anyway (see page 335). The only change I made in this old recipe, besides using the food processor, was to reduce the amounts of cinnamon, butter, and sugar.

CRUST

Enough zwieback to make
   2 cups crumbs (about
   6 ounces)
¾ cup sugar
⅓ cup melted butter
¼ teaspoon cinnamon

FILLING

1½ tablespoons cornstarch
⅔ cup heavy cream
⅓ cup milk
2½ cups cottage cheese
2 tablespoons melted unsalted
   butter
4 large eggs, separated
1 cup sugar
Juice of 1 lemon
Grated rind of 1 lemon
½ teaspoon cinnamon
⅛ teaspoon grated nutmeg

Strawberries for garnish

1. To make the crust, place the zwieback in a food processor with the sugar, melted butter, and cinnamon. Process until fine crumbs are formed.

2. Press the crumb mixture into the bottom and sides of a 9-inch greased springform pan, reserving 2 tablespoons for the top of the torte.

3. To make the filling, dissolve the cornstarch in the cream and milk.

4. Using a food processor, puree the cottage cheese. Add the melted butter, egg yolks, sugar, lemon juice and rind, cinnamon, nutmeg, and cream mixture and puree well.

5. Beat the egg whites until they are stiff, but not dry, and fold into the cheese mixture.

6. Pour the filling into the prepared springform pan. Sprinkle with the reserved 2 tablespoons of crumbs, and bake for 45 minutes to 1 hour in a preheated 325-degree oven. Turn off the oven and leave the cake in for almost 1 hour to cool gradually, to avoid falling. Serve surrounded by and decorated with fresh strawberries.

Yield: 8 servings (D)

Before There Was Lindy's There Was Reuben's Cheesecake

We were the first ones to have the original cream cheesecake at Reuben's Restaurant, then on Broadway and Madison Avenue and Fifty-eighth Street. We made it with Breakstone's cream cheese with whole eggs and cream. Everybody else was making cheesecake with cottage cheese in those days. In 1929 we won the Gold Medal in the World's Fair for our cake. In about 1935 Lindy's went and stole our German chef with the recipe. We were open for years before he went into business. He came out with a very good cheese cake. But he started out by putting in fancy strawberries. Ours was plain. He had a sort of a honky-tonk place but he did very well.

Arnold Reuben, Jr., Little Neck, New York

Both Lindy's and Reuben's were the places where every nocturnal nomad turned up sooner or later. They were the unofficial clubs for the regular members of the acting profession, the cabaret performers, and those whose working hours end when everyone else wakes up.

Like Reuben's the success of Lindy's is attributed to a German émigré. Leo Linderman left school at fourteen to become an apprentice in a Berlin delicatessen. In 1921, eight years after his arrival in America, the go-getter launched Lindy's on Broadway where he marketed deli food so well that it captured the popular imagination. The theater district restaurant quickly became famous for its sandwich creations—smoked turkey and chicken liver, sturgeon and Nova Scotia salmon. It may even have been here where the famous bagels, cream cheese, and lox troika was launched, although his menu of 1939 does not include it.

Linderman's marketing genius is best illustrated with his cheesecake, probably one of the most discussed recipes in America. It was by means of this recipe, an outgrowth of a Kraft promotional Philadelphia Supreme Cheesecake and possibly Reuben's Cheesecake, that "New York Cheesecake" translated as "Jewish cheesecake." To show how famous American cheesecake has become today, at the festival on the mall prior to Bill Clinton's inauguration in 1993, Eli's Cheesecake of Chicago gave away slices of a two-thousand-pound red, white, and blue cheesecake to the eagerly awaiting public.

Lindy's—Or Is It Reuben's?—Cheesecake

A Greek man answered an ad we ran in *The New York Times* for a baker. He said he baked Lindy's cheesecakes. "You get me the ingredients I want—pure cream cheese, eggs, and heavy cream and I'll make you Lindy's cheesecake." He was a gem. He baked Lindy's cheesecake for our restaurant.

> Miriam Perlof, founder, the Country Club
> Restaurant and Pastry Diner, Philadelphia

COOKIE CRUST

1 cup all-purpose flour

¼ cup sugar

1 teaspoon grated lemon rind

½ teaspoon vanilla extract

1 egg yolk

1 stick (½ cup) unsalted butter, chilled and cut into ¼-inch bits

CHEESE FILLING

1¼ pounds softened cream cheese

¾ cup sugar

1½ tablespoons flour

1½ teaspoons grated lemon rind

1 teaspoon grated orange rind

½ teaspoon vanilla extract

3 eggs plus 1 egg yolk

2 tablespoons heavy cream

1. To make the crust, place the flour, sugar, grated lemon rind, vanilla extract, egg yolk, and butter in a large mixing bowl. With your fingertips, rub the ingredients together until they are well mixed and can be gathered into a ball. You can also whirl the ingredients in a food processor. Dust with a little flour, wrap in waxed paper, and refrigerate for at least 1 hour.

2. Place the chilled dough in an ungreased 9-inch springform pan. With your hands, pat and spread the dough evenly over the bottom and about 2 inches up the side of the pan. Bake in the center of a preheated 450-degree oven for 10 minutes. Remove and set aside to cool to room temperature.

3. Lower the oven temperature to 300 degrees. To make the filling, place the cream cheese in a large mixing bowl and beat vigorously with a wooden spoon until it is creamy and smooth. Beat in the sugar, a few tablespoons at a time, and, when it is well incorporated, beat in the flour, lemon and orange rinds, vanilla extract, eggs and egg yolk, and heavy cream.

4. Pour the filling into the cooled cookie crust and bake in the center of the oven for 1 hour or until a toothpick comes out clean when put in the center. Then remove from the oven and set aside to cool in the pan. Then demold.

5. Refrigerate the cheesecake for at least 3 hours before serving.

Yield: at least 12 servings (D)

Alice Medrich's Black and White Cheesecake

One of the most successful high-quality chocolate companies today is Cocolat, founded by Alice Medrich in Berkeley, California, in an area known as the "gourmet ghetto" (Alice Waters's Chez Panisse is nearby).

Born to a Jewish family in Temple City, California, Ms. Medrich received her culinary inspiration from her grandmother, who lived with her. "Sure we had bagels and lox and my mother might doctor up borscht from a jar," she said. "But my parents didn't connect to their heritage or cuisine. I remember it all from my grandmother who made a wonderful chicken soup."

It was only a matter of time for her to create the quintessential chocolate cheesecake with a white filling reminiscent of her childhood tastes of Sara Lee cheesecakes. "I don't like totally chocolate cheesecakes. Bittersweet chocolate and cheesecake combine the tangy and bitter," she said. "By swirling one it doesn't lose the contrast. You taste the vanilla and chocolate like a chocolate sundae."

CRUST

¾ stick (6 tablespoons)
   unsalted butter

½ cup sugar

¾ teaspoon vanilla extract

⅛ teaspoon salt

¼ cup plus 2 tablespoons sifted
   unsweetened cocoa powder

¾ cup all-purpose flour

FILLING

5 ounces bittersweet chocolate,
   cut into bits

¼ cup water

24 ounces cream cheese,
   slightly softened

1¼ cups sugar

½ teaspoon vanilla extract

2 large eggs

1. To make the crust, mix the butter, sugar, vanilla, and salt in the bowl of a food processor and whirl until creamy. Add the cocoa and process until you have a dark, smooth paste. Add the flour and pulse just until incorporated but still crumbly.

2. Firmly pat three-fourths of the mixture into the bottom of an 8-inch springform pan or cheesecake pan with a removable bottom. With a fork toss and spread the remaining one fourth crumbly dough loosely in a shallow baking pan. Place both the bottom crust and the pan of extra dough in a preheated 350-degree oven. Bake for 10 minutes. Remove the baked crumbs. Bake the bottom crust for an additional 5 minutes. Let crust and crumbs cool completely on a rack. Reduce the oven temperature to 325 degrees.

3. Pulverize the cooled crumbs. Store in an airtight container until needed.

4. To make the filling, melt the chocolate with the water in a double boiler, stirring occasionally until the chocolate is melted and smooth. Or, microwave on medium for 1 minute. Stir until smooth and keep warm.

5. Place the cream cheese in the bowl of an electric mixer and beat on medium speed, gradually adding the sugar, until completely smooth. Add the vanilla and the eggs, one by one, beating only until well mixed.

6. Measure and set aside 1 cup of the cheesecake filling. Pour the remaining batter over the baked chocolate crust; set aside.

7. Stir the warm chocolate into the reserved cheesecake batter. Pour the chocolate batter in a thick ring, about ½ inch in from the side of the pan, on top of the plain batter. Use a soup spoon to marble the chocolate. Try not to blend the batters together too much. If necessary, use your finger to wipe the side of the pan clean above the batter after marbling.

8. Bake in the 325-degree oven for 20 to 25 minutes, or until the cheesecake shows signs of puffing around the edges but is still very soft in the center. Remove the cake from the oven and run a thin knife blade carefully around the edges to release the cake from the side of the pan.

9. Cool in the pan, on a rack, covered with an inverted large mixing bowl. Refrigerate, covered with plastic wrap, after it is completely cool. The cake may be made to this point and refrigerated up to 4 days in advance. Unmold the cheesecake. Press reserved cookie crumbs around the sides of the cake, being careful not to get the crumbs on top.

Yield: 12 to 14 servings (D)

Oregon's Kosher Maven's Honey Cake

In Portland, Oregon, a city settled by German-Jewish tradesmen and shopkeepers in the 1840s, one woman is still remembered for her great kosher cooking. The late Runi Hyman used to provide kosher meals for transients and hungry Portlanders from the late 1920s until about 1970.

Because of her great heart she always opened her door to anyone who knocked and asked for a meal. One day someone sent a well-dressed young man to her. The man told her he had been traveling across the country and had left a wife and three sons in the east. Ms. Hyman looked him in the eye and said, "What's a young man with so many family responsibilities doing bumming around the country instead of getting a steady job?" That young man was the singer Jan Peerce.

During World War II she cooked for soldiers. A regular ritual followed each meal. Mrs. Hyman would take a snapshot of each young man. Then the picture would be developed and sent home to the soldier's family.

Although most of her recipes are gone, she shared her traditional honey cake, made for Rosh Hashanah to ensure a sweet New Year but also prepared by honey-cake aficionados for all good occasions.

3 large eggs

1 tablespoon fresh lemon juice

Grated rind of 1 lemon

1/3 cup vegetable oil

1 cup honey

1 cup warm black coffee

3 1/2 cups all purpose flour, sifted

2 1/2 teaspoons baking powder

1 teaspoon baking soda

1/2 teaspoon salt

1/4 teaspoon cream of tartar

1 cup sugar

1 teaspoon cinnamon

1/2 cup slivered almonds

1. Preheat the oven to 350 degrees and grease and flour a 10-inch tube pan.

2. Place the eggs, lemon juice, lemon rind, oil, honey, and coffee in the bowl of an electric mixer. Mix on low speed until well blended. Gradually add the flour, baking powder, baking soda, salt, cream of tartar, sugar, and cinnamon, mixing for about 5 minutes or until well blended. Fold in the slivered almonds.

3. Pour the batter into the tube pan. Bake in the oven for 50 minutes or until a toothpick inserted in the center of the cake comes out clean.

Yield: 1 cake with at least 12 servings (P)

Cousin Jenny's Hungarian Honey Cake

It was years ago that Charles Fenyvesi first told me about this extraordinary layered honey torte. The Jenny described in the box (on the following page) was deported to Auschwitz, where she died. Mr. Fenyvesi's mother experimented for twenty years until she came up with the following formula. Here is the recipe, a tribute to Hungarian Jewry and to Mr. Fenyvesi's late cousin Jenny.

TORTE

2 tablespoons unsalted butter

1 cup sugar

¼ cup milk

3 tablespoons dark wildflower honey

5 cups all-purpose flour

1 tablespoon baking soda

1 large egg

FILLING

¼ cup regular cream of wheat

2 cups milk

1 teaspoon vanilla extract

1¾ sticks (¾ cup plus 2 tablespoons) unsalted butter

1¼ cups sugar

1 large egg

1 cup apricot or sour cherry preserves (about)

1. To make the torte, put the butter, sugar, milk, and honey in a small pan. Warm it over a low heat, beating well, and then let cool.

2. Sift the flour and the baking soda onto a board. Make a well and break the egg into it. Mix thoroughly with your hands, then add the contents of the small pan. Make a dough, kneading a few minutes until the dough is smooth. Divide into 4 balls. Cover and let rest for 1 hour.

3. Using a rolling pin, flatten each ball and roll out into a 10- by 15-inch rectangle. Place on 4 greased cookie sheets and bake in a preheated 400-degree oven until the surface is golden brown, about 15 to 20 minutes. (Watch carefully: The dough burns quickly.) Remove the sheets from the oven and let stand overnight at room temperature. If you do not have 4 cookie sheets, use 2 and then repeat.

4. Before going to bed, prepare the filling. Place the cream of wheat and the milk in a small pan, stirring constantly until thickened, about 2 minutes. Add the vanilla extract.

5. Let cool slightly. Add the butter, sugar, and egg. Beat with a mixer. Cover and refrigerate overnight.

6. The next day, place half of the filling on the first pre-baked sheet of dough. Put the second sheet of dough on top of the first and spread on the apricot or sour cherry preserves. Then put the third sheet on top, spread the remaining filling on it, and finally top with the last sheet. Let stand for at least 6 hours. Cut with a sharp knife into small squares, which is what Mr. Fenyvesi's mother likes, or into diamonds, which is what Jenny preferred.

Yield: 1 cake, serving at least 20 (D)

Honey Cake from Hungary Reconstructed After the Holocaust

Though Cousin Jenny was a versatile baker who liked to try many different recipes, she had one item she served nearly every Sunday: her honeycake. Cut with a sharp knife into precise diamonds, it had a soft, creamy filling which nobody could identify for certain but which was a perfect complement to the layer of preserves, homemade of course. Jenny's favorites were raspberry and plum. To her, raspberries represented innocence, and plum, abundance, and these were two qualities she admired.

Members of the family who travelled widely and sampled the honeycakes of other households and other lands thought that Jenny's honeycake was the softest, the creamiest, and the most delicate honeycake they had ever tasted. They thought it was unquestionably superior to the spicy, heavy, and often dry honeycakes of Romania, made with cloves and cardamom, and topped with almond slivers—which tasted better with a splash of plum brandy or wine—as well as to the gooey concoctions of Yugoslavia, Greece, and Turkey dripping with honey and crammed with walnuts or filberts, or both. Jenny's honeycake was on another level, the connoisseurs decided, it was in a class of its own.

Charles Fenyvesi, *When the World Was Whole, 1990*

Tishpishti *(Nut Cake with Sugar Syrup)*

Like honey cake for Eastern European Jews, this nut cake with a sugar (and originally honey) sauce is a typical celebratory cake for Syrian and Turkish Jews. It is much easier to make than baklava and, I believe, just as good.

CAKE

3 cups all-purpose flour

1½ tablespoons sugar

½ teaspoon cinnamon

½ teaspoon cloves

3 cups finely chopped walnuts

½ cup water

1 cup vegetable oil

SYRUP

1½ cups sugar

2 cups water

Juice of ½ lemon

½ teaspoon cinnamon for sprinkling on the cake

1. To make the cake, mix together the flour, sugar, ½ teaspoon of the cinnamon, the cloves, and the walnuts. Rub with your hands until the ingredients are well blended. Make a well in the center and add the water and the vegetable oil. Knead very well. You can also merely whirl everything in the food processor, making sure that you don't over-process. You want some crunch in the walnuts.

2. Place in a 9-inch round or square greased baking pan and pat the dough down tight. Cut into about twenty-four 2-inch diamond shapes.

3. Bake in a preheated 350-degree oven for 1 hour.

4. After you put the cake in the oven, make the syrup. Mix the sugar, water, and lemon juice in a heavy saucepan. Bring to a boil, then lower the heat, and let the mixture simmer, uncovered, for 1 hour or until it is reduced to one-third of the volume.

5. When the cake is done, pour the syrup over the cake. Make sure that the pan is on top of a larger pan lest the syrup spill over. Cut it again into the same diamond shapes. Let it cool, covered with a clean dish towel. With a knife remove onto wax paper and if you like, place in small cupcake liners to serve. Sprinkle with the cinnamon.

Yield: 24 slices (P)

Basboussa *(Egyptian Cake with Orange Flower Water)* in Providence, Rhode Island

I was first introduced to Egyptian Jews during my teenage years in Providence, Rhode Island. Because of Gamel Abdul Nasser's antipathy towards Israel in the late fifties, many Egyptian Jews fled, some coming to the United States. Because French was the first language of Jews educated at French schools in Egypt, they spoke French. These people often were having a difficult time making ends meet. My father took a liking to one such lady from Alexandria and decided that the way to help her was to have her teach me French. I was not thrilled with the idea of giving up an afternoon a week after school, but I did enjoy the desserts that she prepared for me, especially *basboussa,* a cream-of-wheat cake soaked in a sugar sauce, another Jewish celebratory cake.

CAKE

2 cups cream of wheat

1 teaspoon baking powder

1 cup sour cream or yoghurt

½ cup sugar

3 tablespoons melted unsalted butter

¼ cup bread crumbs for dusting

2 dozen blanched almonds

SYRUP

2 cups sugar

2 cups water

1 tablespoon orange flower water*

1 cup whipped cream

*Obtainable at Middle Eastern stores

1. To make the cake, mix together the cream of wheat and the baking powder in a bowl. Add the sour cream or yoghurt, the sugar, and the melted butter and mix well.

2. Grease a 10-inch round baking pan and dust with the bread crumbs. Pour in the filling and using your hands, pat down into the pan. Make a design of diamonds by scoring with a knife.

3. Place a blanched almond in each diamond. Bake in a preheated 350-degree oven for 30 to 45 minutes or until slightly brown on top.

4. Meanwhile make the syrup by mixing the sugar and water. Bring to a boil in a saucepan and simmer until it forms a syrup and is sticky. Add the orange flower water.

5. As soon as the *basboussa* comes out of the oven pour the syrup over. Let the cake stand until cool. Place the diamond-shape pieces in paper cups. Serve with a dollop of whipped cream.

Yield: about 24 squares (D)

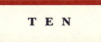
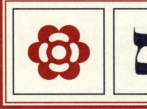

TEN

Cookies, Candy, and Fruit Desserts

Purim. A day snatched from busy lives, and devoted, whole-heartedly to sheer gladness and merrymaking—the day of Esther. Everyone masqueraded. Adults gave painful thought and time to the preparation of costumes, and the balls were really elegant. The robes worn were rich and often very original. And the children possessed the streets and invaded all the houses in the neighborhood, in such costumes as they could devise. Young folks 14, 15 or 16 used to burst into our home, dressed in bizarre garments and my mother always pretended to be surprised and scared, but never were the mountains of delicious Purim cookies missing. And I, a timid little thing, always hid behind my mother, charmed, admiring, interested and always a little afraid.

Jennie Gerstley, "Reminiscences, Chicago, Illinois, 1859–1934," American Jewish Archives

In Europe a peddler was a rarity. Here in one single street I saw more people offering wares than in the largest Jahrmarkt, and more different items than in a hundred Jahrmarkts. Many of the things I saw on sale were simply not to be had in Galicia, or even in Hungary. Some I had never seen before at all. Fruits, for instance. Bananas were new to me, and peaches. Other fruits were unobtainable in Europe. Here they were thrown half eaten into the gutter. In the filth of the East Side I suddenly saw wealth, teeming life. . . . It was vulgar and dirty but it was alive. . . . That afternoon my usual dessert of bananas, after lunch, sent a purposeful thought flashing through my head. An hour later I was out on Hester Street with a pushcart, dispensing bananas to a hungry public.

Louis Borgenicht, The Happiest Man, 1942

Flora Atkin's Dutch Kichelkies *(Little Kichel)*

In nineteenth-century America, *kichlers* or Haman's Ears for Purim Night were small cookies (*kichel* is cookie in Yiddish), sometimes made from a pound-cake batter, deep-fried in butter, and bathed in a sugar syrup flavored with cinnamon and rose water. Notice that butter was used in this age before vegetable shortening.

The Edward Hartogensis family, Washington, D.C. Fanny (far right) was known for her **kichelkies** *from an old family recipe.*

Haman's Ears is also the American name for a *kichel, kichelkies,* or *hazenblosen* (blown-up little pants), thin strips of fried dough sprinkled with confectioners' sugar, similar to the Italian bugie served at Carnivale in February. "When I would ask my grandmother how much red wine to use in her *kichelkies,* she would reply, 'Half an egg shell,' " said Flora Atkin, who enjoys making traditional family recipes for holidays. "She used to say, 'I know my recipe won't die because my granddaughter will carry on the tradition.' " She was right. Before Rosh Hashanah, each year, Mrs. Atkin makes *kichelkies* on an assembly line with three frying pans going at once.

1 large egg

¼ teaspoon salt

¼ cup sweet red wine

½ to 1 cup all-purpose unbleached flour

Vegetable oil or Crisco for deep-frying

Confectioners' sugar

1. Beat the egg well. Then add salt, wine, and gradually the flour until you have a sticky elastic dough, almost like the consistency of molasses.

2. Flour your hands and break off pieces not much bigger than a marble. Roll out paper-thin on a floured surface. Cut in segments approximately 2 by 4 inches (dough the size of a large marble will make about 3), or cut on the diagonal very thin strips or whatever shape you wish.

3. Pour about 2 inches of oil into a heavy frying pan and heat to 375 degrees. Slide the strips carefully into the hot oil. Let cook a few seconds on each side. Soon they will bubble and puff up like *hazenblosen*. Remove with a spatula and drain on paper towels. When cool sprinkle with confectioners' sugar. Eat immediately or let sit, covered well, for one day with plastic wrap.

Yield: about 20 (P)

At Purim Large Quantities of Haman's Three-cornered Cakes Are Being Baked

Meanwhile, in the kitchen (at Purim) large quantities of Haman's three-cornered cakes are being baked, as also rolled cakes with citron and raisins and almonds all pounded together . . . These (gift) plates, as a rule, are filled with oranges, nuts, raisins, and cake, but there are others which use cake and fruit as a cover to conceal a silver dollar or a greenback underneath. These latter plates are intended as a gift either to some poor family on the East Side or some poor relative. All of them are covered neatly with a napkin, and either placed in a basket or carefully made up into a package, and, carrying these, the boys and girls become the unconscious doers of good deeds and pleasant courtesies.

Esther J. Ruskay, *Hearth and Home Essays,* 1905

Mrs. Ruskay wrote beautiful essays on preserving Jewish traditions. To this day these gift baskets or *shalah manot* of fruit, candy, and cookies are a traditional part of Purim. In religious neighborhoods, where every family fetes its neighbors, the house resembles the American Halloween with the goodies that children assemble.

Esther Ruskay, who wrote essays about the glories of a religious life

Fruit-filled Hamantashen from Philadelphia

Haman's pockets, or *Hamantashen,* were brought to this country by Jews from the eastern part of Germany and Eastern Europe. *Hamantashen* are so popular here that at many academic institutions there is an annual *Hamantashen* versus latke debate. The filling for the following *Hamantashen* recipe comes from the *Taste of History: Recipes Old and New* put out by Philadelphia's Historic Spanish and Portuguese Congregation, Kahal Kadosh Mikveh Israel, founded in 1740. With the filling I used my own butter cookie dough, which everyone in my family loves. Although adults like fruit or poppy-seed fillings, my children do not, and they fill the dough with chocolate chips and even make a *Hamantashen* with chocolate chips and peanut butter. I'll stick to this prune filling and leave the chocolate-chip *Hamantashen* to them.

FRUIT FILLING

¾ *cup pitted prunes*

⅓ *cup seedless raisins*

¼ *cup water*

¼ *cup shelled walnuts*

¼ *apple with peel*

Juice and rind of ½ lemon

2 tablespoons sugar

DOUGH

⅔ *cup pareve margarine or*
  butter

½ *cup sugar*

1 large egg

½ *teaspoon vanilla*

2½ to 3 cups unbleached
  all-purpose flour

1 teaspoon baking powder

Dash of salt

1. To make the filling, simmer the prunes and raisins together in the water, covered, for 15 minutes or until the prunes are softened but still firm.

2. Add the nuts, then put the mixture through a grinder or chop in a food processor with the apple. Add the lemon juice and rind and sugar and mix well.

3. To make the dough, cream the margarine or butter with the sugar. Add the egg and vanilla and continue creaming until smooth. A food processor is great for this.

4. Add the flour, baking powder, and salt. Process until a ball of dough is formed.

5. Chill for 2 to 3 hours, or overnight.

6. Taking one fourth of the dough, roll out on a lightly floured board to a thickness of ⅛ inch. Cut into 2½-inch circles. With your finger, brush water around the rim of the circle. Drop 1 teaspoon of filling in the center. Then bring the dough around the filling and press 3 ends together.

7. Bake in a preheated 375-degree oven on a well-greased cookie sheet for 10 to 15 minutes or until the tops are golden.

Yield: 36 cookies (P) with margarine; (D) with butter
Regional Variation: A similar and equally delicious
Hamantashen *filling comes from Natchez, Mississippi.*
Naturally, it includes pecans rather than walnuts.

Ma'amoul *(Syrian Stuffed Cookies)*

This round cookie, often served at Purim by Jews, comes from the Middle East. This particular version from White Plains, New York, has become three-cornered like a *Hamantashen* in this country.

COOKIE DOUGH

2 sticks (1 cup) unsalted butter or margarine

1¾ cups unbleached flour

¼ cup water

FILLING

½ cup ground walnuts

2 tablespoons sugar

1 teaspoon cinnamon

1. Place the butter and the flour in the food processor. Add the water and process. Let sit for 45 minutes and cover with a dish towel. Roll the dough out and cut the pieces with a cookie cutter or glass about 3 inches in diameter.

2. Place the walnuts in a small bowl and add the sugar and cinnamon. Place by teaspoons in the center of the rounds.

3. Lift the dough on 3 sides and pinch the seams to close like a triangle. You can also enclose in a circle.

4. Bake on a greased cookie sheet in a preheated 350-degree oven for about 15 minutes or until the cookies start to turn color.

Yield: 2 dozen cookies (D) or (P)

Old-fashioned Lebkuchen Dallas Style

Jewish food in Dallas came to mean dishes like matzah balls with pecans (see page 113), barbecued brisket (page 178), and *Lebkuchen,* a Bavarian gingerbread with a glazed icing.

A famous *Lebkuchen* baker was Minnie Marcus, whose husband founded the department store Neiman-Marcus. Her recipe appeared in *5000 Years in the Kitchen,* a cookbook first published in 1965 by the Sisterhood of Temple Emanuel in Dallas. "As a hostess to her husband's associates among the fashion and art world, she often baked this cake," read the entry in the cookbook.

It is a perfect pareve dessert and one that tastes better the longer it sits. Citron was used in southern Germany and very old recipes used honey instead of sugar. Chocolate and pecans were added in the United States. Emme Sue Frank, one of Dallas's finest *Lebkuchen* bakers, makes "lepkuchen," as she pronounces it, at her home and sends the cookies as gifts each year to Mrs. Marcus's son Stanley, around the Hanukkah-Christmas holidays.

Emme Sue Frank and her family in Memphis, Tennessee, circa 1948

LEBKUCHEN

4 squares unsweetened chocolate

1½ cups sugar

1 cup molasses

4 large eggs plus 2 large egg yolks

1 teaspoon allspice

½ teaspoon ground cloves

2 teaspoons cinnamon

2½ cups flour

Dash of salt

2 teaspoons baking powder

2 cups chopped pecans

ICING

1 cup sugar

⅓ cup water

Pinch of salt

2 large egg whites

1. To make the cookies, melt the chocolate in a double boiler. Cool.

2. Mix together the sugar and the molasses and add to it the whole eggs, the yolks, and the spices. Beat well.

3. Mix the flour with the dash of salt and the baking powder and stir into the sugar mixture. Fold in the pecans.

4. Cover 2 jelly-roll pans with sloping sides with aluminum foil and then grease. Divide the dough in 2 and spread on the sheets. Bake in a preheated 375-degree oven. After 5 minutes shake the pans. Shake again after 5 more minutes. Bake for 17 minutes in all.

5. Remove from the oven and cool slightly. Then flip the entire cake onto a cookie sheet and flip again onto a cooling board.

6. To make the icing, mix the sugar with the water in a saucepan. Stirring constantly, bring to a boil and continue cooking over medium heat to the soft ball stage, when a small quantity of syrup dropped into ice water forms a ball that does not disintegrate. Cool slightly.

7. Add the salt to the egg whites and beat until stiff. Fold the whites into the sugar mixture and stir over the heat until very white and thick. Cool and spread over the 2 *Lebkuchen* sheets when cool. Cut into 2-inch squares.

Yield: 30 squares (P)

Tip: These keep very well in plastic containers. Whenever I make Lebkuchen *for my family, the cookies vanish instantly.*

Felicia Schlenker's German Nut Crescents with Mississippi Pecans

One of the most popular of the Austrian cookies are *kipferlin,* moon-shaped crescents. Pecans were added in the South whereas northern immigrants made the authentic versions with almonds in the cookies. This particular recipe comes from the late Felicia Schlenker, one of the first Jews to live in Natchez, Mississippi.

*1 cup plus 5 tablespoons
  confectioners' sugar*
1 vanilla bean
*2 sticks (1 cup) unsalted butter
  or margarine, softened*
*2 cups unbleached all-purpose
  flour*
¼ cup ice water
1 cup chopped pecans

1. In a bowl place 1 cup of the confectioners' sugar. Insert the vanilla bean and let sit for several hours before starting this recipe.
2. Using a food processor, mix the remaining 5 tablespoons sugar and the butter. Add the flour, ice water, and pecans. Roll about a teaspoon of the dough into a snake and shape into a crescent. Repeat until all the dough is used up. Place on an ungreased cookie sheet, leaving an inch between cookies.
3. Bake in a preheated 350-degree oven for 10 to 15 minutes. Roll in the vanilla confectioners' sugar and serve.

Yield: 4 dozen cookies (P) or (D)
Note: You can replace the vanilla bean with 1 teaspoon vanilla, and put it in the cookie dough.

*Felicia Schlenker was
probably the first cook to
bring almond crescents to
Natchez, Mississippi.*

Jewish Butter Cookies

The Shops they (German Jews) have taken over on Broadway and 181st Street, from candy stores to five-and-tens, are no different from any others except for the accent of the man behind the counter, and, perhaps, the fact that the windows of their bakeries contain some of the most succulent butter cookies produced in the Western Hemisphere.

Ernest Stock, *Commentary,* June 1951

One of my favorite cookies as a child were my aunt Lisl's butter cookies, sprinkled with crushed almonds. Little did I know that these cookies are called "Jewish" cookies in many languages. *Jodekager* are found in Danish and Danish-American cookbooks as well as in Dutch ("*Jodenkoeken*") and German cookbooks. The Dutch version sometimes includes candied ginger. I found one variation, called "Cincinnati Cookies" with cardamom seeds, cut long rather than round, in a German-Jewish family turn-of-the-century cookbook in Cincinnati.

1½ sticks (¾ cup) unsalted
  butter, softened
½ cup plus 3 tablespoons sugar
1 large egg
½ teaspoon vanilla, aquavit,
  or rose water
1 teaspoon baking powder
3 cups all-purpose flour
Dash of salt
1 egg yolk
1 tablespoon heavy cream
3 tablespoons chopped
  blanched almonds

1. In the base of a food processor mix the butter and ½ cup of the sugar. Add the whole egg and the vanilla or rose water and process.
2. Mix together the baking powder, flour, and salt and add to the butter mixture. Whirl until the dough comes together in a ball. Set aside, covered, in the refrigerater for a few hours.
3. Roll the batter out ¼ inch thin on a floured board and cut into round shapes about 2 inches in diameter. Place on a greased baking sheet, brush with egg yolk mixed with the cream. Sprinkle with 3 tablespoons almonds, and remaining sugar, and bake about 5 to 7 minutes in a preheated 400-degree oven or until a delicate brown.

Yield: about 50 cookies (D)

Hungarian Sour Cream Kipfel from Detroit

There is no other Jewish sweet that has gone more mainstream than *rugelach*. Basically a crescent-shaped cookie that comes from the Yiddish "rugel" (royal), it is also called *kipfel,* cheese bagelach, and cream-cheese horns of plenty in this country. The yeast-based and often butter or sour cream—based dough in Europe was usually rolled out into circles, cut into pie shapes, covered with nuts, raisins, sugar, and cinnamon and then rolled up like pinwheels. It can also be rolled out into a rectangle, covered with filling, rolled up, and cut into circles.

DOUGH

2 cups sifted all-purpose flour

2 sticks (1 cup) unsalted butter

1 teaspoon vanilla

3 tablespoons sour cream

Pinch salt

FILLING

1 cup walnuts

1/2 cup raisins

1/4 cup sugar

Pinch of cinnamon

1/2 teaspoon lemon rind

2 teaspoons raspberry or
   strawberry jam

1. Mix the flour, butter, vanilla, sour cream, and salt in a food processor and process until they come together in a ball. Remove, cover, and refrigerate a few hours or overnight. Divide the dough into 4 balls.

2. Put the filling ingredients in the processor and pulse or process until they form a paste.

3. Roll each ball of dough out to an 8- by 10-inch rectangle and place one-quarter of the filling along a long side. Roll up and then cut in half-inch slices. Place open side down on a greased cookie sheet. You can also roll it into a circle, spread with the topping, and cut into 16 spokes, rolling from the wide to the narrow end like *rugelach* (below).

4. Bake in a preheated 350-degree oven for 20 to 25 minutes or until slightly golden.

Yield: about 5 dozen cookies (D)

Apricot- or Chocolate-Filled Rugelach
(Cream-Cheese Cookies)

The American addition to *rugelach* was cream cheese and the myriad fillings used today. The cream-cheese dough may have been developed by the Philadelphia Cream Cheese Company because the dough is often called Philadelphia cream-cheese dough. One of the early cream-cheese doughs appeared in *The Perfect Hostess,* written in 1950 by Mildred Knopf. Mrs. Knopf, the sister-in-law of Alfred Knopf the publisher, mentioned that the recipe came from Nela Rubinstein, the wife of the famous pianist Arthur Rubinstein.

It was Mrs. Knopf's friend Maida Heatter who put *rugelach* on the culinary map with Mrs. Heatter's grandmother's recipe. It is the most sought after of all Mrs. Heatter's recipes and is the *rugelach* most often found in upscale bakeries nationwide. Here is my own version.

DOUGH

8 ounces cream cheese

2 sticks (1 cup) unsalted butter

½ cup confectioners' sugar

Pinch of salt

½ teaspoon lemon juice

½ teaspoon vanilla

2 cups all-purpose flour

1 large egg

*¼ cup crystallized or
   granulated sugar*

APRICOT FILLING

1 cup apricot jam

*2 tablespoons cake crumbs
   (optional)*

¾ cup walnuts, broken up

OR CHOCOLATE FILLING

*1 cup shaved bittersweet
   chocolate (about 8 ounces)*

¼ cup sugar

1. Place the cream cheese, butter, confectioners' sugar, salt, lemon juice, and vanilla in a food processor. Add the flour and pulse until a very soft dough is formed. Refrigerate for at least an hour.

2. Mix the ingredients for the filling of your choice and divide the dough into 4 balls. Roll the balls out into 4 circles, about ⅛ inch thick and spread with apricot filling or chocolate filling.

3. Cut into pie-shaped pieces an inch wide at the circumference. Roll up from the wide side to the center. Beat the egg and brush the top. Sprinkle with the crystallized sugar and place flat on a greased cookie sheet. (Alternately, roll out each ball to a rectangle, ¼ inch thick. Top with the apricot filling or chocolate filling. Roll each rectangle into a jelly roll and cut into ½-inch pieces. Lay flat on a greased cookie sheet. Beat the egg, brush the tops of each cookie, and sprinkle with the crystallized sugar.)

4. Bake on a greased cookie sheet in a preheated 350-degree oven for 25 minutes or until golden brown.

Yield: about 50 rugelach (D)

Mandelbrot

This recipe for *mandelbrot* (literally almond bread) came from Poland to Galveston, Texas, just after World War I. Because the sweet bread was twice baked, it kept well and was a staple dessert for the Sabbath and for merchants, rabbis, and other itinerant Jews who wanted to take a sweet with them during the week. Of course, in Eastern Europe no chocolate chips were added.

½ cup vegetable oil

¼ cup whiskey

1 cup sugar

3 large eggs

Dash of salt

2 teaspoons baking powder

2¾ cups all-purpose flour

½ teaspoon grated lemon rind

2 teaspoons almond extract

1 teaspoon vanilla

1 cup chopped almonds,
candied fruit, or chocolate
chips, or a combination of
any or all

½ teaspoon cinnamon

1. Mix the oil with the whiskey and all but 2 tablespoons of the sugar. Add the eggs, one at a time, and mix well after each addition. Add the salt, baking powder, flour, lemon rind, and extracts. Mix just to bind and fold in the almonds, candied fruits, or chocolate chips. Cover and place in the refrigerator a few hours or overnight.

2. Remove the dough, divide and shape into 2 long rolls. Then shape each like a half moon about 3 inches wide. Place on a greased cookie sheet, flat side down.

3. Bake in a preheated 350-degree oven for about 30 minutes or until golden.

4. Remove from the oven, slice, place wide side down on the cookie sheet, and sprinkle with the remaining sugar and cinnamon.

5. Raise the oven to 400 degrees and return to oven for about 15 minutes more or until brown.

Yield: about 2 dozen slices (P)

A letter from Poland to Hannah and Harry Lensky of Galveston is as sweet as **mandelbrot.**

Biscotti-Mandelbrot Italian Style

Mandelbrot, kamishbrot, and *biscotti:* three twice-baked cookies. One is Italian. The others are Eastern European Jewish. Is there a connection? Perhaps. "We've thought about the connection," said Peter Pastan, chef-owner of Obelisk, a tiny prix-fixe Italian restaurant in Washington, D.C. "*Mandelbrot* is all over Eastern Europe and in Italy everybody has a different recipe for *biscotti*—some with fennel, some are crunchy; the ones around Siena are ugly but good."

Mr. Pastan, who comes from an American-Jewish family, studied cooking in Italy before opening his mostly Italian restaurant. With a large Jewish population in Piedmont, Italy may have been the place where Jews first tasted *biscotti* and later brought them to Eastern Europe where they called them *mandelbrot,* which means literally almond bread. In the Ukraine, a similar cookie not necessarily with almonds but made at home, *thuskamish,* was served. In Italy they are often eaten as a dessert dipped into wine or grappa. In Eastern Europe Jews dipped them into a glass of tea, and because they include no butter and are easily kept they became a good Sabbath dessert.

When Mr. Pastan's grandmother's *mandelbrot* came out of the oven, it was texturally like his *biscotti,* the only difference being the length of the second baking. He more than doubles the time used for a regular *mandelbrot.*

The first thing you notice when you walk into the Obelisk Restaurant is a long, narrow wooden country table with a still life of food, including a welcoming platter of *biscotti,* or is it *mandelbrot* or maybe *kamishbrot?*

2 cups unbleached flour

1 cup sugar

1 teaspoon baking soda

3 large eggs

½ teaspoon vanilla

6 ounces whole, unblanched
*   almonds*

1. Using a paddle in the bowl of an electric mixer, mix the dry ingredients.
2. Lightly beat the eggs and the vanilla and add to the dry ingredients. Add the nuts.
3. Knead the dough quickly on a well-floured surface. Divide into 2 pieces. Roll each piece into a sausage about 2 inches wide. Lay the strips on a buttered and floured baking pan. Leave several inches between each.
4. Bake for 50 minutes in a 300-degree oven. Let cool for 5 minutes. Remove to a cutting surface and using a sharp knife, cut into diagonal slices every ¾ inch. Lay the bars on their sides on the baking sheets and return to the oven for 35 to 50 minutes until they are nicely browned. Let cool and then store them in a plastic bag.

Yield: 30 cookies (P)

A "Kochbuch" from a Concentration Camp

Anna Stern, who was born in Czechoslovakia, went to Palestine during Hitler's war and came to New York City in the sixties when her only son, David, decided to emigrate. She had left behind in Czechoslovakia her mother, Mina Paechter, who eventually was taken to Theresienstadt, the ghetto-concentration camp. Mrs. Paechter died there, leaving behind a hand-written "*kochbuch.*"

In an effort to pass away hours in the camp, hours when all the women were hungry, cold, and terrified, Mrs. Paechter thought of writing a little book. Together with other Czech-speaking inmates, she carefully, sometimes painfully, put down sixty-five recipes as well as her own poems, using whatever pen or pencil and paper she could find. Later, she sewed together the pages. The recipes evoked memories of better days—the *Gesundheitskuchen,* the good health cake brought to the mothers of newborn babies, the *Linzertortes* from carefree days of tea parties, and the typically Czech Jewish *mazelokich,* a layered matzah and fruit dessert for family-filled days of Passover.

Her cookbook would have been lost had not Mrs. Paechter entrusted it and letters to her children in Palestine to a fellow inmate who survived. Years later, the woman, now an art dealer, living in Teblitz, Czech Republic, happened to give the book to a visiting Israeli. "It belongs to some people named George and Anna Stern," the art dealer said. "Maybe you know them." The Israeli did not, but at a meeting of Czech Jews living in Israel, he learned that the Sterns had left for the United States.

Twenty-five years after her mother died, Mrs. Stern, now in her mid-eighties, received a telephone call in New York telling her of a package and a letter from her late mother. "I was stunned. I didn't touch it for four years," she said.

Eventually she did leaf through the tattered book with much emotional difficulty. Bianca Brown, also a survivor from Theresienstadt, agreed to translate the manuscript of recipes and poems that Mrs. Paechter had written. It will soon be published, a testimony to the celebration of life over the horror of the Holocaust.

Central European Butter Triangles

This easy butter cookie recipe comes from Bianca Brown, the translator of Mrs. Stern's mother's cookbook (see box on page 355). She told me that in Czechoslovakia every Jewish woman had her own version.

1 stick (½ cup) unsalted butter

1 cup all-purpose flour

½ cup pot or cottage cheese

Dash of salt

½ cup thick apricot preserves

1 egg

1 tablespoon water

Confectioners' sugar

1. Place the butter, flour, pot cheese, and salt in a food processor fitted with a steel blade. Process until it forms a ball. Let rest a half hour, covered, in the refrigerator.

2. Roll the dough out as thin as you can with a rolling pin and cut into 2-inch squares. Place a teaspoon full of apricot preserves on each square. Fold into a triangle, crimp the edges, and brush with the egg mixed with the water. Place on a greased cookie sheet and bake in a preheated 375-degree oven for about 15 minutes or until golden. Sprinkle with confectioners' sugar.

Yield: about 36 (D)

Esther Salem Cohen, a famous Syrian-Jewish caterer in Brooklyn

Sarina Roffe's Adjwah (Syrian Date-Filled Crescents)

I love these Syrian cookies. The semolina adds a delightful crunch.

DOUGH

1 cup smead (semolina, not
    semolina flour)

2 cups all-purpose unbleached
    flour

Dash of salt

1 tablespoon vegetable oil

2 sticks (1 cup) unsalted butter
    or margarine

½ to ¾ cup cold water

FILLING

1 pound pitted dates

½ cup chopped walnuts

2 tablespoons orange
    marmalade

1 teaspoon cinnamon

½ cup confectioners' sugar

1. Mix together thoroughly the semolina and the flour. Add the salt, oil, and butter. With a fork or your fingers, mix in the butter and oil until the dough is lumpy. Do not overmix. Add the water, a little at a time, until the dough comes together and is smooth and pliable.

2. Put the dates in a saucepan and add water to barely cover. Cook until soft, about 15 minutes. Mash them in the saucepan to a smooth paste. Lower the heat and, stirring occasionally to avoid sticking, cook about 5 to 10 minutes until the water is mostly absorbed and a thick paste is formed. Add the walnuts and orange marmalade. Season with the cinnamon.

3. Roll the dough into 1-inch balls. Flatten each with a rolling pin or tortilla press. If using a tortilla press, flour or cover with plastic wrap so the dough doesn't stick to the press. Place a tablespoon of dates in the middle of the circle of dough, pressing the dates down on the circle. Fold to form a crescent; the dates should stick out on the edge. Repeat with all the dough.

4. Bake in a preheated 350-degree oven for 20 to 25 minutes on an ungreased cookie sheet or until slightly golden. Adjwah can be frozen. Sprinkle with confectioners' sugar when ready to serve.

Yield: about 3 dozen (D) or (P)

Carrot Candy (Eingemachts)

In Eastern Europe *eingemachts* was the term used to describe all kinds of jams and some-times candy. For Passover beet *eingemachts,* made by mincing beets and boiling them in honey or sugar, was the most popular. In some communities radishes and carrots were used. To this day Jews in the former Soviet Union put up cherries and carrots as jam or candy and eat them as a sweet with their tea. Because white flour has always been scarce in Eastern Europe, these jams are less expensive than cakes and therefore a good alternative that keeps throughout the winter. Although the formulas for making many of the *eingemachts* have disappeared in this country, some like the following carrot candy have lin-gered for special events in families.

1 pound carrots

½ cup water

1 cup sugar plus extra sugar
   for sprinkling

Juice of 2 oranges

Juice of 1 lemon

2 teaspoons ground ginger or to
   taste

½ teaspoon cinnamon

1. Peel and cut the carrots in small chunks. Place in the water and simmer slowly, covered, about 30 minutes or until soft. Mash the cooked carrots with the juice from the cooking process.

2. Mix the carrots with the sugar and the orange and lemon juices. Cook the mixture over a medium heat, stirring constantly, until it comes away from the pot and until most of the liquid has disappeared, about 45 min-utes. Add ginger and cinnamon and mix well.

3. When it is cool enough to handle, put the carrot mix-ture onto a wet board and roll out with a wet rolling pin to a ½-inch thickness. Sprinkle with granulated sugar. Let stand for one day, uncovered, until the top feels dry. Cut into 1-inch strips. Turn and cover the other side of the strips with sugar. Let this dry another day. Keep turning the strips daily until the candy is dry. It may take up to 4 days. After it feels crisp, cut into 1-inch squares, sprinkle again with sugar, and put in little paper cups.

Yield: about 20 squares (P)

Barton's Made Buying Candy a Hollywood Musical

Another tangible contribution of the German Jews to the Washington Heights scene is an excellent candy shop on 181st Street, the original store of the Barton chain which has since spread all over the city, setting an example of orthodoxy by faithfully closing for Sabbath from sundown Friday to sundown Saturday.   Ernest Stock, *Commentary Magazine,* June 1951

"In America, candy was too serious," said the late Stephen Klein, the founder of the Barton Candy chain in a *Commentary* interview in 1952. "I figured a customer should get a pleasure from walking into my store—he should feel he's getting a production as well as a pound of chocolate. He should feel good, like he's in the air, like floating or dancing, like in a big Hollywood musical. So I had my first store designed in light-hearted Viennese style, joyful colors." Mr. Klein was a refugee who had been a candy apprentice in Vienna before fleeing Hitler in 1938. He founded Barton's in 1940 and had fifty shops ten years later. Like many other immigrants he started as a peddler, making candy at night in the kitchen of his apartment, being careful to make it neither too sweet nor too bitter. During the day he sold his kosher chocolates in the garment district.

When he went into mass production, he specialized in making geometrically shaped pieces of candy from molds on a mechanical assembly line. This way he could fill them with liqueurs, an unusual custom in those days.

Eveline Weyl's Chocolate Truffles

The following chocolate truffles recipe comes from a distant cousin of mine who lives in Lexington, Massachusetts.

½ pound imported dark
   bittersweet chocolate
3 tablespoons unsalted butter
   or margarine
2 egg yolks
2 tablespoons coffee
2 tablespoons rum
Cocoa powder

1. Melt the chocolate with the butter in a double boiler. While hot, but with the heat off, add the egg yolks, coffee, and rum. Stir constantly until the mixture cools down.
2. Let sit for 2 to 3 hours in the refrigerator.
3. When firm, roll into small balls the size of a large marble and then dip in cocoa powder.
4. Refrigerate, covered, one to two days before serving.

Yield: about 2 dozen truffles (D) or (P)

Hendricks Schulson Family Coconut Pudding

This recipe may very well have been an adaptation of the Jewish almond pudding (see page 411) created when the Sephardic Jews lived in Recife before they came to New York in the seventeenth century. Jews in Brazil had quickly learned to substitute the readily available coconut and coconut juice for almonds and almond milk in pareve recipes. The early Sephardic immigrants from Brazil brought the recipe to New Amsterdam.

1 whole coconut or 4 cups
   grated coconut
1 cup sugar
4 large eggs, separated
3 tablespoons rum

1. Break the coconut, reserving the water. Shell, peel, and grate the coconut. You should have about 4 cups.
2. Put the sugar and the reserved coconut water, measuring about ½ cup, in a saucepan. If you do not have enough coconut water, add tap water to equal the ½ cup. Stirring constantly, cook over a medium heat for about 5 minutes.
3. Beat the egg yolks well and add to the coconut mixture with the rum.
4. Beat the egg whites until stiff peaks form and fold into the coconut mixture.
5. Place in a greased oval gratin mold and bake in a preheated 350-degree oven for 30 minutes or until the pudding is brown and a toothpick comes out clean when tested. Serve this with sliced tropical fruit like pineapple.

Yield: 4 to 6 servings (P)

Danish-German Rote Gritz at a Boardinghouse in Nineteenth-Century San Francisco

Boardinghouses were a way of life in the nineteenth century. The newspapers were filled with advertisements for rooms to let for Jewish people. One such rooming house was run by Therese Landauer Untermyer of Lynchburg, Virginia. Mrs. Untermyer's husband had died of a heart attack at the news of Lee's surrender at Appomattox. A widow with five children, destitute as a result of the Civil War, she moved in 1867 to New York, where she started a boardinghouse for the sons of southern Jewish families who were studying there.

It was a common practice of widows to take in boarders in cities elsewhere in the country. What follows is a wonderful description of a turn-of-the-century boardinghouse in San Francisco.

Grandma's boarding house was strictly Jewish, that is, it was occupied strictly by Jewish people. But right there the Jewishness of the place ended except for an annual event which was one of the high points of my childhood and undoubtedly started me down the road to being a gourmet.

On the evening of Yom Kippur . . . faithful Jews, the world over, have fasted. And so, being a faithful Jewess, no food was served in Grandma's boarding house on Yom Kippur. . . .

It was here that I first learned, as a boy, about the glories of imported cheese both with and without holes, bagel and lox, herring in sour cream, gefilte fish, cheese blintzes with jelly, anchovies, King Oscar sardines, olives, both green and ripe, soaked in olive oil and garlic, Cresta Blanca sauterne, cracked crab on ice, broiled lobster tails, good coffee and home made pastry such as would cause the proudest chef, French or otherwise, to hang his head in shame, plus other oddments which were intended to make life less painful. . . .

You haven't lived if you haven't eaten, for instance, Grandma's Rote Gritz. Rote Gritz is a dessert of German or possibly Danish origin. The family lived in Germany, close to the Danish border, for as far back as anyone knows, and most of Grandma's dishes were of German origin.

To this day, through two major wars with Germany, and despite my deep and loyal pride as a fourth generation American, I have always felt that there is some hope for a nation that could originate a dish like Rote Gritz.

J. Lloyd Conrich, San Francisco

Rote Gritz *(Berry Pudding)*

4 cups berries such as
  loganberries, raspberries,
  or blackberries
3 cups plus 3 tablespoons
  water
¾ cup sugar
Juice of 1 lemon
3 tablespoons cornstarch
Whipped cream

1. Simmer the berries in 3 cups of water for 10 minutes. While hot, put through a food mill or sieve and add the sugar and lemon juice, adding more sugar if too tart.
2. Mix the cornstarch and remaining 3 tablespoons water. Transfer the berry mixture to the top of a double boiler. Pour the dissolved cornstarch into the juice and stir continuously for 15 minutes while allowing the mixture to bubble.
3. When thickened, pour the juice into 6 dessert glasses. Let cool and solidify. Serve with whipped cream.

Yield: 6 servings (D)
Tip: You can also serve the pudding with ice cream, fresh berries, and a sprig of mint.

Baked Bananas

In the South baked bananas often were served at the Passover table. This recipe is adapted from *What's Cooking with the Millsteins,* a privately published cookbook from Natchez, Mississippi.

6 firm bananas
1 tablespoon lemon juice
½ cup brown sugar
3 tablespoons butter or
  margarine

1. Arrange whole peeled bananas in a buttered baking dish.
2. Sprinkle with lemon juice and brown sugar. Dot with butter. Bake in a preheated 350-degree oven for about 25 minutes or until bananas are hot and sugar is melted. Serve hot with whipped cream.

Yield: 6 servings (D) or (P)

The First Time We Saw Bananas We Ate Them with the Skin On

I saw bananas for the first time. We bought some from a peddler and waited to see how other people ate them. To this day bananas are my favorite fruit.

By Myself I'm a Book! An Oral History of the Immigrant Jewish Experience in Pittsburgh, 1972

While we waited at Ellis Island we ate bologna sandwiches and tomatoes and bananas with the skin on.

National Council of Jewish Women, *My Voice Was Heard, 1981*

Again and again immigrants described their delight at first tasting the banana. But what few people realize is that it was a Jew who first introduced bananas to the United States. According to the *American Hebrew* of May 7, 1909, Solomon J. Marks, one of the largest banana growers in Jamaica, sent the first shipload of bananas from the West Indies to the United States.

After immigrants mastered the art of eating a raw banana, they started cooking them. During the "theme period" of American cookery many Jewish cookbooks featured such novelties as a banana rolled in mayonnaise and crushed pecans and served on a lettuce leaf or an individual "candle" salad, with a pineapple round as a base, a half peeled banana as a candle, and a cherry as a wick. It was seriously presented as a recipe in *Jewish Home Beautiful,* written by Betty D. Greenberg and Althea O. Silverman and first published by The Women's League of the United Synagogue of America in 1941. The authors, taking the lead from such non-Jewish publications as the *Ladies' Home Journal,* suggested an entire Hanukkah environment to go with the candle salad. "The color scheme should be predominantly orange, the usual color of the Hanukkah candles, with green or blue as a complementary color," they wrote. "The centerpiece is a very attractive Menorah set in a circle of orange and green or blue flowers and containing all nine candles. Ribbon streamers lead from the Menorah to gaily wrapped gift packages scattered around the table. Shining new pennies, dreidlach, a Jewish National Fund box and some of the Women's League publications are also properly spaced on the table. Place cards, cut in the form of a hammer with the name on the handle, and individual small candy baskets in the shape of oil cruses filled with Palestinian candy, add a decorative touch. Two large platters of latkes, at least one of which should contain potato latkes, a large Menorah fruit salad, a tray of helzenblozen, a fancy cake, candy, etc. help to complete the festival requirements."

Jell-O—Do Chemical Changes Render Non-kosher Meat Kosher?

What American in the 1920s and '30s could resist the appetizing photographs of gently rippling Jell-O salads in the *Ladies' Home Journal*? The majority of Jews, wanting to embrace everything American, to be part of this new age of science and technology, were open to new products that would shorten their time in the kitchen and these included the new Jell-O desserts.

Quite a stir was made over Jell-O within the Jewish community. "According to our knowledge, Jell-O does not contain any lard or meat shortening," declared a form letter from Jell-O to Jewish homemakers. "The Jewish publications have been carrying the advertising of Jell-O in their columns for the past ten years, and as a result it is used in most Jewish homes, and its popularity among your people has been growing consistently," it continued.

Nevertheless, the Orthodox said that no matter how much of a chemical change the rennet underwent it was still not kosher. Conservatives felt that a chemical change made its original source unimportant. The 1936 *Kosher Food Guide* included an article entitled "Jell-O—Is it Kosher or Trefa?" It said that "Jell-O was absolutely trefa as the gelatine contained in this product is derived from trefa bones and parts of skins, as for instance the skins of hams, etc. As there is unfortunately no kosher animal gelatine produced, we naturally answered to various inquiries about the permissibility of Jell-O or similar products for consumption by Jews, that these articles are trefa." Until certified pareve kosher synthetic gelatins came on the market, Orthodox Jews would not use any junkets, gelatins, or Jell-Os.

Barbara Levin's Banana Strawberry Jell-O Mold

Barbara Levin, wife of Senator Carl Levin of Michigan, used to bring the following strawberry banana Jell-O mold to office picnics when her husband was a city councilman. If you want to update this recipe substitute yoghurt for the sour cream.

3 3-ounce packages strawberry Jell-O

2½ cups water

2 10-ounce packages frozen strawberries, thawed

1 20-ounce can crushed pineapple with juice

4 to 5 bananas

2 cups sour cream or yoghurt

Fresh fruit for garnish

1. Dissolve the Jell-O in boiling water.
2. Add the strawberries and canned pineapple and mix together.
3. Put half of the mixture into a greased 2-quart mold. Refrigerate until almost set. Slice the bananas and place on top of the mold. Spoon the sour cream on top of the banana, leveling with a knife or spoon. Add the remaining Jell-O mixture. Refrigerate overnight. When ready to serve, unmold and garnish with fresh fruit.

Yield: 8 to 10 servings (D)

Compote of Oranges, A Jewish Dish

The following update of "Compote of Oranges, a Jewish Dish" comes from *Mrs. Seely's Cook Book* 1902. Mrs. Seely, who was not Jewish, had the fanciest "intelligence office," what we would call an employment agency, in New York City. She must have gotten this recipe from one of her Jewish clients. It's best made at least a day in advance.

5 seedless oranges

1 cup sugar

⅓ cup brandy

⅔ cup Sabra or other orange liqueur

½ cup slivered toasted almonds

1. Cut off the orange peel in slivers, removing as little of the white as possible. Boil the orange peel in water to cover for 5 minutes. Discard the water.
2. Mix the sugar with 2 cups of water and simmer the peel until tender, about 30 minutes. Remove the peel. Boil the syrup down and add the brandy and the liqueur. Return the peel to the syrup.
3. Slice the oranges, removing the pith, and put in a pretty crystal bowl. Add the peel and the syrup. Sprinkle with the slivered almonds. Chill.

Yield: 6 to 8 servings (P)

Tip: You can also decorate this with mint leaves.

You Don't Have to Be Ill to Eat an Orange

(On the boat to America a lady) offered me an orange. I refused to take it, saying that I was not ill.

"But you don't have to be ill to eat an orange," she said, as she pushed the fruit into my hand.

I was puzzled. The painful memory of my mother's dying came back to my mind. The barber of my Polish home town was also the town's "doctor." When he had prescribed an orange for my mother, everybody knew that she was gravely ill. Oranges were not available in our small town, so that day my father hired a carriage and set out for the neighboring town, which was much bigger. He returned late that night and the whole family crowded around him to see the fruit with their own eyes. We watched him lift the orange carefully out of a straw basket of the kind which peasants used for carrying eggs in. I had seen an orange then for the first time.

Now that the orange was there, nobody knew what to do with it. Was it to be cooked first, or was my mother to eat it raw? Was it to be cut open with a knife, or was it to be peeled by hand? After much deliberation, my father decided to wake up a neighbor of ours, a ninety-year-old woman who, because of her advanced age, my father thought she would know what ought to be done.

About half an hour later my father returned with all the instructions written down in Hebrew characters. The orange was not to be cooked. It was to be peeled by hand and each segment was to be carefully separated from the other and sucked dry by my mother. The peelings were to be scattered all over the room, so that they could fill it with their aroma. When they began to wither, they were to be cooked for a long time and then used for preserves.

Yuri Suhl, *One Foot in America*, 1948

Pineapple Sherbet

For Jews who observe kashrut, sherbet and pareve dairy creamers are very important. "I remember the ice creams and sherbets we used to make," said Meta Buttnick, who grew up in Alaska. "They were strictly pareve and we served them with meat meals. Technology has made these things purchasable, but when we made our own they were sensational!" Of course, today with kosher Tofutti, started by a religious Jew, and kosher sherbets, you don't have to make your own. But not so long ago you did.

1 cup sugar

1 cup warm water

½ cup light corn syrup

2 cups pineapple juice

2 egg whites

1. Bring the sugar and water to a boil. Simmer, uncovered, for 5 minutes. Remove from the heat. Add the corn syrup and chill overnight.
2. Remove from the refrigerator and reserve ⅓ cup of the sugar syrup. Mix the rest with the pineapple juice. Mix well and freeze for several hours.
3. When almost frozen, remove from the freezer. Start beating the whites until frothy. Add the remaining syrup gradually as you beat, and continue beating until the whites are stiff like a meringue. Stir into the sherbet and freeze.

Yield: 6 servings (P)

Rose Zawid's Applesauce with Cranberries

In Europe other berries were often added to apples when making applesauce. This one is especially nice because it makes the applesauce slightly red. Until I learned this recipe I used to add red hots to mine—a trick I learned from a Jewish lady from Mississippi.

¾ pound fresh cranberries

1½ cups water

¾ cup sugar or to taste

4 pounds apples, unpeeled and
    quartered

1. Put all the ingredients into a large saucepan. Simmer, covered, 20 minutes or until the apples are soft.
2. Cool slightly and put through a food mill. Adjust the sugar to taste and serve.

Yield: about 8 cups (P)

Plum Pudding for Hadassah

Portland, Oregon's plum pudding project started in 1928 as a fundraiser for the Hadassah Medical Organization in Jerusalem. By the time they stopped this project in 1942, over two hundred Hadassah volunteers were making four thousand puddings annually. By 1942 the two-pound puddings, which cost from $1.50 to $10 apiece, were shipped coast to coast, as far away as China and Palestine and served on the Union Pacific Railroad.

Starting out as a small project in someone's basement, the volunteer battalion, working from September to December, soon moved to a Hebrew school and later to an empty store. The ladies mixed, measured, cooked, and baked on a regular work schedule, using borrowed huge mixers, stoves, pressure cookers, and a motor corps to deliver within the city. After many years of experimentation the women came up with a recipe that included 150 pounds each of orange peel, cherries, lemon peel, flour, and citron, 500 pounds of bread crumbs, 900 pounds of dates and prunes, 300 pounds of shortening, and 1,500 pounds of raisins. World War II with its war shortages put an end to the project. The plum pudding recipe, divided by 350, is as follows.

4 large eggs

½ cup milk

½ cup all-purpose flour

1 cup bread crumbs

*2 sticks (1 cup) unsalted butter
   or margarine, softened*

1 cup raisins

½ cup currants

¼ cup dates

¼ cup prunes

1 cup sugar

½ teaspoon cinnamon

½ teaspoon nutmeg

½ teaspoon mace

½ tablespoon salt

¼ cup red wine

2 tablespoons brandy

*¼ cup slivered blanched
   almonds*

2 tablespoons candied citron

1. Beat the eggs until light. Add to them ¼ cup each of milk, flour, bread crumbs, and beat in with the butter.
2. Sprinkle the fruit with the remaining flour and mix in by degrees. Then add all but 2 tablespoons of the sugar, the spices, the wine, and brandy. Beat very hard, and stir in the remainder of the milk. Add the remaining bread crumbs.
3. Grease and sprinkle with the remaining sugar a pudding mold, a pound coffee can, or a small baking dish with a cover. Pour the ingredients two thirds of the way up. Cover and place the mold, can, or baking pan on a trivet in a heavy kettle with over 1 inch of boiling water. Cover the kettle tightly. Steam slowly in water for about 4 hours, adding more water if needed.
4. Turn out carefully and before serving, decorate with blanched almonds and sliced citron. Serve with the cold vanilla sauce (page 307), the wine sauce (page 416), or frozen vanilla yoghurt or ice cream. It is delicious.

Yield: 1 plum pudding which serves 8 (D)

Fruit Compote

> We ate lots of stewed fruit such as prunes, dried apples and dried pears called hutzeln. These latter are never seen any more because there is a new process of vaporation now which completely alters the taste. They were sometimes baked in bread we called hutzel-brod, similar to the raisin bread of today.
>
> Jennie Gerstley, "Reminiscences, Chicago, Illinois, 1859–1934,"
> American Jewish Archives

During much of Mrs. Gerstley's life in nineteenth-century and early twentieth-century Chicago fresh fruit was seasonal. Her mother probably dried them as did the immigrants from Eastern Europe, often by sewing them on long strings and hanging them on lines in the sunshine, to use later in compotes, a favorite Sabbath dessert.

Experiment with the following compote. Once you have cooked the fruit, add sliced oranges, strawberries, fresh peaches, slivered almonds, whatever you have in your refrigerator. Simmer a few minutes and serve. Your guests will love this winter dessert.

6 cups water

½ cup sugar or to taste

½ pound dried peaches, apples or pears

¾ pound prunes, pitted

½ cup raisins

1 clove

1 cinnamon stick

1 lemon, quartered

1. Bring the water and the sugar to a boil in a small saucepan.
2. Add the remaining ingredients and simmer, covered, for 30 minutes. Remove the lemon before serving.

Yield: 6 to 8 servings (P)

The Hadassah ladies who, for years, made plum pudding in Portland, Oregon

Figs Alice B. Toklas

I started making compote in the winter months when the fruits were not so good. After I read that Alice B. Toklas liked to serve prunes to Gertrude Stein, I played around with that recipe. I always let my fruits sit in sweet wine left over from Passover. Then I didn't have to worry about adding extra sugar or opening a bottle of wine. Of course my sons make it fancier substituting Port and dry wine for the Manischewitz. Figs Alice B. Toklas was born because figs were more elegant to serve in a restaurant than prunes.

Rochelle Rose, mother of the owners of
Mrs. Simpson's Restaurant, Washington, D.C.

2 pounds dried figs

2 3-inch cinnamon sticks

12 whole cloves

1 cup firmly packed dark
　brown sugar

½ cup firmly packed light
　brown sugar

½ teaspoon grated lemon rind

¼ teaspoon grated orange rind

4 cups Ruby Port

1 cup dry red wine

Whipped cream as an
　accompaniment

1 cup hazelnuts, toasted and
　skinned and chopped, for
　garnish

1. In a saucepan place the figs, cinnamon sticks, cloves, dark and light brown sugars, lemon and orange rinds, Port, and the red wine and simmer the mixture, covered, for 1 hour or until the figs are tender.

2. Let the mixture stand in a cool place for 24 hours and chill it for 2 hours. Serve the figs topped with whipped cream and garnished with the hazelnuts.

Yield: 12 servings (P) without the whipped cream or (D) with

Tip: Mrs. Rose suggests serving the dish as she used to in Chicago: in a very tall cylinder type jar and preparing it up to a week in advance. Store in the refrigerator.

Variation: You can substitute prunes, apricots, raisins, and walnuts for the figs and hazelnuts. Don't cook the walnuts.

ELEVEN

שתיות

Drinks—From Seltzer to California Kosher

Squeeze the raisins in cheesecloth as you would milk a cow.

An old American recipe for making Jewish ritual wine

And thank God that the holidays passed with us in goodness and kashruth, with matzos and with mead from
sugar, with wine from raisins. . . . Like Flengyaner
wine because there is a man here from Flengyan, who is
a brother of Reb Zvi, a son-in-law of the late Reb David,
the shochet, a good man who fears God and he made a
little wine here, to sell, and I bought from him.

Dov Behr Manischewitz, founder of Manischewitz Co.,
in a letter to his father in Russia in 1887

Rum and Shrub

Kosher Lunch—The Identical, corner of Battery and Sacramento, will again during the (Passover) holidays, set a splendid hot lunch. Mrs. Isaacs is celebrated for her excellent cooking. Rum and Shrub in abundance.

The Hebrew Observer, San Francisco, April 19, 1872

Although the above advertisement appeared during the Gold Rush days in San Francisco, rum and shrub was a popular drink during the Revolutionary period. It was made by mixing fresh fruits, such as oranges, in sugar and pouring the combination over rum, a preserving technique that the Arabs taught to the Jews in the medieval period.

When I visited the Topkapi Palace in Istanbul, I saw a room filled with silver sorbet pitchers that had been used during the Ottoman Empire for sorbet or fruit drinks often mixed with white wine. These sorbets (shrubs) eventually became our sherbets.

In Philadelphia rum and shrub was known to be a favorite drink of Benjamin Franklin, a great friend of the Jews. It may have been the drink served at the first kosher public meal in this country, the 1788 picnic celebrating the acceptance of the Constitution in Philadelphia. A separate table was set up with "soused salmon and crackers" for the Jewish attendees who most certainly observed the dietary laws.

1 quart light or dark rum

Rind of lemon or orange, cut into julienne strips

2 cups sugar

4 cups water

1 cup lemon or orange juice

1. Combine the rum with the lemon or orange rind. Let stand, covered with a towel, for 2 days or longer.
2. Combine the sugar and water and bring to a boil. Let simmer, uncovered, for a few minutes. Add to the shrub with the lemon or orange juice. Let stand covered for a few days in a cool place. It lasts for months.

Yield: about 10 cups (P)

Mordecai M. Noah's Temperance Raisin Wine*

"Unfermented liquor or wine free from alcoholic substances . . . is used to the present day at the Passover, (it is) the wine over which the blessing is said," wrote the New York politician and journalist, Mordecai M. Noah, in a letter to the editor of the *New York Evening Star for the Country* in 1838. Mr. Noah deliberately mentioned the "unfermented" liquor because of the

Central Park mineral-water drinkers

strong temperance movement during this period. Although raisin wine is not the same as wine made from grapes, it was one of the early methods of winemaking used by Jews throughout the world since the biblical period.

Mordecai M. Noah's great-grandfather, a famous doctor who fled Portugal during the Inquisition on a boat while guests were eating at a grand luncheon at his home, must have made this same raisin wine. From the eighth century onwards Jews in Europe and the Middle East have made their own raisin wine for Passover.

Early American Jewish handwritten cookbooks, such as that of the Heller family of Richmond, contain recipes for grape wine, including one clearly American version calling for corn and grapes.

Although Southern Jews were some of the first grape growers as well as wine importers in the United States, there was little if any commercially produced kosher wine until after the Civil War. If Jews wanted kosher wine, they made it themselves, sometimes as in Mr. Noah's recipe, without sugar.

> . . . take a gallon demijohn, or stone jug; pick three or four pounds of bloom raisins, break off the stems; put the raisins into the demijohn, and fill it with water. Tie a rag over the mouth, and place the demijohn near the fire, or on one side of the fire-place, to keep it warm. In about a week it will be fit for use, making a pure, pleasant, and sweet wine, free from alcohol. It may last from Sunday to Sunday without getting sour or tart; but it is easy to make a small quantity of wine for each time it is to be used. This is the wine we use on the nights of Passover.

*Some of this information came from Jonathan Sarna, "Passover Raisin Wine, the American Temperance Movement, and Mordecai Noah."

Raisin Wine for Passover

The following recipe with sugar from *The American Hebrew,* March 27, 1896, became an American way of making raisin wine. In other countries dried figs as well as sassafras and licorice were used.

2 pounds raisins

1 pound sugar

1 lemon

6 quarts boiling water

1. Place the raisins, sugar, and the lemon in a large stone or ceramic jar.

2. Add 6 quarts of boiling water and stir every day for a week, covering with a towel.

3. Then strain and bottle. Let sit for another 10 to 12 days.

Yield: about 6 quarts (P)

From Raisin Wine to California Kosher

We were a happy family party. Melodies, food, raisin wine, all were new, peculiar to the festival, not staled by familiarity; never savored upon any other occasion, they reappeared like half-forgotten friends, the delight of whose charm we had only half-remembered.

Harriet Lane Levy, *920 O'Farrell Street,* 1947

In this lovely memoir of turn-of-the-century life in a Jewish home in San Francisco, the raisin wine was either homemade or bought from one of the kosher winegrowers already at work in northern California. Later, during Prohibition, Jewish vintners as well as Beaulieu and Inglenook were allowed to make sacramental wines. Eastern European Jews, skilled in making mead and raisin wine, brought the concept of kosher sweet wine to this country.

Concord grapes thrived in the cold, humid climate and pest-ridden soil of the east. But, because Concords do not usually get sweet enough for adequate fermentation and taste, it is necessary to add sugar or grape juice to complete the process. After Prohibition, kosher wine companies started making wines, using grapes from upstate vineyards and loganberries from Oregon, elderberries from Ireland, and cherries from Yugoslavia.

A Rabbi blessing wine

Kosher wine is a simple process. From the crushing of the grape to the sealing of the bottle, it must be handled only by Sabbath-observant Jews, unless the grape juice is heated to the point of *yayin mevushal,* or "boiled wine," after which anyone can handle it. This wine ferments for about six weeks.

In addition, kosher law dictates that animal products and other non-kosher ingredients may not be used in the processing. Furthermore, kosher-for-Passover wine cannot be vinified with non-wine-grain yeasts. Chlorine or even vodka rather than soap, an animal product, can be used to clean the tanks.

Eugene Herzog, whose family had been making savory kosher wines in Czechoslovakia from 1848 until the Holocaust, came to this country after World War II. "Europeans always drank better dry table wines. It is only in the last fifteen years in America that that tradition has continued," said Philip Herzog, his son. "On the bottles it was inscribed: Herzog's wine," said Phillip Herzog, fifth generation in the family business, rebuilt in America as Royal Kedem Wine Corporation. "Everyone knew it was kosher. We didn't need a sign. There were no grapes in Poland so they made honey wine, like mead."

"There was no concept of kosher wine as there is today," agreed Peter Sichel of Forman and Sichel, whose family had been in the wine business in Germany for over a hundred years. "Having kosher signs on wine is an American institution. So-called kosher wines are an aberration of the modern world."

Like the Sichel and Herzog families, other Jews had been in the wine industry in Europe. "There were a lot of them in Germany. They were distributors, in the retail trade. Since Jews couldn't own property or become farmers it was a natural inclination to go into risk-taking businesses like wine importing where they lived by their wits. Some were better than others," Mr. Sichel continued.

It was Alfred Fromm, a German wine expert living in San Francisco, who helped bring savory kosher wines to this country. "I was asked in the 1950s by the U.S. government to help restructure the wine export business in Israel. I spent a

month there and tasted all the wines. I particularly sought to clean up the cellars and
purchased the right corks and bottles which
were not of good quality at that time," said
Mr. Fromm, in his late eighties. "Samuel
Bronfman, a friend of mine, advised and
helped me to get orders from all the American distributors. Carmel was the first of
the better kosher wines." Today, some
kosher wine companies are marketing and
importing kosher French, Italian, and Alsatian dry varietals.

American kosher wine took a new turn in the 1980s. As the interest in gourmet
food increased and young people who were returning to religion developed
sophisticated palates, a demand grew for good kosher wine from native dry vari-
etal grapes.

And people like Craig Winchell did something about American kosher wine.
Once he started keeping strictly kosher, he discovered that his wine choices were
severely limited. No longer. Mr. Winchell's Gan Eden kosher Chardonnay has
won many gold medals in major wine competitions, as have other dry kosher
wines.

Unlike Mr. Winchell, who became a kosher vintner out of religious observance, Ernie Weir, owner of Hagafen Cellars in Napa Valley, makes kosher wine
out of cultural conviction. "As a Jew I thought that it was important to produce a
first-rate kosher wine," he said. Across from his ranch-style home are the thirteen
acres he is cultivating with grapevines.

Kosher vintners often have to let perfect grape-picking days go by without
removing the grapes. Kosher wine must, among other things, not be made from
Friday sundown to sundown on the Sabbath. To make picking more difficult, Rosh
Hashanah, Yom Kippur, and Sukkot come smack in the middle of the harvest
period. "There can be as many as ten days of holidays during September and October when the grapes are mature," said Mr. Weir.

Holding back does not seem to have hurt Mr. Weir's wines. They have been
served at the White House for state dinners for visiting Israeli officials and have
won gold medals in national competitions. "It's our attention to detail, but it can
be hard if the Jewish holidays coincide with the maturity of the grapes," said Mr.
Weir.

Seltzer: Champagne of the Diaspora

Not wine or beer drinkers by nature, and forbidden to down a deli sandwich with a milk product, Eastern European Jews turned to inexpensive, non-alcoholic seltzer—the "champagne of the proletariat." In the Lower East Side and later, after World War I, in Brooklyn and the Bronx, seltzer would be delivered in blue and green etched crystal bottles from Czechoslovakia.

In neighborhood candy stores you could order a "two cents plain"—a glass of cold seltzer. And in coffee houses on the Lower East Side immigrants would order it, when they were not drinking tea in glasses.

Made from purified tap water filtered through charcoal and paper to remove the residual salt, gassified with carbon dioxide, shot under high pressure into glass bottles, and capped, seltzer should never be confused with the less fizzy mixes that we get in our bottled club sodas today.

One popular seltzer drink was Dr. Brown's Cel-Ray Tonic, which was sold in every Jewish New York deli. This seltzer, filled with celery seeds and sugar, was developed in 1869 by a doctor who treated immigrant children on the Lower East Side. "Generation after generation was weaned on the stuff," said Harry Gold, marketing director of Dr. Brown's. "World War II's population explosion produced children who hungered for Dr. Brown's. Now you can find it in most states." In the early thirties before Coca-Cola became kosher, many Jews started drinking Cel-Ray soda as well as his cream and cherry sodas.

"Two-cents plain" was how
seltzer was often sold.

In Search of the First Chocolate Egg Cream

Another drink created in New York was egg cream, which today includes neither egg nor cream. There are as many theories as to the origins of this drink as there are ways to make it.

One story is that it began at Auster's candy store on Third Street and Avenue D on the Lower East Side in the late 1890s. "In those days a candy store was a gathering place of the working people," said Stanley Auster, grandson of the founder. "Our store had an open front with a marble counter. It was partially enclosed and partially open, especially in the summertime, and we would serve drinks." At that time, before air conditioning, television, and electric ice-cream freezers, people lived in tenements where one five- or six-story building could house two hundred families. People would go out on the street or the fire escape or congregate at a candy store for a seltzer drink. "My grandfather liked to tinker with different drink preparations," he continued. "One day he concocted this refreshing chocolate seltzer drink, using a cocoa base with no milk that turned out to be extraordinarily delicious with a rich, creamy frothy consistency. People loved it." One of his clients—it may have been Boris Thomashevsky, the Yiddish actor—came back from a trip to Europe and told him that he had a drink in Paris called "*chocolat et crème*" that was nowhere as good as Auster's chocolate drink. For the immigrant Louis Auster, "*chocolat et crème*" sounded like chocolate egg cream. Thus, according to Mr. Auster, the eggless chocolate drink was named.

"Not so," retorted Professor Daniel Bell of Harvard University. "Auster did not invent it. He denatured it. It was my Uncle Hymie Fredkin. He had a candy store near Auster's on Second Avenue and St. Marks Place. He was a quiet, doer-type. I worked behind the counter in the late twenties and I watched him tinker. He mixed chocolate syrup, chocolate ice cream and an egg, using that as a binder. Then he added milk and reversed the spigot on the seltzer. He called his drink 'Uncle Hymie's Egg Cream.' It was a very creamy thing and very popular. During the Depression ingredients like eggs and ice cream were too expensive so he kept tinkering and made it with chocolate syrup and milk. The seltzer provided the same sense of frothiness."

And then there is the theory that only Grade A milk would do. This cost two cents more and was much creamier, having Grade A top cream, thus the corruption to egg cream.

Whatever the real origin, egg cream became a New York institution, Jewish by association because it was drunk in Jewish neighborhoods. It traveled as far

In the summer, it was so hot in the tenements that seltzer and

egg creams were welcome drinks.

as South Philadelphia. Chicago Jews drank phosphates—chocolate syrup and seltzer—almost, but not the same.

How did the popularity of the egg cream spread so quickly? "It was easy," continued Mr. Auster, who lives in the Bronx. "Our store was able to serve fifty or sixty people at a shot, right on the sidewalks. On a hot summer's night five hundred people could be served within ten minutes. They'd swap stories and the word spread." Auster's was a hangout for a diverse group of customers, including political leader Louis Lefkowitz and gangster Bugsy Siegel. Eventually there were five Auster candy stores in New York, all serving the same egg cream. Although people still talk about Auster's egg cream, Mr. Auster will not divulge the secret and promised his father he would carry the recipe to his grave.

Brooklyn Egg Creams

To be an egg cream connoisseur you had to have grown up near a candy store watching the soda jerk make his version. "You need a wide-lipped glass," said Mark Siegel, a consultant in Washington and son of a Brooklyn seltzer man. "Part of the process is getting a stream of seltzer at high pressure, to make it foamy. A properly made egg cream has a meringue looking top, like the white of an egg and a chocolatey bottom. You have to fluff it up with high pressure."

Mark Siegel's Brooklyn Egg Cream

½ cup milk

1 12-ounce Coca-Cola glass

¼ cup seltzer

¾ inch Fox's U-Bet or other chocolate flavor syrup

1. Pour milk into a tall, chilled glass. Shoot in the seltzer real hard until a white head reaches the top of the glass.
2. Pour in the syrup very slowly. Gradually stir it on the bottom so as not to disturb the couple of inches of foam on the top. When you pull the spoon out you will have a dark chocolate bottom and a pure white foamy top. Adjust the amount of chocolate depending on the sweetness you want.

Yield: 1 serving (D)

Passover Tastes and Traditions

Matzoth! The original pioneer Matzoth Bakery in this City and State most respectfully announce to their Co-Religionists that their arrangements for manufacturing Matzoth are most perfect. Mr. Adler is the old Pioneer and first Practical Baker in California who undertook to furnish the above article. We will strictly pay obedience to religious duties and invite our customers for inspection. We call special attention to our stock of Cakes, Confectionery and Goose Grease for the Holydays. Particular attention paid to Orders for the Country.　　　　An advertisement in the *Israelite,* San Francisco, 1864

My father presided with great style (over the Passover seder). . . . He would stumble through the first part of the blessing before the meal, then hand the "holy wine" to me for the second part, all the family and guests joined in at the end to sing the tune I had learned at camp. On Passover, when no less than twenty-five people attended, including Jewish girls from Duke that Mother was anxious to fix up with boys from Chapel Hill, he (my father) transformed the table into a jovial city council meeting, calling on each guest to read sections of the Haggadah so that everyone would stay involved. He tried to update the symbols, like comparing the four cups of wine to Roosevelt's four freedoms—which would cause my grandfather Isaac to complain vigorously, but he would plod on, calling on Grandpa to "give the next reading in the original Hebrew."　　　　Eli Evans, *The Provincials,* 1973

Even the most assimilated American Jewish family celebrates the ancient home festival of Passover in one form or another. Many Jews remove all leavening from their homes and eat only matzah for eight days. A reading of the Haggadah—a narration of the Exodus—is a central part of the first (and second) nights of Passover and takes place in homes. The observance was originally a nature festival celebrated by nomadic desert Jews, with a roasted sheep or goat as the central food. "And they shall eat the flesh in that night, roast with fire, and unleavened bread; with bitter herbs they shall eat it" (Exodus 12:8). Centuries later, the peasants of Israel had a spring grain observance, the Festival of Unleavened Bread where the unleavened matzah was served.

Jews taking home free matzahs

After the Exodus the seasonal aspect of the festival was transformed into a freedom holiday representing more closely the history and social and spiritual strivings of the Jewish people. When the Temple in Jerusalem was destroyed in 70 C.E., the celebration moved from the Temple to the home seder. Foods that had been used in the Temple like roasted lamb became the symbolic objects on the seder plate to illustrate the story, the telling of which is even more important than the food. *Pesach* came to mean "passing over," when God passed over the Jewish homes and did not slay the first-born sons in Egypt (Exodus 6). The "*maror,*" bitter herbs, once the first greens of the spring, came to represent the bitterness of slavery. The four cups of wine represent the four divine promises of redemption by God showing them the way out of Egypt.

To my mind, *haroset,* the last symbolic food, represents not only the mortar with which the Israelites, as slaves, used in building Raamses and Pithom in Egypt, it also shows the diversity of the Jewish people. With the dispersion of Jews throughout the world there must be seventy variations of *harosets* with new ones being created every year in America by our Jewish superstar chefs. Regional dispersals have also created differences in the foods that were eaten. Although Sephardim eat all vegetables and some even eat rice at Passover, Askhenazim avoid such vegetables as corn, string beans, and peas. They also refrain from lentils, chick-peas, and other dried beans that either rise or ferment when mixed with water.

Just as each civilization has left its mark on the Passover seder, so has America. We are the first with packaged foods to make cooking more convenient. This country probably has more varied Passover observances than anywhere but Israel.

No matter how assimilated American Jews have become, most have attended or regularly attend a Passover seder. Whereas in the old country it was a family event with few outsiders, the American way of life has created extended and combined family seders, each with a character of its own.

There are still many families like the Smelkinsons of Baltimore, Maryland, who have been holding an ever-growing family seder for the past thirty years with, at last count, ninety relatives. Jackie Smelkinson, with a battalion of family volunteers, makes the meal from scratch and includes old family recipes for gefilte fish, *harosets,* and matzah balls.

In nearby Washington the late justice Arthur Goldberg and his wife, Dorothy, held an annual seder for over forty people. Mrs. Goldberg would prepare a freedom haggadah and everyone sang labor songs. "We moved the furniture out to the garage and set up chairs inside," said the Justice shortly before his death. "The story of the Exodus is the longest strike in history."

Other seders are equally wonderful. There are neighborhood community seders where a new cooperative haggadah is made each year. There are gay seders, lesbian seders, singles seders. There is a seder for Trappist monks led by a rabbi.

At our home-seder, which we have been holding for the past ten years, we include about twenty-five family members and friends. Everyone contributes a dish. The children, between the main course and the dessert, prepare a play for us on the story of Passover. For me, despite all the work entailed in preparing my house and the meal, it is always among our year's most memorable evenings.

One of the essentials of the seder is the plate that must include the following symbolic foods:

Karpas. Celery, parsley, or chervil, to be dipped in salt water, recalls the "sixty myriads" of Israelites oppressed with difficult labor and is also symbolic of rebirth in the springtime.

Zeroa. This roasted shank bone is symbolic of the pascal sacrifice in the Temple in Jerusalem and of the miracle when God passed over the Jewish houses and slew the firstborn of Egypt. Before the last plague, the Israelites were told to smear the blood of a lamb on the doorposts of their houses, so that the Angel of Death would pass over their homes.

Betzah. The roasted egg represents the festival sacrifice brought to the Temple and is a symbol of both fertility in the spring and mourning for the destroyed Temple.

Maror. Horseradish or romaine are the bitter herbs recalling the bitterness of slavery in Egypt.

Haroset. The fruit and nut mixture symbolizes the bricks and mortar with which the Jews worked as slaves in Egypt.

Haroset: Bricks and Mortar from Raisins and Nuts Rolled into Balls

The herbs are placed upon a plate, together with a glass of salt water or vinegar, prepared for Passover, and a mixture made of chopped apples and raisins, and almonds rolled in cinnamon balls; all of these being symbolical of events of the past, in the history of our people.

The Jewish Cookery Book, 1871

In the book of Exodus, at the Passover meal while the Jews were still in Egypt, the Jews sat down to a meal of matzah, bitter herbs, and roast lamb. Although *haroset* was not part of that meal, the fruit and nut compound is served today at every Passover seder throughout the world. Most likely it came into the Passover service during the Greco-Roman period, in which a fruited condiment was part of a feast with meat. Recipes have varied as Jews have wandered throughout the world, ingredients being added depending upon regional availability.

Haroset is one of those recipes learned at a mother's elbow and then passed down from generation to generation. "Our *haroset* is made from raisins, almonds, and one apple," said Emily Nathan whose family recipe has varied little the past three hundred years since her ancestors came to New York. (See page 135 for more on Miss Nathan.) "When I was a child, we ordered the almonds with the skin, putting them in boiling water, blanching them, and then grinding them with raisins in a hand grinder. Just enough apple was added to season the *haroset.* Then the paste was rolled into little balls topped with an almond. It seemed so excessive to me, all that work."

The Nathan family concoction, which closely resembles a Moroccan *haroset* rather than the popular American version made with apples, nuts, and sweet wine, has undergone something of a gastronomic odyssey. Possibly Nathan forebears used dates in the Iberian peninsula before the Inquisition drove them away. They may have soaked the raisins and the dates before using a mortar and pestle to pound them. When they came to the New World, Miss Nathan's ancestors may have substituted first dried and then fresh apples for the rare dates. The Sephardim in Morocco, who made their way to the United States three hundred years after Miss Nathan's ancestors, were able to continue the original recipe in its pure, date-filled form, including the custom of rolling the *harosets* into little balls. Both versions are delicious. Allow at least two balls per guest.

Early American Sephardic Haroset Balls with Raisins, Nuts, and Apple

A Couple of round Balls, about the Bigness of an Egg; they look brown, and are made up of bitter Almonds, pounded and mixed with other Ingredients, and are very soft, and of an indifferent bitterish Taste.

Little Known Facts about the Ritual of the Jews and the Esoteric Folklore of the Pennsylvania-Germans, London, 1753

Although Nathan family members would never use a food processor for their *haroset,* it makes the preparation a little easier than with an old-fashioned grinder.

3 cups raisins

2 cups almonds, blanched

½ apple

½ teaspoon cinnamon or to taste

1. Coarsely grind the raisins and 1½ cups of the almonds. Peel and core the apple and add with the cinnamon; if using a food processor, grind in quick pulses so as not to over-process. Set aside in a bowl.

2. Using your hands, press the mixture into balls the size of large marbles. Press one of the remaining almonds into each *haroset* ball. There will be lots of *haroset* left over; serve in bowls at the table during Passover.

Yield: About 4 dozen balls or 5 cups (P)

An immigrant seder, 1910

Moroccan Haroset Balls with Dates, Raisins, and Nuts

The Passover seder never ceases to amaze me. Millions of Jews all over the world sit down at the same time to more or less the same story being retold in different languages, different melodies, and different customs. At the Moroccan seder the eldest son takes a seder plate covered with a shawl and passes it over the heads of all the guests. Everybody sings "*Bibhilo*" in haste while the person beneath the plate makes a wish. The words are "we are in a rush, we went out of Egypt and we are now free."

Later in the service Moroccans scoop up the *haroset* balls with romaine lettuce, their bitter herb, reminiscent of the bitterness of slavery in Egypt.

2 cups pitted dates

½ cup golden raisins

½ cup dark raisins

½ cup walnuts

1 to 2 tablespoons sweet red Passover wine

1. Process the dates, raisins, and walnuts in a food processor until the mixture is finely chopped and begins to stick together. Add enough wine to make a sticky mass.

2. Line a baking sheet with waxed paper. Drop slightly rounded measuring teaspoonfuls of the mixture onto the lined sheet. Roll each mound with moistened palms into hazelnut-size balls. Refrigerate for at least three hours or until firm.

Yield: Approximately 60 or 3½ cups (P)

American Haroset

The following *haroset* recipe is the most common one made in the United States. What makes it American is the pecans rather than the walnuts or almonds used in Europe.

6 large apples

2 tablespoons sugar (about)

1 teaspoon cinnamon

¼ cup sweet wine

½ cup chopped pecans

1. Core and quarter the apples.

2. Put the apples in a food processor with the remaining ingredients. Process in pulses, leaving a bit of a crunch to the mixture. Adjust seasoning.

Yield: about 5 cups (P)

Tip: This is very similar to the recipe that Doralee Patinkin Rubin, mother of actor/singer Mandy Patinkin, makes at Passover with her grandson. Change and/or add the ingredients here: 2 tablespoons sugar or honey (about); ½ teaspoon ground cloves; ½ teaspoon ground ginger; 1 cup chopped pecans.

Note: In Shreveport, Louisiana, ninety-five-year-old
Isabelle Goldman uses sherry as her wine and adds
raisins. Her recipe came from Alsace in the 1830s.

Halek, A Biblical Date Jam

When the late David Sofaer was a boy in Rangoon, Burma, his mother made *halek* in huge cauldrons over an open fire on one of the verandas surrounding her house. Called *dibis* by the Syrian Jews and *halek* by the Iraqis and Iranians, the recipe for this old Middle Eastern *haroset* consists of a slow reduction of dates to their essence, probably the way date jam, a common sweetener before sugar, and considered the honey from the land of milk and honey, was made in the ancient world. "The servants would stir the jam with long ladles until it reached the consistency of apple sauce," recalled Mr. Sofaer; then it would be strained through folded muslin.

The Sofaer ancestors came to Babylon (now Iraq) during the first exile in 586 B.C.E. In the late nineteenth century Mr. Sofaer's grandfather trekked across Asia to Burma, coming down the Irrawaddy River. Eventually the family moved to Rangoon, Calcutta, and then Bombay, bringing with them the recipes the family had always used.

At Passover the synagogue in Bombay would make matzah and the *halek* in empty wine bottles collected throughout the year. Wealthy families like the Sassoons would contribute the ingredients as a service to the Jewish community.

When the Sofaers moved to New York in 1952, they could not buy *halek* so Mr. Sofaer tried to copy what his mother had made during his childhood in Rangoon. Mozelle Sofaer

Mozelle Sofaer remembers the bread of
affliction at her Iraqi-Indian seder in Berkeley.

lives now in San Rafael, California, following the death of her husband. There she makes *halek* every Passover for her four children, thirteen grandchildren, and four great-grand-children. She has abandoned both cauldron and muslin and uses, instead, a food mill, which makes the task much easier.

10 cups pitted dates, preferably Mejdoul

4 quarts water

2 teaspoons ground anise

3 cups coarsely ground walnuts

1 cup ground almonds

1. Place the dates, water, and anise in a large saucepan. Boil for about one hour, uncovered, until you "take out the goodness of the flavor." For the first 45 minutes stir occasionally and for the last 15 stir frequently. The dates should soften, open up, and reach the consistency of chunky apple sauce.

2. Press the date mixture through a sieve or a food mill. Return the thin, clear syrup to a smaller saucepan and simmer slowly, uncovered, over very low heat for about 3 hours, stirring frequently, until the *halek* thickens enough to coat a spoon.

3. Cool and just before serving place 2 cups of *halek* in a bowl. Sprinkle with half the walnuts and almonds. Reserve the remaining *halek* and nuts separately. Serve as *harosets* at the seder and as a dip for matzah throughout the Passover season.

Yield: 4 cups halek and 4 cups chopped walnuts and almonds (P)

Libyan Haroset

¼ cup walnuts

¼ cup pecans

¼ cup almonds

¼ cup hazelnuts

½ cup raisins

1 cup pitted dates

1½ teaspoons cinnamon

1½ teaspoons allspice

½ teaspoon ginger

1 teaspoon nutmeg

1. Combine all the ingredients using a mortar and pestle or a food processor.

2. Serve the *haroset* with romaine lettuce as the bitter herb.

Yield: about 3 cups (P)

Libyan Haroset
(Made in New York
from the Fruit from Sukkot)

Each Passover in Libya, Z'mira Chen's father would slaughter a sheep and then say blessings over each part. "My mother would clean every part of the sheep herself," said Ms. Chen, who lives in New York and Tel Aviv.

Like many Middle Eastern Jewish communities, Libyan men did all the shopping while the women stayed at home to care for the children. "Sometimes I would go with my father. He would choose the most perfect food."

Each food had its place within the cycle of the year. At Tu b'Shvat, the New Year of the trees, people eat fruits and nuts saved from Sukkot, the harvest season. Some of that fruit is used for pastries at Purim and the rest goes into the *harosets* served in Libyan homes at Passover.

"At the Passover seder," Ms. Chen said, "my father and brothers sat on the floor leaning on pillows at a low table. It's like a Greek or Roman feast. The last day of Passover was the evening for lettuce and flowers. From the afternoon on all the single girls dressed up in white. The boys who wanted to get engaged would take a flower and throw it to one. If she picked up the flower he would talk to her parents. The engaged couple would wait one year to get married." Pausing, she continued, "Even though it may seem chauvinistic there was a special appreciation for women in that world that is no more."

Persian Haroset De-spiced for American Children

Susan Bakhaj, a teacher from Iran, makes Persian *haroset* each year for the children at Adas Israel Synagogue in Washington, D.C. In the spring the traditional pomegranates are difficult to obtain and pistachio nuts are expensive, so Ms. Bakhaj substitutes strawberries, bananas, and walnuts. Because the children do not like spicy foods, she uses cinnamon instead of the cayenne, cloves, and cardamom she would have used in her native land.

1 cup walnuts

1 cup almonds

1 cup raisins

6 strawberries

1 cup dates, pitted

2 apples, cored, pitted, and
*   quartered*

1 banana, cut up

½ cup sweet wine

1 teaspoon cinnamon

¼ teaspoon pepper

Grind all the ingredients together in a food grinder or throw them in a food processor and process until a crunchy paste is formed. Or better yet place in a wooden bowl and allow the youngest member of your family to pound everything with a hand food chopper until it forms the consistency of a crunchy paste.

Yield: 4 cups (P)

Tip: Try serving this with cream cheese on your matzah for breakfast.

Janos Wilder's New American Haroset

Janos Wilder, whose restaurant is located in a national historic landmark on the grounds of the Tucson Museum of Modern Art, cooks French-inspired Southwestern cuisine most of the time. But on Jewish holidays he returns to his California Jewish roots. One of his favorites is this *haroset* with fresh mangoes and Port. "This recipe just happened. I wanted to make something special for Passover, using the ingredients we had around."

2 Granny Smith apples

Juice of ½ lemon

½ cup fresh mango, peeled
*   and diced*

½ cup chopped toasted pecans

½ teaspoon cinnamon

1 tablespoon honey

1 tablespoon Port or sweet wine

1. Peel, core, and dice the apples and sprinkle with the lemon juice.
2. Place all the ingredients in a food processor. Pulse once or twice just to break up. Let sit for the flavors to meld.

Yield: about 2 cups (P)

Passover in Camp: A Reminiscence of the Civil War

The following description of an improvised seder during the Civil War comes from the reminiscences of J. A. Joel, written in 1866 in the *Jewish Messenger:*

In the commencement of the war of 1861, I enlisted from Cleveland, Ohio, in the Union cause. . . . While lying there, [in the mountains of West Virginia] our camp duties were not of an arduous character, and being apprised of the approaching Feast of Passover, twenty of my comrades and co-religionists . . . united in a request to our commanding officer for relief from duty, in order that we might keep the holydays, which he readily acceded to. Our business was to find some suitable person to proceed to Cincinnati, Ohio, to buy us *matzos* [sic]. We were anxiously awaiting to receive our [mazzot] and about the middle of the morning a supply train arrived in camp, and to our delight seven barrels of *matzos*. On opening them, we were surprised and pleased to find that our thoughtful sutler had enclosed two Hagodahs [sic!] and prayer-books. We were now able to keep the [seder] nights, if we could only obtain the other requisites for that occasion. We obtained two kegs of cider, a lamb, several chickens and some eggs. We had the lamb but did not know what part was to represent it at the table; Yankee ingenuity prevailed, and it was decided to cook the whole and put it on the table, then we could dine off it, and be sure we had the right part. The necessaries for the *choroutzes* [sic] we could not obtain, so we got a brick which, rather hard to digest, reminded us, by looking at it, for what purpose it was intended. Horseradish or parsley we could not obtain, but in lieu we found a weed, whose bitterness, I apprehend, exceeded anything our forefathers "enjoyed." The herb was very bitter and very fiery, like cayenne pepper, and excited our thirst to such a degree, that we forgot the law authorizing to drink

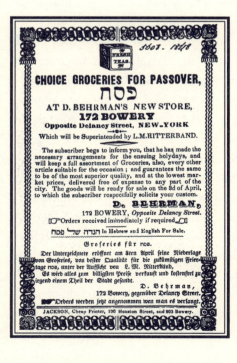

only four cups, and the consequence was we drank up all the cider. Those that drank the more freely became excited, and one thought he was Moses, another Aaron, and one had the audacity to call himself a Pharaoh. The consequence was a skirmish, with nobody hurt, only Moses, Aaron and Pharaoh, had to be carried to the camp, and there left in the arms of Morpheus.

There, in the wild woods of West Virginia, away from home and friends, we consecrated and offered up to the ever-loving God of Israel, our prayers and sacrifice.

Matzah on Both Sides of the Conflict

Another Union soldier, Myer Levy of Philadelphia, wrote his family that he was strolling through the streets of a Virginia town and noticed a little boy sitting on the steps of a house, eating matzah. When he asked the boy for a piece, the child fled indoors, shouting at the top of his lungs, "Mother! There's a damn Yankee Jew outside!" The boy's mother came out immediately and invited the soldier to the seder.

As we can see, Jewish soldiers on both sides of the conflict had to go out of their way to obtain matzah.

Until the 1840s, American Jews would buy matzah directly from their synagogues; there special committees were given the job of shaping them by hand into round or rectangular forms. As bakeries went into the matzah business in the mid-1800s, observant Jews wrote to the chief rabbi of Gleiwitz in Prussia to inquire whether it was lawful to use machinery to manufacture matzah. His affirmative response was published in the New York *Asmonean* on February 28, 1851.

Because of the lack of religious unity, advertisements appeared in the Jewish press throughout the country proclaiming the kashrut of one matzah over another.

After the Civil War many food businesses sprang up, including matzah bakers. In the early 1800s, Augustus Goodman, the scion of a family of matzah bakers in Posen, Poland, settled in Washington, D.C., where he became a baker for the Union Army. In 1865 he moved to Philadelphia where he opened a bakery which eventually became A. Goodman & Sons, Inc.

After the Civil War, editorials appeared in the Jewish press encouraging northerners to forget their ill feelings towards the south and provide their Jewish brethren there, many of whom had lost everything, with matzah for the seder.

Caper-Sauce Fish (Shreveport, Louisiana, Style)

"For seder we always had caper-sauce fish," said Isabelle Wile Goldman, ninety-five, of Shreveport, Louisiana, whose family came from Alsace in the middle of the nineteenth century. "It's just in the past few years that people have worried about cholesterol. People didn't know about it when I was young." This Alsatian recipe, originally made with carp, but in Louisiana made with snapper, is made hotter with cayenne pepper in the poaching liquid. "Caper-sauce fish takes a long time to make, it's expensive, and it's delicious. Now is it so terrible to have eggs once a year?"

FISH

1 4-pound red snapper or grouper, cleaned and gutted

Cold water to cover

1 large onion, quartered

1 celery, diced

1 green pepper, cut in 2-inch chunks

Juice of 1 lemon, plus 1 sliced lemon

Salt and cayenne pepper

SAUCE

3 hard-boiled eggs

3 raw eggs, separated

1½ teaspoons dry mustard

½ cup olive oil

Juice of 1 lemon

½ to 1 3-ounce bottle capers

¼ cup finely chopped onion

2 tablespoons finely chopped celery

2 tablespoons parsley

Salt and cayenne pepper

Parsley for garnish

Lettuce

Pimientos for garnish

1. Wash the fish and place in a poacher or other long pan with a lid. Cover with cold water and remove the fish.

2. Bring the water to a boil and add the onion, celery, green pepper, lemon juice, lemon slices, a generous sprinkling of salt to taste, and cayenne. Bring to a boil and simmer for 15 minutes, covered. Return the fish and simmer, covered, for 15 to 20 minutes, or until the fish flakes with a fork. Drain the fish and cool.

3. To make the caper sauce mash 2 of the boiled egg yolks, add to the raw egg yolks, and beat until creamy with the dry mustard. Add the olive oil a drop at a time, beating well after each addition. Add the lemon juice and continue to beat until creamy. A food processor is great for this. Add the capers, onion, celery, parsley, and mix well. Season to taste with salt and cayenne pepper.

4. Skin and bone the fish and cut into 4-inch squares. Refrigerate for several hours.

5. Before serving, place the snapper on a bed of lettuce. Pour the sauce over the fish, dice the hard-boiled egg whites and grate the remaining egg yolk with a cheese grater. Garnish with parsley and strips of pimiento.

Yield: 6 servings (P)

Cajun Matzah Balls with Green Onions

The following recipe is a perfect example of American regional assimilation. Made the Alsatian or southern German way with broken-up matzah rather than matzah meal, these matzah balls also include red pepper and scallions, called green onions in Louisiana. For more matzah ball recipes, see pages 110 to 113.

1 cup diced green onions
   (scallions)
½ stick (¼ cup) pareve
   margarine
8 regular matzahs
Salt and pepper to taste
Cayenne pepper to taste
2 large eggs, separated
½ cup chopped parsley
1 matzah, toasted and rolled
   into fine crumbs, or ½ cup
   matzah meal, toasted and
   rolled fine

1. Sauté the green onions in the margarine. Cool.
2. Soak the 8 matzahs in water until soft. Drain very well and squeeze out all the water. Place in the skillet with the sautéed green onions. Add the salt, pepper, and cayenne, and 2 well-beaten egg yolks before the mixture gets too hot. Add the parsley and cook, stirring constantly, until the matzah is dry and it leaves the skillet. Cool.
3. Beat the egg whites until they are stiff and fold in.
4. Roll into balls slightly smaller than a walnut. Then roll them in the toasted matzah meal.
5. Lower the matzah balls gently with a slotted soup spoon into gently simmering salted water and simmer them, covered, for 30 to 40 minutes. Lift with a slotted spoon into bowls with chicken soup or drain and serve as a dressing with beef or turkey.

Yield: about 56 matzah balls or 6 to 8 per person (M)

Uzbekistan Zagora *(Fish in Garlic and Coriander Sauce)*

In Brooklyn's Crown Heights, the matzah bakers from Uzbekistan do not forget how sweet it is to be in a land of freedom. For most of their lives they were forced to celebrate Passover in secrecy in Tashkent, where they baked matzah clandestinely at 4 a.m. in their homes. With full voices they can now sing "mitzvah matzah" while kneading and rolling out the dough to quickly make the matzah. No more than eighteen minutes can elapse between the start of mixing specially watched flour and water to the finished product of *shmorah* (watched) matzah emerging from the oven. While the women roll out the dough, they talk, often sharing recipes like their carp in garlic, their Friday night and Passover fish dish. This recipe is adapted from *Sephardic Cooking* by Copeland Marks.

1½ pounds fresh carp,
    flounder, or salmon, filleted

2 teaspoons salt

1 cup water

¼ cup vegetable oil

2 large garlic cloves

3 tablespoons chopped fresh
    coriander

1. Drench the fish with 1 teaspoon of the salt and ½ cup of the water and let stand for 30 minutes. Drain well and dry the slices on paper towels.

2. Heat the oil in a skillet. Add the fish, and fry on both sides over moderate heat for about 4 minutes to crisp the slices. Put the fish on a serving platter and keep it warm.

3. Prepare the sauce by mixing together the garlic, remaining teaspoon salt, coriander, and remaining ½ cup water. Stir this briskly and pour it over the fish, turning the slices over once so that they can absorb the sauce. Serve immediately at room temperature.

Yield: 4 servings (P)

Note: You can also marinate the fish in the sauce and then grill the fish.

Scenes of a matzah factory

Horseradish Special in the U.S. Army: Pesach Seder Supplies—No Chrain—Gefilta

About a week before Passover, 1952, while stationed at an Air Force Head-quarters in Texas, I received an SOS via MARS Radio. The operator said there was an emergency high priority message for me from Ramey Air Force Base in Puerto Rico, but he was unable to decipher it. "Spell it out to me and maybe I'll be able to help." Letter by letter he spelled:

PESACH SEDER SUPPLIES — NO CHRAIN — GEFILTA

Determined to prevent a serious violation of gefilta fish etiquette, I dropped everything and hastened to Shreveport, Louisiana, where I pur-chased three large gallon jars of horseradish. I packed them carefully, almost reverently, and marked the cartons "Religious Articles—Very Holy and Very Important."

Back at my Base I contacted Flight Operations and found a courier plane going to MacDill Air Force Base in Tampa, Florida. From there another courier could bring the precious cargo to Ramey in time for Passover. I went out to speak to the commander of the plane personally, and asked him to deliver the cartons to the Base Chaplain at MacDill. I then got on the direct wire to MacDill and told the Base Chaplain how urgent it was to deliver the "Passover Supplies."

Chaplain Louis Barish, *Rabbis in Uniform:*
The Story of the American Jewish Military Chaplain, 1962

In Germany during World War II, if Jewish servicemen could not receive matzah, they often baked it themselves. For bitter herbs they would gather what was grow-ing or even substitute radishes or other local roots for it.

The bottled horseradish they used with their gefilte fish (see pages 140 to 145 for recipes) may very well have been Gold's. Polish-born Tillie and Hyman Gold were struggling in Brooklyn, selling insurance and wine bricks during the Depres-sion. One day Mr. Gold's cousin, who made a living sharpening knives and grind-ing vegetables, got into an argument and ended up in jail. Hyman bailed him out and the grating machine ended up in the hallway of his house.

One day Mrs. Gold said, "Let me grind up horseradish," which she did in a big black pot keeping the kitchen window open for the fumes to escape. Then she filled jars with the horseradish, vinegar, salt, and sometimes grated beets.

Her husband started selling white and red grated horseradish in small bottles out of a pushcart. Soon business was so brisk that they went full-time into the horseradish-grinding business and have been doing the crying for their customers ever since.

Today the third generation runs Gold's Horseradish, the largest producer of horseradish in the world, out of a factory in Long Island.

Segerman Horseradish Special

Although most people buy prepared horseradish, it is easy to make it yourself. Bernard and Charles Segerman of Chevy Chase, Maryland, have a father-son tradition of growing and grinding horseradish. Hint: before starting this recipe open a window and wear a pair of tight-fitting swimmers' goggles. If you make this once you will never buy commercial horseradish again. For gefilte fish recipes to go with this horseradish see pages 140 to 145.

1 pound thick horseradish
   roots
1 large fresh beet
½ cup white vinegar
¼ cup sugar or to taste

1. Peel the horseradish root, trimming a portion to be used as the symbolic bitter herbs on your seder plate. (Save some for planting too.)
2. Peel the beet. Grate both the beet and the horseradish coarsely by hand or in a food processor.
3. Add the vinegar and sugar to the beet and the horseradish and blend well. Add more vinegar if too dry. Store in a tightly covered container in the refrigerator and serve it with your gefilte fish. It will keep several weeks.

Yield: about 6 cups (P)

Mock Chopped Liver

When Debra Wasserman was a graduate student in international relations at Georgetown University, she was a non-vegetarian pacifist. During a heated discussion a fellow student asked, "How can you be against war and eat meat?" Her protagonist told her about the violence of killing animals, how they have feelings, too. Ms. Wasserman couldn't sleep all night thinking about this conversation. The next day she became a vegetarian. Eleven years later vegetarianism has replaced international relations as her life career. She is now the head of the Jewish Vegetarians of North America.

Once she became a vegetarian, she decided to develop alternatives for dishes like chopped liver. "Especially at Passover it was difficult," she said. "The food is so heavy on eggs and chicken fat." Now she has put together the *No-cholesterol Passover Cookbook,* a slim volume with recipes like this "mock chopped liver." Instead of matzah ball soup she suggests a carrot cream soup using whole carrots and a vegetable-stock puree.

This new kind of vegetarianism that emphasizes self-control, free choice, compassion for animals, sanctity of life, preservation of health, and the Jewish duty to feed the hungry was dubbed "Kashruth of the Counter-Culture" in *Time* magazine.

½ pound mushrooms, chopped

1 small onion, chopped

3 tablespoons vegetable oil

1 cup chopped walnuts

Salt and freshly ground pepper
   to taste

1 tablespoon water

1. Sauté the mushrooms and onion in the vegetable oil over a medium heat until the onion is clear.
2. Turn into a blender or food processor, add the walnuts, salt and pepper, and the water. Process until blended but not too smooth. Serve as a spread with matzah.

Yield: about 1 cup (P)

Baton Rouge Matzah Balls

Some families in Baton Rouge prefer their matzah balls as a vegetable or starch with gravy, rather than with soup. In many homes the hostess will ask the servant to bring out the dumplings, meaning matzah balls. In one Southern Jewish cookbook I found a recipe for matzah ball gumbo! For more on matzah balls, see pages 110 through 113.

¾ cup cold water or chicken
   broth
5 tablespoons melted chicken
   fat or margarine

1. In a saucepan bring the water or chicken broth to a boil and add the chicken fat or margarine. Turn the heat off and beat in the matzah meal.
2. In a bowl mix the onion, eggs, red pepper, salt, and parsley.

1¼ *cups matzah meal*

1 grated onion

3 large eggs

½ *teaspoon red pepper*

½ *teaspoon salt*

¼ *cup chopped parsley*

3. Mix with the meal mixture and let sit for 15 minutes. Cover and chill in the refrigerator for several hours.

4. Grease your hands to keep them from sticking and roll bits of the mixture into balls a little smaller than the size of a walnut. (At this point you can freeze the matzah balls uncooked on a cookie sheet and remove to a plastic freezer bag.)

5. Drop the balls into boiling salted water and cook, covered, for about 30 minutes. Serve floating in your choice of chicken soup.

Yield: about 26 balls, about 6 per person (M)

Egad, Yankee Matzah Balls!
Just Love Them Dixie Dumplings!

I tried matzah balls with nutmeg one year and my family rose up in rebellion.
Helene Blitzer, Baton Rouge, Louisiana

Baton Rouge Jews like their food spicy, even at the seder table. Journalist Carol Anne Blitzer offended the Southern sensibilities of 102-year old Celina Aaron Maas when she showed up to photograph her preparing matzah balls for a Passover story. To help the elderly lady, Mrs. Blitzer brought with her some mixed Manischewitz matzah balls for the picture. Mrs. Maas took one look at them and cried, "Yankee matzah balls!" She then got out a butcher knife and started cutting up green onions and sprinkling on red pepper to stud the dumplings, then molded them into smaller balls for the photograph. Like Mrs. Maas, the two hundred Baton Rouge "old time" Jewish families, most of whom have German and Alsatian roots, prefer their food hot, and they like their matzah balls with some bite. In Baton Rouge there is much discussion over which is the correct and the best-tasting matzah ball. Some make these ecumenical dumplings with matzah meal only, while others use a combination of matzah and matzah meal, following recipes brought to this country over one hundred years ago. Most disdain the mild nutmeg and ginger, which were typically German and are found as spices in matzah-ball recipes in Charleston and elsewhere. All scorn Yankee matzah balls, which are too big and too soft.

Passover Bagels

Bagels have become so much part of the American Jewish scene that Passover bagels, made like cream puffs, add variety to the Passover fare.

½ cup cold water

Pinch of salt

½ cup vegetable oil

1 tablespoon sugar

1 cup matzah meal

3 large eggs

1. Put water, salt, vegetable oil, and sugar in a saucepan and bring to a boil. Beat in the matzah meal at one time. Stir until it forms a ball and remove from the heat. Set aside to cool. Add the eggs, one at a time, beating well after each addition until all are well blended.
2. Drop by heaping tablespoons on a greased pan. Dip your thumb in cold water and make a hole in the center of each. Bake in a preheated 350-degree oven for 30 minutes or until golden.

Yield: 12 bagels (P)

Farfel Kugel at a Seder in the White House?

During the first year of the Clinton administration, White House staffers decided to hold a kosher Passover seder. Sue Fischer of Sue Fischer Catering prepared the meal, which included traditional gefilte fish, matzah ball soup, chicken stuffed with sun-dried tomatoes, and farfel kugel. Here are her recipes.

4 large eggs

6 cups farfel or crushed matzah

4 tablespoons margarine

2 small onions, diced (about 1 cup)

14 medium mushrooms, sliced (about 1½ cups)

4 cups chicken broth

Pinch of marjoram

Black pepper to taste

1. Mix the eggs and the crushed matzah in a bowl. Spread a thin layer of the mixture on a cookie sheet lined with aluminum foil. Place in a preheated, 350-degree oven for about 15 minutes or until the farfel is dry.
2. In the meantime, heat the margarine in a small sauté pan. Add the onions and sauté until limp. Then add the mushrooms and continue cooking until soft.
3. Add the matzah, 1 cup of the chicken broth, a pinch of marjoram, and black pepper to taste. Stirring constantly, continue to add the broth until most of the liquid is absorbed into the matzah. Reduce the heat to low, letting it sit until all the liquid is absorbed. Serve with the chicken with sun-dried tomatoes and *shiitake* mushrooms (see recipe, page 404).

Yield: 8 to 10 servings (M)

Passover Bumuelos

One popular New Mexican dessert is *bumuelos,* similar to the Greek *loukomades* and the *bimuelos* of Sephardic Jews. Possibly the earliest dessert known to mankind, these fried doughnuts, drained and honey coated, were eaten by the ancient Greeks. In New Mexico today they are sometimes made with a rosette iron, fried, and later dipped in a sugar-cinnamon combination. In Istanbul, a Jewish recipe that came to Turkey with the Inquisition is a matzah *bumuelo,* sprinkled with cinnamon and sugar and made in Washington, D.C., each Passover by Ida Dana.

1 cup matzah meal
Dash of salt
1½ cups water
2 large eggs
Kosher-for-Passover vegetable
  oil for deep frying

1. Mix the matzah meal, salt, water, and eggs in a mixing bowl and beat well.
2. Put about 2 inches of oil in a frying pan. Heat until about 375 degrees. Drop the batter by heaping tablespoons into the oil and fry over a medium low heat a few minutes on each side. Drain and serve with hard-boiled eggs or sugar and cinnamon or maple syrup.

Yield: about 12 (P)

Barry Wine's Matzah Salad

This matzah salad, created at the now defunct Quilted Giraffe Restaurant in New York, is the Passover equivalent of the Middle Eastern Fettoosh salad with toasted pita bread. It is delicious, a great accompaniment to pot roast.

10 squares matzah
4 tablespoons chicken fat or
  pareve margarine
1 red pepper, finely diced
1 cucumber, finely diced
2 to 3 teaspoons capers
  (optional)
1 bunch chives, finely chopped
Salt and pepper to taste

1. Run a rolling pin over the matzah to break it up into small pieces no larger than ¼ inch, about the size of matzah farfel.
2. Cook in a dry sauté pan or slightly toast in a 300-degree oven for 10 minutes.
3. Heat the chicken fat or pareve margarine in a saucepan and add peppers and cucumbers. Cook for 1 minute over medium heat.
4. Turn off the heat and add capers and chives.
5. Toss in a mixing bowl with the toasted matzah. Add salt and pepper to taste. Serve at room temperature or slightly warm surrounding the brisket.

Yield: 6 servings (M) or (P)

San Francisco Seder with Scacchi, Roman Layered Vegetable Dish

Carol Field, author of *Celebrating Italy,* comes from a fifth-generation San Francisco Jewish family that arrived with the Gold Rush. While living in Italy on a sabbatical with her architect husband, John, she decided to write a book on festivals. Mrs. Field's description of the food served at a Roman seder meal, which the Italians call *Pasqua Ebraica,* Jewish Easter, is mouth-watering. The Roman feast itself includes such dishes as *bresaoli,* air-dried beef served with hard-boiled eggs, and *carciofi alla giudea,* "artichokes cooked the Jewish way" (see my *Jewish Holiday Kitchen*), and risotto containing asparagus, artichokes, or fresh peas. *Scacchi,* a Sephardic layered dish like lasagna, called *mina* in Turkey, with layers of meat and sautéed vegetables alternating with matzoh, takes the place of pasta and is served at the seder Mrs. Field attends in Berkeley. Try this dish with or without the meat. For garlic lovers who like a lemony taste to their vegetables, this is a real winner.

12 standard matzahs

1 cup olive oil

1 pound chopped ground beef (optional)

Salt and freshly ground pepper to taste

1½ pounds onions, thinly sliced

4 artichokes, or 2 8-ounce cans of artichoke hearts

Juice of 1 lemon, plus ½ cup juice

6 cloves garlic, minced

¾ teaspoon minced rosemary

¾ teaspoon minced sage

2 pounds fresh spinach, cleaned, stemmed, and cooked 4 to 5 minutes in a pot with only the water left on the leaves, then squeezed dry

1. Cover the matzahs with water and let sit until wet and almost crumbling.

2. Warm 1 tablespoon of the olive oil and sauté the chopped ground beef, stirring until it is no longer red. Add salt and pepper, drain, and set aside.

3. Sauté the onions in ¼ cup of the olive oil. Drain and set aside.

4. Clean the artichokes, remove the chokes and fibrous leaves, cook for about 20 minutes in water with lemon, and then sauté the artichokes in ¼ cup olive oil with 2 cloves of garlic, rosemary, sage, and salt to taste. Drain and set aside. If using canned hearts, cut in half.

5. Clean, stem, and cook the spinach for 4 to 5 minutes in a pot with only the water left on the leaves. Squeeze dry. Sauté with 2 more cloves of garlic, the *peperoncino,* nutmeg, salt to taste in ¼ cup of olive oil. Drain and set aside.

6. Lastly, sauté the mushrooms in ¼ cup olive oil, with 2 more cloves garlic and salt to taste added after 3 to 4 minutes.

7. Grease a 9- by 13-inch baking dish and cover the bottom with the sautéed chopped meat if using. Cover with a layer of 3 matzahs. Don't be upset if the matzahs fall apart; it won't matter. Cover with the onions. Layer 3

*1 peperoncino (dried red
chili), seeded and minced*

*½ teaspoon freshly grated
nutmeg*

1 pound mushrooms, sliced

6 large eggs

1 cup beef broth or water

more matzahs on top, alternating with the artichokes, spinach, and mushrooms, and finishing with the mushrooms.

8. Beat together the eggs and the remaining ½ cup lemon juice, and pour over the top of the dish. Add enough of the broth or water to moisten well.

9. Bake in a preheated, 400-degree oven for about 30 minutes or until the mixture is set and cooked through.

Yield: 8 to 10 servings (P) or (M)

The San Francisco earthquake of 1906 did not stop this family from celebrating Passover.

Chicken with Sun-dried Tomatoes and Shiitake Mushrooms

MARINADE

2½ tablespoons kosher-for-
   Passover Dijon mustard

4 tablespoons dry white wine

4 tablespoons kosher-for-
   Passover vegetable oil

2 tablespoons diced shallots

CHICKEN

4 whole chicken breasts, boned

⅓ cup kosher-for-Passover
   vegetable oil

⅓ cup shallots, diced

20 medium shiitake
   mushrooms, sliced (about
   2 cups)

16 sun-dried tomatoes, sliced

1 tablespoon potato starch

Salt to taste

2 cups chicken broth

1 cup non-dairy creamer

1. To make the marinade mix the mustard, wine, oil, and the shallots in a small bowl.

2. Mash the chicken with a wooden pounder and let marinate in the mustard sauce.

3. Melt the oil in a frying pan. Add the shallots and the mushrooms, and stir until the mushrooms are soft. Add the sun-dried tomatoes and a tablespoon or so of the potato starch if the sauce has too much liquid. Add salt to taste. Remove from the heat.

4. Separate half the mushroom mixture to fill the chicken breasts. Place ¼ of this mixture on one end of each breast and roll like a jelly roll on the diagonal so both ends are filled.

5. Bake in a preheated, 400-degree oven for 25 minutes or until done. Cut each breast into 6 slices on the diagonal, allowing 3 slices per portion.

6. To make the sauce, return the remaining half of the mushroom mixture to a sauté pan. Add the chicken broth and stir over a low heat. Continuing to stir, add enough nondairy creamer to make a sauce. If the sauce has too much liquid add a pinch of potato starch. Place the chicken on the plate, cover with the sauce, and serve with the farfel pilav.

Yield: 8 servings (M)

Variation: If you prefer, you can omit the sauce and serve as is. The chicken will be juicy enough with the mushroom stuffing.

Passover Stuffed Boneless Chicken Breast with Apricot Jam

B'nai B'rith Hillel chapters on college campuses have played an important role in introducing many Jewish students to each other and to Jewish food. But there are Hillels and Hillels. The one at the Johnson and Wales Cooking School in Providence, Rhode Island, has more of a culinary challenge than most. Each year the soon-to-be chefs prepare their own seder, cooking the dishes that they present. The following chicken recipe has been very popular.

STUFFING

1 cup boiling water (or ½ cup
water and ½ cup chicken
broth)

3 cups matzah farfel

1 medium onion, chopped

½ green pepper, chopped

3 ribs celery, chopped fine

1 tablespoon kosher-for-
Passover oil

Salt and freshly ground pepper
to taste

3 large eggs, beaten

CHICKEN

6 chicken breasts, boned and
halved

Apricot jam

1. To make the stuffing, pour the boiling water over the farfel and wait until all the water is absorbed. Allow to cool.

2. Meanwhile, sauté the onion, green pepper, and celery in the oil over a medium heat until the onion is soft. Mix together the salt, pepper, and eggs. Set aside while preparing the chicken breasts.

3. Hold each breast half in one hand (skin towards the palm) and spoon about 3 tablespoons of stuffing on top. Pull the skin up around the stuffing and use a toothpick to fasten the breast closed.

4. Place open-side down in a greased ovenproof pan and place a teaspoon of apricot jam on the top of each roll.

5. Bake in a preheated 350-degree oven for 1 hour, uncovered.

Yield: 8 to 12 servings (M)

A Sephardic Rabbi's Seder
with Hand-me-down Recipes from Yugoslavia

Sephardic Rabbi Hayyim Kassorla of Rockville, Maryland, reenacts the Exodus with his children.

When I arrived at Rabbi Hayyim Kassorla's home in Rockville, Maryland, on the second night of Passover, he was dressed in a *galabia,* an Egyptian gown. A Sephardic rabbi born in the Bronx of Yugoslavian parents, Rabbi Kassorla dressed symbolically as a free man, not as a slave in Egypt. We sat around the table with his wife, Jodi, and their three children, sang songs, and told stories from the Haggadah. Romaine, not horseradish, was used for the bitter herbs, parsley was dipped in kosher-for-Passover vinegar (some use lemon juice), rather than salt water.

The *afikomen* (the dessert matzah), instead of being hidden as is the Ashkenazic custom, was wrapped inside a napkin cover, thrown into a sack, and slung over the shoulders of the children. With their provisions on their back, they reenacted the story of the Exodus. In Hebrew and English (sometimes in Arabic and Ladino), the children knocked on a pretend door and asked questions in Hebrew, English, and Ladino. When an adult opened it, someone asked each child, "Who are you?" The response was, "A Hebrew slave from Egypt." "Where are you coming from?" "We're coming from Egypt," they replied. "And where are you going?" "To a land flowing with milk and honey. Even though we don't know where it is we have faith in the Almighty."

The food served at the dinner that followed was pan-Sephardic. Jodi, the rabbi's Ashkenazic wife, is an avid cook who is interested in all the foods of her husband's Sephardic congregants. She is also the author of *The Sephardic Gourmet Cookbook,* compiled by the Magen David Sephardic Congregation Sisterhood in Rockville, Maryland.

Unlike some Ashkenazic Jews who (purposefully) avoid lamb at Passover since the destruction of the Temple in Jerusalem, where the lamb was once sacrificed, Jodi makes a traditional roast lamb breast with rosemary and garlic, a *basmati* rice with pine nuts (some Sephardic Jews can eat rice, based on their own rabbinic opinion), and springtime asparagus.

For Rabbi Kassorla, Passover would not be Passover without *megina,* a meat pie with leeks and matzah from his family's native Monastir, Yugoslavia. Similar to the Turkish Jewish *mina,* a layered matzah pie often prepared with spinach,* the recipe came down from his Yugoslav grandmother to his Rumanian mother, who passed it on to Jodi. Now the rabbi's eight-year-old son Josef says that the wife he chooses has to observe kashrut, be a keeper of the Sabbath, and know how to make his leek pie.

*See my *Jewish Holiday Kitchen.*

Frittada de Pressa *(Sephardic Casserole of Leek and Potatoes)*

This is a dairy version of Rabbi Kassorla's leek pie made by the Capsouto Frères Restaurant in New York. See box, page 409, for more about the restaurant and its seder.

4 large russet (baking) potatoes, peeled and quartered

10 leeks, the white part only, split and washed well

Salt and freshly ground pepper to taste

4 eggs, well beaten, plus 1 egg yolk, beaten

¼ cup grated kosher-for-Passover Parmesan cheese

¼ cup olive oil

1. Bring a pot of salted water to a boil. Peel and quarter the potatoes and add with the leeks. Boil for about 10 to 15 minutes or until tender. Remove from the pot and drain.

2. Mash the potatoes and leeks together in a bowl. Season with salt and pepper, then mix in the eggs and the ¼ cup cheese.

3. Pour 2 tablespoons of the oil into an 8-inch baking pan and swirl to cover the bottom. Place in a preheated, 350-degree oven for just a minute. Spread the potato-leek mixture evenly over the pan and brush the top with the egg yolk mixed with the remaining 2 tablespoons of the oil. Sprinkle on the additional parmesan cheese and bake for 20 minutes.

Yield: 6 servings (D)

Eggplant and Green Pepper Kugel (Casserole)

Here is an eggplant *kugel* for Passover I first tasted in Jerusalem, the world's capital of international eggplant dishes. The recipe was brought there by American immigrants.

*1 large eggplant (about
    2 pounds)*

1 onion, diced

1 green pepper, diced

2 tablespoons pine nuts

¼ cup olive oil

*2 tablespoons chopped fresh
    basil*

*Salt and freshly ground pepper
    to taste*

2 large eggs, lightly beaten

1 matzah, crumbled

*2 tablespoons butter or
    margarine*

1. Peel the eggplant and dice in 2-inch cubes. Cook in simmering salted water to cover until the eggplant is tender—about 20 minutes. Drain and mash.

2. Meanwhile, sauté the onion, pepper, and pine nuts in olive oil over medium heat until the vegetables are tender but not crisp. Combine with the basil and salt and pepper.

3. Mix the eggplant with the lightly beaten eggs as well as the vegetable mixture. Add the matzah and mix well. Place in a greased casserole and dot with butter or margarine. Bake in a preheated 350-degree oven for 35 minutes or until golden brown on top and crusty on the sides.

*Yield: 6 to 8 servings (D) with butter; (P) with
margarine*

Chef Allen's Rhubarb Tsimmes

Few *nouvelle* American chefs are as playful or as comfortable with Floridian Jewish cuisine as is Allen Susser of Chef Allen's in Aventura, Florida. His Passover seder menu says it all: homemade red snapper gefilte fish with sweet carrots, *calabaza,* and jellied consommé; matzah pasta with asparagus, *shiitake,* and farm ripe tomato; slow roasted rack of veal with caramelized shallots; rhubarb tsimmes and hand-grated boniato (a light-colored, sweet potato) pancake, chocolate silk pie with a macaroon crust and mango relish, or poppy-seed cake baked in a brown paper bag with Key lime curd. In the spirit of Passover, Chef Allen donates the profits to the Rose Rosenkrantz Philanthropic League, set up in memory of his grandmother who taught him to cook, to provide Passover foods for the less fortunate.

3 pounds rhubarb

1 cup dried mango, chopped

1 cup dried papaya, chopped

½ cup dates, chopped

1½ cup dry red wine

1 large onion, diced

2 tablespoons butter

1 teaspoon cinnamon

¼ teaspoon allspice

¼ teaspoon cumin

1. Clean and rough chop the rhubarb into 1-inch pieces.
2. In a small sauce pot combine the mango, papaya, and dates, add the red wine, and bring to a boil. Simmer for 5 minutes until the fruit has softened.
3. In a heavy sauce pot sauté the onion in butter for 2 to 3 minutes until translucent. Add the rhubarb.
4. Pour cooked fruit and red wine into the rhubarb pot. Add the cinnamon, allspice, and cumin. Continue to cook over low heat for 10 more minutes.

Yield: 8 servings (P)

Why Is This Night Different from All Other Nights? For One Night a Year Capsouto Frères Restaurant Becomes a Seder Table

"When terrorists bombed a synagogue in Turkey in 1985, killing twenty people, we wanted to do something," said Sami Capsouto, co-owner of Capsouto Frères Restaurant in Manhattan's TriBeCa neighborhood. The Capsouto brothers, of Turkish-Jewish origin, decided to hold a seder in their 110-seat restaurant, and to donate the proceeds to the American Jewish Joint Distribution Committee.

The restaurant usually serves country French cuisine, but for Passover the chef goes Turkish, and Eva Capsouto, the owners' mother, steps into the kitchen and prepares the heirloom recipes of her childhood: an apple and date *haroset,* as well as a *mina* or pie made from matzah, cheese, and eggs; *frittada de pressa* or casserole of leeks and potatoes (see page 407); poached salmon; macaroons; quince paste; and—for the American palate—Passover brownies. These were the recipes—minus the brownies—Mrs. Capsouto made for her sons when they were growing up in Cairo. "The meal that we prepare is what my mother would have served at home," said Sami Capsouto.

Passover Brownies—Good Enough for the Whole Year

These brownies, created by Capsouto Frères for their Passover seder, are moist and delicious all year round.

¾ sticks (¾ cup) unsalted butter or margarine, softened

¾ cup sugar

5 eggs, separated

6 ounces bittersweet chocolate

6 ounces finely ground almonds or almond flour

Pinch of salt

1. Cream the butter and sugar together. Mix in the egg yolks.
2. Melt the chocolate over a double boiler. Cool and add to the butter mixture. Add the finely ground almonds or almond flour.
3. Beat the egg whites with the salt until stiff but not dry. Fold into the batter. Pour into a 9-inch square greased baking tin. Bake in a preheated 350-degree oven for 45 minutes. Cool and cut in squares.

Yield: about 24 brownies (M) or (P)

Pistachio Macaroons

During the American Colonial period Jewish merchants frequently had glass bowls filled with pistachio nuts for visitors in their homes. Sometimes at Passover they made their macaroons with these pistachios instead of almonds.

3 cups shelled pistachio nuts

1 cup sugar

3 egg whites

Sugar for dusting

1. Whirl the pistachio nuts in the food processor until ground but not pureed.
2. Line 2 cookie sheets with parchment paper and set aside. In a medium bowl mix the ground pistachio nuts, sugar, and egg whites. Refrigerate for about 10 minutes. Drop the batter from a tablespoon onto the cookie sheets, leaving ½ inch between macaroons. Bake in a preheated 325-degree oven for 12 to 15 minutes or until lightly brown. Dust with sugar when cool.

Yield: about 2 dozen (P)

Hendricks Schulson Family Almond Pudding

Old recipes for sponge cakes or almond tortes today traveled with the Jews from Spain to Holland and throughout the Ottoman Empire, where sponge cake became known as *pan d'Espana,* the bread of Spain. Mentioned as a Jewish dessert in the 1855 edition of Eliza Acton's *Modern Cookery for Private Families,* "almond pudding" usually includes both bitter and sweet ground almonds or matzah meal, sometimes orange flower water, and always eggs and sugar.

Way back in history, when some enterprising cook figured out how to separate eggs, beating the whites stiff before folding them into the yolks, almond and sugar combinations became puddings and later sponge cakes and tortes. As stone hearths were replaced by more modern ovens and German immigrants of the nineteenth century, both Jewish and non-Jewish, brought more sophisticated baking methods to this country, tortes became complex, sometimes including both coconut and almonds.

4 large eggs, separated

½ cup plus 2 tablespoons sugar

¾ cup ground blanched almonds

½ teaspoon almond extract (optional)

Oil for the pan

Matzah meal for the pan

1 pint strawberries or 1 cup strawberry puree

1. Using an electric mixer beat the egg yolks until they are foamy. Add ½ cup sugar and continue to beat until the egg yolks are very pale and fluffy. Add the almonds and the extract, if using, and mix until well blended.

2. In another bowl beat the egg whites until stiff peaks form.

3. Fold the egg whites into the yolk mixture and turn into an 8-inch soufflé dish or springform pan that has been greased and then dusted with matzah meal. Bake in a preheated 350-degree oven for 35 minutes or until golden. The pudding will rise slightly during cooking; it will settle as it cools. Let cool slightly.

4. Sprinkle the top with the remaining 2 tablespoons of sugar. Top with fresh strawberries or strawberry puree and serve. (You can also use confectioners' sugar, but not at Passover. Confectioners' sugar includes cornstarch and, therefore, is taboo, corn products being prohibited at Passover.)

5. Decorate with fresh strawberries or strawberry puree.

Yield: 6 to 8 servings (P)

Tip: Another old recipe uses orange flower water.

Marmalada of Eggs the Jews' Way
Is a Substitute for Custard at Passover

Jews and Arabs have been making marzipan (almond paste), also called marmalada, as a candy and a decoration for elaborate cakes for more than seven hundred years. In Hannah Glasse's *The Art of Cookery Made Plain and Easy* (1751), a recipe for "A Marmalade of Eggs the Jews Way" included twenty-four egg yolks, pounded almonds, sugar, and orange blossom water. The recipe continued, "This marmalade, mixed with pounded almonds, with orange peel and citron, are made in cakes of all shapes, such as birds, fish and fruit."

In *The National Cookery Book* (1876), a marmalada also appears with only twenty yolks called "A Substitute for Custard in Passover." *Yemas Dobles,* a similar recipe with twelve whole eggs, has come to this country with Sephardic Jews who sojourned in Latin America.

Blanch a pound of almonds, pound them in a mortar and add a quart of water. Put them on the fire with a pound of loaf sugar, and stir in the yolks of twenty eggs, beaten light. Be careful not to let the eggs curdle.

Almond Nougat

Although almonds and almond candy are not uniquely Jewish, Jews tended to put this nut in their sweets as a reminder of their connection to the holy land. In Toledo, Spain, where Jews and Arabs lived for centuries, nougat candy was "the springtime sweet," one of the items served at a community open house in the spring.

Therefore, The *Maimouna* (pronounced *meemojna*) table, whether in Rabat or Rockville, Maryland, includes a potpourri of Moroccan sweets—a couscous with dates, *mouffleta* (Moroccan pancakes), petit fours, jams, Moroccan cookies, baklava, and the more Spanish nougat candy for the end of a Passover Moroccan meal. It is also decorated with symbolic items of a plentiful harvest, such as fresh fava beans, hard-boiled eggs for rebirth, and dates, a bowl of flour, a stalk of new wheat, fresh mint, a dish of honey, and a whole salmon. The nougat candy becomes the link to their past in Toledo. Solange Amsellem's version is considered the best in the greater Washington Moroccan community.

2 *cups sugar*

1 *cup water*

Juice of ½ *lemon*

1 *large egg white*

1 *cup almonds*

1 *cup walnuts*

1. Mix the sugar and water in a saucepan and bring to a boil. Add the lemon juice and simmer over a medium heat about 1 5 minutes or until 2 3 4 to 2 4 0 degrees—the soft ball stage—is reached on a candy thermometer.

2. Place the sugar-water mixture in a mixer and beat until stiff, about 1 5 minutes, adding the egg white gradually after the first few minutes.

3. Meanwhile, toast the almonds for about 1 0 to 1 5 minutes on a cookie sheet in a preheated 3 5 0-degree oven.

4. Carefully fold the walnuts into the nougat mixture and place in a bowl. Decorate with the almonds and serve with a spoon.

Yield: 8 servings (P)

Tip: An American shortcut to this recipe is to roast 1 cup of walnuts and melt 2 6-ounce containers of marshmallow fluff. Fold in the walnuts with the fluff and sprinkle the almonds on top. For a Venezuelan twist, replace the almonds with cashew nuts!

Alabama Lemon Pecan Torte

In the South, Austrian, Alsatian, and German immigrants substituted locally grown pecans in their much-loved almond tortes. The following recipe, which was originally an almond lemon torte in Europe, often served for Passover, became a pecan lemon torte in Alabama. An early version was included in the *20th Century Cookbook,* published in Montgomery, Alabama, in 1 8 9 7, by C. F. Moritz and Adelle Kahn.

TORTE

7 *large eggs, separated*

¾ *cup sugar*

2 *cups coarsely ground pecans*

1 *tablespoon lemon rind*

1 *tablespoon lemon juice*

2 *tablespoons matzah meal*

1. Whisk together the egg yolks and the sugar in a large bowl until blended. Stir in the pecans and the lemon rind.

2. In a separate bowl beat the egg whites and the lemon juice until the whites are stiff but not until dry peaks form. Stir one-fourth of the whites into the yolk mixture. Gently fold in the remaining whites until blended.

3. Scrape into a greased 9-inch springform pan that has been dusted with matzah meal.

Lemon Pecan Torte, cont.

GLAZE

1 large egg yolk

1/3 cup lemon juice

1/2 cup sugar

1 teaspoon unsalted butter or margarine

1 tablespoon lemon rind

4. Bake in a preheated 325-degree oven for 1 hour or until firm to the touch in the center. Cool in the pan on a wire rack for 15 minutes. The cake may sink in the center.

5. Meanwhile, prepare the glaze. Combine the egg yolk, lemon juice, sugar, and butter or margarine in a small saucepan. Bring to simmering over medium heat, whisking constantly. Remove from the heat. Stir in the lemon rind.

6. Poke holes in the top of the cake with long skewers so that the glaze can soak in. With the cake still in the springform pan, spoon the glaze over. Let the cake stand a few minutes until the glaze seeps into the cake. Then remove the cake from the pan by running a thin knife around the rim to release the cake. Garnish with lemon rind, if you wish.

Yield: 8 servings (P) or (D)

Mississippi Praline Macaroons

This is a great recipe for Passover, one that was very popular in Austria and Germany . . . without the pecans. It comes from the cookbook of the late Felicia Schlenker (see page 349).

3 large egg whites

1 cup brown sugar

1 full cup roughly chopped pecans

Butter or margarine for greasing cookie sheet

24 pecan halves for topping

1. Beat the egg whites until they form soft peaks. Gradually add the sugar and beat until the whites are very stiff.

2. Stir in the chopped nuts by hand.

3. Cover a cookie sheet with aluminum foil and grease. Spoon out a heaping teaspoon of batter on the cookie sheet with at least 1 inch between cookies. Then press down flat. Place a pecan half on top. Repeat with the rest of the batter.

4. Bake in a preheated 275-degree oven for about 30 minutes, until the cookies are firm but still shiny.

Yield: about 2 dozen macaroons (P)

Passover Chremslach *(Fritters Stuffed with Currants, Almonds, and Apricots)*

This is an updated version of the *chremslach* passed down in my own family. I have never had a seder without it. A heavier version stuffed with cranberries appeared in many early American Jewish cookbooks as Kentucky *grimslech*.

*3 matzahs, soaked and
    squeezed very dry*

2 tablespoons currants

2 tablespoons chopped almonds

*2 tablespoons chopped dried
    apricots*

3 large eggs, separated

¼ cup matzah meal

⅓ cup sugar

Grated rind of 1 lemon

1 tablespoon lemon juice

*Kosher-for-Passover vegetable
    oil for frying*

1. Mix together the matzahs, currants, almonds, apricots, egg yolks, matzah meal, sugar, lemon rind, and lemon juice.

2. Beat the egg whites until stiff. Fold into the matzah mixture, adding matzah meal to make the mixture hold together.

3. Using an electric skillet or deep fryer, heat about 2 inches of oil to 375 degrees. Drop the mixture by tablespoons and brown a few minutes on each side until they are crisp. Cook only about three at a time. Drain well on paper. Serve at room temperature or crisped up in the oven. The fritters are especially delicious with stewed prunes with orange juice as an accompaniment, if desired. Or use the wine sauce on the following page .

Note: You can make these in the morning, drain on paper, leave out all day, and crisp in the oven just before serving.

Yield: about 2 dozen (P)

A Vineyard and Grape Nursery in Bushberg, Missouri

During the Revolution of 1848 Isidor Bush left Vienna and settled in St. Louis, Missouri, where he joined with his brother-in-law and together they organized the firm of Bush & Taussing, a wholesale grocery business.

To illustrate to the world that a Jew could be interested in agricultural pursuits, Mr. Bush bought one hundred acres of land, which he named Bushberg. Here he planted grapes, establishing a large vineyard and grape nursery on the banks of the Mississippi, twenty-five miles south of St. Louis. Until his death in 1898, he not only produced many thousands of gallons of native wine annually, but he bought grape plantings from all over the world, giving his nurseries a worldwide reputation.

Passover Wine Sauce

This recipe comes from the private family collection of another wine family, the Sichels of New York. Serve with the *chremslach* (on the preceding page).

2 large eggs, separated

3 tablespoons sugar

Juice of 1 lemon

1 cup white wine

½ cup water

2 teaspoons potato starch

1. Mix the egg yolks, sugar, lemon juice, wine, and 1 cup of the water in a medium saucepan and cook over a low heat for 15 to 20 minutes, stirring constantly until it starts to thicken.

2. Mix the potato starch with the remaining half cup water until smooth. Add the wine mixture, beating well to avoid lumps. Boil only until thick, remove from the heat, and cool.

3. Beat the egg whites until stiff and fold into the wine mixture.

Yield: about 6 servings (P)

A Morganthau family gathering in New York

Apple-Cassis Compote in Meringue Shells

As strawberries became available year round, these apple-cassis or rhubarb-strawberry compotes went out of fashion as fillings for meringue shells. They are, however, still a pleasant dessert. The tart compote is a nice contrast to the sweet meringue shells. This comes from the Morgenthau family of New York.

COMPOTE

*12 Stayman or other good
    apples for sauce*

½ cup apple juice

Sugar to taste

*8 to 10 tablespoons cassis
    (black currant) preserves*

MERINGUE SHELLS

3 large egg whites

Dash of salt

¾ cup sugar

1 teaspoon lemon juice

½ teaspoon vanilla

1. To make the compote, peel and core the apples and cut into chunks. Place in a large pot with the apple juice and heat. Simmer, covered, about 20 minutes or until the apples are chunky and soft. Taste and add sugar as needed. (You want this to be tart.)

2. Add 2 tablespoons of cassis preserves per cup of applesauce. Adjust the cassis to the sweetness of the apples.

3. To make the meringue shells, beat the egg whites with a dash of salt on the high speed of an electric mixer just until soft peaks form. Gradually beat in the sugar, ¼ cup at a time, beating well after each addition. Beat in the lemon juice and vanilla. Continue beating 12 minutes longer. The meringue batter should be very thick.

4. With an ice cream scoop or a large spoon, drop mounds of the meringue on a greased cookie sheet, keeping each ball smooth. Make a deep pocket in the center of each by twirling the back of a teaspoon around. Bake in a preheated 200-degree oven for 1 hour. Turn the oven off and leave the meringues for another half hour. Cool and fill them with about ½ cup compote per meringue.

Yield: 8 shells and about 4 cups apple-cassis compote (P)

The Flavor and Aroma of Strawberries Recall Childhood Tastes and Passover Seders

Sometimes, when I am not trying to remember at all, I am more fortunate in extracting the flavors of past feasts from my plain American viands. I was eating strawberries the other day, ripe, red American strawberries. Suddenly I experienced the very flavor and aroma of some strawberries I ate perhaps twenty years ago. I started as from a shock, and then sat still for I do not know how long, breathless with amazement. In the brief interval of a gustatory perception I became a child again, and I positively ached with the pain of being so suddenly compressed to that small being. I wandered about Polotzk once more, with large, questioning eyes; I rode the Atlantic in an emigrant ship; I took possession of the New World, my ears growing accustomed to a new language; I sat at the feet of renowned professors, til; my eyes contracted in dreaming over what they taught; and there I was again, an American among Americans, suddenly made aware of all that I had been, all that I had become—suddenly illuminated, inspired by a complete vision of myself, a daughter of Israel and a child of the universe, that taught me more of the history of my race than ever my learned teachers could understand. . . . All this came to me in that instant of tasting, all from the flavor of ripe strawberries in my tongue.

Mary Antin, *The Promised Land,* 1912

The first strawberries in Jewish homes were eaten at Passover seders as soon as the refrigerated railroad cars brought them there. Later they were used for fund-raisers at places like the forerunner of the 92nd Street Y in New York. Some ultra-Orthodox peel their strawberries at Passover as they do other fruit lest any *hometz* food or product may have touched the berries.

Strawberry Sponge Cake

To this day a typical American-Jewish Passover dessert is a *schaum torte* or meringue torte filled with strawberries. The Passover menu of the venerable *Settlement Cook Book* includes a recipe for a *schaum torte* with whipped cream. No matter that it was a meat meal. Another typical recipe was a sponge cake with strawberries, creating a Passover strawberry shortcake. The following recipe came from the late Beatrice Lopoo Nathanson of Natchez, Mississippi, and, I believe, was adapted from the *Settlement Cook Book*.

8 large eggs, separated

1½ cups sugar

1 cup sifted matzah cake meal

Pinch of salt

½ lemon, grated rind and juice

Matzah flour for dusting

3 cups whipping cream

4 pints strawberries

1. Beat the egg yolks until light. Add the sugar and beat again.
2. Add the matzah meal, a pinch of salt, and grated rind and juice of the lemon.
3. Beat the whites until stiff but not too dry. Fold into the batter. Place in 2 greased 9-inch pans floured with matzah flour.
4. Bake in a preheated 350-degree oven for 45 minutes. Set on a rack and cool. Remove the cakes from the pans.
5. Whip the cream until thick, cut half the strawberries in quarters, and fold into half the whipped cream. Spread this filling between the 2 layers of the cake.
6. Spread the remaining whipped cream over the top and side of the cake. Decorate with the reserved whole strawberries.

Yield: 8 servings (D)

Modern update: Tragara Restaurant in Bethesda, Maryland, macerates the strawberries in Sabra liqueur and sugar before adding. It also uses basically the same cake recipe and bakes it in a jelly-roll pan lined with parchment paper for about 15 minutes in a 400-degree oven. When cool, fill it with strawberries and whipped cream, and then roll.

Frozen Strawberry Meringue Torte

This is a cake that is easy to make, perfect for those watching their cholesterol, and gets rave reviews. Make sure you serve it with the sauce. Judy Wohlberg, the wife of our rabbi, shared the recipe with me.

CRUST

1½ cups crushed almond or
    coconut macaroons
2 tablespoons unsalted butter
    or margarine, melted
½ cup finely chopped nuts,
    such as pecans or walnuts
½ cup sugar

FILLING

2 large egg whites, at room
    temperature
1 cup sugar
2 cups sliced strawberries
1 tablespoon lemon juice
1 teaspoon vanilla extract

SAUCE

10-ounce package frozen sliced
    strawberries
2 tablespoons orange
    marmalade
1 tablespoon currant jelly
1 cup sliced strawberries

1. Process the macaroons and the butter or margarine until coarsely ground in a food processor with a metal blade. Add the nuts and ½ cup of the sugar and process until the mixture begins to hold together. Press into the bottom of a 10- by 3-inch springform pan. Bake in a preheated 350-degree oven for 7 to 10 minutes or until golden. Cool.

2. To make the filling, put the egg whites, sugar, fresh strawberries, lemon juice, and vanilla into the large bowl of an electric mixer. Beat on low speed to blend. Increase to high speed and continue until stiff peaks form when the beaters are withdrawn. Pour into the cooled crust. Cover and freeze until very firm, a minimum of 6 hours. (It may be frozen for 3 weeks.) Serve the torte directly from the freezer as it will not become totally solid.

3. To make the strawberry sauce, slightly defrost the strawberries. Puree the strawberries and the marmalade in a food processor. Mix in the currant jelly. Remove to a bowl and stir in the sliced strawberries. Serve cold. (The sauce may be refrigerated overnight.) Cut the torte in wedges.

Yield: 12 servings (P)

Absolutely Easy and Absolutely Delicious Chocolate Torte

Our whole life revolved around the kitchen. I stayed very close to my parents because my father did his broadcasts from home. A lot of important people came to the house for meals, sometimes for the seder—Winston Churchill, Franklin Delano Roosevelt, J. Edgar Hoover. Everything revolved around eating and cooking. The national news was going on in the house. Our seder was always very proper and very official. One of the desserts was the Queen Mother's Cake. I can't tell you how many people have used that for the seder. I guess it is the official seder dessert. I have used it in two of my books.

Interview with Maida Heatter

Another chocolate torte, as easy as Maida Heatter's, comes from Claudine Ostrow, an Egyptian Jew, living in Chevy Chase, Maryland, who learned it from an Italian chef in Italy. It is delicious!

1 stick (¹/₂ cup) unsalted butter or margarine

8 ounces imported bittersweet chocolate

5 large eggs, separated

³/₄ cup sugar

1 cup ground almonds

TOPPING

Confectioners' sugar or ¹/₄ cup granulated sugar mixed with ¹/₄ teaspoon potato starch

1. Melt the butter or margarine with the chocolate in the top of a double boiler. Cool.
2. Beat the egg yolks with ³/₄ cup of the sugar until they become pale yellow.
3. Mix the cooled butter or margarine and chocolate with the sugar and yolks. Add the nuts.
4. Beat the egg whites until they are stiff but not dry. Fold into the chocolate mixture.
5. Place a pan of water on the bottom shelf of a preheated 375-degree oven. (This makes the torte moister.)
6. Line the bottom and side of a greased 9-inch springform pan with aluminum foil and pour in the filling. Bake for 45 to 50 minutes. Remove from the oven and let sit a few minutes in the pan. Unmold and carefully peel off the foil and place on a plate upside down.
7. Sprinkle with confectioners' sugar during the year and with the ¹/₄ cup granulated sugar ground in a food processor for Passover. (Confectioners' sugar, which contains cornstarch, is not kosher for Passover.)

Yield: 1 torte (D) or (P)

Hungarian Hazelnut Torte

To learn how to prepare some new Passover recipes, Congregation Adath Israel in Riverdale, New York, invited Andre Balog to cook for them. "The younger members wanted to learn new recipes," said Marjory Tolub, one of the organizers. "We also wanted to expose some of the older members to new lighter cooking with a French flavor."

The Hungarian flourless hazelnut torte that he learned from his own grandmother won the older women's approval. "They couldn't get over how light this flourless torte was," said Mr. Balog, a Hungarian-born cooking teacher at the 92nd Street Y.

TORTE

8 large eggs, separated

½ cup sugar

¼ cup orange juice

4 heaping tablespoons matzah meal

4 heaping tablespoons ground hazelnuts

FILLING AND ICING

¾ cup sugar

⅓ cup water

8 egg yolks

2 sticks (1 cup) unsalted butter or pareve margarine, softened

½ cup ground toasted hazelnuts

12 whole, shelled hazelnuts

1. Blend the egg yolks and sugar with an electric mixer until they are smooth in texture and creamy yellow in color. Whisk in the orange juice, the matzah meal, and the ground hazelnuts. Set aside.

2. Whip the egg whites until they are quite firm, then fold into the yolk mixture.

3. Turn into a well-greased 9-inch springform pan and bake in a preheated 350-degree oven for 35 minutes. Cool in the pan.

4. Meanwhile, prepare the icing and filling. Boil the sugar in the water until it is dissolved. Continue boiling slowly over a low heat. Test the thickness of the syrup by dropping a small drop into a glass of cold water. If it holds its shape, it is okay.

5. Beat the egg yolks at medium speed in a bowl and add the boiling sugar syrup, a little at a time, to the yolks while continuing to beat for about 3 or 4 minutes, until light yellow. Beat for 2 or 3 more minutes, until the blend cools. Add the butter or margarine and continue beating at low speed for 5 more minutes. Add the ground hazelnuts.

6. When the baked cake is completely cool, slice it into 2 or 3 layers. Spread each layer evenly with the hazelnut cream as well as the top and the side.

7. Decorate the top with the whole hazelnuts.

Yield: 10 servings (P) or (D)
Note: For a more nouvelle presentation, use a larger springform; for a more traditional, taller layer cake, use a smaller one.

Café Crocodile's Orange Almond Fig Cake

Andree Levy Abramoff, chef owner of Café Crocodile, a tiny Mediterranean restaurant on New York's East Side, kindly shared this orange almond fig cake that she learned from her Greek grandmother. She has added her own touch, by enriching the orange syrup with butter, and she serves it at the restaurant the first and second nights of Passover.

CAKE

10 large eggs, separated

1 cup sugar

1½ cups matzah cake meal

1 teaspoon cinnamon

Zest of 1 orange

⅓ cup orange juice

½ teaspoon allspice

1 cup chopped almonds

10 dried calimyrna figs, chopped up

ORANGE SYRUP

¾ cup brown sugar

½ cup orange juice

1 stick (½ cup) unsalted butter or margarine

Orange slices for garnish

1. Beat the yolks with the sugar until lemony. Add the cake meal, cinnamon, orange zest and juice, allspice, and almonds.

2. Beat the egg whites until stiff peaks form and mix together with the figs. Fold into the yolk mixture.

3. Grease a 10-inch tube pan with oil and pour the batter into the pan. Bake in a preheated 350-degree oven for 50 minutes.

4. Unmold the cake and let it cool. Serve as is or with the orange syrup.

5. To make the syrup, mix the brown sugar and orange juice in a saucepan. Bring to a boil. Add the butter and let melt.

6. When you serve the cake, pour the syrup on each slice and garnish with orange slices.

Yield: 1 cake (P) or (D)

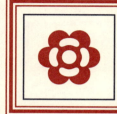 # New Recipes

Collected during the filming of
Jewish Cooking in America with Joan Nathan

All other recipes demonstrated in the series
can be found within the main section of the book.

Turkish Pickled Fish

Known as *garato,* this recipe for lime-cured Sabbath fish was brought to the United States by Turkish Jews. Jenny Sarajevo Edelstein, whose family came to Havana and then to Miami from Istanbul, showed me how she makes it by salting and weighing down tuna, kingfish, bonito, or Spanish mackerel steaks. In Istanbul, Jenny's relatives go to the fish wharf and buy live fish, which they kill and then cure. They then serve this as one of many appetizers on the Sabbath.

*2 pounds tuna, kingfish,
    bonito, or Spanish mackerel,
    cut into about 6 steaks,
    1 inch thick, skin removed*

2 tablespoons salt

1 tablespoon sugar

*1 cup olive oil or enough to
    cover the fish*

Juice of 4 or 5 lemons or limes

*1 large Spanish onion, peeled
    and chopped fine*

*3 tablespoons parsley or
    cilantro, chopped*

1. Sprinkle both sides of the fish steaks generously with salt and the sugar. Place the fish close together in a 9×13-inch plastic pan, making a second layer if needed. Cover the pan tightly with plastic wrap. Place a heavy object, such as a brick, over the fish to weigh it down. Refrigerate the fish for at least 2 days.

2. Rinse off the salt and sugar. Remove all the bones and cut the fish into 1-inch pieces. Place the fish in a bowl and cover with the olive oil. Refrigerate overnight.

3. The next day, drain the oil and pour the lemon or lime juice over the fish. Sprinkle with the onion and then the parsley or cilantro. Serve with toothpicks.

Yield: 8 to 10 servings (P)

Jean Louis Palladin's Smoked Salmon Roll-ups

12 thin slices smoked salmon,
each about 4 inches long
½ pound soft goat cheese
2 tablespoons walnuts, finely
chopped
1 tablespoon chives, chopped
1 cup dill, chopped
1 cup heavy cream or more
Salt and freshly ground pepper
to taste

1. Overlap 3 slices of the salmon lengthwise on a piece of plastic wrap. Then overlap 3 more slices to form an 8-inch-long piece.

2. Put the cheese, walnuts, chives, and 1 tablespoon of the chopped dill in a mixing bowl and mash until well blended, adding a little of the cream if the mixture is too thick. Take half of the cheese and place lengthwise down the salmon on one side. Roll up carefully, close the top ends like a sausage, and wrap the sheet of plastic around the outside. Repeat with the remaining salmon slices and filling. Refrigerate several hours or overnight.

3. When ready to serve, remove the plastic wrap and cut through with a knife at 2-inch intervals. Place 2 pieces open-side-down on a plate and serve with a splash of the dill sauce.

4. To make the dill sauce, bring the remaining cream to a boil in a saucepan. Place the remaining dill in a blender with a few tablespoons of the boiled cream and pulverize. Add the salt and pepper to taste and enough more cream if necessary to make a thin sauce.

Yield: 8 salmon roll-ups or 4 servings as an appetizer (D)

Grilled Eggplant, Pepper, and Tomato Salad

Cookbook author Steve Raichlen has embraced grilling as a way of life at his home in Coconut Grove, Florida. A Jewish cab driver from Gaziantep in southern Turkey taught him the following recipe. Like many Middle Eastern salads, it is best prepared a day or so in advance.

1 medium eggplant (about
  1 pound)
1 large green bell pepper
1 large red bell pepper
4 to 5 plum tomatoes (about
  1 pound)
1 medium onion, chopped fine
  (about ½ cup)
2 cloves garlic, minced
3 tablespoons extra-virgin
  olive oil
2 tablespoons wine vinegar,
  or to taste
½ cup flatleaf parsley, coarsely
  chopped
Salt and freshly ground pepper

1. Preheat the grill to high. Grill the eggplant whole, until very soft and charred all over, using tongs to turn it. The skin should be completely black. Grilling will take 20 to 30 minutes. Char the peppers in the same way, about 10 to 15 minutes, then the tomatoes about 5 minutes. Cook the tomatoes just enough to blister the skins, but not so much that they become soft (the centers should remain firm). Transfer the charred vegetables to a plate to cool.

2. Scrape the charred skin off the eggplant, peppers, and tomatoes with a paring knife. Core and seed the pepper. Dice the vegetables into 1-inch cubes and transfer to a mixing bowl. Stir in the onion, garlic, oil, vinegar, half the parsley, salt and pepper. Just before serving, taste and correct the seasoning. Sprinkle the remaining parsley on top. Serve with grilled pita bread chips.

Yield: 4 to 6 servings (P)

An Ancient Bread from Uzbekistan to Queens

In parts of Queens, New York, the flavor of Judaism has nothing to do with traditional breads like challah or pastries like rugelach. Instead, it has a Moslem touch to it—a reflection of life in the former Soviet Republic of Uzbekistan, where Moslems and Jews have shared the same cuisine for eons.

No Jewish holiday in Uzbekistan, for instance, goes by without the large round of soft, chewy bread that is a cross between pizza and bialy. And in the kosher Uzbekistan Tandoori Bread Bakery in Kew Gardens, owned by Isak Barayev, the ovens—tended by Moslem bakers—are fired up nowadays to turn out these breads, the *lepeshka* of Mr. Barayev's childhood.

When he arrived from Tashkent in 1989, the forty-seven-year-old Mr. Barayev recalls, he found to his disappointment that there was no *lepeshka* anywhere. In 1995 he remedied that. Armed with his green card and a thousand dollars, he flew home, bought two clay tandoori ovens and air-freighted them to Kennedy Airport. Then he installed them in a converted ceramic studio in Kew Gardens at 120-35 83rd Avenue and, in 1996, opened the first kosher bakery to produce the Uzbek specialty.

Word spread quickly through the circle of Uzbek limo drivers who, between rides, double park outside the bakery and rush in to grab a taste of Tashkent.

The bread, first cousin of the biblical flat breads baked on a disk over an open fire, is perhaps as old as the Jewish lineage in Central Asia—2,500 years. The ancestors of the Jews in that region were Babylonians who migrated eastward after the conquest of Jerusalem by the Romans. A later wave came from Persia, trekking to this Silk Road junction between Persia and China, perhaps with the conqueror Genghis Khan. Of the 200,000 Bukharan Jews in the world today, the great majority live in Israel, with only 15,000 still in Central Asia and at least 30,000 in Queens.

"We are called 'Bukharan Jews' because for many centuries Bukhara was the city where our ancestors lived," said Rabbi Itzhak Yehoshoua, chief rabbi of the Bukharan Jews in New York. "And our Judaic language, called Bukharan, is similar to Farsi."

The dough for the *lepeshka*—made from flour, yeast, salt, and water—is stretched into rounds and then the center is pressed with a heavy metal stamp called a *chikech* (the best common approximation of a *chikech* is the "frog" that flower arrangers place in the bottom of a vase to secure the stems). Sprinkled with black and white sesame seeds, the dough is then slapped onto the sides of the clay oven with the help of a large pillowlike potholder. Ten minutes later, the bakers, holding a long stick with a round metal netlike bowl at the end, knock the baked bread off the wall of the oven and into the bowl.

To accompany the bread, the Tandoori Bakery, which has six tables for customers, serves a fragrant vegetable, meat, and spice-infused soup called *lagman* or a tricornered pastry, called a *somsa,* stuffed with potatoes, pumpkin, broccoli, diced beef, or lamb and flavored with cumin and cardamom. Sour salads are accompanied by bottled vinegar in a used cognac bottle, seasoned with hot pepper, garlic, dill, and carrots along with spices brought from Uzbekistan. This condiment reminds the diner of the link to China. Especially for holidays, there is a pilaf called *birched,* a fragrant rice dish flecked with *caloundra* and dill, steamed in a cotton sack so that each kernel of rice remains separate. Sweets served include *halvah,* the candy made from ground sesame seeds and oil, *koulcha,* a sweet yeast cookie, or the everyday *lepeshka* dipped into Marshmallow Fluff and eaten with a glass of Russian tea drunk in Chinese teacups.

As if the experience weren't already authentic enough, Mr. Barayev is likely to don his antique silk robes—a reminder of the Silk Route—play the Turkish guitar, called a *saz,* and sing the monotonic melodies that Bukharan Jews claim originated in the first Temple in Jerusalem. A regular fixture at his bakery, Mr. Barayev plays for customers whenever requested. "Like the bread," he said, "this music is in my soul."

Bukharan Flat Bread *(Lepeshka)*

After I tasted *lepeshka* at a stall at the Carmel Market of Tel Aviv, I asked the baker if a similar bakery existed in the United States. He sent me to a limo driver in Queens named Uri, who directed me to the Uzbekistan Tandoori Bakery. There Charlie Pinsky, my television producer, and I met the Barayev family and the authentic Moslem bakers who, for generations, have been crafting this bread in Tashkent. Although these expert bakers tend to bring their own secret nuances to each production, a fair adaptation of the *lepeshka* can be turned out at home in a conventional oven.

2½ cups lukewarm water

1 package or 1 scant
    tablespoon active dry yeast

2 teaspoons sugar

1 tablespoon salt or to taste

6½ to 7 cups high gluten* or
    bread flour

2 teaspoons white sesame seeds

2 teaspoons black sesame seeds

Ice cubes

*High gluten flour is available at specialty stores. It has even more protein, and, therefore, more gluten than bread flour.

1. In a large bowl or the bowl of a mixer equipped with a dough hook, mix the water, the yeast, and the sugar. Gradually add the salt and 5 cups of the flour, 1 cup at a time, mixing well after each addition.

2. Knead by hand or with a dough hook until the dough is smooth and elastic, adding enough of the remaining flour to prevent sticking.

3. Shape the dough into a ball, and place in a greased bowl, turning to coat. Cover with plastic wrap, and let rise in a warm room until doubled in bulk, at least 1½ hours.

4. Divide the dough into 4 pieces, and shape each piece into a ball. On a floured surface, roll out each ball into a round about 8 inches in diameter. Using a pastry brush, brush each round with cold water. Cover with a towel, and let stand for 30 minutes.

5. Preheat the oven to 500 degrees and place 2 heavy baking sheets in the oven for 10 minutes.

6. Brush the dough with a little oil. Using the heel of your hand, press the dough down in the center, then prick with the tines of a fork to make a design (a flower-arranging frog is perfect for this). Brush the dough with water and then sprinkle each round with the white and black sesame seeds.

7. Remove the baking sheets from the oven. Carefully place 2 rounds on each, leaving space between, and sprinkle lightly with cold water. Bake one sheet at a time on the lowest rack of the oven, and just before you shut the door, put a few ice cubes in a pan on the oven floor to create more steam. Bake until the breads are golden,

12 to 15 minutes. Remove from the oven. Let the loaves rest 10 minutes. Repeat with the second baking sheet. Eat immediately, if possible.

Yield: 4 loaves (P)

Jewish Corn Rye

"Benny Moskovitz is the genuine article," Congressman Sander Levin of Michigan told me. And he is. Mr. Moskovitz, baker and owner of Star Bakery in Oak Park, Michigan, makes all the traditional desserts of my childhood—seven-layer cakes, corn rye, chocolate *babka,* and a thin sugar coated cookie called a *kichel.* Before we filmed at his bakery, I hoped that his personality would shine through on camera. I had already seen that television lights and cameras can be so daunting that many people seem to freeze. Not Mr. Moskovitz. On camera he told me stories I had never heard before. One touched me deeply. He remembered as a boy in Apsha, Czechoslovakia, that his mother started making bread late at night and worked all night long. "She mixed the dough at eleven p.m. and let it rise under the goose-feather quilt on my bed," he said, smiling broadly, and his eyes sparkling behind his owl-shaped eyeglasses. Mr. Moskovitz does not stay up all night making bread for his three traditional Jewish bakeries, but he does start at 5:00 a.m. and works until 5:00 p.m. every day, preserving Old World recipes like the following corn bread, which has also appeared in my *Jewish Holiday Baker* (Schocken).

A Jewish corn bread is very heavy and sour. Grain, *kern* in German and Yiddish, became translated into corn in this country.

3 cups rye sour starter (see page 434)

7 cups bread flour

2¼ cups water

1 teaspoon active dry yeast

1½ tablespoons salt

2 tablespoons caraway seed

5 ice cubes

Cornmeal for dusting

1. Place the sour starter in a large mixing bowl. Add 1¾ cups of the bread flour and ½ cup of the water to keep it wet. Mix and stir down the sides to keep them clean. Cover loosely with plastic wrap and let the mixture sit for 1 hour.

2. Scoop the mixture into the bowl of an electric mixer fitted with the dough hook. Sprinkle the yeast with the remaining 1¾ cups water into the bowl. Then gradually add the remaining flour and the salt as you knead the dough at medium speed, about 5 minutes. If the dough is too stiff, add water. When the dough no longer sticks to the mixer, it is ready. Remove the dough, pat it into a round, and let it rise on a floured work surface for 20 minutes, uncovered.

3. Punch the dough down, and divide it in half. Add caraway seeds to one half, and form both into balls or oblongs. Let them rise 1 more hour on a cookie sheet dusted with flour.

4. Preheat the oven to 400 degrees. You will know when the dough is ready to bake because its texture softens— it becomes soft like a balloon, and when you push on it with your finger, it springs back and does not leave a mark. Slash the loaves ⅛-inch deep a few times with a straight razor or a very sharp knife. Put 5 ice cubes in a pan on the floor of the oven. Before you put the loaves in the oven, brush them with water.

5. Bake the loaves on the middle rack of the oven for 40 to 50 minutes, or until they sound hollow when you tap them on the top. When you remove the loaves, brush with water, or, if you want a shinier loaf, brush with ½ cup water and ½ teaspoon of cornstarch.

Yield: 2 2½-pound loaves (P)

Michael London's Sour Starter and Pumpernickel

Michael London, Brooklyn-born baker extraordinaire, shared with me many old-time bakers' tricks. He told me that the dark color of pumpernickel in the old days came from burned sugar. Today most bakers use caramel coloring. He also related how, on New York's Lower East Side, Jewish bakers left their moistened day-old bread in pickle barrels covered with cheesecloth and their sours in wooden proofing trays. In those days it was against the law to use old soaked ryes because the mash molds so easily. Young children used to sit on top of the pickle barrels and make noise to distract the health inspectors when they came into the stores. Here is Michael London's sour and his pumpernickel bread with the mash, which he makes at Rock Hill Bakehouse near Saratoga Springs, New York, and which he shared with me for *The Jewish Holiday Baker.*

SOUR

2 medium onions, coarsely
chopped

1 tablespoon caraway seeds

1 scant tablespoon (1 package)
active dry yeast*

4 cups water

5 cups medium rye flour†, plus
1 tablespoon for sprinkling

1. Tie the onion and caraway seeds in a knotted cheesecloth bag.

2. Dissolve the yeast in 3½ cups of the water in a small bowl and pour it over 4 cups of the flour in a large bowl. Stir to mix until it attains the consistency of wet cement. Submerge the cheesecloth bag of chopped onions and caraway seeds down into the center of what will become "the sour." Sprinkle the tablespoon of rye flour over the surface. Cover loosely with plastic wrap and set aside overnight, unrefrigerated. The sour needs air to breathe, but not too much, or it will dry out.

3. The next day, remove the onion-caraway bag and discard. The sour should smell somewhat acidic but not rotten after about 15 hours. At this point, feed it (mix it) with the remaining 1 cup flour and ½ cup water, or enough to maintain the thick consistency. Cover again and let the sour sit until the area between "cracks" in the dough spreads. You want to capture as much of its strength as possible.

4. After it rises again, in about 4 hours, you will have about 6 cups. You can begin to use it or continue to build it up (which increases the amount of sour). Use it in the bread now or refrigerate it. You should feed the sour once every 24 hours with at least 1 cup flour and ½ cup water. The sour can stay several days in the refrigerator without being fed, but, as Michael says, never take a sour for granted. It needs to be nourished.

Yield: 6 cups sour (P)

B R E A D

5 slices day-old rye bread,
   crusts removed (about 2½
   cups)

3 cups water

2 cups sour

4 teaspoons blackstrap
   molasses or caramel coloring

2 tablespoons sea salt

2 tablespoons caraway seeds,
   coarsely ground (optional)

1 cup cracked rye or
   pumpernickel flour,[†] plus
   additional for sprinkling

8 cups good bread flour, plus
   additional as needed

1 scant tablespoon (1 package)
   active dry yeast*

4 tablespoons raisins

6 ice cubes

*Although Michael never uses dry yeast, I have used that instead of his wet yeast.

[†]Available at many supermarkets or by mail order from King Arthur Flour's *Baker's Catalogue*

1. In a bowl, crumble the day-old rye bread into 1 cup of the water until the water is absorbed. Crumble it up with your hands; this is what the old-time bakers did. It carries the character of yesterday's bread to today. Remove excess water.

2. In the bowl of an electric mixer fitted with the dough hook, put the rye bread mixture, the remaining 2 cups water, 2 cups of the sour, and the molasses or caramel color. Stir together at low speed until mixed, about 1 minute.

3. Add the sea salt and caraway seeds. Gradually add the cracked rye or pumpernickel flour and the bread flour. Sprinkle the yeast in and stir about 5 minutes, until well incorporated, scraping down the sides of the bowl. Knead by hand for a few minutes, incorporating the raisins into the dough. Place in a greased bowl, brush with oil, and cover, letting the dough rise 1 to 1½ hours, until doubled in volume.

4. Punch the dough down, and if it is still sticky, incorporate more flour as needed. Divide the dough in half, gently form 2 flattened round or oblong loaves, brush with oil, and let them rest 10 to 15 minutes on a floured work surface. Remove the loaves to a cornmeal-dusted cookie sheet, cover very loosely with plastic wrap, and let them rise for another 40 minutes, until doubled in bulk.

5. Preheat the oven to 400 degrees, set a rack in the middle, and put 6 ice cubes in a pan on the floor of the oven.

6. Since rye and pumpernickel love steam, brush or spray the loaves with water. Sprinkle some of the rye flour on top and then, with a single-edged razor or very sharp knife, make 5 cuts in each loaf, shorter ones on the outside, longer in the center. Bake the loaves for 45 to 50 minutes, or until they sound hollow when tapped with a spatula. To keep a shine, brush them afterward with water.

Yield: 2 2½-pound loaves (P)

Cold Transylvanian Cherry Soup

Adam Tihany, the designer-architect who is responsible for the twenty-first-century look of the interiors of so many of America's restaurants, including Boston's Biba, New York's Le Cirque 2000, and most of Wolfgang Puck's Spago restaurants, comes from a Transylvanian Jewish background. His proud mother, Judith, a survivor of the Holocaust who lives in Jerusalem, visits frequently, making the food of his childhood, such as this recipe for sour-cherry soup which, like so many Transylvanian dishes, is half Rumanian and half Hungarian.

2 pounds fresh sour cherries, pitted

2 cinnamon sticks

1 tablespoon all-purpose flour

2 cups natural sour-cherry juice

1 cup sugar, or to taste

1 cup sour cream

1. Cover the cherries with cold water in a saucepan and bring to a boil. Add the cinnamon sticks and simmer about 5 to 10 minutes, until the cherries are soft, but not mushy. Then cool.

2. In a separate saucepan stir the flour into 1 cup of the sour cherry juice, and slowly add a cup of water from the boiled cherries. Bring to a boil, stirring constantly. Remove from the stove and add a second cup of sour cherry juice. Add the cherries and sugar to taste, stirring until the sugar is dissolved. Cool the syrup, remove the cinnamon sticks, and add the sour cream before serving.

Yield: 6 to 8 servings (D)

Milky Way's Lentil Soup with Egg Dumplings

Leah Adler, Steven Spielberg's mom, makes this vegetarian lentil soup at Milky Way, her kosher dairy restaurant in Los Angeles. It is her famous son's favorite item on the menu. "I started the restaurant on a dare in 1977," said Mrs. Adler. "My late husband and I had just become kosher. Today the restaurant gives me a world to inhabit. I am always here by choice. My kids come in and out by chance." What makes this lentil soup different from others is the addition of the egg dumplings, which she spoons into the simmering soup just before serving. I have added herbs as well.

1 large onion, diced

1 stalk celery, diced

4 cloves garlic, minced

2 cups lentils

8 cups water

Salt and white pepper to taste

1 bay leaf (optional)

½ teaspoon thyme (optional)

*1 tablespoon chopped chives
  (optional)*

½ teaspoon oregano (optional)

*2 tablespoons chopped parsley
  (optional)*

2 large eggs

*8 tablespoons all-purpose flour
  (about)*

1. Put the onion, celery, garlic, and lentils in a 4-quart pot, along with the water. Bring to a boil, add salt and white pepper to taste, as well as the bay leaf, thyme, chives, oregano, and parsley.

2. Simmer, partially covered, for about 40 minutes or until the lentils are tender.

3. Just before serving, beat the eggs in a small bowl and slowly add the flour, continually beating with a whisk or spoon, until they reach the consistency of "soft bubble gum."

4. Using a teaspoon, scoop up a small amount of the batter and let it fall off the spoon into the simmering soup. Repeat until the batter is used up. Cover and simmer for a few minutes until the dumplings are puffed. To serve, ladle up the soup with a few dumplings in each bowl.

Yield: about 6 servings with 12 dumplings (P)

Lagman — *Uzbekistan Lamb, Carrot, and Noodle Soup*

This vegetable, meat, and spice-infused soup is first cousin to a meat borscht. It is clearly a Silk Route soup, with its dill and cilantro, but closer to Mongolia than Moscow, and it is traditionally served over homemade spaghetti, rather than a potato. I tasted it at Uzbekistan Tandoori Bread in Queens (see box on page 429) and at the Uzbekistan Restaurant in Los Angeles, also run by Uzbek Jews.

2 tablespoons vegetable oil

1 pound boneless lamb or beef shoulder, cut into ½-inch cubes

3 medium yellow onions, chopped

1 red pepper, diced

6 celery stalks, diced

3 cloves garlic, peeled and minced

8 cups water

2 large carrots, peeled and diced

1 cup fresh or canned (not drained) tomatoes, peeled, seeded, and chopped

1 tablespoon tomato paste

½ teaspoon ground cumin

½ teaspoon cayenne pepper or to taste

Salt and ground pepper to taste

½ pound medium spaghetti

¼ cup fresh cilantro, chopped (for garnish)

¼ cup fresh dill, chopped (for garnish)

1. Heat the oil in a large heavy pot over medium heat. Add meat, brown on all sides, stirring occasionally. Remove with a slotted spoon, and set aside.

2. Add onions, and sauté until translucent, about 10 minutes. Add pepper, celery, and garlic, and sauté for 10 to 15 minutes.

3. Add 8 cups of water and bring to a boil. Return the meat to the pot and add the carrots, tomatoes, tomato paste, cumin, cayenne pepper, and salt and pepper to taste. Simmer for 20 minutes, covered. Skim off any fat that may accumulate.

4. Meanwhile, cook the spaghetti according to the package label.

5. When ready to serve, place a heaping portion of spaghetti into each of 6 serving bowls. Ladle soup over the top, and sprinkle liberally with the fresh cilantro and dill. Serve with Bukharan or other flat bread.

Yield: 6 to 8 servings (M)

Winter Borscht

When I was living in Jerusalem in the early seventies, winter borscht was just that, a hearty cabbage soup eaten during the cold months of December, January, and February. Barbara Kafka's version, which she learned to make from her father who came from Slutzk, one of the towns that disappeared in the Pale of Settlement, includes beets, tomatoes, and a subtle balance between sugar and red-wine vinegar. "My father remembered this borscht from Russia," said Barbara during a taping in her kitchen on New York's Upper East Side. "I tried to recreate it from the winter vegetables my father told me he remembered from his childhood."

This is one of my favorite Sunday-night-dinner dishes, served as a main course with a green salad and a rustic bread. When you try the recipe, taste the soup before adding more sugar as beets vary tremendously in sweetness.

2½ pounds short ribs, chuck, or beef shin with meat, cut across in 2-inch pieces

4 medium beets, scrubbed well and all but 2 inches of stem removed (about 2 pounds)

4 cups canned tomatoes (not plum tomatoes), lightly crushed, with their juice

4 large carrots, peeled and cut across into ½-inch rounds

1 medium onion, peeled and diced

1 medium red cabbage, cored and shredded (about 2 pounds)

8 medium cloves garlic, smashed, peeled, and diced

1 bay leaf

1 cup red wine vinegar

½ cup sugar or to taste

1. Place the beef in a saucepan and cover with water, about 10 cups. Bring to a boil. Skim off any foam and fat that rise to the surface. Lower the heat, and simmer gently for 90 minutes, uncovered. Strain through a fine-mesh sieve, and measure the liquid—there should be about 7 cups. Reserve the liquid and remove the meat. Cut into ½-inch cubes, discarding the bones.

2. While the meat is cooking, place the beets in a medium stockpot with enough water to cover. Bring to a boil. Lower the heat and simmer slowly for 20 minutes, uncovered, or until the tip of a knife easily pierces the beet. Remove the beets. Cool until easily handled, then peel and cut into large matchstick strips and set aside. Strain the cooking liquid from the beets through a coffee filter or fine sieve and reserve 5 cups.

3. Place the tomatoes, carrots, onion, cabbage, garlic, and bay leaf in the 7 cups of reserved liquid from cooking the meat. Bring to a boil. Lower the heat and simmer for 20 minutes, or until the carrots are almost tender.

4. Stir in the beets and simmer for 20 minutes more. Then add the 5 cups reserved beet liquid, the vinegar, sugar, salt and pepper to taste, the meat, and the 1 cup dill. Remove from the heat and allow the flavors to blend for 1 hour or overnight.

5. When ready to eat, remove the bay leaf and reheat the soup. To serve in a traditional manner, place 2 boiled

Winter Borscht, cont.

3 tablespoons kosher salt
   or to taste

Freshly ground pepper to taste

1 cup fresh dill, coarsely
   chopped, plus dill to
   garnish (about 2 bunches)

10 small potatoes, boiled,
   peeled, and cut in half

potato halves in each bowl. Ladle the soup over the potatoes and sprinkle each bowl with additional dill.

Yield: 8 to 10 servings (M)

Fish

Mark Russ Federman's Updated Herring in Parchment Paper

This is a modern twist on Mr. Si Goldman's Herring Fry (see pp. 145–6) using parchment paper instead of the Yiddish newspaper. "When you open the parchment paper and take a whiff it will bring you right back to your roots on the Lower East Side," said Mr. Federman, who has been filleting herring since he was a child. If you think the final result lacks color without printers' ink, use a lot of black pepper!

1 pure salt herring fillet

1 small onion, sliced in rounds

2 tablespoons olive oil

3 cloves allspice, crushed

2 tablespoons unsalted butter, cut in thin slices

2 small new potatoes, boiled, unpeeled, and sliced in 8 rounds

1. Soak the herring overnight in cold water, changing the water twice. Then cut crosswise into 6 pieces.

2. Preheat the oven to 400 degrees. Sauté the onion in the olive oil in a frying pan until golden. Add the allspice.

3. Cut the parchment paper into a circle about 12 inches in diameter. In a long line, adjacent to the diameter fold, layer half the butter. Place half the potatoes on top, then half the onions, and then the herring fillet pieces. Then repeat with the remaining potato, onion, and butter.

4. Fold across the diameter of the paper and make a tight seal, crimping the paper all around the folded edge.

5. Bake on a cookie sheet in the oven for 12 to 15 minutes. To be fancy, bring the fish, still wrapped in the parchment, to the table. Fragrant steam will rise when

you cut it open. To be less fancy, place the cooled herring on a bed of lettuce with some marinated beets.

Yield: 1 to 2 servings, depending on your appetite for herring! (D)

Horseradish-Crusted Bass with Borscht Broth

This cutting-edge fish recipe with playful Jewish accents comes from chef Ed Brown at the Sea Grill Restaurant in New York. It is perfect for the Sabbath-observant or anyone cooking for a dinner party. Because you cook the fish on one side ahead of time, you are technically warming the fish when you place it in the oven and therefore not cooking on the Sabbath. "To me, the tastes are a play on the traditional Eastern European flavors I grew up with in my family on the New Jersey Shore," said Ed.

BASS

6 6-ounce fillets striped bass, boneless and skinless

Salt and freshly ground pepper to taste

1 cup all-purpose flour

3 large eggs

1 cup horseradish root, peeled, grated coarsely lengthwise

2 cups fresh bread crumbs, or slightly crumbled matzah farfel (pulsed briefly in the food processor)

⅓ cup loosely packed flat parsley leaves, roughly chopped

2 tablespoons unsalted butter

2 tablespoons grapeseed or vegetable oil

1. Preheat the oven to 375 degrees and cover a cookie sheet or jelly-roll pan with aluminum foil.

2. Season the fish well with salt and pepper and dredge in the flour, removing any excess. Place the eggs in a flat soup bowl, beat well and then dip the fish fillets in the egg.

3. In a mixing bowl stir together the horseradish, fresh bread crumbs or the matzah farfel, along with the parsley. Remove the fillets from the egg and coat generously with this mixture, patting the fish so it adheres well.

4. In a large skillet over a medium-high heat, add 1 tablespoon of the butter and the oil. When the butter begins to brown, add 3 of the fish fillets, flesh side down first. After about 1½ minutes, or when golden, remove the fillets to the cookie sheet. Add the remaining tablespoon of butter and repeat the procedure with the remaining 3 fillets. You can do this ahead of time.

5. Bake in the oven for about 5 to 8 minutes or until cooked on the second side.

**BORSCHT BROTH
SAUCE**

2 medium beets (about 1
    pound)

3½ tablespoons unsalted butter

1 small white onion, peeled
    and diced

1 cup loosely packed white
    cabbage, shredded

1 tomato, cored, split, seeded,
    and chopped

½ cup dry white wine

1 sprig fresh thyme

1 bay leaf

2 cups fish stock

½ potato, unpeeled and diced

Salt and freshly ground pepper
    to taste

Juice of ½ lemon or to taste

¼ cup sour cream

1. Preheat the oven to 400 degrees and wrap the beets in aluminum foil. Roast for 1½ hours or until very tender. Cool slightly, scrape the peel off with a butter knife, and cut in large chunks.

2. In a medium, nonreactive saucepan melt 2 tablespoons of the butter over medium heat. Add the onion and the cabbage. Lower the heat, cover and sweat until tender, approximately 5 minutes.

3. Add the tomato, wine, thyme, and bay leaf. Simmer, uncovered, and reduce by half, about 5 minutes. Then add the fish stock, the beets, and the potato. Simmer, uncovered, until the potatoes are fully cooked, about 10 to 15 minutes. Remove the herbs and transfer the sauce to a blender. Puree until smooth, approximately 1 minute. Taste and then add the remaining 1½ tablespoon butter, salt, pepper, and lemon juice to taste and pulse for about 15 seconds.

4. At the last minute swirl in the sour cream, but do not incorporate fully. You want to see that swirl. Spoon a puddle of sauce in the center of the plate. Set 1 crusted fillet on top. Serve with horseradish mashed potatoes by adding some prepared horseradish and chopped dill to the mashed potato.

Yield: 6 servings (D)

Meat

Sukkot at the Steinbergs' in Highland Park, Illinois

For Miriam and Mort Steinberg of Highland Park, Illinois, Sukkot, the biblical fall-harvest festival, marking the first rains of the season, is a time to entertain friends and family. For a week they dine in their 15 × 23-foot Sukkah, the kind of hut in which the children of Israel dwelled for seven days "in order that your generations may know that I caused the children of Israel to dwell in tabernacles when I brought them out of the land of Egypt" (Leviticus 23:42–3). In 1982 Mort designed and built the collapsible structure. Its roof is covered with evergreens open to see the sky, according to the biblical injunction. Each year, the Sunday between Yom Kippur and Sukkot, the entire family gathers together to assemble the lattice walls of their hut. Outside, the Steinbergs arrange cornstalks; and inside, they decorate with strings of plastic apples, pears, peaches, and grapes, wooden cranberries, and walnuts—all reminders of the harvest period in ancient Israel.

At their synagogue, the Steinbergs hold the four species mentioned in the Bible: the palm, the myrtle, the willow, and the *etrog* (citron) representing "the fruit of a goodly tree." The *etrog,* according to Leviticus 23:40, must be in perfect condition. "In addition to being a time of thanksgiving for the produce that has been harvested," said Mort, "Sukkot is probably our most family-intensive festival. In our home, everyone gets involved in some aspect."

Miriam's Moussaka

In the kitchen, Miriam Steinberg prepares casserole dishes such as the stuffed cabbage on page 197 or the following moussaka, along with platters of cookies for dessert. "I usually don't like to use fake food in cooking and prefer to make recipes without substitutions," said Miriam, "but I like this moussaka dish so much that I don't mind using nondairy creamer for the sauce." In a kosher home, where milk is never mixed with meat, it was impossible to make a creamy moussaka until the first nondairy creamer was created in 1945. (See box, page 471.)

MEAT SAUCE

2 large onions, diced

1 clove garlic, minced

⅓ cup vegetable oil, plus extra to brush the eggplant

1 pound ground beef or lamb

1 15-ounce can tomato sauce

1 teaspoon chopped parsley

1 teaspoon salt

½ teaspoon oregano

½ teaspoon cinnamon

½ cup dried bread crumbs

2 medium eggplants (about 2 pounds)

TOPPING

4 tablespoons pareve margarine

¼ cup flour

1 teaspoon salt

¼ teaspoon pepper

3 cups nondairy creamer

4 large eggs or egg substitute

Oil for greasing

1. Preheat the oven to 350 degrees.

2. Sauté the onions and garlic in the oil until translucent, about 5 minutes. Add the meat, stirring to break it up, and cook until brown; drain off any excess fat.

3. Add the tomato sauce, parsley, salt, oregano, and cinnamon. Simmer for 30 minutes while proceeding with the recipe. Cool, stir in bread crumbs. Set aside.

4. Slice the eggplant into ½-inch-thick rounds. Brush both sides with oil. Broil for 2 minutes on each side or until golden.

5. Melt the margarine in a saucepan. Remove from the heat and stir in the flour, salt, and pepper. Gradually stir in the nondairy creamer.

6. Return to the heat and slowly bring to a boil, stirring constantly until the mixture thickens. Remove from the heat.

7. Beat the eggs in a small bowl. Beat about ¼ cup of the hot cream sauce into the eggs to warm them so they will not curdle by putting too much hot cream in at once. Slowly add the rest of the hot mixture. Then pour the egg-and-cream mixture back into the saucepan and stir. Cook for 1 minute over low heat. Remove from the heat.

8. Lightly grease a 9×13-inch shallow baking pan. Place half the eggplant slices in the bottom of the pan. Spoon the meat sauce over them. Top with a layer of eggplant and pour the cream sauce over the top. Bake for 1 hour. Let stand for 15 minutes before slicing and serving.

Yield: 10 to 12 (M)

Note: The moussaka may be made in advance and reheated, or frozen ahead. Bake for 90 minutes, uncovered, in a 350-degree oven.

Chicken Adobo with Mojo

Adobo is Cuba's national marinade, a tangy mixture of garlic, cumin, and sour orange juice beloved by Jews and non-Jews alike. (The sour orange is a citrus fruit that looks like an orange but tastes like a lime. If unavailable, use lime juice with a little fresh orange juice for sweetness.) Steve Raichlen sees this dish as a joining together of Cuba and the Columbus Exchange which, of course, included many Jewish crew members.

5 cloves garlic, minced

1/2 teaspoon salt

1/2 teaspoon ground cumin

1/2 teaspoon dried oregano

1/2 teaspoon dried thyme

3/4 cup fresh sour orange juice, or 1/2 cup fresh lime juice and 1/4 cup fresh orange juice

3 tablespoons extra-virgin olive oil

Salt and pepper to taste

2 large boneless, skinless chicken breasts, cut into halves

1/2 cup fresh cilantro or flat leaf parsley, chopped (for serving)

1. Using a mortar and pestle, mash the garlic, salt, cumin, oregano, and thyme into a paste. Slowly stir in the orange juice and the olive oil. Correct the seasoning, adding salt or pepper to taste. The mixture should be highly seasoned. If you don't have a mortar and pestle, puree the ingredients in a blender.

2. Transfer the marinade to a nonreactive baking dish and add the chicken breasts. Cover the dish and marinate the chicken for 1 hour in the refrigerator.

3. Preheat the grill to high.

4. Grill the chicken breasts over high heat until just cooked, about 3 minutes per side, basting with the marinade. Do not baste the last 2 minutes. Sprinkle the chicken breast with the chopped cilantro and serve with fried sweet plantains, black beans, and white rice. Spoon a little of the *mojo* over the chicken and serve the rest on the side for dipping.

Yield: 4 servings (M)

Mojo Sauce

Mojo—pronounced *moho*—is Cuba's national table sauce, a sort of garlicky vinaigrette. To be strictly authentic, you would use the acid juice of the sour orange. (See above.)

⅓ cup olive oil

6 to 8 cloves garlic, sliced thin or minced

⅔ cup fresh sour orange juice or ¼ cup lime juice and 2 tablespoons fresh orange juice

½ cup ground cumin

Salt and freshly ground pepper

1. Heat the olive oil in a saucepan over medium heat. Add the garlic and cook until fragrant and lightly toasted but not brown, about 20 seconds.

2. Add the orange juice, cumin, salt and pepper. Stand back. The sauce may sputter. Bring the sauce to a rolling boil. Correct the seasoning, adding more salt and pepper to taste.

Yield: 1 cup (P)

Ethiopian Spicy Chicken

I met Ethiopian-born Professor Ephraim Isaac many years ago when we were both studying at Harvard University. It was there that he introduced me to *doro wat* chicken, the spicy chicken stew that is usually eaten with *injera* (see page 98), the spongy bread that is the national food of Ethiopia. A linguist living in Princeton, New Jersey, Ephraim makes *wat* for each Shabbat from chicken, beef, or lentils or other legumes. "*Wat* is the name for a special Ethiopian hot sauce," he said. "What makes this version Jewish is the use of oil instead of *ghee* and the fact that we remove the blood by blanching the chicken in boiling water instead of salting and then soaking the meat in cold water." Although commercial ground spices are acceptable in this recipe, the most flavorful and truly authentic Ethiopian *wat* comes from using the freshest spices available and grinding them in a spice mill or mortar and pestle. Ephraim divides spices into three categories—the basic hot spices of peppers; ancient aromatic ones like cardamom, cinnamon, cumin, and coriander; and the medieval ginger, nutmeg, and turmeric. Except for the tomato paste and some of the more modern spices, this dish goes back hundreds, perhaps thousands of years. Who knows? The Queen of Sheba may have made *wat* for King Solomon when she visited him in his Temple in Jerusalem.

Ethiopian Spicy Chicken, cont.

1/3 cup vegetable oil

3 large Spanish onions, diced

1 head garlic, peeled and
   chopped

1 whole chicken, cleaned and
   cut into at least 8 pieces

1 tablespoon salt or to taste

2 cups water

2 to 3 dried red chili peppers
   with the seeds, ground
   (about 1 tablespoon ground
   red pepper)

1 tablespoon freshly ground
   black pepper

1 teaspoon freshly ground
   cumin seeds

1 teaspoon freshly ground
   cinnamon bark

1 teaspoon freshly ground
   coriander

1 teaspoon freshly ground
   cardamom seeds

1 teaspoon freshly ground dry
   ginger root

1 teaspoon freshly ground
   nutmeg

1 teaspoon turmeric

2 to 3 tablespoons tomato paste

Juice of 1/2 lemon

1. Heat 1/4 cup of the vegetable oil in a frying pan and sauté the onions slowly with the garlic, stirring occasionally until the onions are golden brown, about 45 minutes.

2. In a soup pot, bring 3 quarts of water to a boil. Add the chicken pieces and blanch for about 2 minutes to eliminate the forbidden blood in the Jewish Ethiopian way. Using a slotted spoon, remove the chicken pieces from the pot and throw out the water. Sprinkle the chicken with salt and return to the pot with the sautéed onions and garlic. Add 2 cups of water and the remaining oil.

3. Grind all the spices into a mixing bowl and stir with a spoon until well blended. Sprinkle over the chicken in the pot and simmer gently, uncovered, for 30 minutes.

4. To subdue the peppery taste, add the tomato paste and the juice of 1/2 lemon. Simmer another 15 minutes or until the chicken is completely cooked. When ready to eat, place the *injera* on a plate and heap the chicken and the sauce in the center. You can also serve the chicken over rice.

Yield: 6 to 8 servings (M)

Grilled Quail with Poached Quinces

On a steamy hot day in July, while scouting for the television series, we visited Israeli caterer Hava Volman at her row house in Park Slope, Brooklyn. Hava and her Greek-Israeli painter husband Artemis Schwebel prepared a biblical barbecue for us near their one mulberry tree. Both my television producer Charlie Pinsky and I were elated by the flavors of their foods, which were presented on platters crafted by Hava during her other career as a ceramicist. The grilled quail with poached quinces, served over the Egyptian *frik* (a burnt wheat–like bulgur), is as biblical as a dish can be. Hava made the marinade which included a dry rub of *za'atar,* a spice combination of wild thyme, sesame seeds, and sumac, and her husband cooked the quails over an Argentinean grill that he designed and built himself. Hava has catered events for the Israeli Ambassador to the United Nations and the Israeli Consul General in New York. Since it is time consuming and, therefore, expensive to *kasher* a tiny quail, most *schochets* (ritual slaughterers) will not do it today. You must find an adventuresome kosher slaughterer to do this. Otherwise, you can use Cornish hens or even chicken and get great results with this recipe, which I think is one of the best dishes I have ever tasted.

2 tablespoons za'atar*
(approximately)
2 tablespoons sumac*
1 teaspoon cinnamon
1 tablespoon cumin
Salt and freshly ground pepper
to taste
8 quails or 2 Cornish hens,
butterflied, backbone
removed, and flattened
1½ cups dry red wine
1½ cups balsamic vinegar
1½ cups sugar or to taste
4 star anise

*Sumac and *za'atar,* the Middle Eastern spice combination (often made with hyssop, wild marjoram, sumac, and sesame seeds) are available in Middle Eastern grocery stores throughout the country.

1. Mix the *za'atar,* sumac, ½ teaspoon of the cinnamon, the cumin, and salt and pepper to taste and rub into the quail or Cornish hens. Let sit in a bowl, covered, in the refrigerator for about 8 hours or overnight.

2. In a small saucepan stir the red wine, balsamic vinegar, sugar, star anise, cinnamon sticks, cardamom seeds, cloves, black peppercorns, and lemon and orange zests. You may want to wrap the spices in cheesecloth (although Hava does not cover them because she likes to see "the beauty of the spices"). Bring to a boil and then simmer, uncovered, 15 minutes, until the sugar is dissolved and the liquid becomes slightly syrupy.

3. Cut the quinces, pears, or Asian pears in wedges. Add to the liquid and simmer, uncovered, for about 10 minutes or until the fruit is soft but not falling apart. Remove the fruit with a slotted spoon. Reduce the liquid to 2 cups and set aside for about 10 minutes.

4. To prepare the glaze, pour ½ cup of the poaching liquid, the date syrup, and the lemon juice into the bowl of a food processor, along with the chopped shallots, the remaining ½ teaspoon cinnamon, and salt and pepper to taste, and puree.

Grilled Quail with Poached Quinces, cont.

2 cinnamon sticks

1 tablespoon cardamom seeds

2 cloves

1 teaspoon black peppercorns

Zest of 1 lemon

Zest of 1 orange

5 quinces, 5 pears, or 4 Asian pears†

¼ cup halek date syrup‡

Juice of 1 lemon

2 tablespoons chopped shallots

†Since quinces are seasonal, Hava often substitutes Asian pears in this recipe.

‡See page 388 for a recipe for *halek.* This date syrup is also available in Middle Eastern grocery stores.

5. Preheat the grill to medium-high. It is very important to work fast when grilling. Otherwise, Hava says, "the bird will die twice." Broil the herb-encrusted quails breast-side-down for 3 to 4 minutes, then brush both sides with glaze and grill another 3 to 4 minutes on the other side or until cooked. You will need to cook Cornish hens about 7 minutes longer on each side, and chicken pieces 10 minutes longer, until the juices run clear at the leg joints.

6. Serve over *frik,* bulgur pilaf, or couscous, and garnish with the poached fruit.

Yield: 4 to 6 servings, with 2 quails or ½ Cornish hen per person (M)

Note: You can also bake the seasoned Cornish hens for a half hour in a preheated 400-degree oven. Then put the glaze on for 10 to 20 minutes more or until done.

Teheran Pomegranate and Walnut Stew with Chicken in Beverly Hills

When the Soofer family came to Los Angeles from Teheran in the late 1970s, they noticed that many of their compatriots were packing spices and herbs in their suitcases. "Why not import Iranian spices and herbs," they thought. Today their Sadaf, Inc., carries over one thousand items for the American market, including lemon pistachio nuts, garlic pickles, figs, orange blossoms, tarragon, Persian basil, shallots, and mint. The Soofers introduced us to one of their growers, a Moslem Iranian family farming in Oxnard, California. They grow cucumbers, fenugreek, and dill from seeds which they import from Israel or from roots originally brought to the United States by Jewish immigrants from Iran.

One of the dishes, definitely enhanced by Sadaf products, is *fesenjan,* which the Soofer family served us in their home in Beverly Hills. This version of pomegranate and walnut stew with duck or chicken, one of my favorite dishes in the whole world, is flavored with full-bodied pomegranate juice, golden prunes, and dates, all blended with walnuts. The recipe, handed down from generation to generation, is the jewel of Persian cooking. According to Najmieh Batmanglij, the queen of Persian cooking, in the north of Iran *fesenjan* traditionally included walnuts, apricots, and prunes as a sour agent, and in the south included pomegranates. She also said that the affinity between the pomegranate and the duck goes back to ancient Persia. Serve this sauce over *chelou,* the Persian rice on page 460, and enjoy. Instead of boiling the walnuts as Farideh Soofer does, Najmieh suggests just toasting them in a toaster oven until golden and then removing the skin.

2 pounds shelled walnuts

*1 8-ounce package golden prunes**

½ cup pitted dates

4 tablespoons vegetable oil (about)

2 large onions, sliced or chopped

Salt and freshly ground pepper to taste

4 whole boneless and skinless chicken breasts, cut into 2-inch cubes

4 cups pomegranate juice (or to taste)†

*Golden prunes are available at many Middle Eastern grocery stores or by mail order through Sadaf Company, Inc., Los Angeles, California 90058, 1-800-852-4050. If you can't find the golden variety, use regular prunes without pits.

†Some pomegranate juice is sweeter than others, so taste as you go along. If the sauce is too tart add a little sugar.

1. Process the walnuts in the food processor.

2. Remove the pits from the prunes and put them in a saucepan with 1½ cups of water to cover. Simmer, covered, about 10 minutes or until the prunes are softened. Puree the prunes and dates with their cooking water in a food processor.

3. Heat a 6-quart casserole with a cover, add the vegetable oil, and sauté the onions until golden brown. Remove from the pot and set aside.

4. Salt and pepper the diced chicken and brown in the oil remaining in the casserole. Drain on paper towels, removing any excess oil. Return the chicken to the casserole and add the onions, walnuts, prune-and-date mixture, pomegranate juice, and enough water to cover. Simmer, covered, for about 45 minutes, stirring occasionally, adding water if needed. Adjust seasonings and serve over rice.

Yield: 8 to 10 servings (M)

Chef Allen's Boniato Latke

Allen Susser, chef-owner of Chef Allen's in North Miami, uses *boniato,* a Cuban white sweet potato, to make a full-flavored and multitextured Caribbean latke in the same way that many of his Cuban Jewish customers use *boniato* in their potato kugels. Adding a little bit of orange zest and ginger to this recipe is an exciting update to an old standard. Allen serves it with a scallion sour cream.

½ large **boniato*** *or yam, peeled, about ¾ pound*

½ medium Spanish onion, peeled

2 large eggs

½ teaspoon grated orange zest

¼ teaspoon cumin

1 teaspoon kosher salt or to taste

Freshly ground black pepper to taste

¼ teaspoon ground ginger

2 tablespoons fresh cilantro, chopped

⅛ teaspoon crushed dried hot peppers

2 teaspoons matzah meal

1. Grate the *boniato* and onion together on the large holes of a grater into a bowl. Stir in the eggs until well blended. Add the orange zest, cumin, salt, pepper, ginger, cilantro, dried hot peppers, and matzah meal, stirring to mix.

2. In a large heavy frying pan, heat about ½ inch of oil over moderate to high heat. Drop the *boniato* mixture into the oil one heaping tablespoon at a time, being careful not to crowd the pan. Pat the batter down in the center with a wooden spoon, and fry the pancakes until golden brown on one side, then turn and brown the other side. Drain on paper towel and keep warm.

3. Mix the sour cream and the scallions in a small bowl. Serve with the hot *boniato* latkes.

Yield: 8 pancakes (P or D)

Peanut or vegetable oil for frying

½ cup sour cream

3 to 4 scallions, chopped

*Available in Latin American stores.

Eggplant Salad with Pomegranate Juice

One of the hallmarks of Israeli cuisine is its eggplant salads. Hava Volman's, flavored with pomegranate juice, is similar to one that I tasted in New York at the home of a Jordanian friend. Hava uses Chinese white eggplants, which she finds in local markets in Brooklyn. She seasons her salad with her own cilantro puree, which you can use as a garnish with other dishes.

4 large white or purple eggplants (about 1½ pounds)

½ cup pomegranate juice

1 tablespoon fresh ginger, grated

Juice of 1 lemon

3 cloves garlic, grated

Pinch of salt

Pinch of white pepper

2 tablespoons tahini

1 tablespoon cilantro puree (see below)

Seeds of 1 pomegranate

1. Prick each eggplant with a fork. Over an open flame, char the eggplant on all sides. You can do this on a gas stove top, using tongs to turn the eggplant. You can also prick the eggplant, place it on a cookie sheet in a 450-degree oven, and roast about 20 minutes or until soft. Let the eggplant cool slightly before peeling. Put the eggplant pulp in a large bowl, and discard the skin.

2. Using a fork, mash the eggplant, then add the pomegranate juice, ginger, lemon juice, garlic, salt, pepper, tahini, and the cilantro puree, mixing well. Taste and adjust seasonings.

3. Garnish with the pomegranate seeds and serve with wedges of pita bread.

Yield: about 2 cups (P)

CILANTRO PURÉE

3 bunches cilantro leaves, stems removed

¼ cup olive oil (approximately)

½ teaspoon salt or to taste

½ teaspoon cumin

1. Wash and dry the cilantro leaves.

2. Place the leaves in a food processor fitted with a steel blade. Pulse, gradually adding oil, salt, and cumin, until you have a pestolike consistency.

Yield: ½ to ¾ cup (P)

Artichokes Jewish Style

Carciofi alla Giudia, artichokes Jewish style, earned their fame during the regime of Mussolini, who brought heads of state to Piperno, a restaurant in the old Roman ghetto. "The recipe itself has existed since Jews first came to Rome, about two thousand years ago," said Edda Servi Machlin, author of *Classic Cuisine of the Italian Jews* (Giro Press). No one is more adept at making this dish than Edda, having learned it from her mother, who grew up in Rome. "We used the young artichokes, the first of the spring, at our Passover Seder," said Edda. When she prepared *Carciofi alla Giudia* on television with small California artichokes, the crew gobbled up every single morsel.

12 small artichokes

Juice of 2 lemons

2 tablespoons kosher salt or to taste

1 teaspoon freshly ground black pepper or to taste

3 cups extra-virgin olive oil

1. Soak the artichokes in cold water to cover for a few hours or overnight. Edda tosses a few ice cubes on hers. This will make the artichokes crisp and easier to clean.

2. Clean the artichokes. Remove and discard the outer, deep-green leaves at the base of the artichoke until you reach a lighter shade of green. Using a sharp knife, one leaf at a time, cut off the leaves where they change color. Cut the top off. Trim the stem, removing the tough outer green skin. Plunge the cleaned artichoke into clean water mixed with the lemon juice. Continue until you have prepared all the artichokes.

3. Take two artichokes from the water and hit one top against the other. This will open up one of the artichokes. Continue until all artichokes are opened. For the last one, hit it with the bottom of an artichoke.

4. Sprinkle the kosher salt and the black pepper in a small bowl.

5. Coat the artichokes one by one thoroughly, inside and out, with the salt and pepper mixture so that the salt and pepper penetrates the inside leaves.

6. Heat 2 inches of oil in a heavy frying pan until almost smoking, about 375 degrees. Now, add the artichokes, a few at a time, on their sides. You will hear a sizzle when you drop them into the oil. Do not crowd the pan. Using tongs, turn the artichokes so the bottoms are submerged in oil, as they need to cook the longest, and rotate the artichokes until they are golden brown on all sides. It will take about 15 minutes to cook the bottoms. Remove from the oil and drain. Repeat this first cooking step with the rest of the artichokes.

7. Just before serving, reheat the oil and place the artichokes, one at a time, leafy top side down, into the oil. Press down with a fork to allow the leaves to open and get crisp. Remove to a paper towel to drain. Serve immediately.

Yield: serves 6 (P)

Tortillas Stuffed with Vegetarian Portobello "Peking Duck"

This delicious kosher appetizer, substituting portobello mushrooms for Peking duck, is one of the dishes served at the Israeli Embassy in Washington. Sue Fischer of Windows Catering thought of this East-West vegetarian combination when she was eating a duck quesadilla. "Since we do so much kosher dairy, we are always on the lookout for interesting ways to prepare vegetarian dishes," said Mrs. Fischer. "The roasted portobello mushroom has the color and texture similar to roast duck." Instead of marinating the duck in Chinese five-spice seasoning, Mrs. Fischer marinates the mushrooms in this combination of star anise, Szechuan peppercorns, fennel, cloves, and cinnamon.

6 portobello mushrooms, left
    whole without stems, about
    1 pound
1/3 cup vegetable oil
1 teaspoon five-spice Chinese
    seasoning*
2 red bell peppers
2 bunches scallions
18 6-inch flour tortillas
1 1/2 cups hoisin sauce*

*Available in Asian food sections of grocery stores

1. Preheat the oven to 350 degrees. Lightly brush the mushrooms with vegetable oil on top and sprinkle all over with the five-spice powder. Place on a greased cookie sheet and bake about 10 to 15 minutes, or until cooked. Cool and slice into julienne strips.
2. Julienne the red peppers and cut the scallions, including both the white and the green parts, into thin 2-inch strips. Brush a flour tortilla with *hoisin* sauce, top with about 4 portobello strips, 3 red-pepper strips, and a few strips of scallions. Roll up tightly like a jelly roll and place seam-side down in a 9×13-inch pan. Repeat. If not baking right away, cover with plastic wrap.
3. When ready to serve, bake in the oven for 10 to 15 minutes or until heated through.
4. Slice each tortilla diagonally into 3 pieces and serve with *hoisin* sauce on the side for dipping.

Yield: 54 pieces, figuring 3 per person as an appetizer (P)

Hungarian Cheese Latkes

"As a child, I used to eat these cheese latkes when I visited my grandmother," said Lillie Stern Serviansky of Coral Gables, Florida. "Since she died before giving me the recipe, I recreated it through my father's taste memories." Mrs. Serviansky's father and mother came from Hungary to Mexico where Lillie was born. "My grandmother used to tell me that during Roman times the Jewish women who were taken as slaves and concubines would feed these latkes to the Roman soldiers to make them thirsty for wine. Then the women would put poison in the wine. She also told us that the only reason Jews in Central and Eastern Europe switched to potato latkes was because they were so poor they couldn't afford cheese."

2 large eggs

1 cup sugar

8 ounces cream cheese

6 tablespoons large-curd cottage cheese

¾ to 1 cup all-purpose flour

½ teaspoon salt

Vegetable oil for frying

1. Mix the eggs and the sugar in the bowl of a food processor fitted with the steel blade. Add the cheeses, ¾ cup of the flour, and salt. Process until smooth.

2. Heat a nonstick frying pan (any size) and pour in a film of vegetable oil. To test the thickness of the batter, drop about 4 tablespoons into the pan and fry for a few minutes on each side. Do not worry if some of the batter spills out of the pancakes. Just scrape off the excess. If the batter seems too liquid, add flour. When the consistency is correct, continue frying all the pancakes, a few at a time.

3. Drain on a paper towel and serve with a dollop of whipped cream, a spoonful of jam, or a sprinkle of cinnamon sugar.

Yield: about 10 latkes (D)

Italian Crusty Fettuccine

Edda Servi Machlin, author of *Classic Cuisine of the Italian Jews* (Giro Press), prepared *Taglio-lini Colla Crocia*—this savory molded-pasta dish with meat sauce, salami, nuts, and raisins—at her home in Croton-on-Hudson, New York. Mrs. Machlin, whose cookbook is almost as interesting as she is, says the real name of the dish is *Ruota di Faraone,* Pharoah's Wheel, and that it symbolizes the passage of the Israelites through the Red Sea and their deliverance from Egypt. Although the original recipe included tongue, Mrs. Machlin now substitutes kosher salami.

½ cup plus 1 tablespoon extra-virgin olive oil

1 medium onion, finely chopped

1 medium carrot, peeled and finely chopped

1 celery stalk, leaves removed, finely chopped

1 large sprig Italian parsley, finely chopped

1 pound lean ground beef

½ cup dry white wine

⅔ cup (1 6-ounce can) tomato paste

1½ cups beef stock or water

2 tablespoons salt plus salt to taste

6 quarts water

12 ounces fresh egg fettuccine

½ cup beef salami or link chicken sausage, precooked, diced

½ cup dark raisins

½ cup whole almonds

½ cup pine nuts

1. Heat the ½ cup olive oil in a 6-quart pot over a medium flame. Add the onion, carrot, celery, and parsley. Cook until the onion is light brown in color, about 2 to 3 minutes, stirring occasionally.

2. Add the ground beef and continue cooking until the meat has browned thoroughly, stirring occasionally to break it up.

3. Pour in the white wine and increase the heat. Let the wine reduce completely. It will take about 10 minutes.

4. Add the tomato paste, stirring, and continue cooking for 1 to 2 minutes.

5. Pour in the 1½ cups of beef stock or water and cook, covered, over a low heat for 40 to 45 minutes, stirring occasionally. Add salt to taste. The sauce should be thick. If it is too thin, it needs to cook a little longer.

6. In an 8-quart pot bring the 6 quarts of water and 2 tablespoons of salt to a boil. Add the fettuccine and cook until done *al dente,* as instructed on the package.

7. Preheat the oven to 350 degrees and grease a 10-inch round baking dish or bundt pan with the last tablespoon of olive oil.

8. Drain the fettuccine. Place in a large mixing bowl with the salami or sausage, raisins, almonds, pine nuts, and meat sauce. Pour this mixture into the prepared pan. Or, for a prettier effect, mix the meat sauce with the pasta and alternate layers of pasta, salami or sausage, raisins, almonds, and pine nuts, starting and ending with the pasta.

9. Bake for 1 to 1½ hours, or until golden brown all around. Transfer onto a serving dish. Serve immediately.

Yield: 6 to 8 servings (M)

The Vinegar Factory's Kasha, Lentil, and Roasted Vegetable Kugel (Or Loaf)

This flavorful wintertime vegetarian dish with kasha and lentils can be a main course or a vegetable accompaniment. Eli Zabar, not an inherent lover of vegetables, realized that he needed a vegetarian loaf as an alternative to meat and fish loaves at the Vinegar Factory, located at 431 East 91st Street in New York. Mr. Zabar grew up in the West Side food emporium Zabar family. He loves this dish. I have varied it slightly to make it easier for home cooks.

5 cups Spanish or other sweet onions, peeled and diced

1½ cups canola or other vegetable oil

8 medium tomatoes, sliced thin (about 10 cups) or 2 cups sun-dried tomatoes

5 tablespoons salt

4 teaspoons freshly ground black pepper

4 large carrots, peeled and diced (about 3 cups)

3 medium turnips (about 3 cups)

1 large eggplant, diced

2 cups French lentils

8 cups water

1½ cups whole kasha

3 large whole eggs

1⅓ cups vegetable stock

1 teaspoon crushed red pepper

2 tablespoons fresh thyme

1. Put the onions in a sauté pan with ½ cup of the oil. Sauté slowly, until the onions are caramelized, stirring occasionally, for about 20 minutes.

2. Meanwhile, preheat the oven to 350 degrees and put the fresh tomatoes in a mixing bowl. Toss with ½ cup oil and sprinkle with 1 tablespoon of the salt and a teaspoon of the pepper. Place in a single layer in a jelly-roll pan and bake for about 45 minutes, or until golden brown and the juice has evaporated.

3. Toss the carrots, parsnips, turnips, and eggplant in a bowl with the remaining ½ cup oil, 2 tablespoons salt, and 3 teaspoons of pepper. Place on a cookie sheet and bake in the oven for 20 to 30 minutes or until golden brown and tender, but not mushy.

4. Put the lentils in a saucepan with 6 cups of the water and bring to a boil. Boil for about 10 minutes, uncovered, or until tender.

5. Put the kasha in a bowl. Beat 1 of the eggs and add to the kasha, coating it well.

6. Heat a heavy 6-cup saucepan and add the kasha. Stir continuously until toasted, about 1 to 2 minutes. Add remaining 2 cups cold water and cover. Simmer, 10 to 12 minutes, or until the kasha is tender but not mushy.

7. Mix the onions, the roasted tomatoes, carrots, turnips, parsnips, eggplant, lentils, and kasha together in a large bowl. Stir in the remaining 2 eggs, vegetable stock, 2 tablespoons more salt, crushed red pepper, and remaining thyme.

8. Place in a greased 9×13-inch baking dish and bake for 30 to 40 minutes or until light-golden brown and firm to the touch.

Yield: 10 to 12 servings (P)

Caribbean Kugel with Plantains and Ratatouille

This cross-cultural kugel recipe is a winner. Sara Kapustin of Miami learned to make a plantain puree as a crust for a meat *picadillo* (see page 203) from her Puerto Rican relatives. To please her vegetarian daughter, she transformed the recipe and used the puree to encase a ratatouille mixture. I have changed the recipe slightly again, encasing the ratatouille vegetables in the plantains instead of layering them. Use ripe, black plantains for this, as they will be softer and sweeter.

4 quarts water

6 ripe plantains (about 3 pounds)

3 tablespoons olive oil

1 large onion, chopped (about 1 cup)

2 cloves garlic, sliced

1 green bell pepper, chopped

1 large eggplant, unpeeled, diced in 1-inch cubes (about 1⅓ pounds)

4 tomatoes, cut in 1-inch pieces (2 pounds), or one 28-ounce can

2 zucchinis, cut in 1-inch cubes (1 pound)

1 teaspoon sugar

½ cup tomato sauce

Salt and freshly ground pepper to taste

2 large eggs

1. Bring the water to a boil. Peel the plantains, put them in the boiling water, then simmer, covered, until they are soft, 20 to 30 minutes, depending on the ripeness.

2. While the plantains are cooking, heat a frying pan, add the olive oil, and sauté the onion, garlic, and green pepper. Cook until the onion is soft, about 5 minutes. Add the eggplant, tomatoes, zucchinis, sugar, and tomato sauce. Simmer, covered, over a low flame for 45 minutes, or until the vegetables are tender. Season with salt and pepper to taste.

3. Preheat the oven to 350 degrees and grease a 9×13-inch baking dish.

4. Drain the plantains. Put them in a bowl and mash with a fork or potato masher. Either spoon the plantains into the casserole or use your hands to mold half the plantain puree into a thin layer and line the bottom and sides of the casserole.

5. Spoon the vegetables over the plantains. Cover the vegetables with the remaining plantain puree. Beat the eggs and spoon over the top.

6. Bake the casserole on the middle shelf of the oven for 25 to 30 minutes, or until golden brown.

Yield: 10 to 12 servings (P)

Iranian Rice

The goal in making a perfect *chelou,* the crusty Iranian rice, is twofold: to have a crusty bottom, called a *tadig,* and to separate every single morsel of rice. Here the *tadig* is created not from rice alone but from a crisp potato bottom. Although I have given the classic way to make this rice, the Soofer family and many other Iranians, including the Persian cookbook author Najmieh Batmanglij, use an automatic nonstick rice cooker in which you mix 2 cups of well-washed, long-grain rice with 2 cups of water, add a few tablespoons of oil, salt to taste, then cover, and turn on the cooker. The result is perfect and almost effortless.

1 pound basmati long-grain rice

2 tablespoons salt

6 tablespoons vegetable oil

½ cup hot water

½ teaspoon turmeric

2 potatoes, peeled and sliced about ¼ inch thick

1. Fill a 4-quart saucepan with water and bring to a boil. Add the rice and salt. Boil, uncovered, for 7 to 10 minutes over high heat. Stir the water occasionally, being careful not to break the rice grains. Taste the rice after 7 minutes to see whether it is done. The rice will begin to curl. If ready remove immediately and drain in lukewarm water to remove excess starch; otherwise cook 2 to 3 minutes longer, then drain.

2. Heat 4 tablespoons cooking oil mixed with almost ½ cup hot water in a heavy-bottomed saucepan. Add the turmeric. Then place the potato slices all around the bottom of the saucepan. Pour the rice into the pan; cover with a cloth and a lid. Let simmer over a low flame for about 10 minutes.

3. Mound up the rice in the center of the pan and make a deep hole in the center of the mound. (This hole allows the rice to steam.) Mix about 2 more tablespoons of oil with the remaining hot water and sprinkle all around the rice. Cover and simmer for about 20 more minutes.

4. When ready to serve, uncover the pan and stir the rice gently with a spatula to make it fluffy. Turn the rice out onto a warm serving dish in a mound. Then remove the crust and potatoes from the bottom of the pan and serve separately, or heap the potatoes on the rice on the serving platter.

Yield: 6 to 8 servings (P)

Palachinta Tower

Aggi Stern, now of Coral Gables, Florida, comes from a long line of Hungarian bakers. After she survived Auschwitz she returned to Hungary, only to discover that her family had all died. She then moved to Mexico City where she had some relatives.

Palachinta are the crepes or blintzes of Hungary, and this layered tower of crepes, filled with nuts and jam, is one of the jewels of the Hungarian home kitchen. Today, Mrs. Stern makes these every Sunday when her children and her eleven grandchildren come for dinner. She feels that making this crepe cake for her family is an affirmation of love and of the future. Her daughter Lillie, who has absorbed some Mexican culinary influences, often fills individual crepes with jalapeño peppers and a Mexican goat cheese called *cajeta* as a treat for her family.

4 large eggs

1 teaspoon salt

6 tablespoons sugar

10 tablespoons flour

1 cup milk

Vegetable oil for frying

½ cup pecans, finely chopped

1 cup strawberry or apricot preserves

1. Mix together in a bowl the eggs, salt, 4 tablespoons of the sugar, the flour, and the milk, beating until smooth.

2. Heat a 6-inch frying pan over medium heat with a teaspoon of oil. Pour about 2 tablespoons of the batter into the pan or enough to completely cover the bottom of the pan when it is swirled around. After 1 to 2 minutes on one side, flip it to finish cooking. Remove from the pan and set aside to cool. Repeat with the remaining batter, adding small amounts of oil when necessary.

3. Put the chopped pecans and the preserves in separate bowls.

4. Preheat the oven to 350 degrees.

5. Grease a round baking pan, and in the bottom of the pan place 1 crepe. Spoon a film of strawberry preserves

over the crepe. Cover this with another crepe and layer this one with the nuts. Continue to layer the crepes alternately with the preserves and the nuts, finishing with the preserves.

6. Bake on the middle rack of the oven for 15 minutes until the preserves caramelize. Cut as you would a pie.

Yield: approximately 12 crepes or 1 tower (D)

(Raphil's) Rice Pudding

When *Jewish Cooking in America* was first published, my husband could not understand why I did not include rice pudding. I was waiting for Barbara Seldin's recipe from her father's deli in Miami Beach, once located on 41st Street and Arthur Godfrey Road. Here it is. To recreate the mood of Raphil's, where this classic was a fixture, Barbara and her cookbook-writer husband Steve Raichlen set the scene for me. "It is Miami Beach, 1949. Harry Truman is president. The musical *South Pacific* opens on Broadway. Miami Beach is America's favorite winter vacation spot and Raphil's is its premier deli. Founded by Ray Malshik and Phil Seldin, Raphil's plays to standing-room-only crowds during the season. No celebrity—from Frank Sinatra to Sammy Davis Jr.—passes through town without an obligatory sandwich at Raphil's. Company trucks criss-cross the Beach, delivering deli platters to the cream of society. Miami Beach is enjoying its Golden Era and Raphil's is the place to be." Since Raphil's is no longer, we tasted the pudding, sprinkled with toasted Indian nuts, today called pine nuts, in Barbara and Steve's kitchen in Coconut Grove.

1 cup Valencia-style or arborio (short-grain) rice

1 cinnamon stick (2 inches long)

3 strips lemon zest

1 vanilla bean, split

1 can (12 ounces) evaporated milk

1. To wash the rice, put it in a large heavy saucepan with cold water to cover by 2 inches. Swirl it around with a spoon; the water will become cloudy. Pour the water off and add more. Continue rinsing the rice this way until the water runs clear. Drain off the water, leaving the rice in the pan.

2. Add 2½ cups of fresh water, the cinnamon stick, lemon zest, and vanilla bean, and bring to a boil over high heat. Reduce the heat, cover, and gently simmer the rice until most of the water is absorbed, about 20 minutes.

1 can (14 ounces) sweetened
condensed milk
1 whole star-anise pod
(optional)
½ cup raisins, soaked in warm
water to cover
1 to 2 tablespoons sugar, or to
taste
½ cup pine nuts, lightly toasted
Ground cinnamon or freshly
grated nutmeg, for
sprinkling

3. Stir in the evaporated milk. Gently simmer, uncovered, until most of the liquid is absorbed, about 8 minutes. Stir the rice occasionally.

4. Stir in the sweetened condensed milk, and, if using, the star anise and the raisins. Gently simmer, uncovered, until most of the liquid is absorbed and the rice is very tender, about 6 minutes. The pudding should remain very moist. Stir occasionally.

5. Remove the cinnamon stick, lemon zest, vanilla bean, and star-anise pod. Stir in the sugar, to taste. Transfer to a bowl and let the rice pudding cool to room temperature. You can serve it at room temperature or chilled.

6. To serve, transfer the rice pudding to a serving bowl or individual bowls. Sprinkle with the toasted pine nuts and a little ground cinnamon or nutmeg and serve at once.

Yield: 8 servings (D)

Guava Mandelbrot

I thought that I had heard of every kind of *mandelbrot* until I tasted Sophia Grobler's fabulous Cuban version. *Mandelbrot* literally means almond bread, but it also means twice-baked. This jam-filled cookie, a cross between a strudel and a *mandelbrot,* originated in Galicia with Sophia's husband's grandmother. She carried the memory of it with her when she escaped the pogroms and went to Cuba while waiting for a visa for the United States. At first, Cuba was a way station for these immigrants. Then, when they got jobs there, they realized that this land was paradise for them. In Havana, guava replaced the original strawberry jam. "Every Friday she would bake cookies like this," said Mrs. Grobler, who was born in Cuba and now lives in Miami, Florida, with her husband. "She used whatever preserves she could find." You can substitute guava preserves but guava paste, like apricot lekvar, has a more intense flavor. When I was testing the *mandelbrot,* my children gobbled up every single one. Now, that is the sign of a good recipe!

3 large eggs

1 cup plus 3 tablespoons sugar

*¾ cup plus 2 tablespoons
    vegetable oil*

1 teaspoon vanilla

¼ cup orange juice

4¾ to 5 cups all-purpose flour

2 teaspoons baking powder

½ teaspoon salt

1. Preheat the oven to 350 degrees and grease 2 cookie sheets.

2. Put the eggs and 1 cup of sugar in the bowl of an electric mixer, and beat until pale yellow. Add ¾ cup vegetable oil, vanilla, and orange juice, beating well after each addition.

3. Sift together flour, baking powder, and salt, and gradually add to the wet mixture, mixing on medium speed or with a wooden spoon until it forms a soft dough. Divide the dough into 4 pieces and roll out each into a circle about ⅛-inch thick and 12 inches in diameter.

2 cups guava paste or
preserves
½ cup almonds, finely chopped
½ cup walnuts, finely chopped
½ teaspoon cinnamon

4. Brush additional oil over one circle. Using a spatula spread about ½ cup of the guava over the dough, a little thicker than you would spread jam for a sandwich, leaving a ½-inch border. If the paste is difficult to spread, soften it in the food processor armed with the steel blade.

5. Place the almonds and walnuts in a food processor and process until finely chopped but not to a powder.

6. Sprinkle ¼ cup of the nuts over the circle. Roll the dough up lengthwise into a tight jelly roll, fold the ends under, and place on the cookie sheet. Repeat with the other 3 doughs, leaving about 1 teaspoon of nuts.

7. Brush the rolls with oil.

8. Mix together the remaining 3 tablespoons sugar and the cinnamon and sprinkle over each roll, then sprinkle on 1 teaspoon of chopped nuts. Press down slightly on each roll to make a half-moon shape.

9. Bake in the oven for 20 minutes or until golden brown. Remove the *mandelbrot* from the oven. Using a sharp, heavy knife, slice diagonally halfway through into ½-inch-thick slices. Don't worry if the top crumbles slightly. Return to the oven for 10 to 15 minutes or until golden. Remove again, until cool enough to handle, and slice through completely.

Yield: about 48 pieces (P)

Kichel from Czechoslovakia

Generations of children in Oak Park, Michigan, have loved to go to the counter at the Star Bakery for the sugar cookies that Mr. Moskovitz still hands out. My favorite sugar cookie, or *kichel,* at Star Bakery is shaped in a round, rolled in sugar, and then baked.

5 large eggs

½ teaspoon vanilla extract

⅔ cup vegetable oil

1 tablespoon sugar, plus 1 cup
    for rolling

2⅓ cups unbleached all-
    purpose flour

1 teaspoon salt

1. Put the eggs, vanilla, vegetable oil, 1 tablespoon sugar, flour, and salt in the bowl of an electric mixer fitted with the paddle and blend on low speed until incorporated; then beat on high for 5 minutes.

2. Remove the paddle and scrape the batter down the sides of the bowl. Rest the dough in the bowl, covered, until soft and spongy outside, about 1 hour. Then remove from the bowl—it will be sticky—and make a ball out of it.

3. Preheat the oven to 350 degrees and grease 2 cookie sheets.

4. Sprinkle a work surface with some of the remaining sugar, about ⅛-inch deep. Place the dough in the center, flatten it slightly with a rolling pin, and sprinkle the dough liberally with the sugar. Roll the dough to a thickness of ⅛ inch in a rectangle about 18×12 inches. Then, using a dull knife, cut the dough into circles, about 6 inches in diameter. Place each round on the cookie sheets, leaving an inch between each cookie.

5. Bake the *kichel* for 25 to 30 minutes on the middle rack of the oven, until the cookies are hard to the touch and golden brown. (If using one oven, put the cookie sheets on the top and center racks, then switch them midway.) To test for doneness, break a *kichel* in half. If it is doughy or too soft, it is not done yet. Return to the oven for a few minutes more.

Yield: about 20* kichel *(P)

Vin des Deux Morts

Schapiro's Wine on the Lower East Side has been advertising "extra-rich sacramental Passover wine, the kind you can cut with a knife" for several generations. In Highland Park, Illinois, a home winemaker, Mort Steinberg, presses a similar wine that his wife's family has made for generations. Together with his father-in-law, Mort Bernstein, who learned the recipe from *his* father-in-law, Isaac Turner, who learned it from *his* father in Kobryn, near Pinsk, Russia, the two Morts have been producing this sweet wine for over twenty years. Around the holiday of Sukkot, the traditional harvest time for grapes since the biblical period, the Morts travel to a farm in Stevensville, Michigan, to pick Michigan Concord grapes. At the same time of the year that the Steinbergs build their Sukkah, they press the wine which they label Vin des Deux Morts, Père et Gendre et Fils. The wine is poured into barrels and stored in the basement to age until Passover. You will need a wine barrel, a bung, a siphon, a press, and a grape crusher, which you can buy from a wine supply company.

120 pounds Concord grapes
25 pounds sugar (about)

1. Wash the grapes in cold water and remove the stems.
2. Crush the grapes in a grape crusher, letting them fall into a plastic bucket.
3. Cover the bucket with a cloth, and allow the grapes to sit for 1 week in a cool area, such as a basement.
4. At the end of the week, prepare an oak barrel by rinsing it thoroughly and then smoking it with sulfur sticks in order to kill any bacteria. This must be done outdoors, since the fumes from the burning sticks are poisonous. After 20 or 30 minutes, remove the remnants of

the burnt sulfur and wash out the barrel numerous times, making sure no sulfur smell remains.

5. Use a siphon to draw the grape juice off into a large clean bowl, then pour the juice into the prepared barrel. Put the crushed grape pulp into a grape press. Press out as much additional juice as possible and add that to the barrel.

6. Add the sugar, stirring for about 20 minutes or until the sugar is fully dissolved. Cover loosely with the bung (wooden stopper), being sure that gases from fermentation can escape. Place in a cold place such as a basement and wait about 6 months until Passover.

7. Just before Passover, taste the wine. If it's not sweet enough, add sugar slowly, stirring and tasting again. Repeat if necessary. This decision will not be the same each year, as the amount of natural sugar in the grapes varies greatly.

8. Bottle the wine and enjoy. *L'chaim!!!*

Yield: about 9 gallons (P)

Anne Rosenzweig's Matzah Brei

What would American Jewish food be without matzah *brei*—and a strong opinion of how to make it? Anne Rosenzweig is one of the few upscale chefs I know who has this classic Passover morning item on her menu all year long. There are two schools of thought on how to prepare the *brei;* whether to soak the matzah in water whole or to first break it up into small pieces. Anne belongs to the whole-matzah school. Here is her formula, with her hidden ingredient, caramelized onions.

4 tablespoons unsalted butter

2 large onions, diced (about 1 pound)

3 matzah boards/squares

6 large eggs

Salt and pepper to taste

Seasonal foods (optional)*

*Different options: in fall and winter add 4 tablespoons of sautéed wild mushrooms, in the spring smoked salmon and dill, and in the summer wild lilies.

1. Heat 2 tablespoons of the butter in a large frying pan over a low heat. Add the onions and cook very slowly until they are a rich caramel color (about 45 to 50 minutes). Set aside to cool.

2. Dip the unbroken matzah boards in hot water. Remove and squeeze out the excess water.

3. Put the eggs in a medium bowl, whisk with a fork, blending the yolks and whites. Break up the matzah into the eggs, and season with salt and pepper. Let the matzah soak up the eggs, almost completely. Add the cooled onions.

4. Heat the remaining butter in a medium skillet. Add the eggs-and-matzah mixture and cook over medium heat. Let set, about 3 minutes, stirring occasionally. Add seasonal ingredients* right before the eggs are completely done. Serve immediately.

Yield: 4 to 6 servings (D)

Matzah-Meal Pancakes

At Passover and every weekend throughout the year, Washington, D.C., psychiatrist Justin Frank makes *gehatke tsibeles*—thinly chopped onions that are sautéed in butter until they begin to brown, then sprinkled with sugar and vinegar and cooked slowly in a 350-degree oven for a half hour. He serves them with salami and eggs and matzah-meal pancakes. "There are two important facts in the matzah-meal pancakes," he said. "First, the order in which the ingredients are mixed affects the taste; and second, this recipe, which I learned from my mother and grandmother in Los Angeles, predates measuring spoons. Measurements are in eggshells." He may measure in eggshells, but I have translated half an eggshell to equal 2 tablespoons to make it a little easier for you.

6 large eggs

1½ cups water

1½ cups matzah meal

1 teaspoon salt

6 tablespoons unsalted butter
   or margarine

1. Beat the eggs well in a mixing bowl. Then add the water and beat again. Add the matzah meal and the salt and beat once more.

2. Melt 1 tablespoon of the butter in an 8-inch frying pan over low heat. Add about 1 cup of matzah batter to the pan, spreading it into a thin layer. As the top solidifies, after 1 to 2 minutes, flip the pancake with a spatula, and turn off the heat. Serve after 1 minute with maple syrup or sugar.

Repeat with the remaining batter and butter.

Yield: 6 matzah-meal pancakes (D or P)

Coffee Rich, the Miracle Cream from the Soya Bean

"When I first started dating Bob Rich Jr., I came home to my Orthodox grandparents in Cincinnati and told them I was seriously dating someone who was not Jewish," said Mindy Rich, Executive Vice President, Rich Products, and today the wife of Robert Rich Jr. "All that I had to do to make it okay was tell them my fiancé was from the Coffee Rich family because, to my Orthodox grandparents, Coffee Rich, the first frozen nondairy creamer, was a miracle cream. When we got married, my grandmother called my husband personally to make sure that he would put an ad on the back page of her Hadassah program every year."

Rich's Whip Topping, a nondairy product that beats up into a whipped-cream-like topping, was developed in 1945. Coffee Rich, a nondairy coffee creamer, was marketed in 1961. Robert E. Rich Sr., who was in the dairy business in Buffalo, New York, had learned about research done on dairy substitutes conducted by the WPA during the Great Depression—when there were milk shortages—and by the Ford Foundation. Eventually he directed a laboratory team in search of a vegetable-based replacement for whipped cream. He discovered that the soya-bean substance could be frozen, thawed, and then whipped.

Just after World War II, armed with an overnight bag and a container of Whip Topping, Mr. Rich took the train from Buffalo to see a food broker in New York. When he began his presentation the next morning, Mr. Rich was shocked to discover that his product, which he had packed in dry ice and newspaper to keep cold for the journey, had frozen solid. Knowing that dairy cream does not whip after being frozen, he feared his demonstration would fail. Borrowing a knife from one of the salesmen, he cut a few pieces off the solid block and put them in a whipping bowl. To his amazement, it whipped perfectly, and Rich's Whip Topping entered the frozen food industry. Today Rich's is a diversified billion-dollar company and sells the most widely used nondairy toppings in the world. Rich's Whip Topping, immediately hailed as "the miracle cream from the soya bean," revolutionized food processing and opened up a new world of nondairy products to the growing frozen-food industry and to kosher consumers everywhere who want milk with their coffee after a meat meal.

Appendixes

Menus

FRIDAY NIGHT SEPHARDIC DINNER

Homemade Wine
Salmon Pickle with Fennel
Haricot Stew with Beans
Coconut Pudding

OLD SEPHARDIC SABBATH LUNCH

Potted Shad
Chamim
Almond Pudding

JUDAH BENJAMIN DINNER

Asparagus with Hollandaise
Pollo a la Chilindron
Corn Oysters
Dandelion Green Salad
Macaroons
Rum and Shrub

GERMAN-JEWISH NINETEENTH-CENTURY FRIDAY NIGHT DINNER

Berches
Sweet and Sour Carp
Beef Soup with Noodles
Cabbage Salad
Roast Beef
Linzertorte

ALSATIAN DAIRY LUNCHEON MENU

Pickled Salmon
Alsatian Onion Tart
Charlotte à l'Alsatienne

RUSSIAN BRUNCH

Fresh Fruit
Bagels
Bialys
Cream Cheese
Herring Salad with Beets,
   Potatoes, and Apples
Barney Greengrass' Nova Wings,
   Heads, Eggs, and Onions
Noodle *Kugel*
Apricot *Rugelach*

EASTERN EUROPEAN FRIDAY NIGHT DINNER

Challah
Polish Gefilte Fish
Chicken Soup with Matzah Balls
My Mother's Pot Roast
Rumanian Roasted Eggplant
   and Pepper Salad
Hungarian Cabbage and Noodles
Russian Compote
Mandelbrot

PURIM DINNER

Challah
Chicken Soup with Kreplach
Lithuanian *Tzimmes* with Beef and Beets
Kasha Varnishkes
Cucumber Salad
Dutch *Hazenblosen*
Russian *Hamentashen*

TRADITIONAL EVERYDAY WINTER DINNER

Pumpernickel
Hungarian Goulash
Compote

BETTER-THAN-AVERAGE MEAL

Crispy Potato Pancakes
Cranberry Applesauce
Roast Chicken
Dressed-up Apple Strudel

ANARCHIST VEGETARIAN MEAL

String Bean Vegetarian Pâté
Mamaliga
Green Salad
Carrot Candy

AMERICAN JEWISH BRUNCH

Jewish Toast
Pickled Salmon with Sour Cream
Mogen David Bagels
Ruth Raab's Noodle Pudding
Fresh Strawberries
Chocolate Babka

TURN-OF-THE-CENTURY BAT MITZVAH KIDDUSH

Poppy-seed *Kichel*
Gefilte Fish
Horseradish
Raisin Wine
Hot Dogs Back Home

AMERICAN JEWISH BAR MITZVAH BUFFET

Chopped Liver on Ice
Sweet and Sour Meatballs
Potato Knishes
Hot Dogs with Sauerkraut
Roast Chicken
Vegetables
Rice
Strawberry Meringue Torte

HUNGARIAN ROSH HASHANAH DINNER

Peppery Gefilte Fish
Chicken Fricassee
Egg Barley with Mushrooms
Honey Cake

AMERICAN BREAK-THE-FAST MEAL

Challah
Mark Siegel's Whitefish Salad
Herring with Sour Cream
Lick-Your-Fingers *Kugel*
Layered Salad
Lindy's Cheesecake

FIFTIES FRIDAY NIGHT DINNER

Challah
Chicken Soup with Noodles
Chicken Fingers
String Beans
Rice
Crustless Apple Crumb Cake

LUBAVITCHER FRIDAY NIGHT MEAL

Challah
Gefilte Fish
Chicken Soup
Cauliflower *Kugel*
Roast Chicken
Eggplant Salad
Corn and Tomato Salad
Compote
Apple Cake

ISRAELI DINNER

Falafel
Pita
Hummus
Tahina
Eggplant Salad
Hot Sauce
Tabbouleh
Poached Jaffa Oranges

MOROCCAN MAIMOUNA

Sweet Couscous with Dates
Mouffleta
Moroccan Cookies
Baklava
Nougat Candy

GEORGIAN SABBATH DINNER

Georgian *Challah*
Eggplant Salad
Spinach Salad
Pressed and Grilled Chicken
Rice
Vodka
Pickles

SALONIKAN MEAL

Burekas de Berencena
Salonika Sfongato (Spinach and Cheese
    Casserole)
Salad
Tishpishti (Nut Cake with Sugar Syrup)

SYRIAN ROSH HASHANAH DINNER

Lajamene
Lubyeh Black-eyed Peas with Veal
Sweet and Sour Tongue
Pickled Vegetables
Cracked Wheat and Tamarind Salad
Swiss Chard with Chick-peas
Adjwah (Stuffed Date Pastry)
Tishpishti (Nut Cake with Sugar Syrup)

OLD AMERICAN SEPHARDIC PASSOVER MEAL

Nathan Family Harosets
Spicy Fish with Fresh Herbs
    and Vegetables
Albondigas
Bumuelos di Matzah
Almond Pudding
Fresh Strawberries

MY SEDER MEAL

Gefilte Fish
Hollywood Chicken Soup
Fluffy Matzah Balls
Turkey with Mushrooms
    and Chestnuts Farfel Pilau
Southwestern *Tsimmes*
Asparagus Vinaigrette
Chremslach

Claudine Ostrow's Moist
    Chocolate Torte
Fresh Strawberries

THURSDAY NIGHT DINNER

Tuna Casserole or Salmon Croquettes
Salad
Rugelach

NINETEENTH-CENTURY PASSOVER GERMAN DINNER

Stewed Fish *à la Juive*
Chicken Soup with Marrow Balls
Turkey with Chestnut Stuffing
Lemon Pecan Torte and
    Mississippi Praline Macaroons

WASHINGTON MOROCCAN SEDER MEAL

Boulettes de Poissons
Red Pepper Salad
Carrot Salad
Eggplant Salad
Brisket with Olives
Salad
Dates Stuffed with Nuts
Marzipan
Fresh Fruit

SOUTHERN SEDER

New Orleans or Charleston Chicken Soup
Cajun Matzah Balls
Georgian Fried Chicken
Greens
Sponge Cake with Strawberries

Kosher Dry Wines

What follows is a list of some recommended American kosher savory wines to serve at Jewish holidays or any time of the year.

Hagafen Cabernet Sauvignon, Napa Valley, 1989

Hagafen Chardonnay, Napa Valley, 1990, 1991

Baron Herzog Cabernet Sauvignon Reserve

Baron Herzog Special Reserve Chardonnay, 1990

Weinstock Vineyard's Chardonnay, Cabernet Sauvignon, Gamay Beaujolais, White Zinfandel

Gan Eden Cabernet Sauvignon, 1986, 1987, 1988

Lionel Gallula Mount Madrona Napa Valley Chardonnay, 1992

J. Furst, Pinot Noir, Sonoma, 1991

Glossary of Jewish Terms

Adafina Moroccan long-simmering Sabbath stew (*chamim* in Hebrew), similar to *cholent,* made with meat, potatoes, chick-peas, vegetables, rice, etc.

Afikomen Piece of matzah broken off from the middle of three matzot used at the Passover Seder and set aside—and often hidden—to be eaten at the end of the meal.

Albondigas Meatballs in Ladino.

Ashkenazim Central and Eastern European, including Yiddish-speaking, Jews and their descendants.

Avas (*Arbes*) Chick-peas, often eaten at Purim.

Baalei Tchuvah Returnees to the faith.

Bagel A yeast roll with a hole.

Bar Mitzvah Jewish boy who has reached his thirteenth birthday and attained the age of religious duty and responsibilities.

Bat Mitzvah Jewish girl who at twelve years assumes religious duties and responsibilities.

Berches German and Central European *challah* often made from potatoes.

Bialy A baked roll with a center indented and sprinkled with diced onion and often poppy seeds.

Biscocho A Sephardic baked roll with a hole, often filled with coriander or anise seeds and then dipped in sesame seeds.

Blintz A crepe-like pancake with a filling, usually of cream or cottage cheese.

Borscht A soup having fermented or fresh red beet juice as the foundation, often with cabbage or meat or both added.

Borscht Belt A term for the Catskills resorts that catered to a primarily Jewish and mostly kosher clientele.

Brisket A cut of meat consisting of the breast muscles and other tissues with the bones removed.

Burekas A triangular and sometimes round pastry filled with spinach, spinach and cheese, eggplant, or meat, of Turkish origin.

Challah Traditional Sabbath and holiday loaf of white bread, often baked in braided or twisted form. Originally the portion of dough given to the Priests in the time of the Temple. In Jerusalem today, the religious remove a small portion of dough before baking and burn it.

Chametz Any food, drink, and other products made from wheat, barley, rye, oats, corn, or pulses, which by coming into contact with a liquid for more than eighteen minutes either rise or ferment.

Cholent Sabbath stew of slow-baked meat, potatoes, and beans.

Choly American term for challah.

Chremslach Deep-fried fritter made from matzah or matzah meal and served at Passover.

Eingemachts Jam or preserves made from beets, radishes, carrots, cherries or lemons, and walnuts, eaten often at Passover with a spoon and served with tea.

Etrog Fruit of the citron, used with the *lulav* in celebrating Sukkot.

Farfel Noodle dough or matzah in the form of small pellets or granules.

Fasulye A stew of green beans and meat.

Fijuelas Moroccan deep-fried pastry.

Fleishig Made of, prepared with, or used for meat or meat products.

Gefilte fish Stewed or baked fish, stuffed with a mixture of the fish flesh, bread or matzah crumbs, eggs, and seasonings, or prepared in the shape of balls or oval cakes, which are boiled in a fish stock.

Glatt Kosher meat that comes from a kosher, properly slaughtered animal that has no imperfections whatsoever. It also is used to designate certain products and restaurants as kosher which have strict supervision.

Goldene Yoikh Rich, golden chicken soup, traditionally served at weddings.

Grieben Cracklings from goose fat and goose skin, usually salted.

Haggadah The narration of the story of the Exodus from Egypt read at Passover.

Hamantashen Triangular-shaped Purim cookie, filled with prunes, poppy seeds, nuts, and even chocolate chips.

Hanukkah Festival of Lights celebrating the Maccabeean victory over the Seleucids in 164 B.C.E.

Harissa A hot sauce containing dried hot red chilies and other seasonings served with Oriental and Moroccan Jewish food.

Haroset Paste-like mixture of fruit, nuts, cinnamon, and wine eaten during the Passover Seder and symbolic of the mortar the Israelites used in building during Egyptian slavery.

Huevos Haminadav Long-cooked eggs served by Sephardic Jews on the Sabbath and other holidays.

Injera Ethiopian bread made traditionally from *teff.*

Kapparot Symbolic ceremony on the eve of Yom Kippur: a cock, hen, or coin is swung around and offered as ransom in atonement for one's sins.

Karpas Piece of parsley, celery, or lettuce, placed on the seder plate as a symbol of spring or hope, and dipped in salt water in remembrance of the hyssop and blood of the Passover in Egypt.

Kasha Coarse, cracked buckwheat, barley, millet, or wheat or a mush made from that.

Kiddush Ceremony proclaiming the holiness of the incoming Sabbath or festival; it consists of a benediction pronounced customarily before the evening meal over a cup of wine and usually two loaves of challah.

Kishke Beef or fowl casing (derma) stuffed with a savory filling (as of matzah flour, chicken fat, and onion) and roasted.

Kneidlach Soup dumplings made from matzah meal, eggs, chicken fat, and sometimes ground almonds, usually boiled but sometimes fried.

Knish A round or square of rich baking powder or strudel dough, folded over a savory meat, cheese, or potato filling and baked or fried.

Kofta Sephardic meatball or fried patty, generally.

Kosher Sanctioned by Jewish law, ritually fit, clean, or prepared for use according to Jewish law.

Kreplach Triangular pockets of noodle dough filled with chopped or ground meat or cheese, boiled and eaten with soup or fried and eaten as a side dish.

Kuchen Coffee cake usually made from a sweet yeast dough and variously shaped, flavored, and frosted.

Kugel Baked sweet or savory pudding or casserole made of noodles, potatoes, bread, or vegetables and often served on the Sabbath or festivals.

Latke Pancake usually made from grated raw potatoes and eaten at Hanukkah.

Lekakh Honey cake.

Lokshen Egg noodle.

Lox Smoked and salted salmon.

Maror Bitter herbs of horseradish or romaine eaten at Passover in remembrance of the bitterness of slavery.

Matzah Unleavened bread of affliction and freedom eaten at Passover.

Milchig Made of, or derived from, milk or dairy products.

Mohn Poppy seeds.

Ozne Haman Haman's ears in Hebrew. Deep-fried pastry, served with sugar at Purim.

Pan de Espana Lemon sponge cake.

Pareve Made without milk, meat, or their derivatives.

Passover Festival of freedom celebrating the Exodus from Egypt.

Pastel Turnover filled with meat, vegetables, or cheese.

Petcha Calves' foot jelly.

Pirogi Small pastry turnovers stuffed with savory filling.

Purim Festival celebrating the deliverance of the Jews from the machinations of Haman, described in the Book of Esther.

Rosh Hashanah Jewish New Year.

Schalet Dessert pudding often made with apples.

Schnecken A snail-shaped yeast dough baked and filled with nuts, sugar, cinnamon, and sometimes raisins.

Schochet Person officially licensed by rabbinic authority as a slaughterer for food in accordance with Jewish dietary laws.

Seder Home or community service and ceremonial dinner on one and two nights of Passover, commemorating the Exodus from Egypt.

Sephardim Jews and their descendants who settled in Spain and Portugal at an early date and later spread to Greece, the Levant, England, the Netherlands, and the Americas.

Shabbat Sabbath.

Shalah Manot Food portions consisting of at least one fruit and one sweet made from flour, given at Purim.

Shavuot Feast of Weeks, commemorating the revelation of the Law on Mount Sinai; a wheat festival in biblical times.

Shmurah Matzah A matzah made from wheat that has literally been watched since the time of reaping, until it comes in contact with liquid before baking.

Shulkhan Arukh Code of Jewish law.

Sufganiyot Doughnut served in Israel at Hanukkah.

Sukkot Thanksgiving festival, originating as an autumn harvest festival, with eating out of doors, in a *succah*.

Treif Ritually unfit.

Tsimmes Sweetened, baked combination of vegetables or meat and vegetables, often with dried fruits.

Varnishkes Noodles, often square or in America shaped like a bow tie.

Yom Kippur Day of Atonement.

Bibliography

Here is a list of books and articles that were exceptionally helpful in researching this book. (Works cited at the end of each quotation and in the text are not included here.)

Batterberry, Michael, and Ariane Batterberry. *On the Town in New York*. New York: Scribners, 1973.

Chyet, Stanley, F. *Lopez of Newport: Colonial American Prince*. Detroit: Wayne State University Press, 1970.

Cohen, Naomi W. *Encounter with Emancipation: The German Jews in the United States, 1830–1914*. Philadelphia: Jewish Publication Society, 1984.

Da Silva, Cara. "Cookbook of Dream Recipes: A Collection from a Tragic Past." *Newsday*, 15 April 1991.

Diner, Hasia. *A Time for Gathering, The Second Migration*. Baltimore: The Johns Hopkins University Press, 1992.

Dresner, Samuel H. *The Jewish Dietary Laws*. New York: Rabbinical Assembly of America United Synagogue Commission on Jewish Education, 1982.

Elzas, Barnett A. *The Jews of South Carolina*. Columbia, South Carolina: University of South Carolina Press, 1905.

Encyclopedia Judaica. Jerusalem: Keter Publishing House, 1971.

Evans, Eli. *Judah P. Benjamin: The JewishConfederate*. New York: The Free Press, 1988.

———. *The Provincials*. New York: Atheneum, 1973.

Faber, Eli. *A Time for Planting, The First Migration, 1654–1820*. Baltimore: The Johns Hopkins University Press, 1992.

Fabricant, Florence. "Cooking a Pot Roast: Four Well-Spent Hours." *The New York Times*, 5 December 1990.

Feinsilver, Lillian Mermin. *The Taste of Yiddish*. London: Thomas Yousseloff, 1970.

Freedman, Seymour E. *The Book of Kashruth*. New York: Bloch Publishing Company, 1970.

Freund, Miriam K. *Jewish Merchants in Colonial America*. Behrman's Jewish Book House, 1939.

Gaster, Theodor H. *Customs and Folkways of Jewish Life*. New York: W. Sloane Associates, 1955.

———. *Festivals of the Jewish Year*. New York: W. Sloane Associates, 1953.

———. *The Holy and the Profane*. New York: W. Sloane Associates, 1955.

Gastwirt. *Fraud, Corruption, and Holiness.*

Glazer, Ruth. "The Jewish Delicatessen." *Commentary,* February 1946.

Harris, Lis. *Holy Days, The World of a Hasidic Family.* New York: Collier Books, Macmillan Publishing Company, 1985.

Heinze, Andrew R. *Adapting to Abundance.* New York: Columbia University Press, 1990.

Henry, May, and Edith Coyhen. *The Economical Cook.* London, 1889.

Hess, Karen. *Martha Washington's Booke of Cookery.* New York: Columbia University Press, 1981.

The Jewish Encyclopedia. New York and London: Funk and Wagnalls, 1903.

Johnson, Paul. *A History of the Jews.* New York: Harper and Row, 1987.

Kanfer, Stefan. *A Summer World: The Attempt to build a Jewish Eden in the Catskills, from the Days of the Ghetto to the Rise and Decline of the Borscht Belt.* New York: Farrar, Straus and Giroux, 1989.

Karp, Abraham J. *The Jewish Experience in America.* New York: Ktav Publishing House, 1969.

Kirshenblatt-Gimblett, Barbara. *Getting Comfortable in New York: the American Jewish Home, 1880–1950.* New York: The Jewish Museum, 1990.

Kisseloff, Jeff. *You Must Remember This.* New York: Schocken Books, 1989.

Kraut, Alan. "The Butcher, the Baker, the Pushcart Peddler. Jewish Foodways and Entrepreneurial Opportunity in the East European Immigrant Community, 1880–1940." *Journal of American Culture* (1983).

Levy, Esther. *Jewish Cookery Book.* Philadelphia: W. S. Turner, 1871.

Marcus, Jacob Rader. *Early American Jewry.* Philadelphia: Jewish Publication Society of America, 1951.

———. *Memoirs of American Jews, 1775–1865.* Philadelphia: Jewish Publication Society of America, 1955.

———. *United States Jewry,* 3 vols. Detroit: Wayne State University, 1989.

O'Neill, Molly. "Where Seltzer Once Thrived, Few True Fizzes Remain." *The New York Times,* 11 July 1991.

Randolph, Mary. *The Virginia House-wife with Historical Notes and Commentaries by Karen Hess.* Columbia, South Carolina: University of South Carolina Press, 1985.

Sachar, Howard M. *A History of the Jews in America.* New York: Alfred A. Knopf, 1992.

Salaman, Redcliffe. *The History and Social Influence of the Potato.* Cambridge, Eng.: Cambridge University Press, 1949.

Sanders, Ronald. *Shores of Refuge: A Hundred Years of Jewish Emigration.* New York: Henry Holt, 1988.

Sarna, Jonathan D. *Jacksonian Jew.* New York: Holmes and Meier, 1981.

Schoener, Allon. *The American Jewish Album, 1654 to the Present.* New York: Rizzoli, 1983.

Sharfman, I. Harold. *Jews on the Frontier.* Chicago: Pangloss Press, 1977.

Shosteck, Patti. *A Lexicon of Jewish Cooking.* Chicago: Chronicle Books, 1972.

Shosteck, Robert. "Notes on an Early Virginia Physician." American Jewish Archives, 1971.

Simons, Howard. *Jewish Times, Voices of the American Jewish Experience.* Boston: Houghton Mifflin, 1988.

Universal Jewish Encyclopedia. New York: Universal Jewish Encyclopedia, Inc., 1939/40–43.

Index

Numerals in color indicate recipes.
Numerals in *italics* indicate illustrations.

Photographic Credits

The photographs and illustrations reproduced in this book were provided with the permission and courtesy of the following:

Collection of Henry Morganthau III: cover, p. 416

National Yiddish Book Center: endpapers, 32, 37, 212, 293, 364, 376

Library of Congress: 13, 17, 20, 113, 217, 280, 294, 382

Collection of Cathy Sulzberger: 14

Chicago Historical Society: 19, 251

Joseph Jacobs Organization: 22

American Jewish Archives: 22, 170, 366, 373, 395

Broadcast Pioneers Library: 23

American Joint Distribution Committee: 24

Yivo Institute for Jewish Research: 25, 200 (Eliot Elisophon), 257, 379, 385

Collection of Paul Tobin: 47

Bill Aron: 51, 157, 195, 198

Collection of Millie Liniado: 56

Richard Nowitz: 75

Museum of the City of New York: 32, 80, 167, 223

Rhode Island Jewish Historical Society: 96

Charleston Museum: 100

San Francisco Chronicle: 109

Collection of Mr. and Mrs. Isaac Levine: 116

Jewish Agricultural Society: 120

American Jewish Historical Society: 134, 204

Jewish Museum/Art Resource: 162

New York Beef Industry Council, Inc.: 177

National Center for Jewish Film: 221, 283

Western Jewish History Center, Judah L. Magnes Museum: 243, 375, 403

Beck Archives of Rocky Mountain Jewish History, Center for Judaic Studies, University of Denver: 244

Jewish Historical Society of the Upper Midwest: 247

New York Times: 252, 263

Allan Gerson: 260, 377

Abbas Photography: 304

Levi Strauss & Co.: 306

Warshaw Collection, Smithsonian Institution, Museum of American History: 334

Collection of Joseph Ruskay: 345

Collection of Sandra Berler: 349

Collection of Roberta Colton: 353

Collection of Sarina Roffe: 356

Permissions Acknowledgments

The author's recipes "Passover Chremslach" and "Alabama Lemon Pecan Torte" first appeared in *Family Circle,* April 2, 1991. Excerpts from "To Queens from Uzbekistan: A Hanukkah Tradition" by Joan Nathan (*The New York Times,* December 24, 1997) is reprinted by permission of *The New York Times.*

Grateful acknowledgment is made to the following for permission to reprint previously published and unpublished material:

American Jewish Archives: Excerpts from unpublished material from "Jennie Gerstley's Reminiscences, 1859–1934, Chicago, Illinois"; and excerpts from the unpublished memoirs of Sarah Thal. Reprinted by permission of American Jewish Archives.

Gilda Angel: The recipe "Pescado con Ruibarbo" from *Sephardic Holiday Cooking* by Gilda Angel (Decalogue Books), copyright © 1986 by Gilda Angel. Reprinted by permission of the author.

Artisan: The recipe "Winter Borscht" from *Soup, A Way of Life* by Barbara Kafka, copyright © 1998 by Barbara Kafka. Reprinted by permission of Artisan, a division of Workman Publishing Company, Inc.

Jonathan David Publishers, Inc.: Excerpt from "Chaplain Louis Barish" from *Rabbis in Uniform: The Story of the American Jewish Military Chaplain* (1962). Reprinted by permission of Jonathan David Publishers, Inc.

Donald I. Fine, Inc.: Adapted recipe "Fish in Garlic and Coriander Sauce" from *Sephardic Cooking* by Copeland Marks, copyright © 1992 by Copeland Marks. Reprinted by permission of Donald I. Fine, Inc.

Pelican Publishing Co.: The recipe "Chicken Jambalaya" from *Kosher Cajun Cookbook* by Mildred Covert and Sylvia Gerson, copyright © 1987 by Mildred Covert and Sylvia Gerson. Reprinted by permission of Pelican Publishing Co.

Random House, Inc. and *Wolfgang Puck*: The recipe "Jewish Pizza" from *The Wolfgang Puck Cookbook* by Wolfgang Puck, copyright © 1986 by Wolfgang Puck. Reprinted by permission of Random House, Inc., and the author.

Sisterhood of the Persian Hebrew Congregation: The recipe "Tav Bisleh, Green Onion Omelette" from *Persian (Jewish) Cook Book,* contents copyright © 1987. Reprinted by permission.

Deborah Sperling: Excerpt from *A Sampling from Di Grine Kuizine: KlezKamp Cooks* by Deborah Sperling, copyright © 1991 by Deborah Sperling.

Vegetarian Resource Group: The recipe "Mock Chopped Liver" from *No Cholesterol Passover*

A NOTE ABOUT THE AUTHOR

Joan Nathan was born in Providence, Rhode Island. She was graduated from the University of Michigan, where she received a master's degree in French literature and, later, received a master's in public administration at the Kennedy School at Harvard University. For three years she lived in Israel where she worked for Mayor Teddy Kollek of Jerusalem. In New York, she founded the Ninth Avenue Food Festival. Ms. Nathan wrote for *The Washington Post* for eight years and currently contributes articles on international ethnic food and special holiday features to *The New York Times, Food Arts,* and the *B'nai B'rith International Jewish Monthly.* She is the author of *The Jewish Holiday Baker, The Jewish Holiday Kitchen, The Children's Jewish Holiday Kitchen,* and *An American Folklife Cookbook,* and coauthor of *The Flavor of Jerusalem.* Ms. Nathan lives in Washington, D.C., with her husband and their three children.

A NOTE ON THE TYPE

The text of this book was set in a digitized version of a typeface named Perpetua, designed by the British artist Eric Gill (1882–1940) and cut by The Monotype Corporation, London, in 1928–1930. Perpetua is a contemporary letter of original design, without any direct historical antecedents. The shapes of the roman letters basically derive from stonecutting, a form of lettering in which Gill was eminent. The italic is essentially an inclined roman. The general effect of the typeface in reading sizes is one of lightness and grace. The larger display sizes of the type are extremely elegant and form what is probably the most distinguished series of inscriptional letters cut in the present century.

Composed by North Market Street Graphics,
Lancaster, Pennsylvania

Calligraphy by Carole Lowenstein

Printed and bound by Courier Book Companies,
Westford, Massachusetts

Designed by Iris Weinstein

KNOPF COOKS AMERICAN

The series of cookbooks that celebrates the culinary heritage
of America, telling different aspects of our story through
recipes interspersed with historical lore, personal reflections,
and the recollections of old-timers.

Already published:

"Our food tells us where we came from and who we are . . ."